FIRST EDITION

CHALLENGING INEQUALITIES
READINGS IN RACE, ETHNICITY, AND IMMIGRATION

Edited by Hortencia Jiménez

cognella® | ACADEMIC PUBLISHING

Bassim Hamadeh, CEO and Publisher

Kristina Stolte, Acquisitions Editor

Michelle Piehl, Project Editor

Christian Berk, Associate Production Editor

Jess Estrella, Senior Graphic Designer

Trey Soto, Licensing Associate

Joyce Lue, Interior Designer

Natalie Piccotti, Senior Marketing Manager

Kassie Graves, Director of Acquisitions and Sales

Jamie Giganti, Senior Managing Editor

ISBN: 978-1-5165-3313-8 (pbk) / 978-1-5165-3314-5 (br)

cognella® | ACADEMIC PUBLISHING

CHALLENGING INEQUALITIES

READINGS IN RACE, ETHNICITY, AND IMMIGRATION

CONTENTS

Contents
· ·

Wave To Salinas   ix
  By James B. Golden

Preface   xi

Organization of this Textbook   xiii

Dedication   xvi

Acknowledgments   xvii

Readings in Race, Ethnicity, and Immigration   xix

The Increasing Diversity of Immigrant America   xxx

PART I: UNDERSTANDING WHY RACE AND
ETHNICITY STILL MATTER   1

Pacific (A Historian)   2
  By Eduardo Velasquez

Racist America: Racist Ideology as a Social Force   4
  By Joe R. Feagin

Racial Formation: Understanding Race and
Racism in the Post-Civil Rights Era   24

By Michael Omi and Howard Winant

Embracing a Cross-Racial Dialogue   46

By Beverly Daniel Tatum

PART II: CONQUEST, SLAVERY, AND MIGRATIONS   59

Double-Crossed, Double-Bordered   60

By Iris Rodriguez

Contemporary Native American Issues,
1900–Present: An Overview   62

By Rebecca Bales

The Sexual Politics of
Black Womanhood   69

By Patricia Hill Collins

What Race Are Mexicans? A Brief History of the
Racialization of Mexican Americans   96

By Agustin Palacios

Asian Americans: Unity in Diverse Experiences   108

By Wendy Ng

Immigration to a Rising Metropolis   115

By Rudy P. Guevarra Jr.

You Ain't White! The Experience of
Middle Eastern Americans   156

By Rita Stephan

PART III: SOCIAL INSTITUTIONS: MAINTAINING INEQUALITIES

165

Untitled   **166**

By Luis Xago Juárez de Baktun 12

Beyond the White-and-Black, Heteronormative Binary: Black, Latinx, and Indigenous Parallel Experiences of State-Sanctioned Policing   **168**

By Hortencia Jiménez

What Does It Mean to Return Home? Narratives of Hope and Uncertainty   **190**

By Monica Lugo

The Power of (Mis)Representation: Why Racial and Ethnic Stereotypes in the Media Matter   **200**

By Mari Castañeda

All That Refuses to Change   **208**

By Eduardo Velasquez

Undocumented Workers and Precarious Labor   **210**

By Shannon Gleeson

Trapped in the Working Class? Latino Youth Struggle to Achieve the American Dream   **217**

By Karina Chavarria and Veronica Terriquez

Race Frames and Their Impact on the Sense of Belonging of Black Students in a College Community   **226**

By Anita Davis, Angela Frederick, and Christopher Wetzel

Nepantleras in a Community College: Student Mothers Negotiating Mothering, School, and Work   **237**

By Nereida Oliva and Hortencia Jiménez

PART IV: OLD AND NEW CHALLENGES: LOOKING INTO THE FUTURE   251

All in the Name of Assimilation   252
By Celeste Torres

Water Protectors: Stories of Inhabited Territories   254
By Gilliam Jackson, Trey Adcock, and Juan G. Sánchez Martínez

Black and Latinx Millennial Students and Racial Justice Activism in the Age of Black Lives Matter   273
By María Joaquina Villaseñor

White Privilege: Moving Beyond Guilt into Responsibility and Action   285
By Debra Busman

Semillas y Culturas: Foodways in Ethnic Studies   296
By Melissa M. Moreno

From Mexico to the United States: Discovering and Advocating for Social Justice   312
By Cristobal Salinas Jr.

Indigenous Immigrants from the Mexican State of Oaxaca Residing in Monterey County, California: The Search for Meaning and Agency   319
By Renata Funke

Reincarnation   330
By Gloria Anzaldúa

References   332

Wave To Salinas

By James B. Golden

Diamond amid coal cinders,
little city with large expectations,
turns dreams the distance.
When you pass by on 101
wave to Salinas for me.

Warrior-Vikings plant strawberries
in the soiled sun, dirty
fingernail freedom badges,
tans darker than carbon.
Pass by the salad bowl of the world
seasoned with the river
and wave to Salinas for me.

Oh, land of the Esselen
Santa Rita red clay dirt
the Freemont flag-spiked Gabilan Mountains
stagecoach settlement of the West
salt marsh shaken by 1800s Chinese immigrants
migrant Mexican field workers or
Alisal district pickers; where
churches bless crops and flocks—

First Baptist and Presbyterian
Mt. Nebo, Northminster,
Sacred Heart, Madonna Del Sasso
flower the skies or casserole pans
for the hungry down on Soledad; where
school children volunteer as
little silver dollars in the night sky.
At the lettuce cornrows growing in the dust,
have a wave to Salinas for me.

There, the grapes of wrath are stored
in a wine cellar across from
Fresh Express—meeting-place of the
Chavez migrant movement; where
Partners For Peace gather in solidarity
and the NAACP marches the streets
keeping Hartnell supplied with brilliance
and thousands of poets,
because in Salinas everyone is poetry,
and poets know Roy's on North Main
had shakes that grew rosebuds in cheeks,
back before the shadow-colored Central Park
train faded away, when
Fox Theatre was the Saturday nightcap moon
looking over a bevy of Old Town shops at
glimpses of people, our greatest,

living vibrantly in a city of aggie warfare,
the paramount of California landscape
and the burning of a million souls.
When you walk, barefoot, sole-exposed on the
fire beneath our streets,
wave to Salinas
for me.

PREFACE

Teaching courses on the sociology of race and ethnic relations and courses on ethnic studies to hundreds of students over the years has allowed me the opportunity to reflect on my teaching pedagogies and the textbooks used in these courses. Contemporary students' levels of knowledge of issues surrounding racism range from very rudimentary to firsthand experiences, yet most contemporary students lack the language with which to articulate those individual experiences in relation to larger societal structures. Most students find it difficult to see how structural arrangements in society impact the lives of individuals and groups, depending on their race, ethnicity, nationality, religion, gender, sexuality, class, and immigration status. In light of this challenge, *Challenging Inequalities: Readings in Race, Ethnicity, and Immigration* is a book intended for undergraduate courses, such as those on race and racism, education/counseling, history, ethnic studies, introductory sociology, and other general education courses that are taught every semester in the community college and university settings. Students in these courses will develop a critical framework for understanding how and why race still matters. The readings contained herein exhibit the ways in which the social construction of race has shaped the experiences of ethnic and racial groups in the United States, from the nation's founding to the present. I take the position of Cornel West, who notes that in order to understand our multicultural society, we must have a "sense of history and open, honest dialogue." This book seeks to engage such dialogue by offering the reader insights on how the history of racism can be examined at the micro (individual) and macro (institutional) level. The contributors highlight the ways in which race is structured in social institutions, and the ways in which these institutional structures continue to maintain and perpetuate social inequalities.

Challenging Inequalities: Readings in Race, Ethnicity, and Immigration includes chapters by pioneers in the field of race, ethnic groups, and immigration, as well as both established and emerging scholars. Contributing authors come from a wide range of fields of study, such as ethnic studies, Chicanx/Latinx studies, history, educational leadership, immigration, creative writing, sociology, communication studies, and Native American studies;

they have been on the front lines teaching these topics or involved on the ground through their grassroots efforts. *Challenging Inequalities: Readings in Race, Ethnicity, and Immigration* provides chapters that are conceptually and theoretically informed yet accessible to undergraduate and nonacademic audiences. My hope is that this book is used by faculty teaching in different academic institutions, as well as nonacademic audiences, such as practitioners in the fields of social work, racial justice, and civil and immigration rights, or those working in nonprofit organizations and advocacy organizations whose work is crucial in moving toward greater racial equity.

ORGANIZATION OF THIS TEXTBOOK

Challenging Inequalities: Readings in Race, Ethnicity, and Immigration is organized into four parts: (1) Understanding Why Race and Ethnicity Still Matter; (2) Conquest, Slavery, and Migrations; (3) Social Institutions: Maintaining Inequalities; and (4) Old and New Challenges: Looking into the Future. It is composed of a total of twenty-two chapters—seventeen original chapters and five previously published—as well as several poems. Although the structure of the book follows a linear path, the reader can pick and choose the order of readings. The majority of the chapters include resources for teaching in the classroom, such as a list of suggested discussion questions, supplementary readings, website links, and audiovisual aids.

PART I. UNDERSTANDING WHY RACE AND ETHNICITY STILL MATTER

In this section, authors introduce students to the sociohistorical context of race and to ideas regarding racial inequality. Contributors argue that race is a social construction rather than a biological one. Topics covered include the development of racist ideologies in North America, the theory of racial formation, and engaging in critical thinking and racial dialogue about racism.

PART II. CONQUEST, SLAVERY, AND MIGRATIONS

The contributing authors in this section show how historical contexts of conquest and slavery have led to the formation of interethnic and interracial mixing, as well as contemporary contexts of migration. Topics covered include Native American issues with the federal government, the sexual politics of Black women's bodies, the racialization of

Mexican Americans, the demographic composition of Middle Eastern and North African (MENA) Americans and their racial identity, and the mixed-race experiences of people of Filipino-Mexican (Mexipino) descent. This section also examines the issues facing Asian American ethnic groups and the structural discrimination, prejudice, and stereotyping faced by the group as a whole. The chapter by Rudy P. Guevarra Jr. on the overlapping migrations of both Mexicans and Filipinos to the United States resonates today with the discourse that the United States relies on a cheap labor pool and then disposes of it when those workers are perceived as a threat to US economic interests. Rita Stephan's chapter highlights the fact that Middle Eastern Americans in most Census Bureau surveys are categorized as an ethnicity within the White race, a racial identity to which many of them do not subscribe.

PART III. SOCIAL INSTITUTIONS: MAINTAINING INEQUALITIES

This section illuminates how race is structured in social institutions that continue to maintain and perpetuate social inequalities. The focus is on the manner in which institutional practices, policies, and ideologies help maintain systems of oppression. Contributing authors from communication studies, ethnic studies, educational leadership, and sociology focus on the ways in which the institutions of the family, education, the media, the economy, and politics interact with issues of race, class, gender, immigration status, and citizenship.

PART IV. OLD AND NEW CHALLENGES: LOOKING INTO THE FUTURE

This section addresses old challenges of race, ethnicity, and immigration, and also provides current literature on how individuals and groups are working toward racial justice. Topics in this section include undocumented Mexican immigrant women and notions of belonging, indigenous Oaxacans, teaching pedagogies on food justice, and indigenous resistance of activism and advocacy. The chapter by Gilliam Jackson, Trey Adcock, and Juan G. Sánchez Martínez highlights five hundred years of indigenous resistance, with two recent testimonies of activism and advocacy in protecting water: (1) the Cherokee resistance against the Tennessee Valley Authority (TVA) in Western North Carolina during the 1970s, and (2) the struggle against the development of the Dakota Access Pipeline on the Standing Rock Sioux reservation from 2016 through early 2017.

My hope is that this textbook will be used and read by students, professors, and people in communities across the United States who have an interest in race, ethnicity, and immigrant experiences in the United States. As a disclaimer, I do not attest or assert that this textbook provides an exhaustive review of the most current and canonical literature. Rather, I offer the reader a selection of classical and original readings that illustrate how race is structured in social institutions that continue to maintain and perpetuate social inequalities. The book's underlying principle is that structural arrangements in society have an impact on the lives of individuals and groups in society, based on race, ethnicity, nationality, religion, gender, sexuality, and class. As the chapters in this book illustrate, racial prejudice, individual and institutional racism, and systematic and structural racism contribute to racial inequality in our country. This is evident in the criminal justice system, employment, education, and immigration legislation.

DEDICATION

To my husband Luis Santiago-Sotelo, and children Luis, Itzel, and Elena.

ACKNOWLEDGMENTS

First and foremost, this textbook project would not have been a reality without the support of Kristina Stolte, senior field acquisitions editor, and Michelle Piehl, project editor. Thank you for believing in my work and nurturing my ideas for this textbook. Special thanks to the Cognella team: Jess Estrella, senior graphic designer, Karen Wiley, associate production editor, Dani Skeen, marketing coordinator, and many others who worked behind the scenes to make this book possible.

I would like to thank my colleagues who contributed original essays for this anthology: Trey Adcock, Rebecca Bates, Debra Busman, Mari Castañeda, Karina Chavarria, Anita Davis, Angela Frederick, Renata Funke, Shannon Gleeson, Gil Jackson, Monica Lugo, Melissa Moreno, Wendy Ng, Nereida Olivia, Agustin Palacios, Cristobal Salinas, Juan Sánchez, Rita Stephan, Veronica Terriquez, Maria Villaseñor, and Christopher Wetzel. I also want to thank James Golden for granting us permission to use his poem "Wave to Salinas" in this book, as well as Rudy P. Guevarra Jr. for his chapter on becoming Mexipino. ¡Gracias! Special thanks to Luis "Xago" Juarez from Baktun 12, Iris Rodriguez from Xica Media, and Hartnell College sociology students Eduardo Velasquez and Celeste Torres for writing original poems. The original artwork for the book was created by Micah Bazant, a visual artist from the Bay Area who works with social justice movements. Thank you all for setting aside time from your busy schedules to contribute to this book project. It has been an honor to work with you.

I would like to acknowledge the Hartnell College curriculum committee, in particular Carol Kimbrough and LaVerne Cook, for their guidance, support, and approval of several new sociology courses, which in large part inspired the development of this textbook. Completing this textbook was possible through the love, support, and care of friends such as Lisa Castellanos, Mercedes Del Real, Patty Diaz, Angela Frederick, Marnie Glazier, Shannon Gleeson, Monica Lugo, Yoshiko Matsushita-Arao, Hermelinda Rocha-Tabera, and Maria Villaseñor. Special thanks to my dear friend Maria Villaseñor for reading earlier drafts of my introductory chapters and providing feedback, and for your Chicanx Mujerista mentoring throughout the years. To Lisa, for being a sister in my life. Thank you for your unconditional love, patience, and support. Your leadership and commitment to social justice struggles and vision for a better society continue to influence my activist scholarship.

Thank you to my colleagues, Mitzi Alexander, Alma Arriaga, Eric Becerra, Manuel Bersamin, Theresa Carbajal, Jackie Cruz, Liz Estrella, Janet Flores, Peter Gray, Rafael Hernandez, Daniel Lopez, Millicent Madrigal, Monica Massimo, Esmeralda Montenegro-Owen, Gabriela Lopez, Bronwyn Moreno, Augustine Nevarez, Sam Pacheco, Nancy Reyes, Sara Sanchez, Nora Torres-Zuñiga, Ron Waddy, La'Quana Williams, Laura Zavala, and countless other staff, faculty, and administrators with whom I've interacted over the years since I've been at Hartnell College. Special thanks to Dean Celine Pinet for all her support in my professional development, and to faculty and staff in the divisions of Curriculum and Instructional Support, Social and Behavioral Sciences, and Fine Arts. Thank you all for your commitment to student success at Hartnell College.

I want to thank my extended and nuclear family. *A mi mamá y hermanas, gracias por todo su amor, apoyo moral, oraciones, y buenos deceos. ¡Las quiero mucho! Gracias, hermana Patricia, por todo tu apoyo. Gracias, mamá, por todas las comidas deliciosas que hizo mientras estaba con nosotros y por cuidar a sus ñietos. A mi abuelita Clara, tia Florentina, y tio/compadre Eleazar, gracias por todos su cariño, apoyo, y amor.* Special thanks to my *suegros* and *cuñadas* for always making me feel welcomed in the Santiago family. Finally, to my wonderful and beloved husband, thank you for always supporting and nurturing my ideas, projects, and professional development. *Gracias, mi amor, por tu apoyo, paciencia, comprención, y amor.* You have been my rock and foundation ever since we met. To my children, Luis, Itzel, and Elena, thank you for giving me the gift of motherhood, for your unwavering love, compassion, understanding, and for your support. You make my life meaningful and so much fun. *Los quiero mucho; les dedico este libro.*

READINGS IN RACE, ETHNICITY, AND IMMIGRATION

By Hortencia Jiménez

In the United States, race, ethnicity, and immigration have always been omnipresent but have moved unequivocally front and center since the election of Donald Trump to the presidency in 2016. The Southern Poverty Law Center, and the FBI's Uniform Crime Reporting noted 201 hate crime incidents following Trump's election in 2016. The attitudes expressed in these incidents ranged from anti-Black, anti-woman, anti-LGBT, to anti-immigrant and anti-Muslim sentiments. The most commonly-reported location of these incidents occurred in K–12 schools (Staff, 2016).

Students' fears are real and omnipresent as they worry about having their families separated, deported, harassed, and detained. They are worried about their future. This leads to stress and feelings of anxiety and uncertainty that impact students' physical and emotional well-being, as well as schoolwork. Sergio Garcia, an immigration lawyer, captures this well when he says, "there's a lot of anxiety, uncertainty of not knowing what tomorrow holds" (Colvin, 2017). As an instructor, I know this all too well, as I witness it first hand with students at my institution who come to my office and express their fear and uncertainty regarding what will happen once their DACA benefit expires. For those who are citizens, their fears are also real, as they worry that their family and community is being threatened, that their undocumented parents will be deported, or that the permanent legal status of family members will be stripped from them. These fears have not subsided, but rather have increased, since January 20, 2017 when Donald Trump officially became the 45th president of the United States.

A day after Trump's inauguration, people all over the nation and around the world protested and called for protecting for the rights of women, immigrants, Muslim, LGBTQ comunity members, and members of other groups that are likely to be further criminalized and marginalized by the Trump administration. Some estimates note that the Women's March on Washington attracted more than 470,000 people. This number excludes the 670 sister marches around the United States and the world, putting the total number of attendees at more than four million (Women's March, 2017). These events made history. Political scientists from the Universities of Connecticut and Denver say that the Women's March may have been the largest and most peaceful day of protest in recent history (Chenoweth, Pressman, 2017). Between 3.3 million and 4.6 million marchers made their presence known across the United States. The largest single demonstration was in Los Angeles, where as many as 750,000 women took to the streets. Meanwhile, sister protests across the globe attracted nearly 300,000 more attendees—100,000 of which were in London. Marches of solidarity also occurred from Iraq to Antarctica (Broomfield, 2017).

Since his inauguration on Friday, January 20, 2017 Trump has signed more than a dozen executive actions and memorandums that have sent shock waves across the country, yet such actions are not surprising given the xenophobic and nativist rhetoric invoked throughout his campaign. The Border Security and Immigration Enforcement Improvement and the Enhancing Public Safety in the Interior of the United States contain provisions that are deeply alarming to immigrant and refugee communities and advocates alike. For example, these measures call for the construction of detention facilities and increased federal and local-level immigration enforcement. The government will add 5,000 Customs and Border Patrol agents and 10,000 Immigration and Customs Enforcement officers to perform enforcement functions and maintains as well, that it will move forward with the construction of a border wall. These executive orders also urge collaboration between local law enforcement and federal immigration authorities through 287(g) agreements with state governors. Under these executive orders, the Department of Homeland Security (DHS) will publicize a list of jurisdictions that continue to provide sanctuary to undocumented immigrants and such jurisdictions will be ineligible to receive federal grants that are not intended for law enforcement purposes. Additionally, Trump's anti-immigration strategies include publishing a weekly report that lists criminal actions committed by immigrants and establishing an Office for Victims of Crimes Committed by Removable Aliens.

Moreover, under the Protecting the Nation From Terrorist Attacks by Foreign Nationals executive order, the administration immediately denied anyone from seven predominantly Muslim countries (Iran, Iraq, Sudan, Syria, Libya, Somalia, and Yemen) entry to the United States for 90 days and suspended all refugee resettlement for 120 days, with the goal of reducing the number of refugees resettled in the country to 50,000 and an indefinite ban on those fleeing Syria (Vongkiatkajorn and Andres, 2017). Omitted from the list of offending countries are those with links to terrorist attacks such as Saudi Arabia, Egypt, and the United Arab Emirates and Lebanon (Yglesias, 2017). Pundits have questioned whether Trump deliberately left off countries in which he has business interests (Blaine and Horowitz, 2017). On Saturday, January 28th, immediately following the executive order, hundreds of immigrants and refugees were detained by customs officials across the country, while lawyers quickly filed lawsuits against the Trump administration (Yglesias 2017; Vongkiatkajorn and Andres 2017).

Donald Trump's immigration-related executive orders led to mass confusion at the very agencies that were in charge of implementing them—hundreds of airports across the United States. Officials in the Department of Homeland Security initially interpreted the executive actions as not applying to legal green card holders from the seven banned countries, but the Trump White House overruled that reading and declared they were too barred. The confusion continued to reign for people who have nationality or dual citizenship from these countries (Merica, 2017).

Homeland Security notes that on Saturday, January 28, 2017 about 109 people were denied entry while they were already on their way to the United States. When the order was signed, about 173 people were prevented from boarding planes headed to the U.S. Eighty-one people who were stopped were given waivers to enter the U.S (Shear, Kulish, and Feuer, 2017). Lawyers from the American Civil Liberties Union sued the government to block the White House order. Judge Ann M. Donnelly of Federal District Court in Brooklyn ruled in favor of two Iraqi immigrants, followed by another judge, Leonie M. Brinkema of Federal District Court in Virginia, issuing a temporary restraining order for a week to block the removal of people with green cards at the Dulles International Airport (Shear, Kulish, and Feuer, 2017). A federal judge in New York temporarily blocked part of Trump's order on Saturday, January 28, 2017, ruling that citizens of the seven countries who have valid legal visas cannot be removed from the United States. Nonetheless, Immigration and Customs Enforcement has "discretionary authority" to question travelers from Iran, Iraq, Sudan, Syria, Somalia, Libya, and Yemen (Shear, Kulish, and Feuer, 2017).

There have been countless of stories of faculty and students who attend American universities and were blocked from returning to the United States. Stories like that of Hameed Khalid Darweesh, an interpreter who worked on behalf of the United States government, who was detained for 19 hours and eventually released. Nisrin Omer, a legal permanent resident who was held at Kennedy International Airport in New York for several hours before she was released; as well as the circulated case of Nisrin Elamin Abdelrahman, a Ph.D candidate in Anthropology at Stanford University (Shear, Kulish, and Feuer, 2017, Democracy Now, 2017). Nisrim shared her experience of being detained, patted down, and handcuffed with Amy Goodman and Juan Gonzalez on *Democracy Now* on January 30, 2017. The possibility of being deported brought Elamin to tears, as she shared, "That's when I started to cry because I felt like—at that moment, I felt like, 'OK, I'm probably going to get deported.'" Elamin eloquently captures the nuances and complexities, as she lives at the intersection of her various identities as a woman, Black, Muslim, and immigrant:

> "I think this order is a reflection of a larger trend in this country to criminalize black people, to criminalize immigrants, to criminalize Muslims. And as a black Muslim immigrant, I'm really concerned about that. And I do think

that the Somalis and Sudanese, people of African descent who are going to be affected by this, you know, I think they're going to be treated differently." (Democracy Now, 2017)

Feminist and racial scholars contend that we must look at race and gender oppression simultaneously, a concept known as **intersectionality**. Nisrin Elamin reminds us that a narrow lens that focuses on just race and religion is not enough, and we must take into account other crucial aspects of her identity. An intersectional perspective can also shed light on how the executive order can have a devastating impact on immigrants and refugees with disabilities. The Disability Rights Education and Defense Fund (DREDF) condemned the executive order noting that the ban will have an impact on individuals with disabilities and on families who have children with disabilities due to the biased assumptions inherent in the ruling. The underlying premise is that refugees are considered "public charge"—burdens to society who will drain social services. DREDF further notes that the rate of disability among refugees is higher than the general population, and people with disabilities are more likely to be displaced during conflict (Disability Rights Education and Defense Fund, 2017).

It is well documented that emigration and displacement can have emotional consequences for many people. The mental and emotional health of refugees and immigrants is shaped by mental health stressors, the most common being migration experience and discrimination. Recently, the American Psychological Association (APA) issued a statement reminding the Trump administration that these executive orders lead to serious mental health consequences for immigrants and refugees. APA president, Antonio E. Puentes, Ph.D notes that these policies can lead to a "perception of reduced freedom, safety and social connection for those directly affected, as well as for society at large" (American Psychological Association, 2017).

Erez Reuveni from the Justice Department's Office of Immigration Litigation estimates that more than 100,000 visas were revoked, and between one hundred and two hundred people were detained at the nation's airports following Trump's ban on travel from the seven predominantly Muslim countries (Jouvenal, Weiner, and Marimow, 2017). People throughout the country have responded to Trump's executive orders and memoranda, from protesting to calling their local elected officials and state representatives. Thousands of people protested from the East Coast to the West Coast on Saturday, January 28 and Sunday, January 29, 2017 making it the second weekend of demonstrations. News accounts reported protests in at least eight major U.S airports, such as Atlanta, New York, Denver, Chicago, San Francisco, Los Angeles, Colorado, and Dallas, and many more took place in Orlando, Philadelphia, Seattle, San Jose, to name a few (Ellis, 2017). People also protested in other landmarks, such as the White House, Boston's Copley Square, and Battery Park in Manhattan (Grinberg, Park, 2017).

On Friday, February 3, 2017, James Robart, a federal judge in Seattle, Washington issued a temporary nationwide restraining order, effective immediately, stopping Trump's executive order on the grounds that the ban targets Muslims and violates constitutional rights of immigrants and their families. Washington Attorney General Bob Ferguson said in a statement after the ruling that "the Constitution prevailed today. No one is above the law—not even the President" (Seipel, 2017). Attorney General Ferguson noted that there is a high probability that the case may go all the way to the US Supreme Court.

We cannot lose hope, as we are reminded by Attorney General Bob Ferguson that there are federal checks and balances in our country. Groups across the country have been protesting Trump's executive actions ranging from national civil rights organizations, to students, to religious and faith-based communities, to actors, to educators, to government officials. For example, former acting Attorney General Sally Yates ordered the Justice Department on Monday, January 30, 2017 not to defend President Trump's executive order on immigration and refugees in court after the president issued it. Yates was fired shortly thereafter. Her stance did not go unnoticed and hashtags #ThankYouSally, #ThankYouSallyYates, and #SallyYates began circulating around the internet to show support for Yates. She was recently nominated for the John F. Kennedy Profile in Courage Award by Representative Jackie Speier from California (Amatulli, 2017). Other examples of unity are reflected in the more than one hundred Asian American and Pacific Islander (AAPI) organizations coming together, such as the 18MillionRising.org, East Coast Asian American Student Union, and cross-movement groups like Asians for Black Lives San Diego who reject the rhetoric that guides Trump's presidency (Rankin, Kenrya, 2017). Officials such as Governor Jerry Brown (CA), Mayor Ras J. Baraka (Newark, NJ), Mayor Rahm Emanuel (Chicago, IL), Mayor Ed Murray (Seattle, WA), Mayor Eric Garcetti (Los Angeles, CA) and Los Angeles police chief Charlie Beck have joined in their commitment to sanctuary cities (Iyer, Deepa 2017).

More recently, on September 5, 2017 Attorney General Jeff Sessions, announced the end of the Deferred Action for Childhood Arrivals (DACA) program. The Department of Homeland Security will not be receiving new DACA applications and people who already have DACA and whose work permits expire between now and March 5, 2018, will be able to apply for a two-year renewal if they apply by October 5, 2017 (National Immigration Law Center, 2017). It is estimated that over 8,000 million DACA recipients will be left without protection (Colvin, 2017). As scholars, we know that policies, executive actions, and memoranda of the Trump administration have an immediate and long-term impact on the lives of faculty members, students, immigrant and refugee communities, as well as U.S citizens from mixed status families. The reality is that undocumented students and international students will continue to face greater obstacles in reaching their academic success, while taking care of their emotional and physical wellbeing due to the nativist and xenophobic political climate that plagues our country. Professors Anita Casavantes Bradford, Laura E. Enriquez, and Susan Bibler Coutin from the University of California, Irvine wrote in the *Higher Education Journal* that, as educators, we have "the responsibility to mediate the impact of immigration policies on undocumented students" and offered ten suggestions for faculty and administrators to consider. These include:

- being aware of the wide range of people affected by proposed changes to immigration policy
- educating yourself about the laws and policies that impact undocumented students' educational access
- signaling to students that you are supportive
- (re)considering how you discuss immigration-related issues and the current political climate in your classroom
- maintaining student confidentiality and privacy
- using appropriate terminology when discussing immigration issues
- providing resources that will help mediate the financial instability that many students are facing
- offering career and graduate preparation opportunities
- identifying, improving, and referring students to campus and community resources
- identifying and raising awareness about your campus's policies regarding undocumented students

As we move forward in these uncertain and turbulent times, Bradford, Enriquez, and Bibler (2017) provide a blueprint of a few ways that we can support undocumented immigrant students that, although they may seem small steps, can have a big impact on students'day-to-day lives. What else could you do beyond what Bradford, Enriquez, and Bibler identify? What kind of commitment and resources would it take to adequately support students?

DEFINING CONCEPTS

Challenging Inequalities: Readings in Race, Ethnicity, and Immigration utilizes a sociological lens to the study of race, ethnicity, and immigration. **Sociology** is the study of human behavior and central to understanding social life. At the heart of this study, is the application of the **sociological perspective**—an understanding that people's social experiences are connected to broader social contexts in society. This approach welcomes us to examine the connection between individual human behaviour and the social structure of society in which people live. The sociological perspective allows us to examine and reflect how society affects us and our behavior and how we also shape society. These reflections can be examined through two levels of analysis: macro and micro. The **macro level** examines large scale patterns in society, including trends and the role of social institutions, while the **micro level** examines the small-scale patterns of society such as face to face interaction, and the examination of people's everyday life experiences. Sociologists who study race, ethnicity, and immigration often use the terms: migrate, emigrate, and immigrate. These words are commonly employed in social science literature and have similar meanings but are differentiated by some important distinctions. The word **migrate** means to move from one country or region and settle in another; and can imply a permanent or temporary relocation. The key distinction in migration is that it does not require moving to a foreign country; it signals moving to a new region. For example, many farmworkers in the United States migrate during the harvest season. Migration is also used an umbrella term, under which both emigrate and immigrate fall. **Immigrate** implies crossing a political boundary (moving to a new country)—a permanent move and settlement. While immigrate means to move into a country, **emigrate** means to move out of a country; it is the act of leaving a country to live in another (Kenton, Bell 2016). For example, I emigrated from Mexico and now live in the United States (immigrate).

Ethnicity is rooted on notions of shared cultural characteristics (i.e., language, religion, speech patterns, dress styles, food, etc.) allowing for people to self identify as belonging to an ethnic group. There is no scientific foundation to race, there is no biological basis; however, pundits continue to debate race today, from the mapping of the human genome to the concept of race as a scientific foundation. Race is as an ascribed category- an imposed category by social institutions. When sociologists study race, they focus on how race is a social and historical construction endowed with meaning that historically have used to sort and racially classify people to justify colonialism, slavery. exploitation, and genocide. Although **race** is a social construction, it has real and tangible consequences for people living in the United States. Race is a social grouping based on people's physical appearance that affords them a position within a racial hierarchy that values whiteness and places as subordinate anything that is "non-white." In the U.S., in particular, racial categories that differentiate white from non-white originate with slavery and colonialism and are derived from a myth of white racial purity, historically called the "one-drop rule" or the "rule of hypodescent." Race has been associated with human tragedies in U.S history, from slavery, colonization, exploitation and mistreatment, discriminatory policies, to genocide. In this text we use the terms racial and ethnic to acknowledge that race and ethnicity are not mutually exclusive, but rather overlap. The term **people of color** is also used throughout the text to refer to racial and ethnic minorities that have been systematically disenfranchised and been targets of racist, and discriminatory policies.

MINORITY GROUPS OR THE NEW AMERICAN MAJORITY?

Sociologists also use the term **minority group**. Being a member of a minority population has less to do with numbers and more to do with the distribution of resources and power. For example, women are considered to be a separate minority group due to their underrepresentation in politics and positions of power, and yet they are the numerical majority of the U.S population. The overwhelming majority of undergraduate textbooks on race and ethnicity, particularly in the field of sociology define minority groups in terms of their lack of economic and political power. The classic definition by Wagley & Harris (1958) of minority groups has five characteristics:

1. Members of the minority group experience unequal patterns of disadvantage and inequality

2. Members of the minority group share similar physical or cultural characteristics that differentiate them from other groups

3. Membership in the minority group is ascribed, determined by birth

4. Members of the minority group have a strong sense of solidarity/are a self-conscious social unit

5. Members of a minority group generally tend to marry within the same group

Black, Latinx, Asian American and Pacific Islander, and Native American are also referred as racially minoritized groups due to their racial background. **Minoritized** as opposed to minority group according to Benitez (2010, p. 131) is the "process [action vs. noun] of student minoritization." that reflects an understanding of "minority" as a status which is socially constructed in specific societal contexts. Minoritized people endure discrimination, racism, mistreatment and exclusion; they do not choose to be minoritized but rather area created as a minoritized group.

Steve Phillips, a civil rights lawyer and senior fellow at the Center for American Progress, is the author of *Brown is the New White: How the Demographic Revolution Has Created a New American Majority*. Phillips (2016) challenges the minority label that has been used over the last few decades by putting forth the argument that the "New American Majority" is the coalition of progressive people of color (23%) and progressive whites (28%), making them 51 percent of the population and eligible voters. Phillips comments that the discourse around a "majority, minority" nation is problematic on two grounds: first, it presumes that all "White people are and will continue to be at odds with all people of color, which is untrue and unfounded" given the long history of Whites siding with people of color throughout U.S history (p. xii). Second, he argues that focusing on the census projection that by 2044 Whites will be the minority overlooks the importance of aggregating the number of today's people of color (who overwhelmingly are progressive) and progressive Whites. Phillips articulates it this way: "[I]t's this calculation that reveals that America has a progressive, multiracial majority right now that has the power to elect presidents and reshape American politics, policies, and priorities for decades to come. Not in 2044. Not in ten years down the road. Today" (p. xii). It is in this context that Phillips calls for a rearticulation of minority groups to a New American Majority that is composed of multiracial progressive individuals who have the power to elect a president to fight for social change and racial equality in the US.

Phillips (2016) in *Brown Is the New White* calls on the New American Majority and progressives to work together to close the racial wealth gap, invest in public education, enact comprehensive immigration reform, end mass incarceration, debunk the myth of America as the land of equal opportunity, and debunk the myth of poverty as a personal failing. What all this points to is that race, ethnicity, immigration, and people of color matter in the United States and issues surrounding racial equality, health outcomes, educational disparities, and the school to prison pipeline continue to be relevant despite claims of a post-racial society. The idea of race has evolved throughout history and continues to shape the way we think and talk today.

Despite the racial progress this country has made, racism is alive and this book's chapters document some of the ways that ethnic and racial minorities experience this very phenomenon in their daily lives. While the election of Donald Trump to the presidency is fairly recent, completing his first year in January 2018, his anti-immigrant, islamophobia, homophobia rhetoric is not new. Trump's rhetoric and policies enact various forms of violence including discursive, psychological, and violence that affects people's physical safety and material living conditions. The book thus contextualizes the present moment by situating it within a broader historical and sociological framework to underscore the reality that this moment in which we find ourselves did not come out of nowhere, but is in fact the direct result of aggregate influences. Likewise, the resistance through protests and use of the courts and the rule of law, as noted at the beginning of this chapter exist within a broader social context. Just as the history of the United States is bountiful with examples of oppressive conditions, it is replete as well, with examples of individuals and groups that have resisted oppression and challenged the status quo as captured in the chapters of *Challenging Inequalities: Readings in Race, Ethnicity, and Immigration*. This book encourages us to have an honest dialogue and take into account how race has been an essential part of our history and of our contemporary society.

REFERENCES

Amatulli, Jenna. 2017. Sally Yates Has Been Nominated For JFK Profile In Courage Award. The Huffington Post. Retrieved from http://www.huffingtonpost.com/entry/sally-yates-has-been-nominated-for-jfk-profile-in-courage-award_us_5890ed77e4b0c90eff00a249

American Psychological Association. 2017. Trump Administration Orders Pose Harm to Refugees, Immigrants, Academic Research and International Exchange, According to Psychologists. Retrieved from http://www.apa.org/news/press/releases/2017/01/trump-harm-refugees.aspx

Benitez, Michael., Ir. 2010. Resituating culture centers within a social justice framework: Is There room for examining Whiteness? In Lori. D. Patton (Ed.), Culture centers in higher education:Perspectives on identity, theory, and practice (pp. 119–134). Sterling, VA: Stylus.

Blaine, Kyle and Horowitz, Julia. 2017. How the Trump administration chose the 7 countries in the immigration executive order. CNN. http://www.cnn.com/2017/01/29/politics/how-the-trump-administration-chose-the-7-countries/

Bradford, Anita Casavantes, Enriquez, Laura E, and Coutin, Susan Bibler. 2017. 10 Ways to Support Students Facing Immigration Crises. Higher Ed. Retrieved from https://www.insidehighered.com/views/2017/01/31/how-faculty-members-and-administrators-can-help-immigrant-students-essay

Broomfield, Matt. 2017. Women's March against Donald Trump is the largest day of protests in US history, say political scientists. Independent

Chenoweth, Erica, Pressman, Jeremy. 2017. This is what we learned by counting the women's marches. The Washington Post. Retrieved from https://www.washingtonpost.com/news/monkey-cage/wp/2017/02/07/this-is-what-we-learned-by-counting-the-womens-marches/?utm_term=.709e27dce09a

Colvin, Jill. 2017. Trump mulling fate of young immigrants protected by DACA Retrieved from http://www.mercurynews.com/2017/01/29/trump-and-gop-search-for-solution-for-dreamers/

Democracy Now. 2017. Sudanese Stanford Ph.D. Student Speaks Out After Being Detained at JFK Under Trump Muslim Ban. Retrieved from https://www.democracynow.org/2017/1/30/sudanese_stanford_phd_student_speaks_out

Disability Rights Education and Defense Fund. 2017. DREDF Statement on Executive Order on Immigration and Refugees. Retrieved from https://dredf.org/

Ellis, Ralph. 2017. Protesters mass at airports to decry Trump's immigration policies. Retrieved from http://www.cnn.com/2017/01/28/politics/us-immigration-protests/

Grinberg, Emanuella, and Park, Madison. 2017. 2nd day of protests over Trump's immigration policies. Retrieved from http://us.cnn.com/2017/01/29/politics/us-immigration-protests/index.html

Iyer, Deepa. 2017. Trump's Executive Orders on Immigration Met With Criticism and Resistance. Colorlines. Retrieved from https://www.colorlines.com/articles/trumps-executive-orders-immigration-met-criticism-and-resistance

Jouvenal, Justin, Weiner, Rachel, Marimow, Ann E. 2017. Justice Dept. lawyer says 100,000 visas revoked under travel ban; State Dept. says about 60,000. Retrieved from https://www.washingtonpost.com/local/public-safety/government-reveals-over-100000-visas-revoked-due-to-travel-ban/2017/02/03/7d529eec-ea2c-11e6-b82f-687d6e6a3e7c_story.html?postshare=4951486141864761&tid=ss_tw&utm_term=.73d800cd0893

Kenton, Bell. 2017. Open Education Sociology Dictionary. Retrieved from http://sociologydictionary.org/emigration/

Merica, Dan. 2017. How Trump's travel ban affects green card holders and dual citizens http://www.cnn.com/2017/01/29/politics/donald-trump-travel-ban-green-card-dual-citizens/

National Immigration Law Center. 2017. DACA. Retrieved from https://www.nilc.org/issues/daca/

Nahal, Tossi. 2017. Revised Trump executive order may ditch indefinite ban on Syrian refugees. Politico. Retrieved from http://www.politico.com/story/2017/02/trump-immigration-order-revision-235207

Phillips, Steve. 2016. *Brown is the New White: How the Demographic Revolution Has Created a New American Majority*. The New Press, New York.

Rankin, Kenrya. 2017. 100+ AAPI Orgs Vow to Resist the Trump Administration. Colorlines. Retrieved from https://www.colorlines.com/articles/100-aapi-orgs-vow-resist-trump-administration

Seipel, Brooke. 2017. Bush-appointed judge halts Trump travel ban nationwide. *The Hill*. Retrieved from http://thehill.com/blogs/blog-briefing room/news/317884-washington-state-judge-halts-trump-immigration-ban-nationwide

Shear, Michael D, Kulish, Nicholas, Feuer, Alan. 2017. Judge Blocks Trump Order on Refugees Amid Chaos and Outcry Worldwide. New York Times. Retrieved from https://www.nytimes.com/2017/01/28/us/refugees-detained-at-us-airports-prompting-legal-challenges-to-trumps-immigration-order.html

Staff, Hatewatch. 2016. Over 200 Incidents of Hateful Harassment and Intimidation Since Election Day. Southern Poverty Law Center. https://www.splcenter.org/hatewatch/2016/11/11/over-200-incidents-hateful-harassment-and-intimidation-election-day

Yglesias, Matthew, Lind, David. 2017. Read leaked draft of 4 White house executive orders on Muslim ban, end to DREAMer program, and more. Vox

Vongkiatkajorn, Kanyakrit and Andrews, Becca. 2017, 2017. Chaos Breaks Out in the Wake of Trump's "Muslim Ban". Mother Jones http://www.motherjones.com/politics/2017/01/trump-executive-order immigration-refugee-muslim-ban-protest

Wagley, Charles, and Marvin Harris. 1958. *Minorities in the New World: Six Case Studies*. New York: Columbia University Press.

Women's March. 2017. Sister Marches. Retrieved from https://www.womensmarch.com/sisters/

THE INCREASING DIVERSITY OF IMMIGRANT AMERICA

It is not uncommon to hear that in the United States "we are all immigrants." While the phrase is often deployed as a rhetorical gesture of inclusion of people of immigrant backgrounds, it nevertheless obfuscates the reality that some groups in the United States have no understanding of themselves as immigrant groups, or have historical origins in the United States as enslaved or colonized peoples.

The US Census Bureau categorizes the population into five racial categories: White, Black or African American, American Indian or Alaska Native, Asian, and Native Hawaiian or Other Pacific Islander. Of these groups, the largest comprises those who identify as "White alone" (254 million), accounting for 79.7 percent of all people living in the United States. The non-Hispanic, White-alone population is the largest racial and ethnic group and accounts for greater than 50 percent of the nation's total population. However, by 2060, the non-Hispanic, White group is projected to be 309 million, representing 74.3 percent of the total (Ortman and Colby 2015).

A smaller population in the United States is those who identify as Black or "African-American alone"—42 million people, representing 13.2 percent of the total population. Between 2014 and 2060, the Black-alone population is projected to increase from 42 million to 59 million (14 percent). An even smaller group, the American Indian and Alaska Native population, was 3.9 million in 2014, representing 1.2 percent of the total population. The population is projected to increase to 5.6 million by 2060.

Still, the United States has historically and undoubtedly been a country of immigrant settlement. From the founding of the United States to the twentieth century, the population consisted primarily of European immigrants. The face of immigrant America has since changed, largely shaped by policies regarding who can enter. For example, US immigration policies of the 1920s favored immigrants from Western Europe, while making it difficult for people from Southern and Eastern Europe, Asia, and Africa to enter the country. Numerous scholars note that immigration is racialized and can be restrictive or signify openings in the immigration system (Golash-Boza 2015; Portes and Rumbaut 2015). Examples of restrictive discriminatory legislation range from the 1790 Naturalization Act, the Indian Removal Act of 1830, the Chinese Exclusion Act of 1882, the 1907 Gentlemen's Agreement, the Tydings McDuffie Act of 1934, the Japanese Internment of 1942, and Operation Wetback in 1954 to the most recent legislation, such as Arizona's SB 1070, passed in 2010, Alabama's HB 546, passed in 2011, and Texas SB4 passed in 2017. Examples of openings in policy range from the 1865 to 1870 amendments to the Thirteenth, Fourteenth, and Fifteenth Amendments to the Constitution, the Bracero Program of 1943, the 1965 Nationality Act Amendments, and the 1986 Immigration and Reform and Control Act (IRCA), to, most recently, the Deferred Action for Childhood Arrivals (DACA) policy of 2012.

The 1965 Immigration and Nationality Act, also known as the Hart-Cellar Act, abolished the racially biased quotas set forth in the 1924 Oriental Exclusion Act and the Immigration Act of 1924, and introduced a family preference model, setting a universal quota system of twenty thousand immigrants for every country in the world (Golash-Boza 2015). This piece of legislation altered the patterns of sending nations, basically ending a national-origin quota system that gave preference to European migration. The outcome of this was increased racial diversity, with the introduction of immigrants who were coming primarily from Latin America and Asia.

The foreign-born population today accounts for about 42.3 million people, representing 13 percent of the total US foreign born, including naturalized citizens, legal permanent residents, temporary residents, and unauthorized immigrants. By 2060, the foreign-born population is estimated to be 78.2 million (compared to a native-born population of 338.6 million); that's an increase of 36 million, or 85 percent (Ortman and Colby 2015).

As of 2014, European immigrants numbered 4.8 million of the total foreign-born population of 42.3 million. Zong and Batalova (2015b) note that European foreign-born percentages in the United States plunged from 75 percent in 1960 to 11 percent in 2014. As of 2014, there were 55.4 million Hispanics in the United States, comprising 17.4 percent of the total US population.[1] As such, the group is the largest minority group in the country, according to the US Census, with continued growth expected. By 2060, 28.6 percent of the United States is projected to be Hispanic—a little more than one-quarter of the total population. Among all Latinos, there were 14.1 million immigrants in 2000. By 2005, that number reached 16.8 million, and by 2013, there were 19 million Latino

---

1. The US Census has been using the label *Hispanic* since the 1970s, which has been a source of debate over the decades. Hispanic or Latino people are those who classify themselves in one of the specific Hispanic or Latino categories listed on the census questionnaire—"Mexican," "Mexican Am.," "Chicano," or "Puerto Rican," or "Cuban"—as well as those who indicate that they are of "another Hispanic, Latino, or Spanish origin." *Origin* can be viewed as the heritage, nationality group, lineage, or country of birth of the person, or the person's ancestors before their arrival in the United States. People who identify their origin as Hispanic, Latino, or Spanish may be of any race. See https://www.census.gov/population/hispanic/.

immigrants in the United States. A few of the largest groups include Mexicans, Puerto Ricans, Cubans, Salvadorans, Dominicans, Guatemalans, Colombians, Hondurans, Ecuadorians, and Nicaraguans (Lopez and Pattien 2015).

In the 2014 Census, approximately 17 million people (about 5.4 percent) identified their race as "Asian alone." The number of Asian immigrants grew from 491,000 in 1960 to about 12.8 million in 2014. This group is projected to see its share of the total population nearly double, accounting for 38 million (9.3 percent) of the total by 2060. The top five originating countries of Asian immigrants have been India, China, the Philippines, Vietnam, and Korea (Zong and Batalova 2016). The smallest major race group is Native Hawaiian and Other Pacific Islander alone, at 734,000 people, representing 0.2 percent of the total population. The projected population is 1.2 million (0.3 percent) by 2060.

The ten largest immigrant groups come from Mexico, India, the Philippines, China, Vietnam, El Salvador, Cuba, Korea, the Dominican Republic, and Guatemala. California is the principal state of settlement for eight of the ten largest immigrant groups, followed by New York, Texas, Florida, Illinois, and New Jersey (Portes and Rumbaut 2015). Significantly, the population of the United States increasingly identifies as multiracial. People who reported more than one race numbered 8 million and made up about 2.5 percent of the total population in the 2014 Census. The "two or more races" population is projected to be 26 million (6.2 percent) by 2060 (Ortman and Colby 2015).

The United States is the top resettlement country for refugees worldwide. Those qualifying for refugee status can be living in authoritarian, repressive, or conflict-enmeshed nations, experiencing war, or members of social groups who are vulnerable and/or persecuted (Zong and Batalova 2015a). In 2015, the United States resettled 69,933 refugees, and in fiscal year 2013 the country granted asylum status to 25,199 people (the most recent data available). According to estimates by the United Nations High Commissioner for Refugees (UNHCR), by the end of 2014, the number of people displaced within their countries or fleeing international crises reached 59.5 million—the highest level ever recorded (UNHCR Global Trends 2014). By mid-2014, there were more than 1.2 million asylum seekers worldwide (Zong and Batalova 2015a). More than 4.1 million Syrians have sought refuge in other countries, and about 7.5 million have been displaced. The Obama administration responded to the humanitarian crisis by increasing the number of refugees the United States accepts each year, from 70,000 in 2015, to 85,000 in 2016, and 100,000 in 2017 (Zong and Batalova 2015a).

The seven countries (Iran, Iraq, Sudan, Syria, Libya, Somalia, and Yemen) that have been the target of the Trump administration's recent executive order, Protecting the Nation from Foreign Terrorist Entry into the United States, account for about 2 percent of all foreign-born people living in the United States; most have become citizens, a rate higher than that of the foreign-born population in the country as a whole (Fessenden,

Lee, Pecanha, and Singhvi 2017). Southern California has been the destination for a larger number of people from these countries, followed by the Detroit area (both places have substantial Arab and Muslim communities), while Somalis, on the other hand, are widely dispersed (Fessenden et al., 2017). Thousands of Iraqis and Yemenis have settled in the Detroit area, while a large number of Syrians live in Brooklyn, but have also settled in Burbank and Glendale, California, along with the Detroit area. Somalis and Sudanese, on the other hand, tend to be more isolated. Minneapolis has the most Somali-born residents, and Columbus, Ohio, and Seattle also have significant communities. Des Moines, Iowa, has a large number of Sudanese residents, who are also numerous in Texas and Virginia (Fessenden et al. 2017). Residents from the seven predominantly Muslim countries, especially Iranians and the small group of Libyans, are more educated than the rest of the people in the United States (Fessenden et al. 2017). People from Syria and Sudan also tend to be better educated than the national average.

Immigrants and refugees are found throughout the United States; however, immigration to the United States is largely an urban phenomenon, with immigrants concentrated in big cities; nonetheless, undocumented immigrants continue to work in agricultural areas, from California's Central Valley to the dairy farms of upstate New York. These locational decisions reflect historical patterns of settlement (Portes and Rumbaut 2015). The diversification of immigrant settlement patterns has been called "new destination," wherein states that had relatively small immigrant populations prior to 1990 have experienced growing immigrant settlements. New destination states include North Carolina, Georgia, Arkansas, Tennessee, Nevada, South Carolina, Kentucky, Nebraska, Alabama, and Utah (Massey and Capoferro 2008; Zuñiga and Hernandez-Leon 2005). The demographic changes, in terms of both native-born and foreign-born people, illustrate a continuous process of racial, ethnic, and cultural diversification in the United States.

PART I

UNDERSTANDING WHY RACE AND ETHNICITY STILL MATTER

•••

•••

PACIFIC (A HISTORIAN)
     By Eduardo Velasquez

RACIST AMERICA: RACIST IDEOLOGY AS A SOCIAL FORCE
     By Joe R. Feagin

RACIAL FORMATION: UNDERSTANDING RACE AND
RACISM IN THE POST-CIVIL RIGHTS ERA
     By Michael Omi and Howard Winant

EMBRACING A CROSS-RACIAL DIALOGUE
     By Beverly Daniel Tatum

Pacific (A Historian)

• •

By Eduardo Velasquez

After spending years, devoid and thinking,
I am convinced that my history must be somewhere down in the Pacific.

So, I'm poring through books, fiction and non, to see
What authors have left of a time before me.

If schools truly taught the past,
Then why wasn't my grandfather's plight on the map?
A *Bracero* living his life crossing two borders,
Reading his share of Robert Frost,
Saying, "A similar philosophy we shoulder."

Multiply this equation, factor by three,
And you'll only get a fraction of all those who believed
In something as vague as an American Dream,
Who interpreted the dreams of Lady Liberty.

If the U.S. were split into the ethnicities it holds,
Where is my history? In what class is it told?
Revolutionaries might answer, say we must demand it by force,
Diplomats might counter, say we should request by vote.

And in the middle of confusion, boycotts, and class,
I must put all to the side to ask:
What of our History?

I'm looking for words like Corky Gonzales's,
I'm looking for actions of people who tried to fight for balance,
I'm searching for faith for those who believe we can manage,
For philosophers and physicists, who welcomed a challenge.

There are some who say we should live and let live,
But forgetting the past is dangerous,
The acts, justifications of why they did what they did,
Lest we'd be willing for a repeat,
We should teach, understand the reason for these happenings.

So, I'm plunging deep into past,
Of the deep waters that hold my History.

Racist America: Racist Ideology as a Social Force

By Joe R. Feagin

CREATING A RACIST IDEOLOGY

The dramatic expansion of Europe from the 1400s to the early 1900s eventually brought colonial exploitation to more than 80 percent of the globe. The resulting savagery, exploitation, and resource inequalities were global, and they stemmed, as W. E. B. Du Bois has noted, from letting a "single tradition of culture suddenly have thrust into its hands the power to bleed the world of its brawn and wealth, and the willingness to do this."[1] However, for the colonizing Europeans it was not enough to bleed the world of its labor and resources. The colonizers were not content to exploit indigenous peoples and view that exploitation simply as "might makes right." Instead, they vigorously justified what they had done for themselves and their descendants. Gradually, a broad racist ideology rationalized the oppression and thereby reduced its apparent moral cost for Europeans.

An ideology is a set of principles and views that embodies the basic interests of a particular social group. Typically, a broad ideology encompasses expressed attitudes and is constantly reflected in the talk and actions of everyday life. One need not know or accept the entire ideology for it to have an impact on thought or action. Thus, each person may participate only in certain fragments of an ideology. Ideologies are usually created by oppressors to cover what they do, and counterideologies are often developed by the oppressed in their struggle against domination. Here we examine a critical aspect of the social reproduction of systemic racism from one generation to the next. The perpetuation of systemic racism requires an intertemporal reproducing not only of racist institutions and structures but also of the ideological apparatus that buttresses them.

The early exploitative relationships that whites developed in regard to African Americans and Native Americans were quickly rationalized, and they became enduring racist relations. From the beginning, racial oppression has been webbed into most arenas of American life, including places of work and residence, and activities as diverse as eating, procreating, and child rearing. Racist practices in these life worlds create, and are in turn shaped by, basic racist categories in the language and minds of Americans, especially white Americans. A racist ideology has overarching principles and beliefs that provide an umbrella for more specific racist attitudes, prejudices, and stereotypes.

Major ideological frameworks, including racist frameworks, are typically created, codified, and maintained by those at the top of a society, although this construction takes place in ongoing interaction with the views and practices of ordinary citizens. Those with the greater power have the greater ability to impose their own ideas on others. As Karl Marx and Friedrich Engels long ago pointed out, "the ideas of the ruling class are in every epoch the ruling ideas: i.e. the class, which is the ruling material force of society, is at the same time its ruling intellectual force."[2] Elites have dominated the creation, discussion, and dissemination of system-rationalizing ideas in business, the media, politics, education, churches, and government. While there is indeed much popularly generated racist imagery and discourse, even this is usually codified and embellished by the elites. As with most important ideas, if the elites had been opposed to the development of the racist ideology, they would have actively combated it, and it would likely have declined in importance. Thus, in his detailed analysis of the racist ideas and actions of presidents from George Washington to Bill Clinton, Kenneth O'Reilly has shown that conventional wisdom about presidents following a racist populace is wrongheaded. The historical evidence shows that most of the men who control U.S. political institutions have worked hard "to nurture and support the nation's racism."[3] Racist thought did not come accidentally to the United States. It was, and still is, actively developed and propagated.

THE EMERGING ANTIBLACK IDEOLOGY: EARLY VIEWS

For several centuries white ministers, business people, political leaders, academics, scientists, and media executives have developed and disseminated to all Americans a complex and variegated racist ideology that defends the theft of land and labor from Americans of color. The antiblack version of this ideology is the most developed; it has included a variety of religious, scientific, and psychosexual rationalizations for oppression. Although the ideology has been elaborated and changed somewhat over time, in all its variations it has operated to rationalize white power and privilege.

From the 1600s to the 1800s English and other European Protestants dominated the religious scene on the Atlantic coast of North America, and their religious views incorporated notions of European superiority and non-European inferiority. The early English Protestants regarded themselves as Christian and civilized, but those they conquered as unchristian and savage. Religious and cultural imperialism accompanied economic imperialism.

Most of the new colonists from Europe saw themselves as Christian people of virtue and civilization. From the first century of American colonization these Europeans frequently portrayed themselves as "virtuous republicans." They did not, or should not, have the instinctual qualities of the "creatures of darkness," the black and red Calibans they saw in their stereotyped images. Europeans were rational, ascetic, self-governing, and sexually controlled, while the African and Native American others were irrational, uncivilized, instinctual, and uncontrolled.[4] The first non-Europeans with whom many European colonists came into contact were Native Americans. Rationalizing the often brutal destruction of Native American societies, European colonists developed early on some negative images of Native Americans. Native Americans were "uncivilized savages" to be killed off or pushed beyond the boundaries of European American society. Moreover, much white thinking about indigenous peoples in the first centuries alternated between great hostility, such as can be seen in the Declaration of Independence's complaint about "merciless Indian savages," and the paternalism seen in the image of a "noble savage" who was independent of the vices of Europeans. Novelists such as James Fenimore Cooper heralded what they saw as the diversity in character of the "native warrior of North America. In war, he is daring, boastful, cunning, ruthless … in peace, just, generous, hospitable, revengeful, superstitious, modest, and commonly chaste."[5]

EARLY COLOR CODING: THE LINK TO SLAVERY

In the first century of North American slavery the antiblack ideology was becoming ever more developed and comprehensive. The emerging ideology increasingly focused not only on the blackness of the others but also on the whiteness of Europeans. Africans and African Americans were viewed as physically, aesthetically, morally, and mentally inferior to whites—differences that were regarded as more or less permanent. "Whiteness" was created in opposition to "blackness," in comparison to which it was not only different but quite superior. Indeed, from the seventeenth century forward black women, men, and children were "constructed as lazy, ignorant, lascivious, and criminal; Whites as industrious, knowledgeable, virtuous, and law-abiding."[6]

Significantly, the antiblack image was not "out there," but rather in the white mind and emotions. In their thinking and imaging, some whites went so far as to view the dark skin of Africans as a "natural infection" or as "pollution." A leading medical educator of the late 1700s, Dr. Benjamin Rush, thought the dark skin color of African Americans resulted from a type of leprosy that could be cured with medical treatment.[7]

The U.S. Constitution recognized the slave economy and implicitly incorporated an ideology of white supremacy in such provisions as the one that counted an African American as only "three-fifths" of a person. After the new nation was created, the unifying of growing numbers of immigrants from various European countries was done in part through the legal and political doctrines buttressing white privilege and superiority. In the first naturalization law in 1790, the new U.S. Congress made the earliest political statement on citizenship. Naturalization was restricted to "white persons." Whiteness thereby became an official government category; only European immigrants could qualify to become citizens of the new United States. The legal doctrines established by Congress and the courts helped to shape and unify the white consciousness, including that of the nation's leadership.[8]

EMOTIONAL UNDERPINNINGS

From the seventeenth century to the present the ideology justifying antiblack oppression, while overtly cognitive and legally enshrined, has had a strong emotional base. Antiblack attitudes and actions among whites have long been linked to or supported by such emotions as hate, fear, guilt, and repulsion. W.E.B. Du Bois suggested that color barriers are created not only out of overt maliciousness but also by "unconscious acts and irrational reactions unpierced by reason."[9]

For instance, many whites have been emotionally obsessed with what they term "racial mixing." Strong and irrational emotions are evident in the taboos and laws against interracial sex and marriage, which have long been considered to be extremely "unnatural" and "abominable" by many whites. In 1662 the colony of Virginia established the first law against interracial sex, and in 1691 a law against interracial marriage was enforced by banishment. White Virginians, scholars have noted, were very "disturbed by the racial intermingling, especially white-Negro mixtures, and introduced laws to prevent what they saw as the 'abominable mixture and spurious issue' by penalizing whites who engaged in interracial sex."[10] Mixed-ancestry Americans were viewed not only as inferior but also as degrading what Benjamin Franklin called a "lovely" whiteness. As Franklin argued, white "amalgamation with the other color produces a degradation to which no lover of his country, no lover of excellence in the human character can innocently consent."[11] Like most whites of the eighteenth century, Franklin seems to have developed a deep fear of black Americans. A slaveholder for several decades, then a leading abolitionist later in life, Franklin openly opposed slavery not because of its inhumanity but because of its negative impact on the whiteness of the American population. Ironically and significantly, for most of American history it was white men who were the most likely to cross the color line and force sex on black women.

Strong emotions are evident in the white violence that has long targeted black Americans. While most of the bloodthirsty lynchings of black Americans took place after the Civil War, they were preceded before that war by barbaric beatings, rape, torture, and mutilation of Africans and African Americans on slave ships, farms, and plantations. The early white notion that African Americans were "dangerous savages" and "degenerate beasts" played a role in rationalizing this violence. To deserve such treatment "the black man presumably had to be as vicious as the racists claimed; otherwise many whites would have had to accept an intolerable burden of guilt for perpetrating or tolerating the most horrendous cruelties and injustices."[12] After slavery, the racist ideology legitimated lynchings, whose sadistic character suggests deep and shared white emotions of guilt, hatred, and fear.

Fear is central to the ideology and attitudes woven through the system of antiblack oppression. Significantly, of the three large-scale systems of social oppression—racism, sexism, and classism—only racism involves the dominant group having a deep and often obsessively emotional fear of the subordinate group. This is not generally true for men, who dominate women in the system of sexism, nor is it true for the capitalists who exploit workers in the class-stratified capitalist system.

DEVELOPING AN EXPLICIT IDEOLOGY OF "RACE"

The ideology rationalizing exploitation did not develop all at once, but was elaborated as colonialism expanded around the globe. First, as we saw above, the "others" were viewed as religiously and culturally inferior. This brought an early accent on a hierarchy of inferior and superior groups. Later on, those oppressed were seen as distinctive "races" that were inferior in physical, biological, and intellectual terms to Europeans. A clearly delineated concept of "race" as a distinctive pseudobiological category was developed by northern Europeans and European Americans about the time of the American Revolution.

By the late 1700s these hierarchical relations were increasingly explained in overtly bioracial terms. This biological determinism read existing European prejudices back into human biology; then it read that biology as rationalizing social hierarchy. Those at the bottom were less than human; they were alleged to have smaller, and thus inferior, brains. Reflecting on European imperialism in the late nineteenth and early twentieth centuries, Frantz Fanon stressed the point that this colonialism was about much more than labor or resource exploitation, for it involved broad social domination constructed in racist terms. European colonialism created the modern idea of "race" across the globe. "In the colonies the economic substructure is also a superstructure.

The cause is the consequence; you are rich because you are white, you are white because you are rich."[13] This new racist ideology had three important elements: (1) an accent on physically and biologically distinctive categories called "races"; (2) an emphasis on "race" as the primary determinant of a group's essential personality and cultural traits; and (3) a hierarchy of superior and inferior racial groups.

America's prominent theorist of liberty, Thomas Jefferson, contended that black Americans were an inferior "race." In *Notes on the State of Virginia*, written in the late eighteenth century, Jefferson articulated what were the first developed arguments by an American intellectual for black inferiority. Blacks are said to be inferior to whites in reasoning, imagination, and beauty. Blacks are alleged to favor white beauty "as uniformly as is the preference of the Oranootan [Orangutan] for the black women over those of his own species." Blacks are alleged to be more adventuresome than whites because they have a "want of forethought," to be unreflective, and—perhaps most amazing—to feel life's pain less than whites. Blacks are alleged to have produced no important thinkers, poets, musicians, or intellectuals. Improvement in black minds comes only when there is a "mixture with whites," which Jefferson argues "proves that their inferiority is not the effect merely of their condition of life."[14]

SCIENTIFIC RACISM

As early as the 1730s the Swedish botanist and taxonomist, Carolus Linneaus, distinguished four categories of human beings—black, white, red, and yellow. Though he did not explicitly use the idea of "race," he associated skin color with cultural traits—with whites being superior and blacks inferior. Between the 1770s and the 1790s the prominent German anatomist and anthropologist, Johann Blumenbach, worked out a racial classification that became influential. At the top of his list of "races" were what Blumenbach called the "Caucasians" (Europeans), a term he coined because in his judgment the people of the Caucasus were the most beautiful of the European peoples. Lower on the list were the Mongolians (Asians), the Ethiopians (Africans), the Americans (Native Americans), and the Malays (Polynesians). "White" was viewed as the oldest color of mankind, and white had degenerated into the darker skin colors.[15]

The new scientific racism firmly encompassed the notion of a specific number of races with different physical characteristics, a belief that these characteristics were hereditary, and the notion of a natural hierarchy of inferior and superior races. In their broad sweep these racist ideas were not supported by careful scientific observations of all human societies but rather were buttressed with slanted reports gleaned by European missionaries, travelers, and sea captains from their experiences with selected non-European societies. Most scientists of the late eighteenth and early nineteenth centuries, while presenting themselves as objective observers, tried to marshal evidence for human differences that the white imperialists' perspective had already decided were important to highlight.[16]

CELEBRATING AND EXPANDING THE RACIST IDEOLOGY

In the United States distinguished lawyers, judges, and political leaders promoted scientific racism and its white-supremacist assumptions. In the first half of the nineteenth century whites with an interest in slavery dominated the political and legal system. This influence was conspicuous in the infamous *Dred Scott v. John F. A. Sandford* (1857) decision. Replying to the petition of an enslaved black American, a substantial majority of the U.S. Supreme Court ruled that Scott was not a citizen under the Constitution and had no rights. Chief Justice Roger Taney, a slaveholder, argued that African Americans "had for more than a century before [the U.S. Constitution] been regarded as beings of an inferior order, and altogether unfit to associate with the white race, either in social or political relations; and so far inferior, that they had no rights which the white man was bound to respect; and that the negro might justly and lawfully be reduced to slavery for his benefit. He was bought and sold, and treated as an ordinary article of merchandise and traffic, whenever a profit could be made by it. This opinion was at that time fixed and universal in the civilized portion of the white race."[17] The Dred Scott decision showed that the racist ideology was both elaborate and well established.

Senators and presidents played their role in articulating and spreading this ideology. President James Buchanan, a northerner, urged the nation to support the racist thinking of the *Dred Scott* decision. Moreover, several years before he became president, in his debate with Senator Stephen A. Douglas, Abraham Lincoln argued that the physical difference between the races was insuperable, saying, "I am not nor ever have been in favor of the social and political equality of the white and black races: that I am not nor ever have been in favor of making voters of the free negroes, or jurors, or qualifying them to hold office or having them to marry with white people. ... I as much as any other man am in favor of the superior position being assigned to the white man."[18] Lincoln, soon to be the "Great Emancipator," had made his white supremacist views clear, views later cited by southern officials in the 1960s struggle to protect legal segregation and still quoted by white supremacist groups today.

With the end of Reconstruction in 1877 came comprehensive and coercive racial segregation in the South. Distinguished judges, including those on the Supreme Court, played a key role in solidifying the extensive segregation of black Americans and in unifying white defenses of institutionalized racism. In *Plessy v. Ferguson* (1896) a nearly unanimous Supreme Court legitimated the fiction of "separate but equal" for black and white Americans in a case dealing with racially segregated railroad cars. This separate-but-equal fiction was legal for more than half a century, until the 1954 *Brown v. Board of Education of Topeka* decision and until broken down further by the civil rights laws of the 1960s. There was widespread agreement in the elites and in the general white population about the desirability of thorough and compulsory segregation for black men, women, and children.

SOCIAL DARWINISM

In his influential writings Charles Darwin applied his evolutionary idea of natural selection not only to animal development but also to the development of human "races." He saw natural selection at work in the killing of the indigenous peoples of Australia by the British, wrote of blacks as a category between whites and gorillas, and spoke against social programs for the "weak" because they permitted the least desirable people to survive. The "civilized races" would eventually replace the "savage races throughout the world."[19]

During the late 1800s and early 1900s a perspective called "social Darwinism" developed the ideas of Darwin and argued aggressively that certain "inferior races" were less evolved, less human, and more apelike than the "superior races." Prominent social scientists like Herbert Spencer and William Graham Sumner argued that social life was a life-and-death struggle in which the best individuals would win out over inferior individuals. Sumner argued that wealthy Americans, who were almost entirely white at the time, were products of natural selection and essential to the advance of civilization. Black Americans were seen by many of these openly racist analysts as a "degenerate race" whose alleged "immorality" was a racial trait.[20]

By the late 1800s a eugenics movement was spreading among scientists and other intellectuals in Europe and the United States. Eugenicists accented the importance of breeding the "right" types of human groups. Britain's Sir Francis Galton argued for improving the superior race by human intervention. Like Galton, U. S. eugenicists opposed "racial mixing" (or "miscegenation") because it destroyed racial purity. Allowing "unfit races" to survive would destroy the "superior race" of northern Europeans. Those from the lesser races, it was decided, should be sterilized or excluded from the nation. Such views were not on the fringe, but had the weight of established scientists, leading politicians, and major business leaders. Thus, in 1893 Nathaniel S. Shaler, a prominent scientist and dean at Harvard University, argued that black Americans were inferior, uncivilized, and an "alien folk" with no place in the body politic. In social Darwinist fashion, he spoke of their eventual extinction under the processes of natural law.[21]

Scientific racism was used by white members of Congress to support passage of discriminatory congressional legislation, including the openly racist 1924 immigration law excluding most immigrants other than northern Europeans. In this period overtly racist ideas were advocated by all U.S. presidents. Former president Theodore Roosevelt openly favored scientific racism.[22] President Woodrow Wilson was well-known as an advocate of the superiority of European civilization over all others, including those of Africa. As president, Wilson increased the racial segregation of the federal government. Significantly, no less a racist leader than Adolf Hitler would later report having been influenced by Wilson's writings. (In its contemporary sense, the term *racism* first appeared in a 1933 German book by Magnus Hirschfeld, who sought to counter the Nazi and other European racists' notion of a biologically determined hierarchy of races.)[23]

In 1921 President Warren G. Harding, who had once been linked to the Ku Klux Klan, said he rejected any "suggestion of social equality" between blacks and whites, citing a popular racist book as evidence the "race problem" was a global problem. Not long before he became president, Calvin Coolidge wrote in *Good Housekeeping* magazine, "Biological laws tell us that certain divergent people will not mix or blend. The Nordics propagate themselves successfully. With other races, the outcome shows deterioration on both sides."[24] Ideas of white supremacy and rigid segregation were openly advocated by top political leaders.

PERPETUATING THE RACIST IDEOLOGY: CONTEMPORARY AMERICA

Periodically, the racist ideology framed in the first two centuries of American development has shifted somewhat in its framing or emphases. Those in charge have dressed it up differently for changing social circumstances, though the underlying framework has remained much the same. Some new ideas have been added to deal with pressures for change from those oppressed, particularly ideas about government policy. After World War II, aspects of the dominant racist ideology were altered somewhat to fit the new circumstances of the 1950s and 1960s, during which black Americans increasingly challenged patterns of compulsory racial segregation.

In recent decades white elites have continued to dominate the transmission of new or refurbished ideas and images designed to buttress the system of racial inequality, and they have used ever more powerful means to accomplish their ends. The mass media now include not only the radio, movies, and print media used in the past, but television, music videos, satellite transmissions, and the Internet.

Today, for the most part, the mass media are still controlled by whites. Just under 90 percent of the news reporters, supervisors, and editors at newspapers and magazines across the United States are white. On television whites are overrepresented in managerial jobs, and as on-air reporters; they are greatly overrepresented as "experts" in the mass media. Americans of color have only a token presence in the choice and shaping of news reports and media entertainment. The concentration of media control in a few corporations has increased dramatically in recent decades. In the early twenty-first century, fewer than two dozen corporations control much of the mass media, and that number is likely to decrease further. In addition, the mass media, especially television, are substantially supported by corporate advertisers, and advertisers have significant command over programming. Thus, information about racial matters is usually filtered and whitewashed through a variety of elite-controlled organizations. This filtering is not a coordinated conspiracy, but reflects the choices of many powerful whites socialized to the dominant framing in regard to racial issues.[25]

Looking for data and stories, reporters and journalists typically seek out established government, business, academic, and think-tank reports and experts. The right wing of the U.S. ruling class, a large segment, has historically been the most committed to the racist ideology and has pressed for repression of protests against oppression. The liberal wing of the white elite is much smaller and often more attuned to popular movements; it has been willing to liberalize the society to some degree and to make some concessions to protesters for the sake of preserving the society. (The center of the elite has waffled between the two poles.) In the late 1960s and 1970s many experts consulted by top executives in government and the mass media came from think tanks usually espousing the views of those in the center or on the left of the ruling elite. Becoming very concerned about this, wealthy conservatives began in the 1970s to lavishly fund right-wing think tanks and to press aggressively conservative views of U.S. society on universities, politicians, and media owners. In recent years the right-wing think tanks—including the American Enterprise Institute, the Manhattan Institute, and the Heritage Foundation—have been very successful in getting their experts into mainstream discussions and debates. Working alongside a large group of other conservative intellectuals, media experts, and activists, these right-wing think tanks continue to be successful in an indoctrination campaign aimed at shaping public views on racial and other social issues.[26]

Most Americans now get their news from commercial television and radio programs. The largest single source is local news programming.[27] Using these local and national media, the white elites have the capability to mobilize mass consensus on elite-generated ideas and views; this consensus often provides an illusion of democracy. These elites encourage collective ignorance by allowing little systematic information critical of the existing social and political system to be circulated through the media to the general population.

With the national racial order firmly in place, most white Americans, from childhood on, come to adopt the views, assumptions, and proclivities of previous generations and established white authorities. In this manner the system of racism is reproduced from one generation of whites to the next.

INCREASED EQUALITY RHETORIC

From the 1960s onward the rhetoric of racial equality, or at least of an equality of opportunity, grew in volume among members of the white elite, including presidents and members of Congress. The black protests and rebellions of the 1950s and 1960s had an important effect in eradicating not only the system of the legal segregation but also most public defense of racial discrimination by the nation's white leadership. Since the late 1960s most leaders have proclaimed the rhetoric of racial and ethnic equality.

The structural dismantling of a large-scale system of compulsory segregation did require a new equality emphasis in the prevailing racial ideology. However, while the structural position of whites and blacks had changed somewhat, at least officially, most whites—in the elites and the general public—did not seem interested in giving up significant white power or privilege. Thus, the racist ideology was altered in some ways but continued to incorporate many of its old features, and it continued to rationalize white privilege—now under conditions of official desegregation. There had long been some fairness language in the prevailing ideology—for example, most whites thought blacks were treated fairly—but now notions of fairness and equality of opportunity were moved to the forefront. The acceptance by the white elite and public of the principles of equal opportunity and desegregation in regard to schools, jobs, and public accommodations did *not* mean that most whites desired for the federal government to implement large-scale integration of these institutions.

A MORE CONSERVATIVE ORIENTATION: 1969 TO THE PRESENT

Beginning around 1969, with the arrival of Richard Nixon's presidential administration, the rhetoric of equality was increasingly accompanied by a federal government backing off from its modest commitment to desegregation and enforcement of the new civil rights laws. At the local level, there was increased police repression of aggressive dissent in the black community, such as the illegal attacks on Black Panthers and other militant black groups by local police and FBI agents. The old racist images of dangerous black men and black welfare mothers were dusted off and emphasized by prominent white leaders who often spouted the rhetoric of equality at the same time. Moreover, the liberal wing of the white elite, which had provided some funding for the civil rights movement and other social movements of the 1960s, significantly reduced its support for these movements.[28]

By the mid-1970s the right wing of the ruling elite was accelerating its attack on the liberal thinking associated with the new civil rights laws. Since the 1970s a growing number of conservative organizations have worked aggressively in pressing Congress, the federal courts, and the private sector to eviscerate or eliminate antidiscrimination programs such as affirmative action efforts, as well as an array of other government social programs. This signaled the increasing influence on national policy of a more conservative Republican Party that represented, almost exclusively, the interests of white Americans. Moreover, even at the top of the Democratic Party there was also some shift to the right, which could be seen in the relatively modest antidiscrimination policies of the Jimmy Carter and Bill Clinton administrations.

The shift away from government action to remedy discrimination was associated with a reinvigoration of notions about inferior black intelligence and culture. In the 1970s, and increasingly in the 1980s and 1990s, numerous white journalists, politicians, and academics were critical of what they saw as too-liberal views in regard to black Americans and remedies for discrimination and defended arguments about black intellectual or cultural inferiority. In public policy discussions, increasingly led by white conservatives, there was a renewed emphasis on the view that only the individual, not the group, is protected from discrimination under U.S. law.

The federal courts provide an important example of this conservative shift. In the decades since the 1970s these courts have often ruled that group-remedy programs against racial discrimination violate the U.S. Constitution, which they assert only recognizes the rights of individuals, not groups. For instance, in 1989 a conservative Supreme Court handed down a major decision, *City of Richmond, Virginia v J. A. Croson Co.*, which knocked down a local program designed to remedy past discrimination against black and other minority businesses.[29] The high court ruled in favor of a white-run construction company, the plaintiff, which argued that the municipal government had unconstitutionally set aside business for minority companies. The court ruled that the city of Richmond had not made a compelling case for racial discrimination, even though the defendant's statistics showed that in a city whose population was one-half black, *less than 1 percent of the city government's business* went to black-owned firms.

STILL ARGUING FOR BIOLOGICAL "RACES"

In recent years some social and behavioral scientists have joined with certain physical scientists to continue to press for the idea of biological races and to connect that idea to concerns over government social policies. Since the late 1960s several social scientists at leading universities, including Arthur Jensen and Richard Herrnstein, have continued to argue that racial-group differences in average scores on the so-called IQ tests reveal genetic differences in intelligence between black and white Americans. Their views have been influential, especially on white politicians and the white public. In 1969 the *Harvard Educational Review* lent its prestige to a long article by Jensen, a University of California professor. The arguments presented there and Jensen's later arguments in the next two decades have received much national attention, including major stories in *Time, Newsweek, U.S. News and World Report, Life,* and major newspapers. Jensen has argued that on the average blacks are born with less intelligence than whites, and that the "IQ" test data support this contention. In addition, he has suggested that high birth rates for black Americans could result in a lowering of the nation's overall intelligence level.[30]

Perhaps the most widely read example of biological determinism is a 1990s book, *The Bell Curve,* which sold more than a half million copies. Into the twenty-first century it is still being cited and read. Like Jensen, the authors of *The Bell Curve*—the late Harvard University professor Richard Herrnstein and prominent author Charles Murray—argue that IQ test data show that black (and Latino) Americans are inferior in intelligence to whites. Though the authors have no training in genetics, they suggest that this supposed inferiority in intelligence results substantially from genetic differences. Thus, biological differences account to a substantial degree for racial inequalities. The fact that the book has sold many copies and has been widely debated in the media—in spite of the overwhelming evidence against its arguments—strongly suggests that biologically oriented racist thinking is still espoused by a large number of white Americans, including those who are well-educated. Indeed, Herrnstein and Murray explicitly suggest that their views are *privately shared* by many well-educated whites, including those in the elite, who are unwilling to speak out publicly. This book was launched during a major press conference at the conservative American Enterprise Institute. This publicity insured that the book would get much national attention, while antiracist books have generally gotten far less media play.[31]

Racist arguments about contemporary intelligence levels are grounded in nearly four hundred years of viewing blacks as having an intelligence inferior to that of whites. Today, such views are much more than an academic matter. They have periodically been used by members of Congress and presidential advisors in the White House to argue against antidiscrimination and other government programs that benefit Americans of color. Given this elite activity, it is not surprising to find these views in the white public.

Another aspect of older racist views that can be found in new dress is the idea of what one might call "cultural racism"—the view that blacks have done less well than whites because of their allegedly deficient culture with its weak work ethic and family values. As early as the seventeenth century, black Americans were seen as inferior in civilization and morality to white colonists. These blaming-the-victim views have regularly been resuscitated among the white elites and passed along to ordinary Americans as a way of explaining the difficult socioeconomic conditions faced by black Americans.

Since the 1970s leading magazines have published articles accenting some version of this perspective on what came to be called the black "underclass"; the perspective accents the allegedly deficient morality and lifestyle of many black Americans. Prominent author Ken Auletta wrote an influential set of *New Yorker* articles, later expanded in his book *The Underclass.* He accented the black underclass and its supposed immorality, family disorganization, and substandard work ethic.[32] A later article in the *Chronicle of Higher Education* surveyed the growing research on the underclass, noting that "the lives of the ghetto poor are marked by a dense fabric of what experts call 'social pathologies'—teenage pregnancies, out-of-wedlock births, single-parent families, poor educational achievement, chronic unemployment, welfare dependency, drug abuse, and crime—that, taken separately or together, seem impervious to change."[33] To the present day, similar stories designed to explain black problems in cultural terms regularly appear in the local and national media across the nation.

A WHITEWASHED WORLDVIEW

This antiblack ideology links in so many ways to so much of white thought and behavior that we might speak of it as a broad worldview. Seen comprehensively, all the mental images, prejudiced attitudes, stereotypes, fictions, racist explanations, and rationalizations that link to systemic racism make up a white racist worldview, one deeply imbedded in the dominant culture and institutions. The U.S. system of racism is not just something that affects black Americans and other Americans of color, for it is central to the lives of white Americans as well. It determines how whites think about themselves, about their ideals, and about their nation.

In the early 1900s European immigrants to the United States came to accept this worldview and its implicit assumption that being "American" means being white. This has not changed much in the intervening years. Today the term "American" still means "white"—at least for the majority of white Americans, and probably for most people across the globe. One can pick up most newspapers or news magazines and find "American" or "Americans" used in a way that clearly accents *white* Americans. Take this sentence from a news writer in a Florida newspaper: "The American Public isn't giving government or police officers the blind trust it once did."[34] Clearly, "American" here means "white American," for the majority of blacks have never blindly trusted the police.

One research analysis examined all the articles in sixty-five major English-language newspapers for a six-month period and estimated that there were thousands of references to "black Americans" or "African Americans" in the articles. However, in the same newspapers there were *only forty-six* mentions of "white Americans."[35] In almost every case these mentions by newspaper writers occurred in connection with "black Americans," "blacks," or "African Americans." (The exceptions were three cases in which "white Americans" was used in connection with "Native Americans" or "Korean Americans.") A similar pattern was found for major magazines. Not once was the term "white Americans" used alone in an article; if used, it was always used in relation to another racial category. The same study examined how congressional candidates were described in news articles in the two weeks prior to the November 1998 elections. In every case white congressional candidates were *not* described as "white," but black congressional candidates were always noted as being "black."[36] In the United States blackness is usually salient and noted, while whiteness generally goes unmentioned, except when reference is specifically made to white connections to other racial groups.

Being "American" still means, in the minds of many people, including editors and writers in the media, being white. This need not be a conscious process. For several centuries most whites have probably not seen the routines of their everyday lives as framed in white. "Race" is often not visible when one is at the top of the social hierarchy. Today, major social institutions, those originally created by whites centuries ago, are still dominated by whites. Yet from the white standpoint they are not white, just normal and customary. They are not seen for what they actually are—whitewashed institutions reflecting in many of their aspects the history, privileges, norms, values, and interests of white Americans. When whites live in these customary arrangements, they need not think in overtly racist terms. Nonetheless, when whites move into settings where they must confront people of color in the United States or elsewhere, they usually foreground their whiteness, whether consciously or unconsciously.

FEAR OF A MULTIRACIAL, MULTICULTURAL FUTURE

Today, many white analysts still see Western civilization as under threat from groups that are not white or European. Racist thinking is more than rationalizing oppression, for it also represents a defensive response, a fear of losing power to Americans of color. In recent years many advocates of white superiority have directed their attacks at the values or cultures of new immigrants of color coming to the United States, as well as at black Americans. In one recent interview study elite numerous white men openly expressed some fear of the growth of Americans of color in the United States, seeing Western civilization as under threat.[37]

We observe examples of this fear among U.S. politicians and intellectuals. For example, in several speeches and articles Patrick Buchanan, media pundit and once a candidate for the Republican presidential nomination, has argued that "our Judeo-Christian values are going to be preserved and our Western heritage is going to be handed down to future generations and not dumped on some landfill called multiculturalism."[38] Once again, we see the linkage between religion and a strong sense of European supremacy. We also see a concern for the reproduction of the white-dominated system from current to future generations. In addition, Buchanan told one interviewer that "if we had to take a million immigrants in, say, Zulus next year or Englishmen, and put them in Virginia, what group would be easier to assimilate and would cause less problems for the people of Virginia? There is nothing wrong with us sitting down and arguing that issue that we are a European country, [an] English-speaking country."[39] The Zulus, who are Africans, seem to represent in his mind the specter of strange or savage hordes who would not assimilate well into the nation. Ironically, Africans have been in the nation longer than Buchanan's Irish ancestors, and Virginia has been home to African Americans for nearly four centuries.

CONCLUSION

The systemic racism that is still part of the base of U.S. society is interwoven with a strong racist ideology that has been partially reframed at various points in U.S. history, but which has remained a well-institutionalized set of beliefs, attitudes, and concepts defending white-on-black oppression. Until the late 1940s commitment to a white supremacist view of the world was proud, openly held, and aggressive. Most whites in the United States and Europe, led by elites, took pride in forthrightly professing their racist perspectives on other peoples and their racist rationalizations for Western imperialistic adventures. Brutal discrimination and overt exploitation were routinely advocated. Indeed, white domination of the globe was "seen as proof of white racial superiority."[40]

Beginning in the late 1940s, however, the open expression of a white supremacist ideology was made more difficult by a growing American awareness of actions of the racist regime in Nazi Germany. In addition, by the 1950s and 1960s growing black civil rights protests against U.S. racism—with their counterideology of black liberation—and the U.S. struggle with the Soviet Union made the open expression of a white supremacist ideology less acceptable. The dominant racist ideology changed slowly to reflect these new conditions, with a new accent on equality of opportunity and some support for moderate programs to break down the nation's segregated institutions. Still, as we have seen, many aspects of the old racist ideology were dressed up in a new guise, and they persist, with some barnacle-like additions, to the present day. From the beginning, the age-old idea of the superiority of white (Western) culture and institutions has been the most basic idea in the dominant ideology rationalizing oppression.

For some time now, most whites have viewed the last few centuries of societal development in terms of a broad imagery equating "human progress" with Western civilization. We hear or see phrases like "Western civilization is an engine generating great progress for the world" or "Africans have only seen real advancement because of their contacts with Western civilization." Western imperialism's bringing of "civilization" or "democracy" to other peoples is made to appear as an engine of great progress, with mostly good results. However, this equating of "progress" with European civilization conceals the devastating consequences of imperialism and colonialism. The actual reality was—and often still is—brutal, bloody, oppressive, or genocidal in consequence for those colonized. When whites speak of Western civilization as equivalent to great human progress, they are talking about the creation of social systems that do not take into serious consideration the interests and views of the indigenous or enslaved peoples whose resources were ripped from them, whose societies were destroyed, and whose lives were cut short. Images of Western civilization, like the racist ideologies of which they are often part, are too often used to paper over the sordid realities of Western colonialism and imperialism.

DISCUSSION QUESTIONS

1. What is a racist ideology, and when did it first develop in North America?

2. Are elites or the rank-and-file population most responsible for the growth and importance of the racist ideology?

3. Is the racist ideology still important today? How and where?

4. Have prominent presidents and scientists played any important role in the development of racist ideas and notions? If so, how and when?

5. What is social Darwinism, and is it still important in U.S. society today?

NOTES

1. W.E.B. Du Bois, *Dusk of Dawn: An Essay Toward an Autobiography of a Race Concept* (New Brunswick, NJ: Transaction Books, 1984 [1940]), p. 144.

2. Karl Marx and Friederich Engels, *The German Ideology*, ed. R. Pascal (New York: International Publishers, 1947), p. 39.

3. Kenneth O'Reilly, *Nixon's Piano: Presidents and Racial Politics from Washington to Clinton* (New York: Free Press, 1995), p. 11.

4. Ronald T. Takaki, *Iron Cages: Race and Culture in 19th Century America* (Oxford: Oxford University Press, 1990), pp. 11–14.

5. James Fenimore Cooper, *The Last of the Mohicans* (1826), as quoted in Emily Morison Beck, ed., *John Bartlett's Familiar Quotations*, 15th ed. (Boston: Little Brown, 1980), p. 463.

6 . Tomás Almaguer, *Racial Fault Lines* (Berkeley and Los Angeles: University of California Press, 1994), p. 28.

7 . Takaki, *Iron Cages*, pp. 30–34.

8 . See Frances Lee Ansley, "Stirring the Ashes: Race, Class and the Future of Civil Rights Scholarship," *Cornell Law Review* 74 (September, 1989): 993.

9 . W.E.B. Du Bois, *Dusk of Dawn: An Essay Toward an Autobiography of a Race Concept* (New Brunswick, NJ: Transaction Books, 1984 [1940]), p. 6.

10 . A. Leon Higginbotham, Jr., and Barbara K. Kopytoff, "Racial Purity and Interracial Sex in the Law of Colonial and Antebellum Virginia," *Georgetown Law Journal* 77 (August 1989): 1671.

11 . Benjamin Franklin, quoted in Takaki, *Iron Cages*, p. 50; Claude-Anne Lopez and Eugenia W. Herbert, *The Private Franklin: The Man and His Family* (New York: Norton, 1975), pp. 194–95.

12 . George Frederickson, *The Black Image in the White Mind* (Hanover, NH: Wesleyan University Press, 1971), p. 282.

13 . Frantz Fanon, *The Wretched of the Earth* (New York: Grove Press, 1963), p. 32.

14 . Thomas Jefferson, *Notes on the State of Virginia*, ed. Frank Shuffelton (New York: Penguin, 1999 [1785]), pp. 145, 147–48.

15 . William H. Tucker, *The Science and Politics of Racial Research* (Urbana: University of Illinois Press, 1994), pp. 8–9; Ivan Hannaford, *Race: The History of an Idea in the West* (Baltimore: Johns Hopkins University Press, 1996), pp. 205–207.

16 . Audrey Smedley, *Race in North America* (Boulder, CO: Westview Press, 1993), p. 26.

17 . *Dred Scott v. John F. A. Sandford*, 60 U.S. 393, 407–408 (1857).

18 . Abraham Lincoln, "The Sixth Joint Debate at Quincy, October 13, 1858," in *The Lincoln-Douglas Debates: The First Complete, Unexpurgated Text*, ed. Harold Holzer (New York: HarperCollins, 1993), p. 283.

19 . Charles Darwin, quoted in Frederickson, *The Black Image in the White Mind*, p. 30.

20 . See Joe R. Feagin, *Subordinating the Poor: Welfare and American Beliefs* (Englewood Cliffs, NJ: Prentice-Hall, 1975), pp. 35–36; and Frederick L. Hoffman, "Vital Statistics of the Negro," *Arena* 5 (April 1892): 542, cited in Frederickson, *The Black Image in the White Mind*, pp. 250–51.

21. John Higham, *Strangers in the Land* (New York: Atheneum, 1963), pp. 96–152; Tucker, *The Science and Politics of Racial Research,* p. 35.

22. Tucker, *The Science and Politics of Racial Research,* p. 93.

23. See Theodore Cross, *Black Power Imperative: Racial Inequality and the Politics of Nonviolence* (New York: Faulkner, 1984), p. 157; Magnus Hirschfeld, *Racism,* trans. and ed. by Eden and Cedar Paul (London: V. Gollancz, 1938). The book was published in German in 1933.

24. Warren G. Harding and Calvin Coolidge, each quoted in Tucker, *The Science and Politics of Racial Research,* p. 93.

25. David K. Shipler, "Blacks in the Newsroom," *Columbia Journalism Review,* May/June 1998, pp. 81 26–29; Robert M. Entman et al., *Mass Media and Reconciliation: A Report to the Advisory Board and Staff, The President's Initiative on Race* (Washington, DC, 1998); Edward Herman, "The Propaganda Model Revisited," *Monthly Review* 48 (July 1996): 115.

26. Sidney Blumenthal, *The Rise of the Counter-Establishment* (New York: Times Books, 1986), pp. 4–11, 133–70; Peter Steinfels, *The Neoconservatives: The Men Who Are Changing America's Politics* (New York: Touchstone, 1979), pp. 214–77.

27. Franklin D. Gilliam Jr., and Shanto Iyengar, "Prime Suspects: the Effects of Local News on the Viewing Public," University of California at Los Angeles, unpublished paper, n. d.

28. Thomas Ferguson and Joel Rodgers, *Right Turn: The Decline of the Democrats and the Future of American Politics* (New York: Hill and Wang, 1986), pp. 65–66.

29. *City of Richmond, Virginia v. J.A.Croson Co.,* 488 U.S. 469 (1989).

30. Arthur R. Jensen, "How Much Can We Boost IQ and Scholastic Achievement?" *Harvard* 99 *Educational Review* 39 (1969): 1–123.

31. Jean Stefancic and Richard Delgado, *No Mercy: How Conservative Think Tanks and 100 Foundations Changed America's Social Agenda* (Philadelphia: Temple University Press, 1996), p. 34.

32. Ken Auletta, *The Underclass* (New York: Random House, 1982).

33. Ellen K. Coughlin, "Worsening Plight of the Underclass Catches Attention," *Chronicle of Higher Education,* March 1988, A5.

34. I draw here on Nick Mrozinske, "Derivational Thinking and Racism," unpublished research paper, University of Florida, fall, 1998.

35 . The search algorithm did not allow searches for the word "whites" alone, because this picks up the surnames of individuals in the Lexis/Nexis database.

36 . Mrozinske, "Derivational Thinking and Racism."

37 . Rhonda Levine, "The Souls of Elite White Men: White Racial Identity and the Logic of Thinking on Race," paper presented at annual meeting, Hawaiian Sociological Association, February 14, 1998.

38 . Patrick Buchanan, quoted in Clarence Page, "U.S. Media Should Stop Abetting Intolerance," *Toronto Star,* December 27, 1991, A27.

39 . Patrick Buchanan, quoted in John Dillin, "Immigration Joins List of '92 Issues," *Christian Science Monitor,* December 17, 1991, 6.

40 . Frank Furedi, *The Silent War: Imperialism and the Changing Perception of Race* (New Brunswick, NJ: Rutgers University Press, 1998), p. 1.

SELECTED BIBLIOGRAPHY

Cross, Theodore. *Black Power Imperative: Racial Inequality and the Politics of Nonviolence* (New York: Faulkner, 1984).

Du Bois, W. E. B. *Dusk of Dawn: An Essay Toward an Autobiography of a Race Concept* (New Brunswick, NJ: Transaction Books, 1984 [1940]).

Furedi, Frank. *The Silent War: Imperialism and the Changing Perception of Race* (New Brunswick, NJ: Rutgers University Press, 1998).

O'Reilly, Kenneth. *Nixon's Piano: Presidents and Racial Politics from Washington to Clinton* (New York: Free Press, 1995).

Smedley, Audrey. *Race in North America* (Boulder, CO: Westview Press, 1993).

Takaki, Ronald T. *Iron Cages: Race and Culture in 19th Century America* (Oxford: Oxford University Press, 1990.

Tucker, William H. *The Science and Politics of Racial Research* (Urbana: University of Illinois Press, 1994).

Racial Formation: Understanding Race and Racism in the Post-Civil Rights Era

By Michael Omi and Howard Winant

In 1982–83, Susie Guillory Phipps unsuccessfully sued the Louisiana Bureau of Vital Records to change her racial classification from black to white. The descendent of an 18th century white planter and a black slave, Phipps was designated "black" in her birth certificate in accordance with a 1970 state law which declared anyone with at least 1/32nd "Negro blood" to be black.

The Phipps case raised intriguing questions about the concept of race, its meaning in contemporary society, and its use (and abuse) in public policy. Assistant Attorney General Ron Davis defended the law by pointing out that some type of racial classification was necessary to comply with federal record-keeping requirements and to facilitate programs for the prevention of genetic diseases. Phipps's attorney, Brian Begue, argued that the assignment of racial categories on birth certificates was unconstitutional and that the 1/32nd designation was inaccurate. He called on a retired Tulane University professor who cited research indicating that most Louisiana whites have at least 1/20th "Negro" ancestry.

In the end, Phipps lost. The court upheld the state's right to classify and quantify racial identity.[1]

Phipps's problematic racial identity, and her effort to resolve it through state action, is in many ways a parable of America's unsolved racial dilemma. It illustrates the difficulties of defining race and assigning individuals or groups to racial categories.

It shows how the racial legacies of the past—slavery and bigotry—continue to shape the present. It reveals both the deep involvement of the state in the organization and interpretation of race, and the inadequacy of state institutions to carry out these functions. It demonstrates how deeply Americans both as individuals and as a civilization are shaped, and indeed haunted, by race.

Having lived her whole life thinking that she was white, Phipps suddenly discovers that by legal definition she is not. In U.S. society, such an event is indeed catastrophic.[2] But if she is not white, of what race is she? The state claims that she is black, based on its rules of classification,[3] and another state agency, the court, upholds this judgment. Despite the classificatory standards that have imposed an either-or logic on racial identity, Phipps will not in fact "change color." Unlike what would have happened during slavery times if one's claim to whiteness was successfully challenged, we can assume that despite the outcome of her legal challenge, Phipps will remain in most of the social relationships she had occupied before the trial. Her socialization, her familial and friendship networks, her cultural orientation, will not change. She will simply have to wrestle with her newly acquired "hybridized" condition. She will have to confront the "other" within.

The designation of racial categories and the assignment of race is no simple task. For centuries, this question has precipitated intense debates and conflicts, particularly in the U.S.—disputes over natural and legal rights, over the distribution of resources, and indeed, over who shall live and who shall die.

A crucial dimension of the Phipps case is that it illustrates the inadequacy of claims that race is a mere matter of variations in human physiognomy, that it is simply a matter of skin "color." But if race cannot be understood in this manner, how can it be understood? We cannot fully hope to address this topic—no less than the meaning of race, its role in society, and the forces that shape it—in one chapter, nor indeed in one book. Our goal in this chapter, however, is far from modest: we wish to offer at least the outlines of a theory of race and racism.

WHAT IS RACE?

There is a continuous temptation to think of race as an essence, as something fixed, concrete and objective. And there is also an opposite temptation: to imagine race as a mere illusion, a purely ideological construct that some ideal non-racist social order would eliminate. It is necessary to challenge both these positions, to disrupt and reframe the rigid and bipolar manner in which they are posed and debated, and to transcend the presumably irreconcilable relationship between them.

The effort must be made to understand race as an unstable and "decentered" complex of social meanings constantly being transformed by political struggle. With this in mind, let us propose a definition: *race is a concept that signifies and symbolizes social conflicts and interests by referring to different types of human bodies.* Although the concept of race invokes biologically-based human characteristics (so-called "pheno-types"), selection of these particular human features for purposes of racial signification is always and necessarily a social and historical process. In contrast to the other major distinction of this type, that of gender, there is no biological basis for distinguishing among human groups along the lines of race.[4] Indeed, the categories employed to differentiate among human groups along racial lines reveal themselves, upon serious examination, to be at best imprecise, and at worst completely arbitrary.

If the concept of race is so nebulous, can we not dispense with it? Can we not "do without" race, at least in the "enlightened" present? This question has been posed often, and with greater frequency in recent years.[5] An affirmative answer would of course present obvious practical difficulties: it is rather difficult to jettison widely held beliefs, beliefs which moreover are central to everyone's identity and understanding of the social world. So the attempt to banish the concept as an archaism is at best counterintuitive. But a deeper difficulty, we believe, is inherent in the very formulation of this schema, in its way of posing race as a problem, a misconception left over from the past, and suitable now only for the dustbin of history.

A more effective starting point is the recognition that despite its uncertainties and contradictions, the concept of race continues to play a fundamental role in structuring and representing the social world. The task for theory is to explain this situation. It is to avoid both the utopian framework that sees race as an illusion we can somehow "get beyond," and also the essentialist formulation that sees race as something objective and fixed, a biological datum.[6] Thus we should think of race as an element of social structure rather than as an irregularity within it; we should see race as a dimension of human representation rather than an illusion. These perspectives inform the theoretical approach we call racial formation.

RACIAL FORMATION

We define racial formation as *the sociohistorical process by which racial categories are created, lived out, transformed, and destroyed.* Our attempt to elaborate a theory of racial formation will proceed in two steps. First, we argue that racial formation is a process of historically situated projects in which human bodies and social structures are represented and organized. Next we link racial formation to the evolution of hegemony, the way in which society is organized and ruled. Such an approach, we believe, can facilitate understanding of a whole range of contemporary controversies and dilemmas involving race, including the nature of racism, the relationship of race to other forms of differences, inequalities, and oppression such as sexism and nationalism, and the dilemmas of racial identity today.

From a racial formation perspective, race is a matter of both social structure and cultural representation. Too often, the attempt is made to understand race simply or primarily in terms of only one of these two analytical dimensions.[7] For example, efforts to explain racial inequality as a purely social structural phenomenon are unable to account for the origins, patterning, and transformation of racial difference. Conversely, many examinations of racial difference—understood as a matter of cultural attributes a la ethnicity theory, or as a society-wide signification system, a la some poststructuralist accounts—cannot comprehend such structural phenomena as racial stratification in the labor market or patterns of residential segregation.

An alternative approach is to think of racial formation processes as occurring through a linkage between structure and representation. Racial projects do the ideological "work" of making these links. A racial project is simultaneously an interpretation, representation, or explanation of racial dynamics, and an effort to reorganize and redistribute resources along particular racial lines. Racial projects connect what race means in a particular discursive practice and the ways in which both social structures and everyday experiences are racially organized, based upon that meaning. Let us consider this proposition, first in terms of large-scale or macro-level social processes, and then in terms of other dimensions of the racial formation process.

RACIAL FORMATION AS A MACRO-LEVEL SOCIAL PROCESS

To interpret the meaning of race is to frame it social structurally. Consider for example, this statement by Charles Murray on welfare reform:

> My proposal for dealing with the racial issue in social welfare is to repeal every bit of legislation and reverse every court decision that in any way requires, recommends, or awards differential treatment according to race, and thereby put us back onto the track that we left in 1965. We may argue about the appropriate limits of government intervention in trying to enforce the ideal, but at least it should be possible to identify the ideal: Race is not a morally admissible reason for treating one person differently from another. Period.[8]

Here there is a partial but significant analysis of the meaning of race: it is not a morally valid basis upon which to treat people "differently from one another." We may notice someone's race, but we cannot act upon that awareness. We must act in a "color-blind" fashion. This analysis of the meaning of race is immediately linked to a specific conception of the role of race in the social structure: it can play no part in government action, save in "the enforcement of the ideal." No state policy can legitimately require, recommend, or award different status according to race. This example can be classified as a particular type of racial project in the present-day U.S.—a "neoconservative" one.

Conversely, to recognize the racial dimension in social structure is to interpret the meaning of race. Consider the following statement by the late Supreme Court Justice Thurgood Marshall on minority "set-aside" programs:

> A profound difference separates governmental actions that themselves are racist, and governmental actions that seek to remedy the effects of prior racism or to prevent neutral government activity from perpetuating the effects of such racism.[9]

Here the focus is on the racial dimensions of social structure—in this case of state activity and policy. The argument is that state actions in the past and present have treated people in very different ways according to their race, and thus the government cannot retreat from its policy responsibilities in this area. It cannot suddenly declare itself "color-blind" without in fact perpetuating the same type of differential, racist treatment.[10] Thus, race continues to signify difference and structure inequality. Here, racialized social structure is immediately linked to an interpretation of the meaning of race. This example too can be classified as a particular type of racial project in the present-day U.S.—a "liberal" one.

These two examples of contemporary racial projects are drawn from mainstream political debate; they may be characterized as center-right and center-left expressions of contemporary racial politics.[11] We can, however, expand the discussion of racial formation processes far beyond these familiar examples. In fact, we can identify racial projects in at least three other analytical dimensions: first, the political spectrum can be broadened to include radical projects, on both the left and right, as well as along other political axes. Second, analysis of racial projects can take place not only at the macro-level of racial policy-making, state activity, and collective action, but also at the level of everyday experience. Third, the concept of racial projects can be applied across historical time, to identify racial formation dynamics in the past. We shall now offer examples of each of these types of racial projects.

THE POLITICAL SPECTRUM OF RACIAL FORMATION

We have encountered examples of a neoconservative racial project, in which the significance of race is denied, leading to a "color-blind" racial politics and "hands off" policy orientation; and of a "liberal" racial project, in which the significance of race is affirmed, leading to an egalitarian and "activist" state policy. But these by no means exhaust the political possibilities. Other racial projects can be readily identified on the contemporary U.S. scene. For example, "far right" projects, which uphold biologistic and racist views of difference, explicitly argue for white supremacist policies. "New right" projects overtly claim to hold "color-blind" views, but covertly manipulate racial fears in order to achieve political gains.[12] On the left, "radical democratic" projects invoke notions of racial "difference" in combination with egalitarian politics and policy.

Further variations can also be noted. For example, "nationalist" projects, both conservative and radical, stress the incompatibility of racially-defined group identity with the legacy of white supremacy, and therefore advocate a social structural solution of separation, either complete or partial.[13] As we saw in Chapter 3, nationalist currents represent a profound legacy of the centuries of racial absolutism that initially defined the meaning of race in the U.S. Nationalist concerns continue to influence racial debate in the form of Afrocentrism and other expressions of identity politics.

Taking the range of politically organized racial projects as a whole, we can "map" the current pattern of racial formation at the level of the public sphere, the "macro-level" in which public debate and mobilization takes place.[14] But important as this is, the terrain on which racial formation occurs is broader yet.

RACIAL FORMATION AS EVERYDAY EXPERIENCE

Here too racial projects link signification and structure, not so much as efforts to shape policy or define large-scale meaning, but as the applications of "common sense." To see racial projects operating at the level of everyday life, we have only to examine the many ways in which, often unconsciously, we "notice" race.

One of the first things we notice about people when we meet them (along with their sex) is their race. We utilize race to provide clues about who a person is. This fact is made painfully obvious when we encounter someone whom we cannot conveniently racially categorize—someone who is, for example, racially "mixed" or of an ethnic/racial group we are not familiar with. Such an encounter becomes a source of discomfort and momentarily a crisis of racial meaning.

Our ability to interpret racial meanings depends on preconceived notions of a racialized social structure. Comments such as, "Funny, you don't look black," betray an underlying image of what black should be. We expect people to act out their apparent racial identities; indeed we become disoriented when they do not. The black banker harassed by police while walking in casual clothes through his own well-off neighborhood, the Latino or white kid rapping in perfect Afro patois, the unending faux pas committed by whites who assume that the nonwhites they encounter are servants or tradespeople, the belief that nonwhite colleagues are less qualified persons hired to fulfill affirmative action guidelines, indeed the whole gamut of racial stereotypes—that "white men can't jump," that Asians can't dance, etc. etc.—all testify to the way a racialized social structure shapes racial experience and conditions meaning. Analysis of such stereotypes reveals the always present, already active link between our view of the social structure—its demography, its laws, its customs, its threats—and our conception of what race means.

Conversely, our ongoing interpretation of our experience in racial terms shapes our relations to the institutions and organizations through which we are imbedded in social structure. Thus we expect differences in skin color, or other racially coded characteristics, to explain social differences. Temperament, sexuality, intelligence, athletic ability, aesthetic preferences, and so on are presumed to be fixed and discernible from the palpable mark of race. Such diverse questions as our confidence and trust in others (for example, clerks or salespeople, media figures, neighbors), our sexual preferences and romantic images, our tastes in music, films, dance, or sports, and our very ways of talking, walking, eating, and dreaming become racially coded simply because we live in a society where racial awareness is so pervasive. Thus in ways too comprehensive even to monitor consciously, and despite periodic calls—neoconservative and otherwise—for us to ignore race and adopt "color-blind" racial attitudes, skin color "differences" continue to rationalize distinct treatment of racially-identified individuals and groups.

To summarize the argument so far: the theory of racial formation suggests that society is suffused with racial projects, large and small, to which all are subjected. This racial "subjection" is quintessentially ideological. Everybody learns some combination, some version, of the rules of racial classification, and of her own racial identity, often without obvious teaching or conscious inculcation. Thus are we inserted in a comprehensively racialized social structure. Race becomes "common sense"—a way of comprehending, explaining, and acting in the world. A vast web of racial projects mediates between the discursive or representational means in which race is identified and signified on the one hand, and the institutional and organizational forms in which it is routinized and standardized on the other. These projects are the heart of the racial formation process.

Under such circumstances, it is not possible to represent race discursively without simultaneously locating it, explicitly or implicitly, in a social structural (and historical) context. Nor is it possible to organize, maintain, or transform social structures without simultaneously engaging, once more either explicitly or implicitly, in racial signification. Racial formation, therefore, is a kind of synthesis, an outcome, of the interaction of racial projects on a society-wide level. These projects are, of course, vastly different in scope and effect. They include large-scale public action, state activities, and interpretations of racial conditions in artistic, journalistic, or academic fora,[15] as well as the seemingly infinite number of racial judgments and practices we carry out at the level of individual experience.

Since racial formation is always historically situated, our understanding of the significance of race, and of the way race structures society, has changed enormously over time. The processes of racial formation we encounter today, the racial projects large and small which structure U.S. society in so many ways, are merely the present-day outcomes of a complex historical evolution. The contemporary racial order remains transient. By knowing something of how it evolved, we can perhaps better discern where it is heading. We therefore turn next to a historical survey of the racial formation process, and the conflicts and debates it has engendered.

THE EVOLUTION OF MODERN RACIAL AWARENESS

The identification of distinctive human groups, and their association with differences in physical appearance, goes back to prehistory, and can be found in the earliest documents—in the Bible, for example, or in Herodotus. But the emergence of a modern conception of race does not occur until the rise of Europe and the arrival of Europeans in the Americas. Even the hostility and suspicion with which Christian Europe viewed its two significant non-Christian "others"—the Muslims and the Jews—cannot be viewed as more than a rehearsal for racial formation, since these antagonisms, for all their bloodletting and chauvinism, were always and everywhere religiously interpreted.[16]

It was only when European explorers reached the Western Hemisphere, when the oceanic seal separating the "old" and the "new" worlds was breached, that the distinctions and categorizations fundamental to a racialized social structure, and to a discourse of race, began to appear. The European explorers were the advance guard of merchant capitalism, which sought new openings for trade. What they found exceeded their wildest dreams, for never before and never again in human history has an opportunity for the appropriation of wealth remotely approached that presented by the "discovery."[17]

But the Europeans also "discovered" people, people who looked and acted differently. These "natives" challenged their "discoverers'" preexisting conceptions of the origins and possibilities of the human species.[18] The representation and interpretation of the meaning of the indigenous peoples' existence became a crucial matter, one which would affect the outcome of the enterprise of conquest. For the "discovery" raised disturbing questions as to whether all could be considered part of the same "family of man," and more practically, the extent to which native peoples could be exploited and enslaved. Thus religious debates flared over the attempt to reconcile the various Christian metaphysics with the existence of peoples who were more "different" than any whom Europe had previously known.[19]

In practice, of course, the seizure of territories and goods, the introduction of slavery through the encomienda and other forms of coerced native labor, and then through the organization of the African slave trade—not to mention the practice of outright extermination—all presupposed a worldview which distinguished Europeans, as children of God, full-fledged human beings, etc., from "others." Given the dimensions and the ineluctability of the European onslaught, given the conquerors' determination to appropriate both labor and goods, and given the presence of an axiomatic and unquestioned Christianity among them, the ferocious division of society into Europeans and "others" soon coalesced. This was true despite the famous 16th-century theological and philosophical debates about the identity of indigenous peoples.[20]

Indeed debates about the nature of the "others" reached their practical limits with a certain dispatch. Plainly they would never touch the essential: nothing, after all, would induce the Europeans to pack up and go home. We cannot examine here the early controversies over the status of American souls. We simply wish to emphasize that the "discovery" signaled a break from the previous proto-racial awareness by which Europe contemplated its "others" in a relatively disorganized fashion. In other words, we argue that the "conquest of America" was not simply an epochal historical event—however unparalleled in its importance. It was also the advent of a consolidated social structure of exploitation, appropriation, domination. Its representation, first in religious terms, but soon enough in scientific and political ones, initiated modern racial awareness.

The conquest, therefore, was the first—and given the dramatic nature of the case, perhaps the greatest—racial formation project. Its significance was by no means limited to the Western Hemisphere, for it began the work of constituting Europe as the metropole, the center, of a series of empires which could take, as Marx would later write, "the globe for a theater."[21] It represented this new imperial structure as a struggle between civilization and barbarism, and implicated in this representation all the great European philosophies, literary traditions, and social theories of the modern age.[22] In short, just as the noise of the "big bang" still resonates through the universe, so the overdetermined construction of world "civilization" as a product of the rise of Europe and the subjugation of the rest of us, still defines the race concept.

FROM RELIGION TO SCIENCE

After the initial depredations of conquest, religious justifications for racial difference gradually gave way to scientific ones. By the time of the Enlightenment, a general awareness of race was pervasive, and most of the great philosophers of Europe, such as Hegel, Kant, Hume, and Locke, had issued virulently racist opinions.

The problem posed by race during the late 18th century was markedly different than it had been in the age of conquest, expropriation, and slaughter. The social structures in which race operated were no longer primarily those of military conquest and plunder, nor of the establishment of thin beachheads of colonization on the edge of what had once seemed a limitless wilderness. Now the issues were much more complicated: nation-building, establishment of national economies in the world trading system, resistance to the arbitrary authority of monarchs, and the assertion of the "natural rights" of "man," including the right of revolution.[23] In such a situation, racially organized exploitation, in the form of slavery, the expansion of colonies, and the continuing expulsion of native peoples, was both necessary and newly difficult to justify.

The invocation of scientific criteria to demonstrate the "natural" basis of racial hierarchy was both a logical consequence of the rise of this form of knowledge, and an attempt to provide a more subtle and nuanced account of human complexity in the new, "enlightened" age. Spurred on by the classificatory scheme of living organisms devised by Linnaeus in *Systema Naturae* (1735), many scholars in the eighteenth and nineteenth centuries dedicated themselves to the identification and ranking of variations in humankind. Race was conceived as a biological concept, a matter of species. Voltaire wrote that "The negro race is a species of men (sic) as different from ours ... as the breed of spaniels is from that of greyhounds," and in a formulation echoing down from his century to our own, declared that "If their understanding is not of a different nature from ours ..., it is at least greatly inferior. They are not capable of any great application or association of ideas, and seem formed neither for the advantages nor the abuses of philosophy".[24]

Jefferson, the preeminent exponent of the Enlightenment doctrine of "the rights of man" on North American shores, echoed these sentiments:

> In general their existence appears to participate more of sensation than reflection. ... [I]n memory they are equal to whites, in reason much inferior ... [and] in imagination they are dull, tasteless, and anomalous. ... I advance it therefore ... that the blacks, whether originally a different race, or made distinct by time and circumstances, are inferior to the whites. ... Will not a lover of natural history, then, one who views the gradations in all the animals with the eye of philosophy, excuse an effort to keep those in the department of Man (sic) as distinct as nature has formed them?[25]

Such claims of species distinctiveness among humans justified the inequitable allocation of political and social rights, while still upholding the doctrine of "the rights of man." The quest to obtain a precise scientific definition of race sustained debates that continue to rage today. Yet despite efforts ranging from Dr. Samuel Morton's studies of cranial capacity[26] to contemporary attempts to base racial classification on shared gene pools,[27] the concept of race has defied biological definition.

In the 19th century, Count Joseph Arthur de Gobineau drew upon the most respected scientific studies of his day to compose his four-volume *Essay on the Inequality of Races* (1853–1855).[28] He not only greatly influenced the racial thinking of the period, but his themes would be echoed in the racist ideologies of the next one hundred years: beliefs that superior races produced superior cultures and that racial intermixtures resulted in the degradation of the superior racial stock. These ideas found expression, for instance, in the eugenics movement launched by Darwin's cousin, Francis Galton, which had an immense impact on scientific and sociopolitical thought in Europe and the United States.[29] In the wake of civil war and emancipation, and with immigration from southern and Eastern Europe as well as East Asia running high, the U.S. was particularly fertile ground for notions such as social darwinism and eugenics.

Attempts to discern the scientific meaning of race continue to the present day. For instance, an essay by Arthur Jensen that argued that hereditary factors shape intelligence not only revived the "nature or nurture" controversy, but also raised highly volatile questions about racial equality itself.[30] All such attempts seek to remove the concept of race from the historical context in which it arose and developed. They employ an essentialist approach that suggests instead that the truth of race is a matter of innate characteristics, of which skin color and other physical attributes provide only the most obvious, and in some respects most superficial, indicators.

FROM SCIENCE TO POLITICS

It has taken scholars more than a century to reject biologistic notions of race in favor of an approach that regards race as a social concept. This trend has been slow and uneven, and even today remains somewhat embattled, but its overall direction seems clear. At the turn of the century Max Weber discounted biological explanations for racial conflict and instead highlighted the social and political factors that engendered such conflict.[31] W. E. B. DuBois argued for a sociopolitical definition of race by identifying "the color line" as "the problem of the 20th century."[32] Pioneering cultural anthropologist Franz Boas rejected attempts to link racial identifications and cultural traits, labeling as pseudoscientific any assumption of a continuum of "higher" and "lower" cultural groups.[33] Other early exponents of social, as opposed to biological, views of race included Robert E. Park, founder of the "Chicago school" of sociology, and Alain Leroy Locke, philosopher and theorist of the Harlem renaissance.[34]

Perhaps more important than these and subsequent intellectual efforts, however, were the political struggles of racially defined groups themselves. Waged all around the globe under a variety of banners such as anti-colonialism and civil rights, these battles to challenge various structural and cultural racisms have been a major feature of 20th century politics. The racial horrors of the 20th century—colonial slaughter and apartheid, the genocide of the holocaust, and the massive bloodlettings required to end these evils—have also indelibly marked the theme of race as a political issue par excellence.

As a result of prior efforts and struggles, we have now reached the point of fairly general agreement that race is not a biologically given but rather a socially constructed way of differentiating human beings. While a tremendous achievement, the transcendence of biologistic conceptions of race does not provide any reprieve from the dilemmas of racial injustice and conflict, nor from controversies over the significance of race in the present. Views of race as socially constructed simply recognize the fact that these conflicts and controversies are now more properly framed on the terrain of politics. By privileging politics in the analysis that follows we do not mean to suggest that race has been displaced as a concern of scientific inquiry, or that struggles over cultural representation are no longer important. We do argue, however, that race is now a preeminently political phenomenon. Such an assertion invites examination of the evolving role of racial politics in the U.S. This is the subject to which we now turn.

DICTATORSHIP, DEMOCRACY, HEGEMONY

For most of its existence both as a European colony and as an independent nation, the U.S. was a racial dictatorship. From 1607 to 1865–258 years—most nonwhites were firmly eliminated from the sphere of politics.[35] After the civil war there was the brief egalitarian experiment of Reconstruction which terminated ignominiously in 1877. In its wake followed almost a century of legally sanctioned segregation and denial of the vote, nearly absolute in the South and much of the Southwest, less effective in the North and far West, but formidable in any case.[36] These barriers fell only in the mid-1960s, a mere quarter-century ago. Nor did the successes of the black movement and its allies mean that all obstacles to their political participation had now been abolished. Patterns of racial inequality have proven, unfortunately, to be quite stubborn and persistent.

It is important, therefore, to recognize that in many respects, racial dictatorship is the norm against which all U.S. politics must be measured. The centuries of racial dictatorship have had three very large consequences: first, they defined "American" identity as white, as the negation of racialized "otherness"—at first largely African and indigenous, later Latin American and Asian as well.[37] This negation took shape in both law and custom, in public institutions and in forms of cultural representation. It became the archetype of hegemonic rule in the U.S. It was the successor to the conquest as the "master" racial project.

Second, racial dictatorship organized (albeit sometimes in an incoherent and contradictory fashion) the "color line," rendering it the fundamental division in U.S. society. The dictatorship elaborated, articulated, and drove racial divisions not only through institutions, but also through psyches, extending up to our own time the racial obsessions of the conquest and slavery periods.

Third, racial dictatorship consolidated the oppositional racial consciousness and organization originally framed by marronage[38] and slave revolts, by indigenous resistance, and by nationalisms of various sorts. Just as the conquest created the "native" where once there had been Pequot, Iroquois, or Tutelo, so too it created the "black" where once there had been Asante or Ovimbundu, Yoruba or Bakongo.

The transition from a racial dictatorship to a racial democracy has been a slow, painful, and contentious one; it remains far from complete. A recognition of the abiding presence of racial dictatorship, we contend, is crucial for the development of a theory of racial formation in the U.S. It is also crucial to the task of relating racial formation to the broader context of political practice, organization, and change.

In this context, a key question arises: In what way is racial formation related to politics as a whole? How, for example, does race articulate with other axes of oppression and difference—most importantly class and gender—along which politics is organized today?

The answer, we believe, lies in the concept of *hegemony*. Antonio Gramsci—the Italian communist who placed this concept at the center of his life's work—understood it as the conditions necessary, in a given society, for the achievement and consolidation of rule. He argued that hegemony was always constituted by a combination of coercion and consent. Although rule can be obtained by force, it cannot be secured and maintained, especially in modern society, without the element of consent. Gramsci conceived of consent as far more than merely the legitimation of authority. In his view, consent extended to the incorporation by the ruling group of many of the key interests of subordinated groups, often to the explicit disadvantage of the rulers themselves.[39] Gramsci's treatment of hegemony went even farther: he argued that in order to consolidate their hegemony, ruling groups must elaborate and maintain a popular system of ideas and practices—through education, the media, religion, folk wisdom, etc.—which he called "common sense." It is through its production and its adherence to this "common sense," this ideology (in the broadest sense of the term), that a society gives its consent to the way in which it is ruled.[40]

These provocative concepts can be extended and applied to an understanding of racial rule. In the Americas, the conquest represented the violent introduction of a new form of rule whose relationship with those it subjugated was almost entirely coercive. In the U.S., the origins of racial division, and of racial signification and identity formation, lie in a system of rule that was extremely dictatorial. The mass murders and expulsions of indigenous people, and the enslavement of Africans, surely evoked and inspired little consent in their founding moments.

Over time, however, the balance of coercion and consent began to change. It is possible to locate the origins of hegemony right within the heart of racial dictatorship, for the effort to possess the oppressor's tools—religion and philosophy in this case—was crucial to emancipation (the effort to possess oneself). As Ralph Ellison reminds us, "The slaves often took the essence of the aristocratic ideal (as they took Christianity) with far more seriousness than their masters."[41] In their language, in their religion with its focus on the Exodus theme and on Jesus's tribulations, in their music with its figuring of suffering, resistance, perseverance, and transcendence, in their interrogation of a political philosophy that sought perpetually to rationalize their bondage in a supposedly "free" society, the slaves incorporated elements of racial rule into their thought and practice, turning them against their original bearers.

Racial rule can be understood as a slow and uneven historical process that has moved from dictatorship to democracy, from domination to hegemony. In this transition, hegemonic forms of racial rule—those based on consent—eventually came to supplant those based on coercion. Of course, before this assertion can be accepted, it must be qualified in important ways. By no means has the U.S. established racial democracy at the end of the century, and by no means is coercion a thing of the past. But the sheer complexity of the racial questions U.S. society confronts today, the welter of competing racial projects and contradictory racial experiences that Americans undergo, suggests that hegemony is a useful and appropriate term with which to characterize contemporary racial rule.

RACE, RACISM, AND HEGEMONY

Parallel to the debates on the concept of race, recent academic and political controversies about the nature of racism have centered on whether it is primarily an ideological or structural phenomenon. Proponents of the former position argue that racism is first and foremost a matter of beliefs and attitudes, doctrines and discourse, which only then give rise to unequal and unjust practices and structures.[42] Advocates of the latter view see racism as primarily a matter of economic stratification, residential segregation, and other institutionalized forms of inequality that then give rise to ideologies of privilege.[43]

From the standpoint of racial formation, these debates are fundamentally misguided. They discuss the problem of racism in a rigid "either-or" manner. We believe it is crucial to disrupt the fixity of these positions by simultaneously arguing that ideological beliefs have structural consequences, and that social structures give rise to beliefs. Racial ideology and social structure, therefore, mutually shape the nature of racism in a complex, dialectical, and overdetermined manner.

Even those racist projects that at first glance appear chiefly ideological turn out upon closer examination to have significant institutional and social structural dimensions. For example, what we have called "far right" projects appear at first glance to be centrally ideological. They are rooted in biologistic doctrine, after all. The same seems to hold for certain conservative black nationalist projects that have deep commitments to biologism.[44] But the unending stream of racist assaults initiated by the far right, the apparently increasing presence of skinheads in high schools, the proliferation of neo-Nazi websites on the Internet, and the appearance of racist talk shows on cable access channels, all suggest that the organizational manifestations of the far right racial projects exist and will endure.[45]

By contrast, even those racisms that at first glance appear to be chiefly structural upon closer examination reveal a deeply ideological component. For example, since the racial right abandoned its explicit advocacy of segregation, it has not seemed to uphold—in the main—an ideologically racist project, but more primarily a structurally racist one. Yet this very transformation required tremendous efforts of ideological production. It demanded the rearticulation of civil rights doctrines of equality in suitably conservative form, and indeed the defense of continuing large-scale racial inequality as an outcome preferable to (what its advocates have seen as) the threat to democracy that affirmative action, busing, and large-scale "race-specific" social spending would entail.[46] Even more tellingly, this project took shape through a deeply manipulative coding of subtextual appeals to white racism, notably in a series of political campaigns for high office that have occurred over recent decades. The retreat of social policy from any practical commitment to racial justice, and the relentless reproduction and divulgation of this theme at the level of everyday life—where whites are now "fed up" with all the "special treatment" received by nonwhites, etc.—constitutes the hegemonic racial project at this time. It therefore exhibits an unabashed structural racism all the more brazen because on the ideological or signification level it adheres to a principle to "treat everyone alike."

In summary, the racism of today is no longer a virtual monolith, as was the racism of yore. Today, racial hegemony is "messy." The complexity of the present situation is the product of a vast historical legacy of structural inequality and invidious racial representation, which has been confronted during the post-World War II period with an opposition more serious and effective than any it had faced before. The result is a deeply ambiguous and contradictory spectrum of racial projects, unremittingly conflictual racial politics, and confused and ambivalent racial identities of all sorts.

DISCUSSION QUESTIONS

1. In recent years civil rights advocates have brought suit against companies like CSX railroad and Fleet Bank on the grounds that they profited from from African slavery in their early years. For example, the lawsuits alleged that corporate ancestors of CSX used slave labor to lay railroad track and to build railroad facilities; they charged that corporate ancestors of Fleet Bank (which merged with Bank of America in 2004) insured plantation owners' "property" (the slaves themselves) in the antebellum South against the risk of slaves running away.

In your view what merit do these lawsuits have? Should contemporary corporations be liable for their predecessors' collaboration with slavery? Are the descendents of slaves entitled to compensation because their ancestors' labor was (allegedly) coerced by CSX's antecedents or because their ancestors' bodies were (allegedly) insured by Fleet's corporate founders against loss to their slavemasters? Is the black community as a whole entitled to such compensation?

2 . The United States is becoming a lot less white. Projecting current population (and immigration) trends forward to the year 2050, the US Census Bureau predicts that in 2050, the population will be about 25% Latino/Hispanic, 17% black, and 9% Asian American. In many of the largest cities in the US, whites are already a minority. The state of California, which was about 75% white in 1975, was only about 42% white in 2007.

What are the implications of these population trends for racial formation in the United States? How in your view will the country adapt to these patterns? For example, do you foresee a greater acceptance among whites of their minority status? Or do you think there will be greater hostility to members of "other" groups? What racial projects do you expect whites to be carrying out as a result of their declining proportion of the US population?

3 . In 2005 white families' average net worth (the monetary value of investments savings, and property belong to these families) was approximately 11X the average net worth of black families. This inequality in wealth distribution had grown significantly over the four decades since the passage of civil rights legislation in the 1960s.

In your view what accounts for the continuing (and in some ways increasing) gap between blacks and whites in the present, supposedly "color-blind" era?

4 . In 1997 golf star Tiger Woods referred to himself as "Cablinasian" on the Oprah Winfrey TV program. He said that it bothered him when people referred to him as black, since he is one-fourth black, one-fourth Thai, one-fourth Chinese, one-eighth white and one-eighth American Indian.

Discuss Woods's self-identification as a racial project. In what ways is he situating himself in the US racial mosaic? What are the implications for him (and for other Americans) of his invention of a "Cablinasian" identity?

5 . Starting in the 1970s, and more intensively since then, many politicians, academics, and public figures have argued that the United States is becoming a "color-blind" society. (The term actually goes back to Justice Harlan's dissent in the landmark *Plessy v. Ferguson* decision of 1896.) Yet survey results continue to show persistent beliefs in black inferiority, laziness, and criminality.

Is there a discrepancy here, or can these two trends be reconciled? Discuss these views on race as conflicting or overlapping racial projects.

NOTES

1. *San Francisco Chronicle*, September 14, 1982, May 19, 1983. Ironically, the 1970 Louisiana law was enacted to supersede an old Jim Crow statute which relied on the idea of "common report" in determining an infant's race. Following Phipps' unsuccessful attempt to change her classification and have the law declared unconstitutional, a legislative effort arose which culminated in the repeal of the law. See *San Francisco Chronicle*, June 23, 1983.

2. Compare the Phipps case to Andrew Hacker's well-known "parable" in which a white person is informed by a mysterious official that "the organization he represents has made a mistake" and that "… [a]ccording to their records …, you were to have been born black: to another set of parents, far from where you were raised." How much compensation, Hacker's official asks, would "you" require to undo the damage of this unfortunate error? See Hacker, *Two Nations: Black and White, Separate, Hostile, Unequal* (New York: Charles Scribner's Sons, 1992), pp. 31–32.

3. On the evolution of Louisiana's racial classification system, see Virginia Dominguez, *White By Definition: Social Classification in Creole Louisiana* (New Brunswick: Rutgers University Press, 1986).

4. This is not to suggest that gender is a biological category while race is not. Gender, like race, is a social construct. However, the biological division of humans into sexes—two at least, and possibly intermediate ones as well—is not in dispute. This provides a basis for argument over gender divisions—how natural?" etc.—which does not exist with regard to race. To ground an argument for the "natural" existence of race, one must resort to philosophical anthropology.

5. "The truth is that there are no races; there is nothing in the world that can do all we ask race to do for us. … The evil that is done is done by the concept, and by easy—yet impossible—assumptions as to its application." (Kwame Anthony Appiah, *In My Father's House: Africa in the Philosophy of Culture* (New York: Oxford University Press, 1992.) Appiah's eloquent and learned book fails, in our view, to dispense with the race concept, despite its anguished attempt to do so; this indeed is the source of its author's anguish. We agree with him as to the non-objective character of race, but fail to see how this recognition justifies its abandonment. This argument is developed below.

6. We understand essentialism as *belief in real, true human essences, existing outside or impervious to social and historical context*. We draw this definition, with some small modifications, from Diana Fuss, *Essentially Speaking: Feminism, Nature, & Difference* (New York: Routledge, 1989), p. xi.

7 . Michael Omi and Howard Winant, "On the Theoretical Status of the Concept of Race," in Warren Crichlow and Cameron McCarthy, eds., *Race, Identity, and Representation in Education* (New York: Routledge, 1993).

8 . Charles Murray, *Losing Ground: American Social Policy, 1950–1980* (New York: Basic Books, 1984), p. 223.

9 . Justice Thurgood Marshall, dissenting in *City of Richmond v. J.A. Croson Co.*, 488U.S. 469 (1989).

10 . See, for example, Derrick Bell, "Remembrances of Racism Past: Getting Past the Civil Rights Decline," in Herbert Hill and James E. Jones, Jr., eds., *Race in America: The Struggle for Equality* (Madison: The University of Wisconsin Press, 1993), pp. 75–76; Gertrude Ezorsky, *Racism and Justice: The Case for Affirmative Action* (Ithaca: Cornell University Press, 1991), pp. 109–111; David Kairys, *With Liberty and Justice for Some: A Critique of the Conservative Supreme Court* (New York: The New Press, 1993), pp. 138–41.

11 . Howard Winant has developed a tentative "map" of the system of racial hegemony in the U.S. circa 1990, which focuses on the spectrum of racial projects running from the political right to the political left. See Winant, "Where Culture Meets Structure: Race in the 1990s," in idem, *Racial Conditions: Theories, Politics, Comparisons* (Minneapolis: University of Minnesota Press, 1994).

12 . A familiar example is use of racial "code words." Recall George Bush's manipulations of racial fear in the 1988 "Willie Horton" ads, or Jesse Helms's use of the coded term "quota" in his 1990 campaign against Harvey Gantt.

13 . From this perspective, far right racial projects can also be interpreted as "nationalist." See Ronald Walters, "White Racial Nationalism in the United States," *Without Prejudice* I, 1 (Fall, 1987).

14 . Howard Winant has offered such a "map" in "Race: Theory, Culture, and Politics in the United States Today," in Marcy Darnovsky et al., eds., *Contemporary Social Movements and Cultural Politics* (Philadelphia: Temple University Press, 1994).

15 . We are not unaware, for example, that publishing this work is in itself a racial project.

16 . Although the Inquisition pioneered racial anti-semitism with its doctrine of "limpieza de sangre" (the claim that Jews could not be accepted as converts because their blood was "unclean"), anti-semitism only began to be seriously racialized in the 18th century, as George L. Mosse shows in *Toward the Final Solution: A History of European Racism* (New York: Howard Fertig, 1978).

17 . As Marx put it:

The discovery of gold and silver in America, the extirpation, enslavement, and entombment in mines of the aboriginal population, the beginning of the conquest and looting of the East Indies, the turning of Africa into a warren for the commercial hunting of blackskins, signalized the rosy dawn of the era of capitalist production. These idyllic proceedings are the chief momenta of primitive accumulation. (Karl Marx, *Capital*, Vol. I (New York: International Publishers, 1967), p. 751.)

David E. Stannard argues that the wholesale slaughter perpetrated upon the native peoples of the Western hemisphere is unequalled in history, even in our own bloody century. See his *American Holocaust: Columbus and the Conquest of the New World* (New York: Oxford University Press, 1992).

18. Winthrop Jordan provides a detailed account of the sources of European attitudes about color and race in *White Over Black: American Attitudes Toward the Negro, 1550–1812* (New York: Norton, 1977 [1968]), pp. 3–43.

19. In a famous instance, a 1550 debate in Valladolid pitted the philosopher and translator of Aristotle, Gines de Sepulveda, against the Dominican Bishop of the Mexican state of Chiapas, Bartolome de Las Casas. Discussing the native peoples, Sepulveda argued that

In wisdom, skill, virtue and humanity, these people are as inferior to the Spaniards as children are to adults and women to men; there is as great a difference between them as there is between savagery and forbearance, between violence and moderation, almost—I am inclined to say, as between monkeys and men (Sepulveda, "Democrates Alter," quoted in Tsvetan Todorov, *The Conquest of America: The Question of the Other* (New York: Harper and Row, 1984), p. 153).

In contrast, Las Casas defended the humanity and equality of the native peoples, both in terms of their way of life—which he idealized as one of innocence, gentleness, and generosity—and in terms of their readiness for conversion to Catholicism, which for him as for Sepulveda was the true and universal religion (Las Casas, "Letter to the Council of the Indies," quoted ibid, p. 163). William E. Connolly interrogates the linkages proposed by Todorov between early Spanish colonialism and contemporary conceptions of identity and difference in Identity/Difference: Democratic Negotiations of Political Paradox (Ithaca: Cornell University Press, 1991), pp. 40–48).

20. In Virginia, for example, it took about two decades after the establishment of European colonies to extirpate the indigenous people of the greater vicinity; 50 years after the establishment of the first colonies, the elaboration of slave codes establishing race as prima facie evidence for enslaved status was well under way. See Jordan, *White Over Black*.

21. *Capital*, P. 751.

22. Edward W. Said, *Culture and Imperialism* (New York: Alfred A. Knopf, 1993).

23. David Brion Davis, *The Problem of Slavery in The Age of Revolution* (Ithaca: Cornell University Press, 1975).

24. Quoted in Thomas F. Gossett, *Race: The History of an Idea in America* (New York: Schocken Books, 1965), p. 45.

25. Thomas Jefferson, "Notes on Virginia" [1787], in Merrill D. Peterson, *Writings of Thomas Jefferson* (New York: The Library of America, 1984), pp. 264–66, 270. Thanks to Prof. Kimberly Benston for drawing our attention to this passage.

26. Proslavery physician Samuel George Morton (1799–1851) compiled a collection of 800 crania from all parts of the world which formed the sample for his studies of race. Assuming that the larger the size of the cranium translated into greater intelligence, Morton established a relationship between race and skull capacity. Gossett reports that "In 1849, one of his studies included the following results: the English skulls in his collection proved to be the largest, with an average cranial capacity of 96 cubic inches. The Americans and Germans were rather poor seconds, both with cranial capacities of 90 cubic inches. At the bottom of the list were the Negroes with 83 cubic inches, the Chinese with 82, and the Indians with 79." Gossett, *Race: The History of an Idea in America*, p. 74. More recently, Steven Jay Gould has reexamined Morton's data, and shown that his research data were deeply, though unconsciously, manipulated to agree with his "a priori conviction about racial ranking." Gould, *The Mismeasure of Man* (New York: W. W. Norton, 1981), pp. 50–69.

27. Definitions of race founded upon a common pool of genes have not held up when confronted by scientific research which suggests that the differences *within* a given human population are every bit as great as those *between* populations. See L. L. Cavalli-Sforza, "The Genetics of Human Populations," *Scientific American*, (September 1974), pp. 81–89.

28. A fascinating summary critique of Gobineau is provided in Tsvetan Todorov, *On Human Diversity: Nationalism, Racism, and Exoticism in French Thought*, trans. Catherine Porter (Cambridge, MA: Harvard University Press, 1993), esp. pp. 129–40.

29. Two good histories of eugenics are Allen Chase, *The Legacy of Malthus* (New York: Knopf, 1977); Daniel J. Kelves, *In the Name of Eugenics: Genetics and the Uses of Human Heredity* (New York: Knopf, 1985).

30. Arthur Jensen, "How Much Can We Boost IQ and Scholastic Achievement?" *Harvard Educational Review*, 39 (1969), pp. 1–123.

31. See Weber, *Economy and Society*, Vol. I (Berkeley: University of California Press, 1978), pp. 385–87; Ernst Moritz Manasse, "Max Weber on Race," *Social Research*, Vol. 14 (1947), pp. 191–221.

32. DuBois, *The The Souls of Black Folk* (New York: Penguin, 1989 [1903]), p. 13. Du Bois himself wrestled heavily with the conflict between a fully sociohistori-cal conception of race, and the more essentialized and deterministic vision he encountered as a student in Berlin. In "The Conservation of Races" (1897) we can see his first mature effort to resolve this conflict in a vision which combined racial solidarity and a commitment to social equality. See Du Bois, "The Conservation of Races," in Dan S. Green and Edwin D. Driver, eds., *W. E. B. Du Bois On Sociology and the Black Community* (Chicago: University of Chicago Press, 1978), pp. 238–49; Manning Marable, *W. E. B. Du Bois: Black Radical Democrat* (Boston: Twayne, 1986), pp. 35–38. For a contrary, and we believe incorrect reading, see Appiah, In *My Father's House*, pp. 28–46.

33. A good collection of Boas's work is George W. Stocking, ed., *The Shaping of American Anthropology, 1883–1911: A Franz Boas Reader* (Chicago: University of Chicago Press, 1974).

34. Robert E. Park's *Race and Culture* (Glencoe, IL: Free Press, 1950) can still provide insight; see also Stanford H. Lyman, Militarism, *Imperialism, and Racial Accommodation: An Analysis and Interpretation of the Early Writings of Robert E. Park* (Fayetteville: University of Arkansas Press, 1992); Locke's views are concisely expressed in Alain Leroy Locke, *Race Contacts and Interracial Relations*, ed. Jeffrey C. Stewart (Washington, DC: Howard University Press, 1992), originally a series of lectures given at Howard University.

35. Japanese, for example, could not become naturalized citizens until passage of the 1952 McCarran-Walter Act. It took over 160 years, since the passage of the Naturalization Law of 1790, to allow all "races" to be eligible for naturalization.

36. Especially when we recall that until around 1960, the majority of blacks, the largest racially-defined minority group, lived in the South.

37. The construction of whiteness and its tropes of identity is explored in numerous studies, far too many to cite here. Some outstanding examples are Toni Morrison,

Playing In The Dark: Whiteness and the Literary Imagination (Cambridge, MA: Harvard University Press, 1992); Michael Paul Rogin, *Fathers and Children: Andrew Jackson and the Subjugation of the American Indian* (New York: Knopf, 1975; Richard Drinnon, *Facing West: The Metaphysics of Indian-hating and Empire-building* (Minneapolis: University of Minnesota Press, 1980).

38 . This term refers to the practice, widespread throughout the Americas, whereby runaway slaves formed communities in remote areas, such as swamps, mountains, or forests, often in alliance with dispossessed indigenous peoples.

39 . Antonio Gramsci, *Selections from the Prison Notebooks*, edited and translated by Quintin Hoare and Geoffrey Nowell Smith (New York: International Publishers, 1971), p. 182.

40 . Anne Showstack Sassoon, *Gramsci's Politics*, 2nd. ed. (London: Hutchinson, 1987); Sue Golding, *Gramsci's Democratic Theory: Contributions to Post-Liberal Democracy* (Toronto: University of Toronto Press, 1992).

41 . Ralph Ellison, *Shadow and Act* (New York: New American Library, 1966), p. xiv.

42 . See Miles, *Racism*, p. 77. Much of the current debate over the advisability and legality of banning racist hate speech seems to us to adopt the dubious position that racism is primarily an ideological phenomenon. See Mari J. Matsuda et al, *Words That Wound: Critical Race Theory, Assaultive Speech, and the First Amendment* (Boulder, CO: Westview Press, 1993).

43 . Or ideologies which mask privilege by falsely claiming that inequality and injustice have been eliminated. See Wellman, *Portraits of White Racism*.

44 . Racial teachings of the Nation of Islam, for example, maintain that whites are the product of a failed experiment by a mad scientist.

45 . Elinor Langer, "The American Neo-Nazi Movement Today," *The Nation*, July 16/23, 1990.

46 . Such arguments can be found in Nathan Glazer, *Affirmative Discrimination*, Charles Murray, *Losing Ground*, and Arthur M. Schlesinger, Jr., *The Disuniting of America*, among others.

Embracing a Cross-Racial Dialogue

"We were struggling for the words."

By Beverly Daniel Tatum

Some people say there is too much talk about race and racism in the United States. I say that there is not enough. In recent years, news headlines have highlighted the pervasiveness of the problem. There have been race riots in Los Angeles and St. Petersburg, Florida. A thirteen-year-old Black boy was beaten into a coma by White youths who caught him riding his bicycle in their Chicago neighborhood. Anti-immigrant legislation in California has led to the public harassment of Latino citizens. Anti-Asian violence has increased dramatically. Precipitated by the damaging publicity incurred by the release of tape recordings in which Texaco officials used racial slurs to describe Black employees, Texaco agreed to pay $176.1 million to settle a race discrimination lawsuit, the largest such settlement in history.[1] Carl Rowan, a respected Black journalist, authored a book titled *The Coming Race War in America: A Wake-Up Call* in which he warns of the growing threat of White supremacist militia groups plotting to ignite racial conflict.[2]

What is happening here? We need to continually break the silence about racism whenever we can.[3] We need to talk about it at home, at school, in our houses of worship, in our workplaces, in our community groups. But talk does not mean idle chatter. It means meaningful, productive dialogue to raise consciousness and lead to effective action and social change. But how do we start? This is the question my students ask me. "How do I engage in meaningful dialogue about racial issues? How do I get past my fear? How do I get past my anger? Am I willing to take the risk of speaking up? Can I trust that there will be others to listen and support me? Will it make a difference anyway? Is it worth the effort?"

THE PARALYSIS OF FEAR

Fear is a powerful emotion, one that immobilizes, traps words in our throats, and stills our tongues. Like a deer on the highway, frozen in the panic induced by the lights of an oncoming car, when we are afraid it seems that we cannot think, we cannot speak, we cannot move.

What do we fear? Isolation from friends and family, ostracism for speaking of things that generate discomfort, rejection by those who may be offended by what we have to say, the loss of privilege or status for speaking in support of those who have been marginalized by society, physical harm caused by the irrational wrath of those who disagree with your stance? My students readily admit their fears in their journals and essays. Some White students are afraid of their own ignorance, afraid that because of their limited experience with people of color they will ask a naive question or make an offensive remark that will provoke the wrath of the people of color around them.

"Yes, there is fear," one White woman writes, "the fear of speaking is overwhelming. I do not feel, for me, that it is fear of rejection from people of my race, but anger and disdain from people of color. The ones who I am fighting for." In my response to this woman's comment, I explain that she needs to fight for herself, not for people of color. After all, she has been damaged by the cycle of racism, too, though perhaps this is less obvious. If she speaks because *she* needs to speak, perhaps then it would be less important whether the people of color are appreciative of her comments. She seems to understand my comment, but the fear remains.

Another student, a White woman in her late thirties, writes about her fears when trying to speak honestly about her understanding of racism.

> Fear requires us to be honest with not only others, but with ourselves. Often this much honesty is difficult for many of us, for it would permit our insecurities and ignorances to surface, thus opening the floodgate to our vulnerabilities. This position is difficult for most of us when [we are] in the company of entrusted friends and family. I can imagine fear heightening when [we are] in the company of those we hardly know. Hence, rather than publicly admit our weaknesses, we remain silent.

These students are not alone in their fear-induced silence. Christine Sleeter, a White woman who has written extensively about multicultural education and antiracist teaching, writes:

> I first noticed White silence about racism about 15 years ago, although I was not able to name it as such. I recall realizing after

having shared many meals with African American friends while teaching in Seattle, that racism and race-related issues were fairly common topics of dinner-table conversation, which African Americans talked about quite openly. It struck me that I could not think of a single instance in which racism had been a topic of dinner-table conversation in White contexts. Race-related issues sometimes came up, but not *racism*.[4]

Instead, Sleeter argues, White people often speak in a kind of racial code, using communication patterns with each other that encourage a kind of White racial bonding. These communication patterns include race-related asides in conversations, strategic eye contact, jokes, and other comments that assert an "us-them" boundary. Sleeter observes,

> These kinds of interactions seem to serve the purpose of defining racial lines, and inviting individuals to either declare their solidarity or mark themselves as deviant. Depending on the degree of deviance, one runs the risk of losing the other individual's approval, friendship and company.[5]

The fear of the isolation that comes from this kind of deviance is a powerful silencer. My students, young and old, often talk about this kind of fear, experienced not only with friends but with colleagues or employers in work settings. For instance, Lynn struggled when her employer casually used racial slurs in conversation with her. It was especially troubling to Lynn because her employer's young children were listening to their conversation. Though she was disturbed by the interaction, Lynn was afraid and then embarrassed by her own silence:

> I was completely silent following her comment. I knew that I should say something, to point out that she was being completely inappropriate (especially in front of her children) and that she had really offended me. But I just sat there with a stupid forced half-smile on my face.

How could she respond to this, she asked? What would it cost her to speak? Would it mean momentary discomfort or could it really mean losing her job? And what did her silence cost her on a personal level?

Because of the White culture of silence about racism, my White students often have little experience engaging in dialogue about racial issues. They have not had much practice at overcoming their inhibitions to speak. They notice that the students of color speak about racism more frequently, and they assume they do so more easily. One White woman observed,

> In our class discussion when White students were speaking, we sounded so naive and so "young" about what we were discussing. It was almost like we were struggling for the words to explain ourselves and were even speaking much slower than the students of color. The students of color, on the other hand, were extremely well aware of what to say and of what they wanted to express. It dawned on me that these students had dealt with this long before I ever thought about racism. Since last fall, racism has been a totally new concept to me, almost like I was hearing about it for the first time. For these students, however, the feelings, attitudes and terminology came so easily.

This woman is correct in her observation that most of the people of color in that classroom are more fluent in the discourse of racism, and more aware of its personal impact on their lives than perhaps she has been. But she is wrong that their participation is easy. They are also afraid.

I am reminded of an article written by Kirsten Mullen, a Black parent who needed to speak to her child's White teachers about issues of racial insensitivity at his school. She wrote, "I was terrified the first time I brought up the subject of race at my son's school. My palms were clammy, my heart was racing, and I could not have done it without rehearsing in the bathroom mirror."[6] She was afraid, but who would advocate for her son if she didn't? She could not afford the cost of silence.

An Asian American woman in my class writes about the difficulty of speaking:

> The process of talking about this issue is not easy. We people of color can't always make it easier for White people to talk about race relations because sometimes they need to break away from that familiar and safe ground of being neutral or silent. … I understand that [some are] trying but sometimes they need to take bigger steps and more risks. As an Asian in America, I am always taking risks when I share my experiences of racism; however, the dominant culture expects it of me. They think I like talking about how my parents are laughed at at work or how my older sister is forced to take [cancer-causing] birth control pills because she is on welfare. Even though I am embarrassed and sometimes get too emotional about these issues, I talk about them because I want to be honest about how I feel.

She has fears, but who will tell her story if she doesn't? For many people of color, learning to break the silence is a survival issue. To remain silent would be to disconnect from her own experience, to swallow and internalize her own oppression. The cost of silence is too high.

Sometimes we fear our own anger and frustration, the chance of losing control or perhaps collapsing into despair should our words, yet again, fall on deaf ears. A Black woman writes:

> One thing that I struggle with as an individual when it comes to discussions about race is the fact that I tend to give up. When I start to think, "He or she will never understand me. What is the point?" I have practically defeated myself. No human can ever fully understand the experiences and feelings of another, and I must remind myself that progress, although often slow and painful, can be made.

A very powerful example of racial dialogue between a multiracial group of men can be seen in the award-winning video *The Color of Fear*.[7] One of the most memorable moments in the film is when Victor, an African American man, begins to shout angrily at David, a White man, who continually invalidates what Victor has said about his experiences with racism. After viewing the video in my class, several students of color wrote about how much they identified with Victor's anger and how relieved they were to see that it could be expressed without disastrous consequences. An Asian American woman wrote:

> I don't know if I'll ever see a more powerful, moving, on-the-money movie in my life! …Victor really said it all. He verbalized all I've ever felt or will feel so eloquently and so convincingly. When he first started speaking, he was so calm and I did not expect anything remotely close to what he exhibited. When he started shouting, my initial reaction was of discomfort. Part of that discomfort stemmed from watching him just going nuts on David. But there was something else that was embedded inside of me. I kept thinking throughout the whole movie and I finally figured it out at the end. Victor's rage and anger was mine as well. Those emotions that I had hoped to keep inside forever and ever because I didn't know if I was justified in feeling that way. I had no words or evidence, solid evidence, to prove to myself or others that I had an absolute RIGHT to scream and yell and be angry for so many things.

The anger and frustration of people of color, even when received in smaller doses, is hard for some White people to tolerate. One White woman needed to vent her own frustrations before she could listen to the frustration and anger of people of color. She wrote:

> Often I feel that because I am White, my feelings are disregarded or looked down upon in racial dialogues. I feel that my efforts are unappreciated. … I also realize that it is these feelings which make me want to withdraw from the fight against racism altogether. … [However,] I acknowledge the need for White students to listen to minority students when they express anger against the system which has failed them without taking this communication as a personal attack.

Indeed, this is what one young woman of color hoped for:

> When I'm participating in a cross-racial dialogue, I prefer that the people I'm interacting with understand why I react the way that I do. When I say that I want understanding, it does not mean that I'm looking for sympathy. I merely want people to know why I'm angry and not to be offended by it.

In order for there to be meaningful dialogue, fear, whether of anger or isolation, must eventually give way to risk and trust. A leap of faith must be made. It is not easy, and it requires being willing to push past one's fear. Wrote one student,

> At times it feels too risky … but I think if people remain equally committed, it can get easier. It's a very stressful process, but I think the consequences of not exploring racial issues are ultimately far more damaging … .

THE PSYCHOLOGICAL COST OF SILENCE

As a society, we pay a price for our silence. Unchallenged personal, cultural, and institutional racism results in the loss of human potential, lowered productivity, and a rising tide of fear and violence in our society. Individually, racism stifles our own growth and development. It clouds our vision and distorts our perceptions. It alienates us not only from others but also from ourselves and our own experiences.

Jean Baker Miller's paper "Connections, Disconnections and Violations" offers a helpful framework for seeing how this self-alienation takes place.[8] As Miller describes, when we have meaningful experiences, we usually seek to share those experiences with someone else. In doing so, we hope to be heard and understood, to feel validated by the other. When we do not feel heard, we feel invalidated, and a relational disconnection has taken place. We might try again, persisting in our efforts to be heard, or we may choose to disconnect from that person. If there are others available who will listen and affirm us, disconnection from those who won't may be the best alternative. But if disconnection means what Miller calls "condemned isolation," then we will do whatever we have to in order to remain in connection with others. That may mean denying our own experiences of racism, selectively screening things out of our consciousness so that we can continue our relationships with reduced discomfort. As a person of color, to remain silent and deny my own experience with racism may be an important coping strategy in some contexts but it may also lead to the self-blame and self-doubt of internalized oppression.[9]

The consequences are different but also damaging for Whites. As we have seen, many Whites have been encouraged by their culture of silence to disconnect from their racial experiences. When White children make racial observations, they are often silenced by their parents, who feel uncomfortable and unsure of how to respond. With time the observed contradictions between parental attitudes and behaviors, or between societal messages about meritocracy and visible inequities, become difficult to process in a culture of silence. In order to prevent chronic discomfort, Whites may learn not to notice.

But in not noticing, one loses opportunities for greater insight into oneself and one's experience. A significant dimension of who one is in the world, one's Whiteness, remains uninvestigated and perceptions of daily experience are routinely distorted. Privilege goes unnoticed, and all but the most blatant acts of racial bigotry are ignored. Not noticing requires energy. Exactly how much energy is used up in this way becomes apparent with the opportunity to explore those silenced perceptions. It is as though a blockage has been removed and energy is released.

According to Miller, when a relationship is growth-producing, it results in five good things: increased zest, a sense of empowerment, greater knowledge, an increased sense of self-worth, and a desire for more connection. In interviews done with White teachers who were leading discussions with others about racism, there was abundant evidence of these benefits. Said one, "The thing that's happened for me is that I'm no longer afraid to bring [race] up. I look to bring it up; I love bringing it up." This educator now brings these issues up regularly with her colleagues, and they, like she, seem to feel liberated by the opportunity for dialogue. Describing a discussion group in which participants talked about racial issues, she said, "It was such a rich conversation and it just flowed the whole time. It was exciting to be a part of it. Everybody contributed and everybody felt the energy and the desire."

Another participant described the process of sharing the new information she had learned with her adult son, and said, "There's a lot of energy that's going on in all sorts of ways. It feels wonderful." Yet another described her own exploration of racial issues as "renewal at midlife." The increased self-knowledge she experienced was apparent as she says, "I'm continuing to go down the path of discovery for myself about what I think and what I believe and the influences I've had in my life. … It impacts me almost every moment of my waking hours." These benefits of self-discovery are made available to them as the silence about racism is broken.

It is important to say that even as good things are generated, the growth process is not painless. One of the White teachers interviewed described the early phase of her exploration of racism as "hell," a state of constant dissonance. Another commented, "I get really scared at some of the things that come up. And I've never been so nervous in my life as I have been facilitating that antiracist study group." A third said, "How do I feel about the fact that I might be influencing large groups of people? Well, in a way, I'm proud of it. I'm scared about it [too] because it puts me out in the forefront. It's a vulnerable position." The fear is still there, but these pioneers are learning to push past it.[10]

FINDING COURAGE FOR SOCIAL CHANGE

Breaking the silence undoubtedly requires courage. How can we find the courage we need? This is a question I ask myself a lot, because I too struggle with fear. I am aware of my own vulnerability even as I write this book. What will writing it mean for my life? Will it make me a target for attack? How will readers respond to what I have to say? Have I really said anything helpful? Silence feels safer, but in the long run, I know that it is not. So I, like so many others, need courage.

I look for it in the lives of others, seeking role models for how to be an effective agent of change. As a person of faith, I find that the Bible is an important source of inspiration for me. It is full of stories of change agents, whose lives inspire me. Moses and Esther are two favorites. Because I am a Black woman, I am particularly interested in the lives of other Black women who have been agents of change. I find strength in learning about the lives of Harriet Tubman, Sojourner Truth, Ida B. Wells, Zora Neale Hurston, Fannie Lou Hamer, Rosa Parks, and Gloria Wade-Gayles, to name a few. I also want to know about the lives of my White allies, past and present: Angelina and Sarah Grimke, Clarence Jordan, Virginia Foster Durr, Lois Stalvey, Mab Segrest, Bill Bradley, and Morris Dees, for example. What about Black men and other men and women of color, Asian, Latino, American Indian? W. E. B. DuBois, Thurgood Marshall, Ronald Takaki, Maxine Hong Kingston, Cesar Chavez, Wilma Mankiller, Joel Spring, Mitsuye Yamada, Nellie Wong? Yes, those examples and many unnamed others are important, too. I am filling in the gaps in my education as quickly as I can.

I have heard many people say, "But I don't know enough! I don't even recognize most of those names. I don't have enough of the facts to be able to speak up about racism or anything else!"They are not alone. We have all been miseducated in this regard. Educating ourselves and others is an essential step in the process of change. Few of us have been taught to think critically about issues of social injustice. We have been taught not to notice or to accept our present situation as a given, "the way it is." But we can learn the history we were not taught, we can watch the documentaries we never saw in school, and we can read about the lives of change agents, past and present. We can discover another way. We are surrounded by a "cloud of witnesses" who will give us courage if we let them.

Do you feel overwhelmed by the task? When my students begin to recognize the pervasiveness of racism in the culture and our institutions, they begin to despair, feeling powerless to effect change. Sometimes I feel overwhelmed, too. The antidote I have found is to focus on my own sphere of influence. I can't fix everything, but some things are within my control. While many people experience themselves as powerless, everyone has some sphere of influence in which they can work for change, even if it is just in their own personal network of family and friends. Ask yourself, "Whose lives do I affect and how? What power and authority do I wield in the world? What meetings do I attend? Who do I talk to in the course of a day?" Identify your strengths and use them.

If you are a parent, what conversations have you had with your children about these issues? What books are sitting on their bookshelves? Do you know what discussions are taking place at your child's school? If you are a teacher, what dialogue is taking place in your classroom? Regardless of your subject matter, there are ways to engage students in critical thinking about racism which are relevant to your discipline. Have you considered what they might be? If you like to write letters to friends, have you written any letters to the editor, adding to the public discourse about dismantling racism? Have you written to broadcasters protesting programming which reinforces racial stereotypes? If you are an extrovert, have you used your people skills to gather others together for dialogue about racism? If you are an athlete, what language and behavior do you model in the locker room? If you are a board member, what questions do you raise at the meetings? Who sits on the board with you? What values and perspectives are represented there? If you are an employer, who is missing from your work force? What are you doing about it?

"What if I make a mistake?" you may be thinking. "Racism is a volatile issue, and I don't want to say or do the wrong thing." In nearly twenty years of teaching and leading workshops about racism, I have made many mistakes. I have found that a sincere apology and a genuine desire to learn from one's mistakes are usually rewarded with forgiveness. If we wait for perfection, we will never break the silence. The cycle of racism will continue uninterrupted.

We all want to "do the right thing," but each of us must determine what our own right thing is. The right thing for me, writing this book, may not be the right thing for you. Parker Palmer offers this wisdom about doing the "right thing": "Right action requires only that we respond faithfully to our own inner truth and to the truth around us … If an action is rightly taken, taken with integrity, its outcomes will achieve whatever is possible—which is the best that anyone can do."[11]

You may be saying, "I *am* a change agent. I am always the one who speaks up at the meetings, but I'm tired. How do I keep going?" This is an important question, because a genuine commitment to interrupting racism is a long-term commitment. How can we sustain ourselves for the long haul? One thing I have learned is that we need a community of support. We all need community to give us energy, to strengthen our voices, and to offer constructive criticism when we stray off course. We need to speak up against racism and other forms of oppression, but we do not have to speak alone. Look for like-minded others. Organize a meeting for friends or colleagues concerned about racial issues. Someone else will come. Attend the meetings others have organized. Share your vision. Others will be drawn to you. Your circle of support does not have to be big. It may be only two or three other people with whom you can share the frustrations of those meetings and the joys of even the smallest victories. Even those who seem to be solo warriors have a support network somewhere. It is essential. If you don't have such a network now, start thinking about how to create one. In the meantime, learn more about that cloud of witnesses. Knowing that history can sustain you as well.

We all have a sphere of influence. Each of us needs to find our own sources of courage so that we will begin to speak. There are many problems to address, and we cannot avoid them indefinitely. We cannot continue to be silent. We must begin to speak, knowing that words alone are insufficient. But I have seen that meaningful dialogue can lead to effective action. Change is possible. I remain hopeful.

NOTES

1. S.Walsh, "Texaco settles race suit," *Washington Post* (November 16, 1996).

2. C.A. Rowan, *The coming race war in America: A wake-up call* (Boston: Little, Brown, 1996).

3. In the same way, we need to break the silence about sexism, anti-Semitism, heterosexism and homophobia, classism, ageism, and ableism. In my experience, once we learn to break the silence about one ism, the lessons learned transfer to other isms.

4. C. Sleeter, "White racism," *Multicultural Education* (Spring 1994): 6.

5. Ibid., p. 8.

6. K. Mullen, "Subtle lessons in racism," *USA Weekend* (November 6–8, 1992): 10–11.

7. L. M. Wah (Producer/director), *The color of fear* [Video] (Oakland, CA: Stir-Fry Productions, 1994).

8. J. B. Miller, "Connections, disconnections, and violations," *Work in Progress, No. 33* (Wellesley, MA: Stone Center Working Paper Series, 1988).

9. B. D. Tatum, "Racial identity and relational theory: The case of Black women in White communities," *Work in Progress, No. 63* (Wellesley, MA: Stone Center Working Paper Series, 1992).

10. An in-depth discussion of the relational implications of working against racism for these female educators can be found in Tatum and Knaplund, "Outside the circle."

11. P. Palmer, *The active life: Wisdom for work, creativity, and caring* (New York: HarperCollins, 1990), p. 115.

PART II

CONQUEST, SLAVERY, AND MIGRATIONS

DOUBLE-CROSSED, DOUBLE-BORDERED

By Iris Rodriguez

CONTEMPORARY NATIVE AMERICAN ISSUES, 1900–PRESENT: AN OVERVIEW

By Rebecca Bales

THE SEXUAL POLITICS OF BLACK WOMANHOOD

By Patricia Hill Collins

WHAT RACE ARE MEXICANS? A BRIEF HISTORY OF THE RACIALIZATION OF MEXICAN AMERICANS

By Agustin Palacios

ASIAN AMERICANS: UNITY IN DIVERSE EXPERIENCES

By Wendy Ng

IMMIGRATION TO A RISING METROPOLIS

By Rudy P. Guevarra Jr.

YOU AIN'T WHITE! THE EXPERIENCE OF MIDDLE EASTERN AMERICANS

By Rita Stephan

Double-Crossed, Double-Bordered

By Iris Rodriguez

"The *wasichu* paradigm and its borders
Son malas hierbas, envenenosas.
They go against life and nature's order.

"They spread and invade people like weeds.
Pero son malas plantas.
They come from bad seeds,"

Abuela said one day,
with her hair braided tight
as she sat barefoot under the mesquite tree.

"*De los dos lados* we've been double-crossed, double-bordered
in English *y en español.*
Indian? Mexican? Hyphenated American?
¿Mestizo? ¿Mexica? No. *Mexica-no.*"

She looked down at her feet.

"*Somos familia.* Clans upon clans.
Regardless of what they name us,
we are the grandchildren of these lands.
And protecting them is part of our sacred responsibility."

She looked up, eagle eyes piercing through me.

"We defend the land, the earth; we defend ourselves.
We must reconnect with our old ways to become free
of the death-eating ways of the *wasichu* mentality.

"The fate of the entire world lives in our hands, *mija*.
We can save the planet, you and me
and all the warriors waking up with us
precisamente from where we are, inside the machine."

Contemporary Native American Issues, 1900– Present: An Overview

• •

By Rebecca Bales

On April 1, 2016, a prayer circle of women formed where a pipeline was planned. These women called themselves "Water Protectors." By summer, their prayer circle grew to become the largest gathering of indigenous people in modern history. Standing Rock Sioux member and tribal historian LaDonna Brave Bull Allard succinctly stated the reasons for the prayer circle: "The water is female; water is life, and so we as women must stand with the water. … We stand in prayer and in civil disobedience. We stand because we must protect our children and grandchildren" (Taub 2016). Resistance to the Dakota Access Pipeline (DAPL) grew because its planned path cuts under the Missouri River and threatens the water source for more than eighteen million people. The pipeline also came within a few miles of the Standing Rock Sioux reservation and desecrated sacred sites in its path. The severity of the Water Protectors' concerns brought indigenous people together from all over the globe. Lakota, Cheyenne, Arapahoe, Cherokee, Apache, and many other North American Natives traveled and sent support to the camp. Support also came worldwide from the Sami of Norway, the Mayans of Central America, the Mäori of New Zealand, and the Aztecs of Mexico. *Mni wiconi*—"Water is life" in the Lakota language—is the mantra for this gathering.

The history of Native Americans in North America is cyclical in nature, as the protest against the DAPL demonstrates. Non-Natives moved onto Native lands, destroyed sacred sites (including grave sites), and asserted power over the land and the people for the past five hundred years. At the end of the nineteenth century, the dominant society believed that Native Americans would disappear forever through military action and assimilation. Boarding schools pulled Native children from their homes and families with the intent to, as founder of the Carlisle Indian Industrial school Henry Pratt stated, "kill the Indian…and save the man" (Iverson, 1998, 21). Belief in the "Vanishing Indian" triggered a series of land grabs and resource acquisitions that tried to undermine Native American cultures.

In 1906, President Theodore Roosevelt signed into law the Antiquities Act, which preserved sites on federal land, including Native American ruins and petroglyphs. Native communities saw this as an opening to argue for their sacred lands. By the 1920s, conflict arose as it became clear that Native peoples were not going away—indeed, they were fighting to hold on to their cultures, traditions, and lands while adjusting to some parts of assimilation. Federal policy shifted as well when C. Hart Meriam was tasked with assessing and reporting on reservation conditions in the 1920s. His 1928 report became the basis for the Indian New Deal formed under President Franklin Roosevelt's administration. For many Nations, this "new deal" offered a different relationship with the federal government.

While Native Americans continued to struggle with assimilation policies and poor living conditions, there was never a question of their readiness to serve the United States in military campaigns: Native Americans have fought in every war in which the United States has engaged. In both World War I and World War II, Native soldiers became critical to the success of the United States. Indigenous languages (which the United States once tried to destroy through assimilation) served to confuse the enemy—the enemy could not break codes in these languages. Thirty-three Native Nations and more than four hundred Native individuals have participated in code talking during modern-day wars, In particular, the two world wars. The Comanche, Choctaw, and Cherokee were critical in WWI; the Lakota, Meskwaki, Seminole, Comanche, and Navajo fought and transmitted codes in WWII. The Navajo Code Talkers, in particular, played an indispensable role in the Pacific arena, especially when they transmitted "SURIBACHI," signaling the US victory over the Japanese on the island of Iwo Jima. When these heroes returned home, they and their service went unrecognized, as the United States believed that it would need these languages again in future military conflicts. They finally received recognition in the early 1970s. Native Americans have also taken their place in the current conflicts of the Middle East as well. For example, the second casualty (and first Native woman to die in combat) of the Iraq War was a Hopi woman, Lori Ann Piestewa. She died on March 23, 2003, when her unit was ambushed in Nasiriyah, Iraq.

As Natives fought and sacrificed for a country with a track record of trying to destroy their cultures and sovereignty, the years after World War II proved to be traumatic. Indian Relocation and Termination directly struck at the heart of Native communities. The government sought to convince Natives residing on reservations that their best opportunity was to remove to urban areas. With promises of good employment, housing, and education, many Natives moved to cities, including Chicago, Minneapolis, Los Angeles, Denver, and San Francisco. Once there the promises rarely materialized, as the Mankiller family of Mankiller Flats, Oklahoma, experienced in the 1950s. A young Wilma Mankiller faced the struggles and discrimination of relocating to the San Francisco Bay Area. Mankiller took the opportunity that the activism of the 1960s offered by becoming involved in Native American issues in the Bay Area. In the early 1970s, she returned to Oklahoma, where she continued working for her community and where she eventually ran successfully for Principal Chief of the Cherokee Nation, the first woman to hold that position in the modern era.

Mankiller's experiences were not unique. Having no established communities like those of other ethnic groups, many fell into despair and depression in cities, which often led to drug and alcohol abuse. Lacking resources in cities, Native Americans established "Friendship Houses," places where Native people could gather and find resources to help their transition to urban living. Those remaining on the reservation struggled to maintain their economic bases, their sovereignty, and their traditions. When the federal government implemented the Termination policy through House Concurrent Resolution 108, which sought to strip Native Nations of their federal status and recognition, some Nations lost their economic livelihood and control of their resources. The Menominee of Wisconsin, whom the United States stripped of their federal recognition, experienced a sharp decline in their economic base (especially lumber) and their traditional rights to hunting and fishing. In 1968 the Menominee sued to regain their rights; in 1973 under the leadership of Ada Deer, the federal government reinstated recognition.

The failed policies of the first half of the twentieth century and developing Civil Rights Movement in the 1960s inspired a new generation of young Natives and brought in a new era of self-determination. Their focus, however, differed significantly from other groups' goals. Protection and defense of sovereignty, traditions, and culture (as well as resistance to police and federal violence, poor conditions on reservations and in urban areas, and broken treaties) fueled Native aspirations and the resulting "Red Power Movement." On March 9, 1964, shortly after the closing of the prison on Alcatraz Island, a group of Bay Area Natives led by Lakota Richard McKenzie briefly occupied Alcatraz under the 1868 Treaty of Fort Laramie stipulation that federal land no longer being used as the government had intended was to be returned to Native peoples. This set the stage for the 1969 occupation, when more than eighty Natives occupied the island for nineteen months. Those involved included Chippewa Adam Fortunate Eagle, Mohawk Richard Oakes, and Shoshone-Bannock LaNada Means War Jack. This occupation also fueled the activism of Wilma Mankiller.

While the activism in California shed a national and international light on Native American issues, it was the poor urban and reservation conditions, as well as the growing prison population, that spurred the creation of the American Indian Movement (AIM) in 1968 Minneapolis. Urban areas seldom offered opportunities for Native youth, many of whom ended up in prison, a traumatic and painful consequence of the Relocation policy. Once they served time and gained their release, it became apparent that those scarce opportunities dwindled to almost nothing. In an effort to address this and other issues concerning Natives (sovereignty, treaty rights, poverty, etc.) a group of young men in Minneapolis founded AIM—Anishinaabe Dennis Banks, Ojibwes Clyde, Vernon Bellecourt, and George Mitchell strove to bring attention to the devastation that federal policy had inflicted on Native communities throughout the United States.

With the formation of AIM, activism across the nation brought Natives together. In 1972, a cross-country caravan of Native Americans traveled to Washington, DC, to address violations of treaty rights, poverty, and poor housing. The takeover of the Bureau of Indian Affairs building was meant to force President Richard Nixon to meet with Native Americans to address these concerns. In addition to the march on Washington, AIM went to reservations with the intention of helping those in need. In 1973, as violence escalated on the Pine Ridge reservation, AIM members took a stand at Wounded Knee, where, eighty-three years earlier the 7th Cavalry massacred more than three hundred Lakota. The siege took place in the town of Wounded Knee and lasted seventy-one days. In the following years, the federal government systematically targeted AIM members; as John Trudell, spokesman for AIM, stated, "Maybe we broke even, right … it instilled a lot of pride in Indian People. And we needed something like that as a people. … But what it did for us as a movement, it was the beginning of the diffusion of the focus. Because we then got tied up in the courts. The hunt became more intense. We may be one of the very few organizations in this country that basically every member of the organization was at one point, at one time or another charged with a criminal act" (*Incident at Oglala* 1992).

By the latter 1980s, as Native communities and individuals continued the struggle to maintain their cultures and sovereignty, control of natural resources and desecration of land and sacred sites took center stage. When Theodore Roosevelt signed the 1906 Antiquities Act into law, it did not ensure protection of Native American graves and the materials in them. With the growth of the academic discipline of anthropology during the late nineteenth and early twentieth centuries, scholars felt no qualms about digging up the ancestors and funerary objects of the indigenous peoples of North America to study. Grave robbing became a way for scholars to make a name, leading to universities and museums acquiring ancestral remains and funerary objects, regardless of the protest of many Native Americans. The Smithsonian in Washington, DC, for example, became the most prominent institution, housing more than eighteen thousand Native American remains. Native Nations waited more than eighty years before the federal government heard and acted on requests to protect and preserve the ancestors and sacred grave sites. The Native American Graves Protection and Repatriation Act (NAGPRA) was passed in 1990, stipulating that all Native American ancestral remains and funerary objects be returned (repatriated) to their Nations once tribal affiliation was determined. NAGPRA authorized the ancestors' return to their homelands for proper interment. This issue has not been completely resolved, as some remains and funerary objects remain institutionalized due to "unknown origins."

The twenty-first century brought new challenges to and opportunities for Native Americans. Currently, the federal government recognizes 350 Native Nations, and states recognize an additional 200 Nations. Resistance to the dominant society and the federal government's determination to disempower Native communities continues, but some progress has occurred. President Barack Obama's presidency saw a shift in the federal government's interaction with Native American Nations throughout the United States. On May 19, 2008, prior to Obama's election to the presidency, the Crow Nation adopted Obama, conferring upon him the name Barack Black Eagle. His administration actively sought to address Native Nations on their own terms while navigating the complexity of federal Indian policy and resource management. The Obama administration coined its work with Native Americans as "Generation Indigenous" ("Gen-I"), and created the first initiative that directly responded to needs of Native American youth. Although many issues remained unaddressed under his administration, President Obama ensured that Native Americans were included in a very visible way when he spoke about and worked on race relations in the United States.

Native Americans were once again unsure how their relationship with the federal government would develop when Donald Trump took office in 2017. Administrative appointments cast an uncertain pall over issues of resources, land use, trust, sovereignty, and mutual respect. The main issue looming over Native Nations is the threat of privatization of reservations for their vast resources. According to many spiritual leaders and others, this move directly threatens Native sovereignty and access to resources, as demonstrated by the Dakota Access Pipeline issue. The questions that arise for the future lie in how the transition from the Obama administration to the Trump administration is impacting Native lives, sovereignty, traditions, resources, and culture. As of March 2017, the Standing Rock Water Protectors dispersed on order of the Trump administration, and the Dakota Pipeline resumed construction; areas around the ancient urban center of Chaco Canyon in New Mexico are targeted for hydraulic fracturing (fracking), which most likely will cause irreparable damage to the sacred site; and the Tohono O'odham in Arizona are gearing up to fight Trump's proposed wall along the US-Mexican border, which will bisect their reservation and block their people from visiting sacred sites and ancestral burials.

Native Nations in North America vary in their distinct cultures and worldviews, but all find commonality in their relationship to the land, their historical struggle against colonialism, and their present relationship with the United States. The issues indigenous peoples faced in the late nineteenth and early twentieth centuries are the same issues indigenous peoples face in the twenty-first century: struggles over federal recognition, land use, economic development, environmental concerns, unemployment, poverty, and, perhaps most important, the fight to maintain their sovereignty. But like those resilient people of a century (and more) ago, Native Nations continue to preserve their own traditions, cultures, communities, and identities. The Haudenosaunee (Iroquois) of the Northeast continue to function under their own constitution brought to them by the Great Peacemaker—the clan mothers still hold important political and social roles, and the people travel around the world on their own passports. The Winnebago have reintroduced ancient, traditional ways of caring for the buffalo and their environment. The result is a shift in their diets back to what they had known for centuries; in the process, their physical health has improved. The California Basket Weavers Association continues to pass on traditional basket-weaving techniques to the younger generation and, in the process, contributes to the maintenance of traditional gathering places. Continuing the cycle of resistance, preservation, and conservation, as well as the struggle to improve poor conditions on the reservation and in urban areas, brings Native American people together. These people are integral to the growth and development of the Americas, often serving as the conscience of those who now inhabit their ancestral homelands. Even though they have not chosen this role, their fight, their worldviews, and their tenacious spirits remain a testament to their connectedness to the land and the ancestors. The circle remains unbroken.

DISCUSSION QUESTIONS

1. What are important issues affecting Native Americans, and how have they responded to them? Why are these issues important to Native Americans?

2. How have Native Americans addressed federal policy over time? Were these responses successful? Why or why not?

3. What role do Native American women play in their communities and in their struggles to maintain sovereignty? What does this tell you about Native American women and their status in their societies?

4. How does understanding Native American history inform our understanding of US history?

WEBSITE LINKS

http://indiancountrymedianetwork.com

www.nativeweb.org

www.native-languages.org/languages.htm

AUDIOVISUAL MATERIALS

Incident at Oglala. Directed by Michael Apted. Miramax Films, 1992.
We Shall Remain: American Through Native Eyes. Directed by Chris Eyer and Sharon Grimberg. PBS, 2009.

SUGGESTIONS FOR FURTHER READING

Alfred, Taiaiake. 2009. *Peace, Power, Righteousness: An Indigenous Manifesto*. Oxford: Oxford University Press.
Gray, Christine K. 2015. *The Tribal Moment in American Politics: The Struggle for Native American Sovereignty*. Lanham, MD: Altamira Press.
Horse Capture, George, Duane Champaign, and Chandler C. Jackson, eds. 2007. *American Indian Nations: Yesterday, Today, and Tomorrow*. Lanham, MD: Altamira Press.

REFERENCES

Incident at Oglala. Directed by Michael Apted. Miramax Films, 1992.
Iverson, Peter. 1998. *"We Are Still Here": American Indians in the Twentieth Century*. Wheeling, IL: Harlan Davidson.
Taub, Pat. 2016. "The Women of Standing Rock." *The Bullshitist*, November 30. https://bullshit.ist/the-women-of-standing-rock-d193dcac88e1#.kdxa4d84x.

The Sexual Politics of Black Womanhood

By Patricia Hill Collins

> Even I found it almost impossible to let her say what had happened to her as she perceived it … And why? Because once you strip away the lie that rape is pleasant, that children are not permanently damaged by sexual pain, that violence done to them is washed away by fear, silence, and time, you are left with the positive horror of the lives of thousands of children … who have been sexually abused and who have never been permitted their own language to tell about it.
>
> Alice Walker 1988, 57

In *The Color Purple* Alice Walker creates the character of Celie, a Black adolescent girl who is sexually abused by her stepfather. Writing letters to God and forming supportive relationships with other Black women help Celie find her own voice, and her voice enables her to transcend the fear and silence of her childhood. By creating Celie and giving her the language to tell of her sexual abuse, Walker adds Celie's voice to muted yet growing discussions of the sexual politics of Black womanhood. But when it comes to other important issues concerning Black women's sexuality, U.S. Black women have found it almost impossible to say what has happened.

As Evelynn Hammonds points out, "Black women's sexuality is often described in metaphors of speechlessness, space, or vision; as a 'void' or empty space that is simultaneously ever-visible (exposed) and invisible, where black women's bodies are already colonized" (1997, 171). In response to this portrayal, Black women have been silent. One important factor that contributes to these long-standing silences both among African-American women and within Black feminist thought lies in Black women's lack of access to positions of power in U.S. social institutions. Those who control the schools, news media, churches, and government suppress Black women's collective voice. Dominant groups are the ones who construct Black women as "the embodiment of sex and the attendant invisibility of black women as the unvoiced, unseen—everything that is not white" (Hammonds 1997, 171).

Critical scholarship also has approached Black women's sexuality through its own set of assumptions. Within U.S. Black intellectual communities generally and Black studies scholarship in particular, Black women's sexuality is either ignored or included primarily in relation to African-American men's issues. In Black critical contexts where Black women struggle to get gender oppression recognized as important, theoretical analyses of Black sexuality remain sparse (Collins 1993b; 1998a, 155–83). Women's studies scholarship demonstrates a predilection for placing Black women in comparative frameworks. Interested in building coalitions among women across differences of race, theorists typically add Black women into preexisting feminist frameworks, often to illustrate how Black women "have it worse." Everyone has spoken for Black women, making it difficult for us to speak for ourselves.

But suppression does not fully explain African-American women's persistent silences about sexuality. U.S. Black women have been discouraged from analyzing and speaking out about a host of topics. Why does this one remain so difficult? In response, Paula Giddings identifies another important factor, namely, the "last taboo" of disclosing "not only a gender but a sexual discourse, unmediated by the question of racism" (Giddings 1992, 442). Within this taboo, to talk of White racist constructions of Black women's sexuality is acceptable. But developing analyses of sexuality that implicate Black men is not—it violates norms of racial solidarity that counsel Black women always to put our own needs second. Even within these racial boundaries, some topics are more acceptable than others—White men's rape of Black women during slavery can be discussed whereas Black men's rape of Black women today cannot. In her essay "Remembering Anita Hill and Clarence Thomas: What Really Happened When One Black Woman Spoke Out," Nellie McKay explains why Black women have remained silent concerning issues of sexuality:

> In all of their lives in America ... black women have felt torn between the loyalties that bind them to race on one hand, and sex on the other. Choosing one or the other, of course, means taking sides against the self, yet they have almost always chosen race over the other: a sacrifice of their self-hood as women and of full humanity, in favor of the race.
>
> (McKay 1992, 277–78)

"Taking sides against the self" requires that certain elements of Black women's sexuality can be examined, namely, those that do not challenge a race discourse that historically has privileged the experiences of African-American men. The cost is that other elements remain off-limits. Rape, incest, misogyny in Black cultural practices, and other painful topics that might implicate Black men remain taboo.

Yet another factor influencing Black women's silences concerns the potential benefits of remaining silent. For example, during the early-twentieth-century club movement, White women were much more successful in advancing analyses of intraracial gender relations and sexuality than were Black women. In a context of virulent racism, public disclosure could leave Black men and women vulnerable to increased sexual violence at the hands of White men. White women who forwarded a gendered analysis faced no such fears. In situations such as these, where regulating Black women's bodies benefited systems of race, class, and gender alike, protecting the safe spaces for Black women's self-definitions often required public silences about seemingly provocative topics. This secrecy was especially important within a U.S. culture that routinely accused Black women of being sexually immoral, promiscuous jezebels. In a climate where one's sexuality is on public display, holding fast to privacy and trying to shut the closet door becomes paramount. Hine refers to this strategy as a culture of dissemblance, one where Black women appeared to be outgoing and public, while using this facade to hide a secret world within. As Hine suggests, "only with secrecy, thus achieving a self-imposed invisibility, could ordinary black women accrue the psychic space and harness the resources needed to hold their own in the often one-sided and mismatched resistance struggle" (Hine 1995, 382). In contexts of violence where internal self-censorship was seen as protection, silence made sense.

The convergence of all of these factors—the suppression of Black women's voice by dominant groups, Black women's struggles to work within the confines of norms of racial solidarity, and the seeming protections offered by a culture of dissemblance—influences yet another factor shaping patterns of silence. In general, U.S. Black women have been reluctant to acknowledge the valuable contributions of Black lesbian feminist theory in reconceptualizing Black women's sexuality. Since the early 1980s, Black lesbian theorists and activists have identified homophobia and the toll it takes on African-American women as an important topic for Black feminist thought. "The oppression that affects Black gay people, female and male, is pervasive, constant, and not abstract. Some of us die from it," argues Barbara Smith (1983, xlvii). Despite the increasing visibility of Black lesbians as parents (Lorde 1984, 72–80; Williams 1997), as academics (Davenport 1996), as activists (Gomez and Smith 1994), within lesbian history (Kennedy and Davis 1993, 113–31), and who have publicly come out (Moore 1997), African-Americans have tried to ignore homosexuality generally and have avoided serious analysis of homophobia within African-American communities.

In this context, Black lesbian theorizing about sexuality has been marginalized, albeit in different ways, both within Black intellectual communities and women's studies scholarship. As a result, Black feminist thought has not yet taken full advantage of this important source of Black feminist theory. As a group, heterosexual African-American women have been strangely silent on the issue of Black lesbianism. Barbara Smith suggests one compelling reason: "Heterosexual privilege is usually the only privilege that Black women have. None of us have racial or sexual privilege, almost none of us have class privilege, maintaining 'straightness' is our last resort" (1982b, 171). In the same way that White feminists identify with their victimization as women yet ignore the privilege that racism grants them, and that Black men decry racism yet see sexism as being less objectionable, heterosexual African-American women may perceive their own race and gender oppression yet victimize lesbians, gays, and bisexuals. Barbara Smith raises a critical point that can best be seen through the outsider-within standpoint available to Black lesbians—namely, that intersecting oppressions of sexuality, race, gender, and class produce neither absolute oppressors nor pure victims.

The widely publicized 1992 Supreme Court Justice confirmation hearings of Clarence Thomas shattered this multifaceted silence. During the hearings, Anita Hill, a lawyer and former employee of Thomas during his years of heading up the Equal Employment Opportunity Commission, accused Thomas of sexually harassing her. For days, the U.S. public remained riveted to their television sets, listening to the details of Hill's accusations concerning Thomas's alleged abuse of power, and Thomas's ingenious rebuttals. The hearings were remarkable in several ways—their highly public, televised format, the similar race/class backgrounds and politically conservative ideologies shared by Thomas and Hill, and the public disclosure of sexually explicit material. By putting questions of race, gender, class, and sexuality on public display, the hearings served as a powerful catalyst to break longstanding silences.

The reactions to the hearings highlighted significant differences among White women and Black men that left African-American women scrambling to find ways to avoid "taking sides against the self" (Crenshaw 1992). White American women routinely viewed the hearings as a landmark event that placed the largely hidden issue of sexual harassment on the national agenda. Seeing a shared sisterhood around issues of sexual harassment in the workplace, they regarded Anita Hill's race as of little concern. Instead, her Blackness operated as an unearned bonus—it buttressed claims that regardless of skin color and other markers of difference, all women needed to rally together to fight sexual harassment. In contrast, U.S. Blacks viewed the event through the lens of racial solidarity whereby Hill's testimony violated Black "family secrets" about abusive Black men. For many African-American men and women, the integrity of Hill's claim became erased by her transgression of airing "dirty laundry" in public. Even if Thomas was a sexual harasser, some argued, out of solidarity with Black men

Hill should have kept her mouth shut. Cultural critic Lisa Jones describes a common reaction: "What happened to Hill sent a more forceful message than her face on the tube: Speaking out doesn't pay. A harassed woman is still a double victim, and a vocal, critical black woman is still a traitor to the race" (Jones 1994, 120).

African-American women found themselves caught in the middle, with issues of sexuality on public display. For many, Anita Hill's dilemma had a familiar ring. For one, images of a row of affluent White men sitting in judgment of both Anita Hill's and Clarence Thomas's sexual narratives smacked of pervasive silencing by dominant groups. Throwing in her lot with White women seemed foolish, because discourses of gender had long ignored the special circumstances of Black women. Because she had to live with the consequences of sexual harassment, the code of silence mandated by racial solidarity also had not served Anita Hill well. No place appeared to exist for Anita Hill's story, because long-standing silences on Black women's sexuality had failed to provide one.

Much has been written about the 1992 hearings, much of it by U.S. Black women (see, e.g., Morrison 1992; Smitherman 1995). Within this discourse lies a new readiness to explore how social constructions of Black women's sexualities must become more central to Black feminist thought. Following patterns established by Black feminist-influenced studies of work, family, controlling images, and other core themes of Black feminism, much of this work contextualizes analyses of Black women's sexualities within structural power relations. Treating race, class, gender, and sexuality less as personal attributes and more as systems of domination in which individuals construct unique identities, Black feminist analyses routinely identify multiple oppressions as important to the study of Black women's sexualities. For example, Black feminist thinkers have investigated how rape as a specific form of sexual violence is embedded in intersecting oppressions of race, gender, and class (Davis 1978, 1981, 1989; Crenshaw 1991). Reproductive rights issues such as access to information on sexuality and birth control, the struggles for abortion rights, and patterns of forced sterilization require attention to how nation-state policies affect U.S. Black women (Davis 1981; Roberts 1997; Collins 1999b). Black lesbians' work on homophobia investigates how heterosexism's impact on African-American women remains embedded in larger social structures (Lorde 1982, 1984; C. Clarke 1983; Shockley 1983; Barbara Smith 1983, 1998b). This contextualization in power relations generates a particular kind of social constructionist argument, one that views Black women's sexualities as being constructed within an historically specific matrix of domination characterized by intersecting oppressions. In understanding these Black feminist contextualizations, it may be more appropriate to speak of the *sexual politics of Black womanhood*, namely, how sexuality and power become linked in constructing Black women's sexualities.

BLACK WOMEN, INTERSECTING OPPRESSIONS, AND SEXUAL POLITICS

Due in large part to the politicized nature of definitions themselves, questions of sexuality and the sexual politics in which they participate raise special concerns. What is sexuality? What is power? Both of these questions generate widespread debate. Moreover, analyzing questions of sexuality and power within an interpretive framework that takes intersecting oppressions into account can appear to be a daunting task.

Whereas sexuality is part of intersecting oppressions, the ways in which it can be conceptualized differ. Sexuality can be analyzed as a freestanding system of oppression similar to oppressions of race, class, and gender. This approach views heterosexism as a system of power that victimizes Black women in particular ways. Within heterosexism as a system of oppression, African-American women find that their distinctive group placement within hierarchies of race, class, and gender shapes the experiences of Black women as a collectivity as well as the sexual histories of individual Black women.

A second approach examines how sexualities become manipulated *within* class, race, nation, and gender as distinctive systems of oppression and draw upon heterosexist assumptions to do so. Regulating Black women's sexualities emerges as a distinctive feature of social class exploitation, of institutionalized racism, of U.S. nation-state policies, and of gender oppression. In essence, this approach suggests that both the sexual meanings assigned to Black women's bodies as well as the social practices justified by sexual ideologies reappears across seemingly separate systems of oppression.

Yet another approach views sexuality as a specific site of intersectionality where intersecting oppressions meet. Studying Black women's sexualities reveals how sexuality constitutes one important site where heterosexism, class, race, nation, and gender as systems of oppression converge. For Black women, ceding control over self-definitions of Black women's sexualities upholds multiple oppressions. This is because all systems of oppression rely on harnessing the power of the erotic. In contrast, when self-defined by Black women ourselves, Black women's sexualities can become an important place of resistance. Just as harnessing the power of the erotic is important for domination, reclaiming and self-defining that same eroticism may constitute one path toward Black women's empowerment.

HETEROSEXISM AS A SYSTEM OF POWER

One important outcome of social movements advanced by lesbians, gays, bisexuals, and transgendered individuals has been the recognition of hetero-sexism as a system of power. In essence, the political and intellectual space carved out by these movements challenged the assumed normality of heterosexuality (Jackson 1996; Richardson 1996).

These challenges fostered a shift from seeing sexuality as residing in individual biological makeup, to analyzing heterosexism as a system of power. Similar to oppressions of race or gender that mark bodies with social meanings, heterosexism marks bodies with sexual meanings. Within this logic, *heterosexism* can be defined as the belief in the inherent superiority of one form of sexual expression over another and thereby the right to dominate.

When it comes to thinking about Black women's sexualities, what is needed is a framework that not only analyzes heterosexism as a system of oppression, but also conceptualizes its links to race, class, and gender as comparable systems of oppression. Such a framework might emphasize two interdependent dimensions of heterosexism, namely, its symbolic and structural dimensions. The symbolic dimension refers to the sexual meanings used to represent and evaluate Black women's sexualities. For example, via the "hoochie" image, Black women's sexualities are seen as unnatural, dirty, sick, and sinful. In contrast, the structural dimension encompasses how social institutions are organized to reproduce heterosexism, primarily through laws and social customs. For example, refusing to prosecute Black women's rapists because the women are viewed as sexual "freaks" constitutes a social practice that reinforces and shapes these symbolic structures. While analytically distinct, in actuality, these two dimensions work together.

In the United States, assumptions of heterosexuality operate as a hegemonic or taken-for-granted ideology—to be heterosexual is considered normal, to be anything else is to become suspect. The system of sexual meanings associated with heterosexism becomes normalized to such a degree that they are often unquestioned. For example, the use of the term *sexuality* itself references *hetero*sexuality as normal, natural, and normative.

The ideological dimension of heterosexism is embedded in binary thinking that deems heterosexuality as normal and other sexualities as deviant. Such thinking divides sexuality into two categories, namely, "normal" and "deviant" sexuality, and has great implications for understanding Black women's sexualities. Within assumptions of normalized heterosexuality, two important categories of "deviant" sexuality emerge. First, *African* or *Black* sexuality becomes constructed as an abnormal or pathologized heterosexuality. Long-standing ideas concerning the excessive sexual appetite of people of African descent conjured up in White imaginations generate gender-specific controlling images of the Black male rapist and the Black female jezebel, and they also rely on myths of Black hypersexuality. Within assumptions of normalized heterosexuality, regardless of individual behavior, being White marks the normal category of heterosexuality. In contrast, being Black signals the wild, out-of-control hyperheterosexuality of excessive sexual appetite.

Within assumptions of normalized heterosexuality, *homosexuality* emerges as a second important category of "deviant" sexuality. In this case, homosexuality constitutes an abnormal sexuality that becomes pathologized as heterosexuality's opposite. Whereas the problem of African or Black sexual deviancy is thought to lie in Black hyperheterosexuality, the problem of homosexuality lies not in an excess of heterosexual desire, but in the seeming absence of it. Women who lack interest in men as sexual partners become pathologized as "frigid" if they claim heterosexuality and stigmatized as lesbians if they do not.

Under Eurocentric ideologies, normalized heterosexuality thus becomes constructed in contrast to two allegedly deviant sexualities, namely, those attributed to people of African descent and those applied to lesbians and gays, among others. The binary fundamental to heterosexism, namely, that dividing alleged normal sexuality from its deviant other dovetails with binaries that underlie other systems of oppression. The important binaries introduced in Chapter 3's discussion of Black women's objectification—white/black, male/female, reason/emotion, and mind/body—now become joined by a series of sexual binaries: madonna/whore, real woman/dyke, real man/faggot, and stud/sissy. These sexual binaries in turn receive justification via medical theories (normal/sick), religious beliefs (saved/sinner), and state regulation (legal/illegal).

All of this influences the actual system of sexual regulation in the United States, where ideas about normalized heterosexuality permeate a range of social institutions. Despite the similarities that characterize constructions of African/Black sexuality and homosexuality, these sexualities differ in their characteristic modes of regulation. Black people experience a highly visible *sexualized racism*, one where the visibility of Black bodies themselves reinscribes the hypervisibility of Black men and women's alleged sexual deviancy. Because U.S. understandings of race rely on biological categories that, while renegotiated, cannot be changed—skin color is permanent—Black hyper-sexuality is conceptualized as being intergenerational and resistant to change.

The seeming intractability of the stigma of Blackness in turn shapes possible responses to this socially constructed yet highly visible deviancy.[1] Because biological traits are conceptualized as permanent, reformist strategies are unlikely to work. In this context, containment strategies of all sorts rise in importance. For example, racial segregation in housing, schools, employment, and public facilities not only benefits some groups of Whites economically—it also keeps allegedly hypersexual Blacks separated from Whites. Maintaining physical distance need not be the sole strategy. Blacks have long worked in close proximity to Whites, but Blacks and Whites alike were discouraged from seeing one another as friends, neighbors, lovers, and, most important, legal sexual partners. In a context where Black bodies signal sexual deviancy, laws against intermarriage and other components of racial segregation ensured that the deviancy could be simultaneously exploited yet contained.

Because the nature of the threat is deemed different, forms of control for lesbians, gays, and other sexually stigmatized groups differ from those of sexualized racism.

Homophobia flourishes in a context where the invisibility of the alleged deviancy is perceived to be the problem. Whereas the fears associated with racism lie in ideas projected upon highly visible, objectified Black bodies, the fears underlying homophobia emerge from the understanding that *anyone* could be gay or lesbian. Reminiscent of the proximate racism of anti-Semitism, one where, for example, Nazi scientists spent considerable time trying to find ways to identify Jewishness, homophobia constitutes a proximate fear that anyone could at any time reveal himself or herself as gay or lesbian.

The panoply of responses to the alleged deviancy of homosexuality also match the nature of the perceived threat. Containment also operates, but differently. For example, the medical profession has been assigned the reformist strategy of counseling gays and lesbians to better cope with normalized heterosexuality. Hate crimes punish individuals, but such crimes make an example of a visible homosexuality in order to drive the rest back into the closet. Recognizing that homosexuality most likely cannot be eliminated, the intended effect is to remove it from public and thereby legitimated space. Laws forbidding gay and lesbian marriages coupled with resistance to gays and lesbians having and raising children seem designed to stop the "spread" of homosexuality. Within this logic of the proximate threat, efforts to keep gays, lesbians, and other sexual minorities "in the closet" and "hidden" seem designed to contain the threat within.

Making heterosexism as a system of oppression more central to thinking through Black women's sexualities suggests two significant features. First, different groups remain differentially placed within heterosexism as an overarching structure of power. As I discuss later in this chapter and the next, African-American women's group history becomes crafted in the context of the specificity of the U.S. matrix of domination. Black women's particular group history within heterosexism intersects with that of other groups. For example, constructions of Black male and female sexuality are linked—they are similar yet different. Similarly, middle-class White women's sexuality could not be constructed as it is without corresponding controlling images applied to U.S. Black women. Moreover, this collective U.S. Black women's history does not eliminate further specification of group histories within the larger collectivity of African-American women, e.g., Black lesbians, adolescent Black women, older Black women, Black women who must rely on social welfare programs, and so on. Instead, it specifies the contours of sexual meanings that have been attributed to Black women. Considerable diversity exists among U.S. Black women as to how the symbolic and structural dimensions of heterosexism will be experienced and responded to.

A second significant feature concerns the space created for Black women's individual agency. Because African-American women express a range of sexualities, including celibate, heterosexual, lesbian, and bisexual, with varying forms of sexual expression changing throughout an individual's life course, Black women's self-definitions become essential. It is important to stress that both the symbolic and structural dimensions of heterosexism are always contested. Individual African-American women construct sexual meanings and practices within this overarching structure of heterosexual power relations. Thus, the individual agency of any one U.S. Black woman emerges in the context of larger institutional structures and particular group histories that affect many others. For individual Black women, the struggle lies in rejecting externally defined ideas and practices, and claiming the erotic as a mechanism for empowerment.

SEXUALITY WITHIN DISTINCTIVE SYSTEMS OF CLASS, RACE, GENDER, AND NATION

Analyzing how heterosexism as a system of oppression victimizes Black women constitutes one major approach to examining sexuality. A second approach explores how sexualities constructed in conjunction with an unquestioned heterosexism become manipulated within class, race, gender, and nation as distinctive systems of oppression. For example, the controlling image of jezebel reappears across several systems of oppression. For class oppression, the jezebel image fosters the sexual exploitation of Black women's bodies through prostitution. The jezebel image reinforces racial oppression by justifying sexual assaults against Black women. Gender ideology also draws upon the jezebel image—a devalued jezebel makes pure White womanhood possible. Overseeing these relationships are nation-state policies that because they implicitly see Black women as jezebels, deny Black women equal treatment under the law. Unmarried Black mothers have struggled to gain social welfare benefits long available to White women (Amott 1990), Black adolescents are more likely than White women to receive Norplant and other contraceptive methods that assume they cannot control their sexual libidos (Roberts 1997, 104–49), and as Anita Hill found out, Black women's claims of being sexually harassed and raped are often discounted. Thus, each system has a vested interest in regulating sexuality and relies on symbolic and structural practices to do so.

Examining how regulating Black women's sexuality functions to support each system constitutes one way of investigating these relationships. Controlling Black women's bodies has been especially important for capitalist class relations in the United States. When it comes to U.S. Black women's experiences, two features of capitalism remain noteworthy. First, Black women's bodies have been objectified and commodified under U.S. capitalist class relations. The objectification of Black women discussed in Chapter 4 and the subsequent commodification of those objectified bodies are closely linked—objectifying Black women's bodies turns them into commodities that can be sold or exchanged on the open market. Commodified bodies of all sorts become markers of status within class hierarchies that rely on race and gender. For example, healthy White babies are hot commodities in the U.S. adoption market, while healthy Black babies often languish in foster care. A second feature of U.S. capitalist class relations concerns how Black women's bodies have been exploited. Via mechanisms such as employment discrimination, maintaining images of Black women that construct them as mules or objects of pleasure, and encouraging or discouraging Black women's reproduction via state intervention, Black women's labor, sexuality, and fertility all have been exploited.

Not only are commodification and exploitation linked, patterns of exploiting Black women's sexuality have taken many forms. In some cases, the entire body itself became commodified. For example, slave auctions brokered the commodified bodies of both Black women and men—bodies could be bought and sold on the open market. In other cases, parts of the body could be commodified and sold for profitability. Barbara Omolade introduces this notion of specialized commodification where "every part of the black woman" was used by the White master. "To him she was a fragmented commodity whose feelings and choices were rarely considered: her head and her heart were separated from her back and her hands and divided from her womb and vagina" (Omolade 1994, 7). Black women's sexuality could be reduced to gaining control over an objectified vagina that could then be commodified and sold. The long-standing interest in Black women's genitalia within Western science seems apt here in that reducing Black women to commodified genitalia and vaginas effectively treats Black women as potential prostitutes. Similarly, current portrayals of Black women in popular culture—reducing Black women to butts—works to reinscribe these commodified body parts. Commodifying and exploiting Black women's wombs may be next. When a California judge rejected African-American Anna Johnson's claim that the White baby she had carried in her womb entitled her to some rights of motherhood, the message seemed clear—storage lockers and wombs constitute rental property (Hartouni 1997).

Regulating Black women's sexuality has certainly been significant within racist discourse and practice. In the United States, because race has been constructed as a biological category that is rooted in the body, controlling Black sexuality has long been important in preserving racial boundaries. U.S. notions of racial purity, such as the rule claiming that one drop of Black "blood" determines racial identity, required strict control over the sexuality and subsequent fertility of Black women, White women, and Black men. Although explicitly a means to prevent Blacks and Whites from associating in public accommodations, racial segregation in the South rested upon a deep-seated fear that "social mixing would lead to sexual mixing" (d'Emilio and Freedman 1988, 106). These mechanisms of control affected diverse population groups differently. Affluent White men typically enjoyed access to the bodies of all women and removed other men from sexual competition. The creation of a class of "angry White men" in the aftermath of social reforms of the 1960s and 1970s reflects, in part, the deterioration of White supremacist practices that gave White men such power (Ferber 1998). Wealthy White women were valued for a premarital virginity that when "lost" in the context of heterosexual marriage, ensured that all children would be biologically "White." Regardless of social class, Whites were encouraged to fear racial amalgamation, believing that it would debase them to the status of other races (d'Emilio and Freedman 1988, 86). In this context, Black men were constructed as sexually violent beasts, a view that not only justified their persecution by the state (Berry 1994), but was used to deny them access to White women's bodies. Black women's sexuality found no protections. Thus, notions of White supremacy relied on a notion of racial difference where "difference would be largely based on perceptions of sexual difference, and ... the foundation of sexual difference lay in attitudes about black women" (Giddings 1995, 417).

Regulating Black women's sexuality also constituted a part of gender oppression. Dividing women into two categories—the asexual, moral women to be protected by marriage and their sexual, immoral counterparts—served as a gender template for constructing ideas about masculinity and femininity. The major archetypal symbols of women in Western thought construct women's sexuality via a tightly interwoven series of binaries. Collectively, these binaries create a sexual hierarchy with approved sexual expression installed at the top and forbidden sexualities relegated to the bottom. Assumptions of normal and deviant sexuality work to label women as good girls or bad girls, resulting in two categories of female sexuality. Virgins are the women who remain celibate before marriage, and who gain license to engage in heterosexual sexual practices after marriage. In contrast, whores are the unmarried women who are willingly "screwed." Whether a woman is an actual virgin or not is of lesser concern than whether she can socially construct herself as a "good" girl within this logic. Racializing this gender ideology by assigning all Black women, regardless of actual behavior, to the category of "bad" girls simplifies the management of this system.

It is important to remember that what appear to be natural and normal ideas and practices concerning sexuality are in fact carefully manufactured and promoted by schools, organized religions, the news media, and, most importantly, government policies. The local, state, and federal branches of the U.S. government may appear to be removed from issues of sexuality, but via their taxation, social welfare, and other policies, the U.S. nation-state in effect regulates which sexualities are deemed legitimate and which are not. For example, U.S. nation-state policies shape understandings of which citizens shall be afforded privacy. Affluent families living in suburban gated communities are provided with far more privacy and government protection than are poor families who live in urban public housing, where police intrude on family privacy more often than they protect it. In a similar fashion, Black women's sexuality has been constructed by law as public property—Black women have no rights of privacy that Whites must observe. As Barbara Omolade suggests, "White men used their power in the public sphere to construct a private sphere that would meet their needs and their desire for black women, which if publicly admitted would have undermined the false construct of race they needed to maintain public power. Therefore, the history of black women in America reflects the juncture where the private and public spheres and personal and political oppression meet" (Omolade 1994, 17).

REGULATING BLACK WOMEN'S BODIES

Sexuality can be conceptualized as a freestanding system of oppression similar to oppressions of race, class, nation, and gender, as well as part of each of these distinctive systems of oppression. A third approach views sexuality as one important social location that joins these distinctive systems of oppression. This conceptualization views sexuality as conceptual glue that binds intersecting oppressions together. Stated differently, intersecting oppressions share certain core features. Manipulating and regulating the sexualities of diverse groups constitutes one such shared feature or site of intersectionality.

In this context, investigating efforts to regulate Black women's bodies can illuminate the larger question of how sexuality operates as a site of intersectionality. Within this larger endeavor, Black women's experiences with pornography, prostitution, and rape constitute specific cases of how more powerful groups have aimed to regulate Black women's bodies. These cases emphasize the connections between sexual ideologies developed to justify actual social practices and the use of force to maintain the social order. As such, these themes provide a useful lens for examining how intersecting oppressions rely on sexuality to mutually construct one another.

PORNOGRAPHY AND BLACK WOMEN'S BODIES

> For centuries the black woman has served as the primary pornographic "outlet" for White men in Europe and America. We need only think of the black women used as breeders, raped for the pleasure and profit of their owners. We need only think of the license the "master" of the slave women enjoyed. But, most telling of all, we need only study the old slave societies of the South to note the sadistic treatment—at the hands of white "gentlemen"—of "beautiful young quadroons and octoroons" who became increasingly (and were deliberately bred to become) indistinguishable from white women, and were the more highly prized as slave mistresses because of this.
>
> (Walker 1981, 42)

Alice Walker's description of the rape of enslaved African women for the "pleasure and profit of their owners" encapsulates several elements of contemporary pornography. First, Black women were used as sex objects for the pleasure of White men. This objectification of African-American women parallels the portrayal of women in pornography as sex objects whose sexuality is available for men (McNall 1983). Exploiting

Black women as breeders objectified them as less than human because only animals can be bred against their will. In contemporary pornography women are objectified through being portrayed as pieces of meat, as sexual animals awaiting conquest. Second, African-American women were raped, a form of sexual violence. Violence is typically an implicit or explicit theme in pornography. Moreover, the rape of Black women linked sexuality and violence, another characteristic feature of pornography (Eisenstein 1983). Third, rape and other forms of sexual violence act to strip victims of their will to resist and make them passive and submissive to the will of the rapist. Female passivity, the fact that women have things done to them, is a theme repeated over and over in contemporary pornography (McNall 1983). Fourth, the profitability of Black women's sexual exploitation for White "gentlemen" parallels pornography's financially lucrative benefits for pornographers (Dines 1998). Finally, the actual breeding of "quadroons and octoroons" not only reinforces the themes of Black women's passivity, objectification, and malleability to male control but reveals pornography's grounding in racism and sexism. The fates of both Black and White women were intertwined in this breeding process. The ideal African-American woman as a pornographic object was indistinguishable from a White woman and thus resembled the images of beauty, asexuality, and chastity forced on White women. But inside was a highly sexual whore, a "slave mistress" ready to cater to her owner's pleasure.[2]

Contemporary pornography consists of a series of icons or representations that focus the viewer's attention on the relationship between the portrayed individual and the general qualities ascribed to that class of individuals. Pornographic images are iconographic in that they represent realities in a manner determined by the historical position of the observers and by their relationship to their own time and to the history of the conventions which they employ (Gilman 1985). The treatment of Black women's bodies in nineteenth-century Europe and the United States may be the foundation upon which contemporary pornography as the representation of women's objectification, domination, and control is based. Icons about the sexuality of Black women's bodies emerged in these contexts. Moreover, as race and gender-specific representations, these icons have implications for the treatment of both African-American and White women in contemporary pornography.

I suggest that African-American women were not included in pornography as an afterthought but instead form a key pillar on which contemporary pornography itself rests. As Alice Walker points out, "The more ancient roots of modern pornography are to be found in the almost always pornographic treatment of black women who, from the moment they entered slavery … were subjected to rape as the "logical" convergence of sex and violence. Conquest, in short" (1981, 42).

One key feature about the treatment of Black women in the nineteenth century was how their bodies were objects of display. In the antebellum American South, White men did not have to look at pornographic pictures of women because they could become voyeurs of Black women on the auction block. A chilling example of this objectification of the Black female body is provided by the exhibition, in early-nineteenth-century Europe, of Sarah Bartmann, the so-called Hottentot Venus. Her display formed one of the original icons for Black female sexuality. An African woman, Sarah Bartmann was often exhibited at fashionable parties in Paris, generally wearing little clothing, to provide entertainment. To her audience she represented deviant sexuality. At the time European audiences thought that Africans had deviant sexual practices and searched for physiological differences, such as enlarged penises and malformed female genitalia, as indications of this deviant sexuality. Sarah Bartmann's exhibition stimulated these racist and sexist beliefs. After her death in 1815, she was dissected, with her genitalia and buttocks placed on display (Gilman 1985).

Sander Gilman explains the impact that Sarah Bartmann's exhibition had on Victorian audiences:

> It is important to note that Sarah Bartmann was exhibited not to show her genitalia—but rather to present another anomaly which the European audience … found riveting. This was the steatopygia, or protruding buttocks, the other physical characteristic of the Hottentot female which captured the eye of early European travelers. … The figure of Sarah Bartmann was reduced to her sexual parts. The audience which had paid to see her buttocks and had fantasized about the uniqueness of her genitalia when she was alive could, after her death and dissection, examine both.
>
> (1985, 213)

In this passage Gilman unwittingly describes how Bartmann was used as a pornographic object similar to how women are represented in contemporary pornography. She was reduced to her sexual parts, and these parts came to represent a dominant icon applied to Black women throughout the nineteenth century. Moreover, the fact that Sarah Bartmann was both African and a woman underscores the importance of gender in maintaining notions of racial purity. In this case Bartmann symbolized Blacks as a "race." Her display also served to buttress notions of European nations as "civilized" as opposed to the backward colonies that were incapable of development (Fausto-Sterling 1995). In the creation of the icon applied to Black women, notions of gender, race, nation, and sexuality were linked in overarching structures of political domination and economic exploitation.

The pornographic treatment of the bodies of enslaved African women and of women like Sarah Bartmann has since developed into a full-scale industry. Within pornography, all women are objectified differently by racial/ethnic category. Contemporary portrayals of Black women in pornography represent the continuation of the historical treatment of their actual bodies (Forna 1992). African-American women are usually depicted in a situation of bondage and slavery, typically in a submissive posture, and often with two White men. A study of fifty-four videos found that Black women more often were portrayed as being subjected to aggressive acts and as submitting after initial resistance to a sexual encounter. Compared with White women, Black women were shown performing fellatio on their knees more often (Cowan and Campbell 1994). Russell (1993, 45–49) reports that Black women are equated with snakes, as engaging in sex with animals, as incestuous, and as lovers of rape, especially by White men. As Bell observes, these settings remind us of "the trappings of slavery: chains, whips, neck braces, wrist clasps" (1987, 59). White women and women of color have different pornographic images applied to them. The image of Black women in pornography is almost consistently one featuring them breaking from chains. The image of Asian women in pornography is almost consistently one of being tortured (Bell 1987, 161).

The pornographic treatment of Black women's bodies challenges prevailing assumptions that since images of White women prevail in pornography, racism has been grafted onto pornography. African-American women's experiences suggest that Black women were not added into a preexisting pornography, but rather that pornography itself must be reconceptualized as a shift from the objectification of Black women's bodies in order to dominate and exploit them, to one of media representations of all women that perform the same purpose. Notions of biological determinism claiming that people of African descent and women possess immutable biological characteristics marking their inferiority to elite White men lie at the heart of both racism and sexism (Halpin 1989; Fausto-Sterling 1992). In pornography these racist and sexist beliefs are sexualized. Moreover, African-American women's pornographic treatment has not been timeless and universal but emerged in conjunction with European colonization and American slavery (Torgovnick 1990; McClintock 1995). The profitability of pornography thus serves capitalist class relations.

This linking of views of the body, social constructions of race and gender, pornography's profitability, and conceptualizations of sexuality that inform Black women's treatment as pornographic objects promises to have significant implications for how we assess contemporary pornography. Pornography's significance as a site of intersecting oppressions promises new insights toward understanding social injustice.

Investigating racial patterns in pornography offers one route for such an analysis. Black women have often claimed that images of White women's sexuality were intertwined with the controlling image of the sexually derogated Black woman: "In the United States, the fear and fascination of female sexuality was projected onto black women; the passionless lady arose in symbiosis with the primitively sexual slave" (Hall 1983, 333). Comparable linkages exist in pornography (Gardner 1980). Alice Walker provides a fictional account of a Black man's growing awareness of the different ways that African-American and White women are objectified in pornography: "What he has refused to see—because to see it would reveal yet another area in which he is unable to protect or defend black women—is that where white women are depicted in pornography as 'objects,' black women are depicted as animals. Where white women are depicted as human bodies if not beings, black women are depicted as shit" (Walker 1981, 52).

Walker's distinction between "objects" and "animals" is crucial in untangling gender, race, and class dynamics in pornography. Within the mind/body, culture/nature, male/female binaries in Western social thought, objects occupy an uncertain interim position. As objects, White women become creations of culture—in this case, the mind of White men—using the materials of nature—in this case, uncontrolled female sexuality. In contrast, as animals, Black women receive no such redeeming dose of culture and remain open to the type of exploitation visited on nature overall. Black women's portrayal in pornography as caged, chained, and naked creatures who possess "panther-like," savage, and exotic sexual qualities (Forna 1992) reinforces this theme of Black women's "wildness" as symbolic of an unbridled female sexuality. In a context where Whiteness as symbolic of both civilization and culture is used to separate objects from animals, racial difference constructed on the bedrock of sexuality becomes the distinguishing feature in determining the type of objectification women will encounter.

While the sexual and racial dimensions of being treated like an animal are important, the economic foundation underlying this treatment is critical. Under capitalist class relations, animals can be worked, sold, killed, and consumed, all for profit. As "mules," African-American women become susceptible to such treatment. The political economy of pornography meshes with this overarching value system that objectifies, commodifies, and markets products, ideas, images, and actual people. Pornography is pivotal in mediating contradictions in changing societies (McNall 1983). It is no accident that racist biology, religious justifications for slavery and women's subordination, and other explanations for nineteenth-century racism and sexism arose during a period of profound political and economic change. Symbolic means of domination become particularly important in mediating contradictions in changing political economies. The exhibition of Sarah Bartmann and Black women on the auction block were not benign intellectual exercises—these practices defended real material and political interests. Current transformations in international capitalism require similar ideological justifications. Contemporary pornography meshes with late-twentieth-century global transformations of postcolonialism in a fashion reminiscent of global changes associated with nineteenth-century colonialism (Dines 1998).

Publicly exhibiting Black women may have been central to objectifying Black women as animals and to creating the icon of Black women as animals. Yi-Fu Tuan (1984) offers an innovative argument about similarities in efforts to control nature—especially plant life—the domestication of animals, and the domination of certain groups of humans.

Tuan suggests that displaying humans alongside animals implies that such humans are more like monkeys and bears than they are like "normal" people. This same juxtaposition leads spectators to view the captive animals in a special way. Animals acquire definitions of being like humans, only more openly carnal and sexual, an aspect of animals that forms a major source of attraction for visitors to modern zoos. In discussing the popularity of monkeys in zoos, Tuan notes: "Some visitors are especially attracted by the easy sexual behavior of the monkeys. Voyeurism is forbidden except when applied to subhumans" (1984, 82). Tuan's analysis suggests that the public display of Sarah Bartmann and of the countless enslaved African women on the auction blocks of the antebellum American South—especially in proximity to animals—fostered their image as animalistic.

This linking of Black women and animals is evident in nineteenth-century scientific literature. The equation of women, Blacks, and animals is revealed in the following description of an African woman published in an 1878 anthropology text:

> She had a way of pouting her lips exactly like what we have observed in the orangutan. Her movements had something abrupt and fantastical about them, reminding one of those of the ape. Her ear was like that of many apes. ... These are animal characters. I have never seen a human head more like an ape than that of this woman.
>
> (Halpin 1989, 287)

In a climate such as this, it is not surprising that one prominent European physician even stated that Black women's "animal-like sexual appetite went so far as to lead black women to copulate with apes" (Gilman 1985, 212). Late-twentieth-century science has had difficulty shedding itself of these deep-seated beliefs. The association of Africa, animals, and seemingly deviant sexualities within AIDS discourse speaks to the persistence of these ideas (Hammonds 1986; Watney 1990). As Paula Giddings suggests, the fact that "respectable journals would make connections between green monkeys and African women, for example, or trace the origin of AIDS to African prostitutes—the polluted sexual organs of black women—reveals our continued vulnerability to racist ideology" (Giddings 1992, 458).

The treatment of all women in contemporary pornography has strong ties to the portrayal of Black women as animals. In pornography women become non-people and are often represented as the sum of their fragmented body parts. Scott McNall observes:

> This fragmentation of women relates to the predominance of rear-entry position photographs. ... All of these kinds of photographs reduce the woman to her reproductive system, and, furthermore, make her open, willing, and available—not

> in control. … The other thing rear-entry position photographs
> tell us about women is that they are animals. They are animals
> because they are the same as dogs—bitches in heat who can't
> control themselves.
>
> (McNall 1983, 197–98)

This linking of animals and women within pornography becomes feasible when grounded in the earlier debasement of Black women as animals.

Developing a comprehensive analysis of Black women's placement in pornography and of pornography itself as a site of interesecting oppressions offers possibilities for change. Those Black feminist intellectuals investigating sexual politics imply that the situation is much more complicated than that advanced within Western feminism in which "men oppress women" because they are men. Such approaches implicitly assume biologically deterministic views of gender and sexuality and offer few possibilities for change. In contrast, the willingness of Black feminist analyses of sexual politics to embrace intersectional paradigms provides space for human agency. Women are not hard-wired as victims of pornography, nor are men destined uncritically to consume it. In the short story "Coming Apart," Alice Walker describes one Black man's growing realization that his enjoyment of pornography, whether of White women as "objects" or Black women as "animals," degraded him:

> He begins to feel sick. For he realizes that he has bought some of
> the advertisements about women, black and white. And further,
> inevitably, he has bought the advertisements about himself. In
> pornography the black man is portrayed as being capable of
> fucking anything … even a piece of shit. He is defined solely by
> the size, readiness and unselectivity of his cock.
>
> (Walker 1981, 52)

Walker conceptualizes pornography as a mechanism within intersecting oppressions that entraps everyone. But by exploring an African-American *man's* struggle to understand his participation in pornography, Walker suggests that a changed consciousness is essential to social change. If Black men can understand how pornography affects them, then other groups enmeshed in the same system are equally capable of similar shifts in consciousness and action.

Because pornography as a way of thinking is so deeply ingrained in Western culture, it is difficult to achieve this changed consciousness and action. Reacting to the same catalyst of the Anita Hill hearings, Black feminist theorist Patricia Williams was intrigued by Clarence Thomas's claims that he admired Malcolm X. A friend's comment that Malcolm X wasn't just a role model but had become the "ultimate pornographic object" sent Williams to the library in search of work on pornography. Her subsequent description of pornography shows it to be a way of thinking that, she argues, has no necessary connection to sex. Williams came to see pornography as "a habit of thinking" that replays relationships of dominance and submission. For Williams, pornography:

> permits the imagination of the voyeur to indulge in auto-sensation that obliterates the subjectivity of the observed. A habit of thinking that allows that self-generated sensation to substitute for interaction with a whole other human being, to substitute for listening or conversing or caring … the object is pacified, a malleable "thing" upon which to project.
>
> (Williams 1995, 123)

Sadly, this "way of thinking" persists even among self-proclaimed progressive thinkers. I have seen three public uses of Sarah Bartmann's image. The first was by a White feminist scholar who refused to show the images without adequately preparing her audience. She knew that graphic images of Black women's objectification and debasement, whether on the auction block as the object of a voyeuristic nineteenth-century science, or within contemporary pornography, would be upsetting to some audience members. Initially, I found her concern admirable yet overly cautious. Then I saw the reactions of young Black women who saw images of Sarah Bartmann for the first time. Even though the speaker tried to prepare them, these young women cried. They saw and felt the connections among the women exhibited on the auction block, the voyeuristic treatment of Sarah Bartmann, the depiction of Black women in pornography, and their own daily experiences of being under sexual surveillance. I quickly changed my opinion of my colleague's concern—she was right.

The remaining two uses of Sarah Bartmann's image illustrate the contradictions and ironies in contemporary scholarship. A prominent White male scholar who has done much to challenge scientific racism apparently felt few qualms at using a slide of Sarah Bartmann as part of his PowerPoint presentation. Leaving her image on screen for several minutes with a panel of speakers that included Black women seated on stage in front of the slide, this scholar told jokes about the seeming sexual interests of the White voyeurs of the nineteenth century. He seemed incapable of grasping how his own twentieth-century use of this image, as well as his invitation that audience members become voyeurs along with him, reinscribed Sarah Bartmann as an "object … a malleable 'thing'" upon which he projected his own agenda. When I questioned him about his pornographic use of the slide, his response was telling. Just as pornographers hide behind the protections of "free speech," so did this prominent scholar. He defended his "right" to use public domain material in any way he saw fit, even if it routinely offended Black women and contributed to their continued objectification.

The final use illustrates yet another limitation of failing to see pornography via the lens of intersecting oppressions. In this case, I attended a conference on race and ethnicity where a prominent Black male scholar presented his analysis of the significance of the changing size of Black bodies portrayed in racist iconography. Once again, the slide show began, and there she was again. Sarah Bartmann's body appeared on the screen, not to provide a humorous interlude, but as the body chosen to represent the nineteenth-century "raced" body. Again, the audience was allowed a lengthy, voyeuristic peek at Bartmann, all the while listening to how this particular "raced" body illustrated my colleague's latest insight about body size. Despite the fact that we stared at a half-naked Black woman, he made no mention of gender, let alone how this particular "raced" and "gendered" body has been central to the pornographic treatment of Black women. As much as I hated to violate the unspoken norm of racial solidarity, during the discussion period, I questioned these omissions. After a brief and disapproving silence, he dismissed my question. In a derisive tone suggesting that I had somehow missed the profundity of his argument, this arrogant individual replied, "I'm concerned about race here, not gender!"

Sadly, both my White male colleague and his Black male counterpart had apparently developed "habits of thinking" that allowed them to use their imaginations "to indulge in auto-sensation that obliterates the subjectivity of the observed." Certainly Black women's subjectivity, both Sarah Bartmann's and my own, were obliterated by how these two men used her image. Instead, I was invited to objectify myself in order to develop the objectivity that would allow me to participate in her objectification. I could become either a laughing voyeur of Bartmann's debasement or a voyeur of her "raced" yet ungendered body, but a voyeur all the same. Apparently, among some thinkers, some habits of thinking are extremely hard to break.

PROSTITUTION AND THE EXPLOITATION OF BLACK WOMEN'S BODIES

In *To Be Young, Gifted and Black*, Lorraine Hansberry creates three characters: a young domestic worker; a chic, professional, middle-aged woman; and a mother in her thirties. Each speaks a variant of the following:

> In these streets out there, any little white boy from Long Island or Westchester sees me and leans out of his car and yells—"Hey there, *hot chocolate!* Say there, Jezebel! Hey you—'Hundred Dollar Misunderstanding'! YOU! Bet you know where there's a good time tonight ..." Follow me sometimes and see if I lie. I can be coming from eight hours on an assembly line or fourteen hours in Mrs. Halsey's kitchen. I can be all filled up that day with

three hundred years of rage so that my eyes are flashing and my flesh is trembling—and the white boys in the streets, they look at me and think of sex. They look at me and that's all they think. ... Baby, you could be Jesus in drag—but if you're brown they're sure you're selling!

(Hansberry 1969, 98)

Like the characters in Hansberry's fiction, all Black women are affected by the widespread controlling image that African-American women are sexually promiscuous. The pervasiveness of this image is vividly recounted in Black activist lawyer Pauli Murray's description of an incident she experienced while defending two women from Spanish Harlem who had been arrested for prostitution: "The first witness, a white man from New Jersey, testified on the details of the sexual transaction and his payment of money. When asked to identify the woman with whom he had engaged in sexual intercourse, he unhesitatingly pointed directly at me, seated beside my two clients at the defense table!" (Murray 1987, 274). Murray's clients were nonetheless convicted.

Not just White men, but Black men have been involved in finding ways to profit from Black women's bodies. During an interview with Brother Marquis from the group 2 Live Crew, Black cultural critic Lisa Jones realizes that "hoochie mama" and other songs by this group actually constitute "soft porn." Jones's interview with Brother Marquis reveals the important links among pornography, the marketing of Black women's images, and the exploitation of Black women's bodies. In defending the misogynist lyrics of 2 Live Crew's music, Brother Marquis states:

I'm not gonna try to disrespect you and call you all those names like I do on those records. I would never do that to a young lady, especially a sister. I'm degrading you to try to get me some money. ... And besides, you let me do that. You got pimps out here who are making you sell your body. Just let me talk about you for a little while, you know what I'm saying? And make me a little money.

(Jones 1994, 243)

Brother's Marquis's explanation displays familiar rationalizations. He divided women into two categories of good girls and "hoochies." In his mind, if Black women are devalued within prostitution already, what harm can it do to *talk* about debasing Black women, especially if he can profit from such talk?

Within Brother Marquis's logic, images of Black women as jezebels and "hoochies" do little harm. Yet this controlling image has been vital in justifying the negative treatment that Black women encounter with intersecting oppressions. Exploring how the image of the African-American woman as prostitute has been used by selected systems of oppression illustrates how sexuality links the three systems. But Black women's treatment also demonstrates how prostitution operates as a site of intersectionality.

Yi-Fu Tuan (1984) suggests that power as domination involves reducing humans to animate nature in order to exploit them economically or to treat them condescendingly as pets. Domination may be either cruel and exploitative with no affection or may be exploitative yet coexist with affection. The former produces the victim—in this case, the Black woman as "mule" whose labor has been exploited. In contrast, the combination of dominance and affection produces the pet, the individual who is subordinate and whose survival depends on the whims of the more powerful. The "beautiful young quadroons and octoroons" described by Alice Walker were bred to be pets—enslaved Black mistresses whose existence required that they retain the affection of their owners. The treatment afforded these women illustrates a process that affects all African-American women: their portrayal as actual or potential victims and pets of elite White males.[3]

African-American women simultaneously embody the coexistence of the victim and the pet, with survival often linked to the ability to be appropriately subordinate. Black women's experiences as unpaid and paid workers demonstrate the harsh lives victims are forced to lead. While the life of the victim is difficult, pets experience a distinctive form of exploitation. Zora Neale Hurston's 1943 essay, "The 'Pet' Negro System," speaks contemptuously of this ostensibly benign situation that combines domination with affection. Writing in a Black oratorical style, Hurston notes, "Brother and Sisters, I take my text this morning from the Book of Dixie. ... Now it says here, 'And every white man shall be allowed to pet himself a Negro. Yea, he shall take a black man unto himself to pet and cherish, and this same Negro shall be perfect in his sight'" (Walker 1979a, 156). Pets are treated as exceptions and live with the constant threat that they will no longer be "perfect in his sight," that their owners will tire of them and relegate them to the unenviable role of victim.

Prostitution represents the fusion of exploitation for an economic purpose— namely, the commodification of Black women's sexuality—with the demeaning treatment afforded pets. Sex becomes commodified not merely in the sense that it can be purchased—the dimension of economic exploitation—but also in the sense that one is dealing with a totally alienated being who is separated from and who seemingly does not control her body: the dimension of power as domination (McNall 1983). Commodified sex can then be appropriated by the powerful. When the "white boys from Long Island" look at Black women and *all* they think about is sex, they believe that they can appropriate Black women's bodies. When they yell, "Bet you know where there's a good time tonight," they expect commodified sex with Black women as "animals" to be better than sex with White women as "objects." Both pornography and prostitution commodify sexuality and imply to the "white boys" that all African-American women can be bought.

Prostitution under European and American capitalism thus exists within a complex web of political and economic relationships. Gilman's (1985) analysis of the exhibition of Sarah Bartmann as the "Hottentot Venus" suggests another intriguing connection between race, gender, and sexuality in nineteenth-century Europe—the linking of the icon of the Black woman with the icon of the White prostitute. While the Hottentot woman stood for the essence of Africans as a race, the White prostitute symbolized the sexualized woman. The prostitute represented the embodiment of sexuality and all that European society associated with it: disease as well as passion. As Gilman points out, "It is this uncleanliness, this disease, which forms the final link between two images of women, the black and the prostitute. Just as the genitalia of the Hottentot were perceived as parallel to the diseased genitalia of the prostitute, so ... the power of the idea of corruption links both images" (1985, 237). These connections between the icons of Black women and White prostitutes demonstrate the interdependence of race, gender, and sexuality in shaping European understandings of social class.

In the American antebellum South both of these images were fused in the forced prostitution of enslaved African women. The prostitution of Black women allowed White women to be the opposite; Black "whores" make White "virgins" possible. This race/gender nexus fostered a situation whereby White men could then differentiate between the sexualized woman-as-body who is dominated and "screwed" and the asexual woman-as-pure-spirit who is idealized and brought home to mother (Hoch 1979, 70). The sexually denigrated woman, whether she was made a victim through her rape or a pet through her seduction, could be used as the yardstick against which the cult of true womanhood was measured. Moreover, this entire situation was profitable.

The image of the lesbian can also be linked with that of the prostitute and with images of Black women as the embodiment of the Black "race." Christian notes that Black women writers broadened the physical image of lesbians: "The stereotypical body type of a black lesbian was that she looked mannish; ... she was not so much a woman as much as she was a defective man, a description that has sometimes been applied to any Negroid-looking or uppity-acting black woman" (1985, 191). Note Christian's analysis of the links among gender, race, and sexuality. Lesbianism, an allegedly deviant sexual practice, becomes linked to biological markers of race and looking "mannish." These links also reinforce constructions of Black women's sexualities as deviant—the co-joining of Black heterosexual women's sexual deviancy as lying in their excess sexual appetite with the perceived deviancy of Black lesbians as lying in their rejection of what makes women feminine, namely, heterosexual contact with men.

RAPE AND SEXUAL VIOLENCE

Force was important in creating African-American women's centrality to American images of the sexualized woman and in shaping their experiences with both pornography and prostitution. Black women did not willingly submit to their exhibition on Southern auction blocks—they were forced to do so. Enslaved African women could not choose whether to work—they were beaten and often killed if they refused. Black domestics who resisted the sexual advances of their employers often found themselves looking for work where none was to be found. Both the reality and the threat of violence have acted as a form of social control for African-American women (Collins 1998d).

Rape has been one fundamental tool of sexual violence directed against African-American women. Challenging the pervasiveness of Black women's rape and sexual extortion by White men has long formed a prominent theme in Black women's writings. Autobiographies such as Maya Angelou's *I Know Why the Caged Bird Sings* (1970) and Harriet Jacobs's "The Perils of a Slave Woman's Life" (1860/1987) from *Incidents in the Life of a Slave Girl* record examples of actual and threatened sexual assault. The effects of rape on African-American women is a prominent theme in Black women's fiction. Gayl Jones's *Corregidora* (1975) and Rosa Guy's *A Measure of Time* (1983) both explore interracial rape of Black women. Toni Morrison's *The Bluest Eye* (1970), Alice Walker's *The Color Purple* (1982), and Gloria Naylor's *The Women of Brewster Place* (1980) all examine rape within African-American families and communities. Elizabeth Clark-Lewis's (1985) study of domestic workers found that mothers, aunts, and community othermothers warned young Black women about the threat of rape. One respondent in Clark-Lewis's study, an 87-year old North Carolina Black domestic worker, remembers, "nobody was sent out before you was told to be careful of the white man or his sons" (Clark-Lewis 1985, 15).

Rape and other acts of overt violence that Black women have experienced, such as physical assault during slavery, domestic abuse, incest, and sexual extortion, accompany Black women's subordination in intersecting oppressions. These violent acts are the visible dimensions of a more generalized, routinized system of oppression. Violence against Black women tends to be legitimated and therefore condoned while the same acts visited on other groups may remain nonlegitimated and non-excusable. Historically, this violence has garnered the backing and control of the state (James 1996). Specific acts of sexual violence visited on African-American women reflect a broader process by which violence is socially constructed in a race- and gender-specific manner. Thus Black women, Black men, and White women experience distinctive forms of sexual violence. As Angela Davis points out, "It would be a mistake to regard the institutionalized pattern of rape during slavery as an expression of white men's sexual urges. ... Rape was a weapon of domination, a weapon of repression, whose covert goal was to extinguish slave women's will to resist, and in the process, to demoralize their men" (1981, 23).

Angela Davis's work (1978, 1981, 1989) illustrates this effort to conceptualize sexual violence against African-American women as a site of intersecting oppressions. Davis suggests that depicting African-American men as sexually charged beasts who desired White women created the myth of the Black rapist. Lynching emerged as the specific form of sexual violence visited on Black men, with the myth of the Black rapist as its ideological justification. The significance of this myth is that it "has been methodically conjured up when recurrent waves of violence and terror against the black community required a convincing explanation" (Davis 1978, 25). Black women experienced a parallel form of race- and gender-specific sexual violence. Treating African-American women as pornographic objects and portraying them as sexualized animals, as prostitutes, created the controlling image of jezebel. Rape became the specific act of sexual violence forced on Black women, with the myth of the Black prostitute as its ideological justification.

Lynching and rape, two race/gender-specific forms of sexual violence, merged with their ideological justifications of the rapist and prostitute in order to provide an effective system of social control over African-Americans. Davis asserts that the controlling image of Black men as rapists has always "strengthened its inseparable companion: the image of the black woman as chronically promiscuous. And with good reason, for once the notion is accepted that black men harbor irresistible, animal-like sexual urges, the entire race is invested with bestiality" (1978, 27). A race of "animals" can be treated as such—as victims or pets. "The mythical rapist implies the mythical whore—and a race of rapists and whores deserves punishment and nothing more" (Davis 1978, 28).

Black women continue to deal with this legacy of the sexual violence visited on African-Americans generally and with our history as collective rape victims. One effect lies in the treatment of rape victims. Such women are twice victimized, first by the actual rape, in this case the collective rape under slavery. But they are victimized again by family members, community residents, and social institutions such as criminal justice systems which somehow believe that rape victims are responsible for their own victimization. Even though current statistics indicate that Black women are more likely to be victimized than White women, Black women are less likely to report their rapes, less likely to have their cases come to trial, less likely to have their trials result in convictions, and, most disturbing, less likely to seek counseling and other support services.

Another effect of this legacy of sexual violence concerns the significance of Black women's continued silences concerning rape. But Black women's silence about rape obscures an important issue: Most Black women are raped by Black men. While the historical legacy of the triad of pornography, prostitution, and the institutionalized rape of Black women may have created the larger social context within which all African-Americans reside, the unfortunate current reality is that many Black men have internalized the controlling images applied to Black women. Like Brother Marquis, they feel that if they as individuals do not rape women, they contribute little to the overall cultural climate that condones sexual violence. These beliefs allow them to ignore Black women's rape by other Black men, their own culpability in fostering Black women's objectification as pornographic objects, and, in some cases, their own behavior as rapists. For example, Black women and men often disagree as to whether Nola Darling, the sexually liberated heroine in Spike Lee's acclaimed film *She's Gotta Have It*, was raped. Men disbelieve Nola's protestations and see her protest as serving to heighten the sexual pleasure of her male partner. In contrast, many women see her re-action as typical for those of a rape victim. Recognizing that it is useless to protest, Nola Darling submits. Was Nola Darling raped? Do the sexual politcs of Black womanhood that construct jezebels and "hoochies" have any grounding in reality? The answers to both questions may lie in who has the power to define.

NOTES

1. The perceived deviancy of sexual outlaws has been addressed in characteristic ways: if possible, fix it (the reformist posture); if it cannot be fixed, at least contain it so that disease will not infect the so-called healthy population (ghettoization, segregation); and if reform and elimination fail, then eliminate it by stamping out the deviant practices if not the actual people themselves (the genocidal impulse).

2. Offering a similar argument about the relationship between race and masculinity, Paul Hoch (1979) suggests that the ideal White man is a hero who upholds honor. But inside lurks a "Black beast" of violence and sexuality, traits that the White hero deflects onto men of color.

3. Any group can be made into pets. Consider Tuan's (1984) discussion of the role that young Black boys played as exotic ornaments for wealthy White women from the 1500s to the early 1800s in England. Unlike other male servants, the boys were the favorite attendants of noble ladies and gained entry into their mistresses' drawing rooms, bedchambers, and theater boxes. Boys were often given fancy collars with padlocks to wear. "As they did with their pet dogs and monkeys, the ladies grew genuinely fond of their black boys" (p. 142). In addition, Nancy White's analysis in Chapter 5 of the differences between how White and Black women are treated by White men uses this victim/pet metaphor (Gwaltney 1980, 148).

What Race Are Mexicans? A Brief History of the Racialization of Mexican Americans

By Agustin Palacios

INTRODUCTION: MEXICAN AMERICANS AND THE UNITED STATES CENSUS

Latinos, including Mexican Americans,[1] do not fit neatly within the United States' racial classification system. In the 2010 US Census, one-third of all Latinos (more than eighteen million) checked the "some other race" box. Many of these Latinos did not see themselves represented by the "Black," "White," or other available racial categories. Part of the confusion might have to do with the fact that for many Latinos, cultural or national identity is more salient than biological ancestry. People in Mexico, for example, are uncomfortable talking about race, or referring to themselves in racial terms; instead, discussions center around skin color (Sue 2013).

The 2010 census asked about Latino ethnicity and race in two separate questions. The first question asked, "Is this person Hispanic, Latino, or [of] Spanish origin?" It also noted that "For this Census, Hispanic origins are not races." The second question asked, "What is this person's race?" Out of the 31.8 million Mexican Americans counted in the census, 52 percent, or 16.8 million, self-identified as White (Ennis,

---

1. In this paper, I include both Mexican immigrants and US-born Mexican Americans under the term *Mexican American*. I do so because both the immigrant and the US-born Mexican have been racialized in similar ways.

Ríos-Vargas, and Albert 2011).[2] The second largest racial identification was "some other race" at 12.5 million, or about 40 percent.[3] The census defined "White" as those "having origins in any of the original peoples of Europe, the Middle East, or North Africa." At the same time, Latino/Hispanic was defined as anyone of "Cuban, Mexican, Puerto Rican, South or Central American, or other Spanish culture or origin regardless of race." The definition of Latino/Hispanic as having Spanish culture might have suggested to Latinos that they should mark the White category. Scholar Julie A. Dowling's study of Mexican American racial identification in Texas found that for some Mexican Americans, White identification functions more as a defense strategy than a true reflection of their personal identity. Some Mexican Americans choose to identify as "White" in government forms in an attempt to avoid social discrimination. These Mexican Americans perceive that being White in the United States comes with some privileges, one of them being the opportunity to be seen as a full American. Their White identification thus functions as a claim for inclusion into American society (Dowling 2014).

In this chapter, I provide a condensed transnational history of Mexican Americans, with a focus on race. A discussion of Mexican Americans and race should include references to Mexico's history, given that Mexican immigrants bring with them their own ideas of race, which they in turn use to negotiate their racialization in the United States. This chapter works in broad historical strokes, and just as when viewing one of Diego Rivera's enormous murals, the reader should be able to step back to better appreciate the complex history of Mexican racialization. I will discuss Mexico's racial diversity, as well as the significance of its colonial history and the US-Mexico War to Mexican Americans' ideas of race. I also provide a discussion on how the Chicano movement transformed Mexican Americans' identity. The last section of the chapter provides a discussion of how Mexican immigration continues to complicate ideas about Mexicans and race in the United States. The reader should take this chapter as an introduction to the complex topic of Mexican American racialization, as well as a way to begin to understand why what seems like a simple question—"What race are Mexicans?"—is at times difficult to answer within the United States's racial classification system.

---

2. In 2014, there were about 34.5 million people of Mexican descent in the United States, making up about 64 percent of the overall Latino population in the country (source: http://factfinder.census.gov/faces/tableservices/jsf/pages/productview.xhtml?src=bkmk).

3. Mexican Americans also marked the categories of American Indian and Alaskan Native (460,098), Black or African American (296,778), Asian (101,654), and Native Hawaiian and Other Pacific Islander (24,600). A separate 1,576,372 Mexican Americans marked two or more races (see Ennis et al. 2011).

MEXICO'S RACIAL DIVERSITY

It has been noted by historians that there were no "Indians" in the Americas before European colonization. The Spanish imposed the label "Indian" on a diverse population that never saw itself as such. To be assigned the "Indio" category in colonial society meant being subjected to forced labor and having tribute obligations (Quijano 2000). The Spanish conquistadores did not see themselves as "White," either; their identities were composed of the diverse ethnic groups of Spain, including Catalans, Basques, and Castilians. Having been colonized by North African Moors for more than seven hundred years, the Spanish settlers were a mixed group to begin with, far from any conception of "White" purity.

The Catholic Church and the Crown encouraged the Spanish settlers to mix with the indigenous population.[4] This was deemed necessary for the establishment of political control and the conversion of the Indians to Christianity. But despite the Crown's professed Christian intentions, the religious justification for conquest contrasted with the widespread sexual violence against indigenous women; these rapes produced mixed-race offspring who had the stigma of illegitimacy and of being the products of rape. The Spanish also imported a large number of enslaved Black Africans to meet the colony's growing labor needs. In fact, for much of the sixteenth and seventeenth centuries, there were more Africans than there were Europeans (Aguirre Beltrán [1946] 1972). Although war, disease, and dangerous working conditions significantly reduced the indigenous population during the colonial period, indigenous people made up the great majority of the population at least until 1810.[5] Today's Mexican population reflects this racial diversity. A 2015 national poll found that out of 119.5 million Mexicans, 25.7 million (21.5 percent) self-identified as indigenous, and 1.38 million (1.2 percent) self-identified as *afrodescendientes*, or *Afro-mestizo* (the mixed-race descendants of Black Africans).[6]

---

4. In contrast to Mexico's more fluid racial system, the United States had a much more rigid racial structure that saw race as fixed and immutable. In some Southern states, there were "one drop" rules that classified mixed race children, no matter their physical appearance, as non-White if one of their ancestors was Black or Native American. There was also a strong aversion against racial mixing in the United States, with many states passing antimiscegenation laws that prohibited Blacks and Indians from marrying Whites. People who disobeyed could be sentenced to prison terms, and in the South, racial lines were at times enforced through lynching. Not until 1967 in the case of *Loving v. Virginia* did the Supreme Court rule that antimiscegenation laws were unconstitutional.

5. In the 1570 census, there were 6,644 Europeans, 20,569 Africans, 3,366,860 indigenous population, and 15,939 mestizos. In contrast, in 1810, there were 15,000 Europeans, 10,000 Africans, 3,676,281 indigenous people, and 2,421,073 mestizos (Aguirre Beltrán [1946] 1972).

6. See *Instituto Nacional de Estadística y Geografía* (2015).

MESTIZAJE AND *MULATAJE*

Mexicans today are the descendants, to various degrees, of indigenous, European, and African peoples. In the Spanish colonies, the term *casta* was commonly used to refer to Indians, Blacks, and people of mixed racial descent. The *sistema de castas* presumed to track the amount of Whiteness, Indianness, and Blackness of each mixed offspring. In contrast to the New England colonies, which racialized individuals under the "one drop" rule, in the Spanish colonies, the offspring of two distinct racial groups created a third ethno-racial category, called *castas*. Depending on who was doing the classification, there could be more than fourteen different *casta* categories (Mörner 1967). The mixed offspring of the Spanish and Indians were called *mestizos/as*, and the mixture of Spanish and Black were called *mulatos/as*. There was also mixing between Africans and indigenous people; their offspring were called *zambo* (knocked-kneed) or *lobo* (wolf).

The first mestizos were the children of Spanish conquistadores and indigenous women. A few of them inherited the noble status of their parents, but the majority of them were seen as illegitimate misfits. Family lineage, place of residence, ability to speak Spanish, phenotype, and class also influenced mestizas/os' place in the social hierarchy. The children of enslaved Africans could be born free if their mother was free. Given that the Catholic Church opposed racial restrictions to marriage, slaves often chose Indian wives so that their children would be born free.

Following Mexican independence in 1821, Mexico abolished slavery and all racial classifications (even the 2010 census did not ask Mexicans about race or ethnicity). The intent was that the population would begin to see themselves primarily as Mexican. Mexico defined itself as a mestizo country and embarked on a nation-building project that relied on homogenization through racial and cultural mixing. The nation-building project rested on the belief that racial and cultural homogeneity was necessary for national unification and progress. The nationalist project was successful to the extent that most mestizos/as identify primarily as Mexican today.

MEXICAN RACIALIZATION AFTER 1848

Racialization refers to the historical, social, and political process through which individuals and groups are assigned to racial categories (Omi and Winant [1986] 2015). The theory of racialization highlights the fact that race is a social construction, the result of history and cultural, political, and economic processes, not biological ones. As Omi and Winant point out, "[al]though the concept of race invokes seemingly biologically based human characteristics (so-called phenotypes), selection of the particular human features for purposes of racial signification is always and necessarily a social and historical process" (110). Although there are differences in skin color, hair texture, and other visible physical features, what these features mean, as well as the value that we give them, is socially constructed.

When discussing the history of Mexican racialization, historians usually begin with the US-Mexico War (1846–1848) and the ways in which Mexicans were racialized through citizenship laws and social customs. The United States declared war on Mexico in May 1846, following violent clashes between US and Mexican military in disputed territory claimed by both Texas and Mexico. US expansionism was driven by the belief in Manifest Destiny, an expansionist ideology based on the idea of racial supremacy and the Puritan notion of being God's chosen people (Gómez 2007). Manifest Destiny and the war profoundly shaped the way in which the United States racialized Mexicans. The war propaganda often portrayed Mexicans as treacherous, low types as a way to justify dispossessing them of their land.

The colonization of Mexico's northern territory involved the displacement of the indigenous and Mexican population. They were displaced so that the new settlers could gain access to their land (Acuña 2014; Menchaca 2003; Montejano 1987). European Americans were quick to settle in the conquered territories, looking for gold and other economic opportunities. With the exception of New Mexico, Mexican Americans quickly became a minority population, subjected to a system of racial hierarchy that privileged Whiteness. Even wealthy Tejanos and Californios who had previously enjoyed respect and high status now faced social discrimination. Such is the case of Juan Seguín, who had been a captain in the Texas Army of Independence, served in the Texas Senate, and was mayor of San Antonio. Seguín had to flee with his family to Mexico in 1842 because Anglo settlers were angry that Seguín defended the rights of fellow Tejanos (Montejano 1987).[7]

As part of the Treaty of Guadalupe Hidalgo that ended the war, the tens of thousands of Mexicans residing in the ceded territories were granted US citizenship, with all its rights and privileges (Griswold del Castillo 1990). Citizenship was important because it gave Mexicans the right to electoral participation, access to the protection of the criminal justice system, and the right to hold onto and accumulate property. Because at the time of the treaty only those considered to be "free White persons" were eligible for citizenship (per the Naturalization Act of 1790), Mexicans became "White by law" (García 2009; Gómez 2007; Gross 2006). Rather than changing the law to allow non-Whites to have access to citizenship, the federal government instead decided

---

7. The story of Mariano Vallejo is a good example of how prominent Californios lost much of their wealth and status following the war. Vallejo had been a military general and politician, and had amassed vast property. Following the Bear Flag Revolt in 1846, Vallejo was imprisoned by the Anglo rebels. After his release from prison, he found that much of his land had been claimed by squatters. The long legal battles to defend his property ended up costing him most of his wealth and land. For more on Vallejo, see Ronald Takaki's book *A Different Mirror* (1993), chapter 7, "Foreigners in Their Native Land."

to classify Mexicans as legally White, regardless of their racially mixed background. This move was strongly debated in Congress. There were congressmen, like Senator John C. Calhoun, who opposed granting US citizenship to Mexicans because of their Indian heritage. Calhoun believed that Mexicans were racially inferior and incapable of self-government, and that their inclusion would undermine American democracy. It is worth remembering that not until the passage of the Fourteenth Amendment in 1868 were African Americans granted citizenship, but the amendment explicitly excluded Native Americans. At the time, Native Americans were not considered part of American society and had been pushed off to reservations. Because of their mixed Indian ancestry, Mexicans became the targets of anti-Indian racism.

Despite the Treaty of Guadalupe Hidalgo, the federal government left it up to the states to determine citizenship requirements for their population. According to California's 1849 territorial laws, having half or more "Indian" blood made an individual non-White. This meant that Mexican mestizos were categorized as White. But once California became admitted as a state, the law was changed so that only one-fourth of Indian blood would make a person non-White (Menchaca 2003). Mexicans who were first eligible for citizenship were now racialized as ineligible Indians. Although the law called for a more nuanced racial classification of Mexican Americans, to most Euro-American society, Mexican Americans were simply "Mexicans" and thus non-White. In particular, Mexicans with dark skin and straight black hair were racialized as Indian and unworthy of equality.

In 1896, Ricardo Rodriguez filed to become a naturalized citizen in the state of Texas. Rodriguez was a Mexican immigrant who had resided in Texas for ten years (De Leon 1979). His citizenship application was challenged by two San Antonio attorneys on the grounds that he was an Indian, and thus ineligible for naturalization. The attorneys stated that it was necessary to deny Rodriguez's citizenship application "to prevent newly arrived Mexicans from voting" (as cited in De Leon 1979, 1). A central question under debate was whether Rodriguez was Indian or primarily Indian, and thus ineligible for naturalization. The lawyers pointed out, "A Mongolian is not a 'person'; an Indian is not a 'person'; a woman is not a 'person'; is an Aztec a 'person,' from the suffrage standpoint?" (1979, 2).[8] In the cross-examination, Rodriguez was asked whether he was Spanish or Indian. He said no to both. Instead, he affirmed that he was a "pure-blooded Mexican" (1979, 3). The judge decided to grant Rodriguez citizenship, not based on his race, but based on the legal precedent that when Texas joined the Union in 1845, Tejanos had acquired US citizenship. This eligibility for citizenship had been reaffirmed by the Treaty of Guadalupe Hidalgo.

---

8. Although at the time Euro-American women were eligible for citizenship, they did not have any political rights and could not vote. Women did not receive suffrage until the passage of the Nineteenth Amendment in 1920.

In the face of social exclusion, and up to the dismantling of Jim Crow segregation in the 1960s, Mexican Americans held onto and asserted their legal Whiteness as a way to protect themselves. Because Mexicans were in theory White, they could become naturalized citizens, attend White schools, marry White partners, and also vote in the Democratic Party's White primary. In practice, however, their acceptance was uneven, and Mexican Americans often experienced de facto segregation, disenfranchisement, and racism. In comparison to Euro Americans, Mexican Americans often received lower wages, attended segregated and poorly funded schools, and lived in the poorer areas of town (Acuña 2014; Muñoz [1989] 2007).

THE RACIALIZATION OF MEXICANS AND THE MEDIA

Mass media also contributed to the negative racialization of Mexican Americans. With the advent of Hollywood's movie industry in the 1910s, Mexicans became some of Hollywood's first bad guys. It was common to see them portrayed as "greasers," the treacherous and depraved antagonists of the White male protagonists (Ramirez Berg 2002). Through scripting, costuming, and makeup, Mexican Americans were depicted on the big screen as criminals, as having low intelligence, and as a people driven primarily by primal emotions and desires. Through repetition, these images became ingrained in the American social imaginary. Stereotypes in the media serve an ideological component; they justify inequality in the eyes of mainstream society. As Charles Ramirez Berg points out, "stereotypes flatten, homogenize, and generalize individuals within a group, emphasizing sameness and ignoring individual agency and variety" (2002, 16). This negative racialization of the Mexican-origin population was used to justify their social segregation. "One way of thinking about the ideological component of stereotyping is to consider stereotypes as vestiges of the colonial system. Within that regime, once the native is 'known' (i.e., set and defined by the colonizer in stereotypical terms), 'discriminatory and authoritarian forms of political control are considered appropriate'" (2002, 21). Although European colonization happened long ago, the system of racialization and representation has managed to reproduce itself in contemporary society.

THE CHICANO MOVEMENT

It is important to highlight that the Mexican American population has always resisted their subordination, oppression, and social exclusion. In the nineteenth century, they formed mutual-aid organizations, joined labor unions, and fought for their right to participate in the political process (Acuña 2014). Some Mexican Americans resorted to social banditry, as was the case of New Mexico's Gorras Blancas (White Caps), a clandestine group who tore up railroad track and cut the fences of Euro-American settlers as a way to protest the encroachment of their lands. In the first half of the twentieth century, many Mexican Americans fought in World War I and World War II; many of those veterans were emboldened to fight for the better of their community. They formed civil rights organizations, such as the League of United Latin American Citizens (LULAC) and the American GI Forum. Through these organizations, Mexican Americans were able to win important legal battles against residential and school segregation (*Mendez v. Westminster*, 1946/1947), as well as to challenge their exclusion from juries (*Hernandez v. Texas*, 1954).

By the mid-1960s, Mexican American youth began calling themselves Chicanos/as and found a new sense of racial pride rooted in their mixed-race and Indian heritage. As Chicano scholar and movement activist Carlos Muñoz points out, "the Chicano Movement was a historic first attempt to shape a politics of unification on the basis of a nonwhite identity and culture and on the interests of the Mexican American working class" ([1989] 2007). In a February 1970 column written by Chicano journalist Ruben Salazar for the *Los Angeles Times* ("Who Is a Chicano? What Is It the Chicanos Want?"), Salazar captured the meaning of Chicano/a:

> A Chicano is a Mexican-American with a non-Anglo image of himself. He resents being told Columbus "discovered" America when the Chicano's ancestors, the Mayans and the Aztecs, founded highly sophisticated civilizations centuries before Spain financed the Italian explorer's trip to the "New" world. (Salazar 1995, 235)

Chicanos/as begin learning Mexican culture and history. They took a strong interest in indigenous spirituality and cultural symbolism, incorporating these into their art, murals, poetry, and theater. Chicanos such as playwright Luis Valdez, poet Alurista, and activist Rodolfo "Corky" Gonzales saw in Mexican culture the continuation of indigenous culture. They hoped that Mexican indigenous culture would serve as an antidote to the internalization of racism and White supremacy that had convinced some Chicanos/as to deny their *mestizaje* in favor of White identification.[9] The Chicano Movement was successful in institutionalizing Chicano Studies departments at the university level and removing some of the social barriers that had kept Mexican American as second-class citizens.

---

9. See, for example, Valdez's poem "Pensamiento Serpentino: A Chicano Approach to the Theater of Reality" (1971), Alurista's preamble to the *El Plan Espiritual de Aztlán* (1969), and Gonzales's poem "I Am Joaquin" (1967).

RACIALIZATION AND MEXICAN IMMIGRATION

Ideas about race and immigration have always intersected in US political discourse. During the late eighteenth century and early nineteenth century, adherents of scientific racism[10] were successful in limiting the number of Eastern Europeans entering the country, and of completely halting Asian immigration (Omi and Winant [1986] 2015). They believed that our immigration policy should be guided by the recognition of a presumed racial hierarchy that reflected each race's physical and mental ability. These pseudo-scientists believed that it was in the best interest of the country to allow only Western Europeans to migrate.

Although there were restrictions against Asian and European immigration up until 1965, Mexicans were often exempted because they were needed to work in agriculture, on the railroad, and in other industries. About 4.5 million Mexican guest workers were brought to the United States during the Bracero Program (1942–1964), a binational agreement between the United States and Mexico (Gamboa 2005). Many of these guest workers were subjected to fumigations with DDT (a pesticide) and intrusive medical inspections. Because of the United States's proximity to Mexico, these workers were expected to return to Mexico after their contract, and, thus, not become part of American society.

The 1980s saw a rise in Mexican and Central American migration to the United States. During this time, old anti-immigrant sentiments were revived, with many calling for a closed border between Mexico and the United States. Latino/a immigrants were portrayed in the media and by politicians as national threats. In their alarmist narratives, these conservatives conjured images of deviant and inferior Latino bodies to produce fears of overpopulation, economic crisis, social decay, criminality, and genetic inferiority. Leo Chavez calls this anti-immigrant discourse the "Latino threat narrative," that is, the popular myth that Latinos are a threat to the well-being of US society (Chavez 2008). The Latino threat narrative continues to be reproduced, most recently by President Donald Trump, who during his presidential campaign went on record making wide generalizations about Mexican immigrants, calling them criminals, drug dealers, and "rapists."[11]

---

10. The two main branches of late nineteenth- and early twentieth-century scientific racism were Social Darwinism and Eugenics. Social Darwinists believed that the different races of the world were in constant struggle, and that this struggle formed part of a larger process of natural selection where ultimately only the strongest would survive. Eugenics was the pseudo-scientific belief that humans could intervene in human evolution by preventing the lower, and/or less evolved, types from reproducing, while at the same time encouraging the reproduction of superior types. For a discussion of European scientific racism, see Mike Hawkins's *Social Darwinism in European and American Thought, 1860–1945: Nature as Model and Nature as Threat* (1997).

11. In his June 16, 2015, presidential campaign announcement speech, Donald Trump said, "When Mexico sends its people, they're not sending their best. They're not sending you. They're not sending you. They're

This negative racialization of Mexicans, as well as other Latinos, is dangerous because it is used to justify harsh immigration policies that separate families and disrupt communities. This racialization can even promote violence against immigrants because it portrays them as dangerous criminals. Draconian anti-immigrant laws, such as those passed in Alabama (HB 56, 2011) and in Arizona (SB 1070, 2010), have been used to legalize racial profiling and deny social services, including health and schooling, for undocumented children. Although the Supreme Court has found aspects of these laws to be unconstitutional, the fact that the laws passed their state legislatures is proof that Latino immigrants continue to be easy scapegoats for this country's problems.

WHAT RACE ARE MEXICANS?

Now we return to our earlier question, "What race are Mexicans?" The answer is that "Mexican" is not a race but an ethnic or national origin group that has been racialized throughout history.[12] The ethnic category "Mexican" has been commonly understood as a racial category, in part, because Mexican Americans have for a very long time been relegated to second-class citizenship. The problem is not so much that there is confusion about what race Mexican Americans are, or that Mexicans confuse ethnicity with race. The problem is the widespread social belief that a person's race can tell us something meaningful about his or her worth as a human being, or about his or her mental and physical dispositions.

DISCUSSION QUESTIONS

1. At the conclusion of the US-Mexico War, why was it important to the Mexican government that Mexicans who were remaining in the ceded territories be granted US citizenship?

2. How has the racialization of Mexican Americans affected their social incorporation into US society?

---

sending people that have lots of problems, and they're bringing those problems with us. They're bringing drugs. They're bringing crime. They're rapists. And some, I assume, are good people."

12. Puerto Rican scholar Ramón Grosfoguel argues that race and ethnicity cannot be understood as two different forms of identity and that we should instead pay attention to how ethnicities are racialized in the United States. He states, "The association of 'Puerto Rican' and 'African American' identity in the Euro-American imaginary with racist stereotypes such as laziness, criminality, stupidity, and uncivilized behavior has important implications in the labor market, seriously affecting the new immigrants' opportunities. They constitute what I called 'racialized ethnicities'" (Grosfoguel 2004, 323).

3 . How does the US racial system compare to Mexico's racial system?

4 . Discuss the ways in which Mexican immigrants have been racialized.

AUDIOVISUAL MATERIALS

"Book Talk: Julie A. Dowling Presents 'Mexican Americans and the Question of Race'" (UCLA Chicano Studies Research Center): https://youtu.be/TQkAx04jjGo

A Class Apart (documentary film): www.pbs.org/wgbh/americanexperience/films/class

"How Scientific Racialization Shapes Mexican Immigration Policies, 1848–Present" (lecture by Natalia Molina, University of California Television [UCTV]): www.youtube.com/watch?v=hROEFW7n83s

Latino Americans (documentary film): www.pbs.org/latino-americans/en

SUGGESTIONS FOR FURTHER READING

Haney-López, I. F. 2003. *Racism on Trial: The Chicano Fight for Justice.* Cambridge, MA: Belknap Press.

Molina, N. 2014. *How Race Is Made in America: Immigration, Citizenship, and the Historical Power of Racial Scripts.* Berkeley: University of California Press.

Pew Research Center. 2015. "Census Considers New Approach to Asking about Race—By Not Using the Term at All." *Fact Tank*, June 18. http://www.pewresearch.org/fact-tank/2015/06/18/census-considers-new-approach-to-asking-about-race-by-not-using-the-term-at-all.

Saenz, R., N. Rodriguez, and D. G. Embrick. 2015. *The International Handbook of the Demography of Race and Ethnicity.* Dordrecht, Netherlands: Springer.

Velázquez, M. E., and G. Iturralde Nieto. 2012. *Afrodescendientes en México: Una Historia de Silencio y Discriminación.* México, DF: Consejo Nacional para Prevenir la Discriminación.

REFERENCES

Acuña, R. F. 2014. *Occupied America: A History of Chicanos.* Upper Saddle River, NJ: Prentice Hall.

Aguirre Beltrán, G. [1946] 1972. *La Población Negra de México: Estudio Etnohistórico.* México: Fondo de Cultura Económica.

Chavez, L. R. 2008. *The Latino Threat: Constructing Immigrants, Citizens, and the Nation.* Palo Alto, CA: Stanford University Press.

De Leon, A. 1979. *In Re Ricardo Rodriguez: An Attempt at Chicano Disenfranchisement in San Antonio, 1896–1897.* San Antonio, TX: Caravel Press.

Dowling, J. A. 2014. *Mexican Americans and the Question of Race*. Austin: University of Texas Press.

Ennis, S. R., M. Ríos-Vargas, and N. G. Albert. 2011. *The Hispanic Population: 2010*. Washington, DC: US Department of Commerce, Economics and Statistics Administration, US Census Bureau.

Gamboa, E. 2005. "On the Nation's Periphery: Mexican Braceros and the Pacific Northwest Railroad Industry, 1943–1946." In *Mexican Americans & World War II*, edited by M. Rivas-Rodriguez, 269–289. Austin: University of Texas Press.

García, I. M. 2009. *White but Not Equal: Mexican Americans, Jury Discrimination, and the Supreme Court*. Tucson: University of Arizona Press.

Gómez, L. E. 2007. *Manifest Destinies: The Making of the Mexican American Race*. New York: New York University Press.

Griswold del Castillo, R. 1990. *The Treaty of Guadalupe Hidalgo: A Legacy of Conflict*. Norman: University of Oklahoma Press.

Grosfoguel, Ramón. 2004. "Race and Ethnicity or Racialized Ethnicities? Identities within Global Coloniality." *Ethnicities* 4(3): 315–336.

Instituto Nacional de Estadística y Geografía (México). 2015. *Encuesta Intercensal 2015: Estados Unidos Mexicanos: Principales Resultados*. http://www.inegi.org.mx/est/contenidos/proyectos/encuestas/hogares/especiales/ei2015/doc/eic_2015_presentacion.pdf.

Menchaca, M. 2003. *Recovering History, Constructing Race: The Indian, Black, and White Roots of Mexican Americans*. Austin: University of Texas Press.

Montejano, D. 1987. *Anglos and Mexicans in the Making of Texas, 1836–1986*. Austin: University of Texas Press.

Mörner, M. 1967. *Race Mixture in the History of Latin America*. Boston: Little, Brown and Company.

Muñoz, C. [1989] 2007. *Youth, Identity, Power: The Chicano Movement*. London: Verso.

Omi, M., and H. Winant. [1986] 2015. *Racial Formation in the United States*. 3rd ed. New York: Routledge.

Quijano, A. 2000. "Coloniality of Power, Eurocentrism, and Latin America." *Nepantla: Views from South* 1(3): 533–580.

Ramirez Berg, C. 2002. *Latino Images in Film: Stereotypes, Subversion, Resistance*. Austin: University of Texas Press.

Salazar, R. 1995. *Border Correspondent: Selected Writings, 1955–1970*. Edited by M. T. García. Berkeley: University of California Press.

Sue, C. A. 2013. *Land of the Cosmic Race: Race Mixture, Racism, and Blackness in Mexico*. Oxford: Oxford University Press.

Asian Americans: Unity in Diverse Experiences

By Wendy Ng

Asian Americans[1] are a varied and diverse population comprising many cultural, social, religious, and ethnic groups. The US Census defines the Asian population as people from the Far East and Southeast Asia or the Indian subcontinent, including the Chinese, Filipino, Asian Indian, Vietnamese, Korean, Japanese, Cambodian, Hmong, Laotian, Pakistani, and Thai communities, as well as other Asian groups (Hoeffel et. al. 2012). Because of this diversity, it is difficult to generalize about the entire Asian American experience, but the early histories of different Asian ethnic groups' immigration have many similarities. Asian immigrants experienced the pull factors of immigration to the United States similar to those of European immigrants: perceived opportunities and a chance to make a better life. They also experienced the push factors of immigration—they were pushed because of social, economic, or environmental conditions that made them look elsewhere to make a temporary or permanent home. Many migrants from Asia might have come to the United States with the idea that they would eventually return to their home country—that this was a temporary sojourn—or, in the case of war, they left their homes as refugees or political asylum seekers.

This chapter provides an overview of the significant historical events that have affected Asian Americans and their incorporation into American society. In addition to looking at immigration history, we will look at a sample of some Asian group experiences, and also look at concepts such as stereotyping and discrimination and how they have adversely affected the Asian American community.

---

1. As noted, Asian Americans are a diverse group, and this chapter does not attempt to provide a comprehensive overview of all Asian American ethnic group experiences. You are encouraged to seek out other sources that provide additional information on ethnic groups not detailed in this chapter.

ASIAN IMMIGRATION HISTORY AND STRUCTURAL DISCRIMINATION

Sociologists refer to *discrimination* as "behavior by which one group prevents or restricts a minority group's access to scarce resources" (Doob 1999, 261). *Structural discrimination* is also referred to as *institutional discrimination*, in which the behavior stems from the larger society, not from an individual person. So, for example, the US government may pass laws that result in discrimination toward one group or another. It's important to note here that sociologists discuss discrimination in the context of minority and majority group relations and that these social relations result from the amount of power held by one group over another. There has been substantial material on discrimination and the African American experience, but Asian American discrimination has often been overlooked. The long history of changing immigration and citizenship laws have affected Asian immigrant groups in different ways and point to how Asian Americans experience past structural discrimination.

The Chinese were the first ethnic group that had a federal law excluding their immigration, through the 1882 Chinese Exclusion Act. While Chinese laborers were prohibited from immigrating, Chinese merchants, their wives, and students were still able to enter the country. Chinese exclusion meant that immigrant Chinese had to find other ways to secure their entry into the United States; it also made it difficult for them to establish families unless they could be identified as merchants.

Following Chinese exclusion, immigration from Japan to the United States increased. While there were never any direct immigration laws excluding the Japanese, the 1907 Gentlemen's Agreement limited immigration of laborers from Japan. While the agreement was never formally ratified by Japan and the United States, it slowed the flow of Japanese immigration as Japan limited passports to Japanese laborers. Finally, in an attempt to deal with the large-scale migration from both Europe and Asia, Congress passed the Johnson-Reed Act, also commonly known as the National Origins Act of 1924, which set restrictive immigration quotas for different countries throughout the world. The law also stated that "aliens ineligible for citizenship" would be excluded from the immigration quotas, thus virtually eliminating immigration from most of Asia until the mid-twentieth century.

Filipinos have a long history in the United States that extends back to the sixteenth century, when Filipino "Manila Men" jumped ship from the Spanish galleons that sailed into Louisiana. The Philippines was a colony of Spain, but was annexed to the United States after the Spanish-American War in 1898. Filipinos had no country, but were considered "US nationals," not quite US citizens, but also not citizens of an independent nation. Thus, the early immigration of Filipinos to the United States occurred in the 1920s and 1930s. In 1934, Congress passed the Tydings-McDuffie Act, which was designed to establish the Philippines as an independent country, but also limited Filipino immigration to the United States.

When the United States suddenly entered World War II, Japanese Americans—both citizens and noncitizen aliens who lived on the West Coast in California, Oregon, and Washington—were forced to move from their homes to so-called internment camps built in isolated areas throughout the West, Southwest, and Southeast. While they were called internment camps or relocation centers, the reality was that they were incarceration centers, where the living environment was closely monitored and limited. Although some individuals were able to leave (college students and others who had the means to relocate to the Midwest and East), most individuals did not have the resources to resettle their families elsewhere.

During World War II, with the Chinese as an ally, the US government's attitude toward Chinese immigrants changed, and in 1943, the Chinese Exclusion Act was repealed. While this was a landmark decision, it did not drastically increase Chinese immigration, because the immigration quotas instituted in 1924 allowed for only a token 105 immigrants per year to be admitted to the country.

Finally, in 1965, the US Congress enacted sweeping legislation to change the original quotas that had been in place since the 1920s. The Immigration and Nationality Act of 1965 (the Hart-Cellar Act) provided preference categories for individuals who wanted to immigrate that were based on skills and family reunification. Quotas, which had once been used to restrict immigration from various countries, became less restrictive, which resulted in increasing immigration from Asia.

Based on this immigration overview, different Asian ethnic groups experienced discrimination in different ways, depending on historical events (e.g., World War II) and the relationship between the United States and Asian immigrants' home countries. Citizenship laws changed after World War II, and Asians who were once ineligible for naturalized US citizenship could take the oath of citizenship and participate fully in American democracy.

STEREOTYPING AND ANTI-ASIAN VIOLENCE

Stereotyping is often based on a preconceived notion or view of an individual or group. It can be also be an overgeneralized image or opinion. Stereotyping in its extreme forms can result in a range of negative behaviors and attitudes held by majority-group populations toward Asian ethnic groups—which is sometimes termed as *anti-Asian sentiment*. On one end of the spectrum, anti-Asian sentiment in the form of stereotyping may manifest itself as derogatory images, jokes, and names. While many attribute this to ignorance, stereotyping can result in unrealistic expectations of behavior that may have detrimental consequences. The "model minority" stereotype has often been used to describe many Asian ethnic groups. It's an image that focuses on Asian Americans as a hardworking and successful minority group that has been able to overcome discrimination. Critics of the stereotype suggest that this image holds Asian Americans as "models" in comparison to other racial and ethnic minorities, without an understanding of the complex practices of structural discrimination and how it affects racial and ethnic minority groups in different ways.

Even with a "model minority" stereotype, Asian Americans can still be subjected to severe forms of anti-Asian sentiment. These attitudes can escalate into discriminatory behavior and practices by social institutions; these can be intentional or unintentional, but they have real consequences for the individuals who are being stereotyped. Even a simple stereotype, such as "all Asians look alike" or the idea that Asian Americans are successful, can cause behaviors resulting in discrimination or violence.

In its most severe form, anti-Asian discrimination resulting from stereotyping can result in violence directed toward Asian Americans. In 1982, Vincent Chin was bludgeoned to death with a baseball bat by two unemployed autoworkers, Ronald Ebens and his stepson Michael Nitz. Ebens and Nitz encountered Chin at a bar in Detroit, where racial slurs and arguments were exchanged between them. The 1983 trial of Ebens and Nitz resulted in their receiving probation and a fine of $3,780 (Zia 2000). Chin's case drew national and international attention because of the perpetrators' light sentence, and Asian Americans across the country became socially and politically involved in an effort to bring justice for Vincent Chin. This resulted in a movement to pressure the US Justice Department to look into whether Chin's civil rights had been violated. Chin's murder is an extreme example of anti-Asian violence—one in which he was mistakenly identified as Japanese and then blamed for the unemployment of US autoworkers, which had been caused by global social and economic conditions.

The 9/11 terrorist attacks increased the attention on the South Asian community in the United States. This is a diverse community that encompasses several religious and ethnic groups, including Muslims, Hindus, Sikhs, and Christians. In the wake of 9/11, on September 15, 2001, a Sikh gas station owner, Balbir Singh Sodhi of Mesa, Arizona, was murdered. His killer, Frank Roque, was charged with a hate crime and first-degree murder and sentenced to death, which was later commuted to life in prison (Chang 2008). Ten years after Sodhi's death, there were still those who did not believe that Sodhi was a "victim" of 9/11, and the Arizona legislature made an attempt to remove his name from a plaque memorializing Arizonans who had died as a result of 9/11. This controversial legislation was eventually vetoed by the state governor (SALDEF 2011). Organizations such as the Sikh American Legal Defense and Education Fund (SALDEF) and South Asian Americans Leading Together (SAALT) are concerned with the social and political climate and the increasing hostilities toward South Asians (SALDEF 2011; SAALT 2010).

The deaths of both Vincent Chin and Balbir Sodhi reflect the view of Asian Americans as being "forever foreigner" (Tuan 1999), never fitting into the social landscape as Americans or citizens. Questions such as "Where are you from?" or "Where were you born?" assume that Asians are from "somewhere else," no matter how many generations of their family may have lived in the United States. This continued stereotype of Asians as the "stranger" (Takaki 1998) and "foreigner" (Tuan 1999) stems from long held anti-foreign sentiment that has existed throughout American history.

NEW ASIAN IMMIGRATION

Asian American immigration has increased dramatically since the changes in federal immigration laws in 1965. The ending of the Vietnam War in 1975 led to refugee populations coming from Vietnam, Cambodia, and Laos. Furthermore, the changing economic global expansion among the United States, Pacific Rim countries, and the Indian subcontinent has increased migration from those countries, especially from the Philippines, China, and South Asia. This new immigration, as well as the increase in refugee populations, makes it difficult to generalize about new Asian Americans, as they are a socially, economically, and ethnically varied group (SEARAC 2011).

The fall of Saigon and the end of the Vietnam War in 1975 brought refugees to the United States from throughout Southeast Asia. The initial refugees were from Vietnam, but were soon followed by ethnic groups from Laos and Cambodia. The flow of refugee immigration from Southeast Asia spanned almost twenty-five years, and each ethnic group came under different circumstances and with varying degrees of resources to enable their settlement in the United States. The first refugees who arrived immediately after the fall of Saigon were resettled throughout the United States, sometimes in isolated communities that had very little exposure to Asian immigrants. Over time, however, many refugee settlers would move to communities where there were larger Vietnamese and Asian populations. Thus, today, the largest populations of Southeast Asians (Vietnamese, Cambodian, and Hmong) live in California, Texas, Washington, and Minnesota (SEARAC 2011).

From 2000 to 2010, the Asian American population grew by 9.5 percent, which was the largest percentage of growth compared to other racial and ethnic groups in the United States for that time period (Hoeffel et al. 2012). The growth is due to not only refugee immigration but also increasing immigration from sending countries whose economies have grown and expanded. The growth of industry in China and India, particularly in the high-tech sector, has led to increasing transnational migration of individuals who live both in the United States and in Asia. In addition, the US need for workers from other countries has also spurred migration from the Philippines of people in the healthcare field, as well as domestic and childcare workers. Throughout the United States, there has been growth in South Asian migration from Pakistan, Afghanistan, and Bangladesh. Some migration has resulted from employment expansion in the United States and H1-B visa policies. This type of non-immigrant visa allows US companies to employ specialty workers in technical fields; it has been used in the fields of science, engineering, and medicine. Thus, the resulting Asian demographic is exceedingly diverse, not only in terms of ethnicity, but in terms of education, religion, economic status, and social class. The reasons for new Asian and South Asian immigration are similar to those of the early Chinese, Japanese, and Filipino immigrants who came in the late nineteenth and early twentieth centuries. The pull to migrate lies in the shared dream and vision that opportunity abounds in America.

CONCLUSION: ASIAN AS AMERICANS

The theme of this chapter focused on varied Asian immigrant experiences, structural discrimination, stereotyping, and anti-Asian violence. Among the commonalities are the facts that Asian American immigrants have been subjected to various forms of inequality based on their racial, ethnic, or citizenship status. These have been historic forms of inequality, such as immigration and citizenship laws. In the more recent time period, the global political climate has produced prejudice and stereotyping, resulting in anti-Asian violence, such as the murders of Vincent Chin and Balber Singh Sodhi.

Asian immigrants from the past and of recent years have become a part of the American social fabric. They are not just temporary residents; they have shown that that they are part of the growing diversity we find in the American population. As this chapter demonstrates, their struggles and triumphs document the resiliency of our American immigrant experience.

DISCUSSION QUESTIONS

1 . In what ways can you compare Asian American immigrant experiences to the experiences of other ethnic groups in America?

2 . Discuss how structural discrimination affects Asian American immigrant experiences.

3 . Discuss and explain how and why Asian Americans are considered to be a diverse ethnic group. How do historical experiences account for this?

4 . What are the recent experiences of Asian Americans that explain their diversity?

SUGGESTIONS FOR FURTHER READING

Chan, S. 1991. *Hmong Means Free: Life in Laos and America*. Philadelphia, PA: Temple University Press.

Do, H. D. 1999. *The Vietnamese Americans*. Westport, CT: Greenwood.

Lam, A. 2005. *Perfume Dreams: Reflections on the Vietnamese Diaspora*. Berkeley, CA: Heyday Books.

REFERENCES

Chang, M. 2008. "Life after 9/11." *Hyphen: Asian America Unabridged*, August 1. http://hyphenmagazine.com/magazine/issue-15-road-trip-fall-2008/life-after-911.

Doob, C. B. 1999. *Racism: An American Cauldron*. New York: Longman.

Hoeffel, E. M., S. Rastogi, M.O. Kim, and H. Shahid. 2012. *The Asian Population: 2010*. Washington, DC: US Department of Commerce. www.census.gov/prod/cen2010/briefs/c2010br-11.pdf.

Sikh American Legal Defense and Education Fund (SALDEF). 2011. *The First 9/11 Backlash Fatality: The Murder of Balbir Singh Sodhi*. http://saldef.org/issues/balbir-singh-sodhi/#.V85B_4Xsebg.

South Asian Americans Leading Together (SAALT). 2010. *From Macacas to Turban Toppers: The Rise in Xenophobic Racist Rhetoric in American Political Discourse*. Takoma Park, MD: Author. http://saalt.org/wp-content/uploads/2012/09/From-Macacas-to-Turban-Toppers-Report.small_.pdf.

Southeast Asia Resource Action Center (SEARAC). 2011. *Southeast Asian Americans at a Glance*. http://www.sjsu.edu/registrar/docs/major_minor_more_than_90.pdf.

Takaki, R. 1998. *Strangers from a Different Shore: A History of Asian Americans*. New York: Little, Brown and Company.

Tuan, M. 1999. *Forever Foreigners or Honorary Whites? The Asian Ethnic Experience Today*. New Brunswick, NJ: Rutgers University Press.

Zia, H. 2000. *Asian American Dreams: The Emergence of an American People*. New York: Farrar, Straus and Giroux.

Immigration to a Rising Metropolis

By Rudy P. Guevarra Jr.

When Jesus "Chuey" Garcia came to the United States in 1927 from Guanajuato, Mexico, he ended up working as a cook for twenty-five cents an hour at an El Paso restaurant. From there, he migrated to San Diego, where he worked picking tomatoes and celery for fifteen cents an hour. He also worked various other unskilled jobs, such as digging ditches. He was disillusioned. "Why did I come? My hands looked like the bottom feet of a horse." Ultimately, Jesus Garcia ended up going back to his trade as a cook, and by 1956 he worked his way into owning his own restaurant, Chuey's Cafe. Since its opening at the corner of Main and Crosby Streets (now Cesar Chavez Parkway), Chuey's has been a cultural institution in Barrio Logan, a predominately Chicano community in Southeast San Diego.[1] Jesus Garcia was not alone in his journey to San Diego to toil in the fields and ditches of a growing city that required cheap, manual labor to sustain its economic boom.

Like Jesus, thousands of Mexicans and Filipinos came to San Diego and other areas of California and the Pacific West Coast from the 1900s to the 1930s seeking employment opportunities in the United States. Most Mexicans and Filipinos who arrived were "birds of passage," hoping to make enough money to go back to their homeland, purchase property, and live out their lives among their families and friends.[2] What both groups did not realize, however, was how larger forces of colonialism and global migrations were influencing their lives.

This chapter will explore the colonial relationships and legal immunities that Mexicans and Filipinos utilized to come to the United States during the early twentieth

Rudy P. Guevarra Jr., "Immigration to a Rising Metropolis," *Becoming Mexipino: Multiethnic identities and Communities in San Diego*, pp. 13-40, 174-183. Copyright © 2012 by Rutgers University Press. Reprinted with permission.

century in order to feed the growing demand for labor that cities like San Diego needed to support their growth. As newcomers to San Diego, they formed both sedentary and fluctuating communities that followed overlapping migratory labor patterns across the Pacific West Coast. The cultural records that emerge from these communities examine how Mexicans and Filipinos began establishing themselves in San Diego.[3] As their numbers increased, by the 1930s there was a cry for their exclusion and, ultimately, expulsion from the United States. Those who survived the repatriation efforts of the Great Depression continued to be the community anchors for subsequent Mexican and Filipino immigrants who settled in San Diego.

MECHANISMS OF MIGRATION

The overlapping migrations of both Mexicans and Filipinos to the United States, and San Diego in particular, are intimately tied to histories of colonialism and immigration policies, which have been both facilitators and responses to globalization. First colonialism and then neocolonialism dictated the relationships between Mexico, the Philippines, and the United States. After the U.S.-Mexican War of 1846–1848, Mexico lost half its territory—now the U.S. Southwest. Since then Mexico and the continental United States have maintained a close network of economic and political ties, which fashioned itself as a colonial relationship. As historian Gilbert González notes, U.S. capitalist interests have dominated economic institutions in Mexico, leaving it dependent on foreign interests. U.S.-built railroads of the nineteenth century (and later, twentieth-century highways), moving in a north-to-south direction, linked both countries.[4] This, along with economic opportunities, facilitated the flow of Mexicans into the United States to meet its labor demands throughout the twentieth century. Its proximity to Mexico would ensure a limitless supply of cheap labor. In the Philippines, however, a more intensive form of colonialism and neocolonialism occurred, which had specific implications for Filipino migrants.

As the United States expanded its empire across the Pacific at the end of the nineteenth century, it illegally seized the Hawaiian Kingdom, and then the Philippine Islands, which had already declared their independence from Spain. The Philippine-American War of 1898 began and continued through the 1910s. The war was just the beginning of an enduring colonial relationship between the United States and the Philippines. As military campaigns came to an end, the U.S. education system was the next step in pacifying Filipinos after their military defeat in the Philippine-American War. Philippine nationalist Renato Constantino called it the "miseducation" of the Filipinos under U.S. colonialism in order to mold them into good colonial subjects.[5] With the Philippines as a colonial possession, there was now a labor pool of inexpensive, brown bodies to travel across the Pacific to the continental United States as colonial subjects.

As an economically dependent and U.S. military–inundated country, the Philippines provided both laborers and sailors to travel within the confines of United States and its territories. Given their status as U.S. nationals, Filipinos could move freely in what historian Dorothy Fujita-Rony called the "colonial empire."[6]

In the twentieth century, these neocolonial relationships enabled the United States, and California in particular, to draw upon a cheap labor pool when needed, then to dispose of it when workers were seen as a threat to America's economic, racial, and moral interests. Indeed, as historian Mae Ngai notes, both Mexicans and Filipinos became part of an "imported colonialism" as the result of the United States' geopolitical power, which has influenced global structures of migration. As a transnational (Mexicans) and transpacific (Filipinos) labor force, both groups "challenged cultural and political norms across a broad spectrum, from the properties of interracial sex to nation-bounded definitions of the working class."[7] This colonial relationship defined how the United States saw both Mexican and Filipino workers, who could be counted on during periods of wartime, but ruthlessly betrayed when economic times threatened white wealth.

Immigration policies were used as legal justification to exclude Asians, while bringing in thousands of Mexican and Filipino laborers to work in California's agricultural, fish-canning, and service industries and on the railroads. Although the United States initially relied on Chinese, then Japanese labor, the American Federation of Labor and civic and social organizations soon called for the end of Asian immigration. An anti-Asian movement ensued, which pressured local, state, and national politicians to act. As a result, Asian immigrants became the first targets of racially motivated legal exclusion. First, the Chinese Exclusion Act of 1882, then the Gentlemen's Agreement in 1907–1908, and finally the Immigration Acts of 1917 and 1924 signaled the end of Chinese, Japanese, Indian, and other Asian immigration to in California.[8] The outcome produced a demand for another cheap labor source. Since Mexicans and Filipinos were both exempt from the 1924 Immigration Act, they were the logical groups to replace Asian farm workers. Thus, after 1910 Mexicans were the primary source of labor to meet the expansive growth of California agriculture.[9] As colonial subjects with U.S. national status, Filipinos also had no immigration restrictions. They could travel freely within the territorial jurisdiction of the Untied States. This enabled them to come by the thousands to California.[10] At the same time these events were unfolding, San Diego's city leaders and boosters were moving to secure it as a military city in the West, which enabled federal money to pour in and shape its infrastructure, making it a major metropolitan city. These structures, in turn, needed a workforce to meet the demands for growth and prosperity. Mexicans and Filipinos filled that need.

SAN DIEGO: AN EMERGING METROPOLIS IN THE WEST

San Diego is California's southernmost city, neighboring Tijuana, Mexico. As California's second largest city and the nation's eighth largest, San Diego is home to one of the largest naval stations in the country and has one of the largest economies in the world.[11] The navy continues to be an important part of San Diego's economy as a major metropolitan city. Defense spending, for example, continues to pour into San Diego, contributing more than 11.7 billion dollars a year to fuel its military installations and civilian workforce.[12] As the gateway to California, San Diego shares a border with Tijuana, Mexico; these two border towns are nestled in one of the world's largest economic zones. San Diego's location thus ensures the continued growth of the Mexican population, now the largest nonwhite ethnic minority in the county. As a naval town and port city, San Diego has also been an area of settlement for Filipinos since the early twentieth century as the United States extended its empire across the Pacific from its western shores. It is currently home to the second largest Filipino population in the country.[13]

San Diego has a rich, complex history, yet little is known about the city or its racial and ethnic communities. When we look at the history of San Diego's economic and social development, for example, we tend to hear the same narrative regarding the role of Alonzo Horton, William Kettner, John D. Spreckels, and other founding fathers of the city, whose visions for San Diego were grand indeed.[14] One cannot ignore how these visionaries sought after vital federal aid for the development of a city that would one day become home to one of the largest military bases in the United States and a center where agriculture, fish canning, ship building, and other wartime industries thrived. Although the nineteenth century saw the foundation being laid for the city, the early twentieth century was a turning point in San Diego's development, as Kettner expanded beyond Horton's and Spreckels's original visions of growth. Kettner secured federal and military spending to develop San Diego into a naval center that became headquarters to the Eleventh Naval District.[15] Construction, agriculture, mining, infrastructure, fish canning, and other industries also thrived during the early to mid twentieth century in San Diego as the population doubled every decade as a result of the navy's increasing labor demands. The favorable climate of San Diego, which was advertised in the 1880s as a cure for many health problems, also contributed to its population growth.[16]

Although we may look to the visionaries and admire the risks they took and fortunes they spent to see their vision become reality, we must not ignore the labor force that actually built the city. Indeed, tens of thousands of workers labored relentlessly, risking their lives in the process of building San Diego and its infrastructure, brick by brick, building by building, and industry by industry. It was the rank-and-file workers who toiled in the rock quarries, brickyards, construction sites, mines, railroads, fish canneries, and agricultural fields so that visionary dreams could become a physical reality. They, I argue, risked just as much and lost their own fortunes along the way, sometimes even their lives. They are the true unsung heroes and heroines in the development of San Diego as a metropolitan city in the West and should be included in the larger narrative of the region's history.

These early industries relied heavily on manual labor, both unskilled and semi-skilled, performed by predominately by nonwhite immigrants. From the early use of Italian, Portuguese, Chinese, and Japanese labor in the late nineteenth to early twentieth centuries, the workforce shifted to become primarily Mexican and Filipino. Although San Diego's economy relied primarily on the navy and defense-related industries during World War II, during its formative years in the early twentieth century, San Diego's economy relied heavily on agriculture and fish canning. As early as the 1920s, agriculture was among the top industries in San Diego, as was the fishing industry, which included several canneries.[17]

California's rapid development during the twentieth century, however, was facilitated by wartime expansion. This was fueled by shipbuilding and aircraft production, especially during World War II. San Diego was no different. Given that San Diego has one of the ten best natural harbors in the world and could hold most of the U.S. Pacific fleet, the navy eyed the city with its prime location and friendly climate. Thus, with the help of men like William Kettner, San Diego established longstanding economic ties to the navy, soon earning the reputation as the "Gibraltar of the Pacific" when it became home to the largest naval station in the country.[18] By the late 1920s and well into the 1930s, San Diego was also gaining a reputation as the "air capital of the West," with Consolidated Aircraft, Solar, and Ryan among the major companies making it their home.[19]

As a result of San Diego's diverse industries, economic and population booms signaled the expansive growth and ensured that San Diego experienced less economic turmoil than other cities, especially during the Great Depression.[20] City boosters and officials, such as Spreckels and, more so, Kettner, were able to continue to gain federal money to create and expand the urban infrastructure of San Diego. This money was also tied to the navy since it was "the primary instrument in the course of urban development."[21] San Diego's industries were so prosperous that between 1939 and 1943 it rose from seventy-ninth in the nation to twenty-eighth as an industrial center. By the 1940s, San Diego became a fast-paced city, leaving behind its image as a "sleepy navy town" or "sleepy border town" and became a "wartime metropolis." San Diego was now an important supplier to the West's regional economy, what Abraham Shragge called a "Federal city."[22]

The need for labor was crucial for San Diego to continue its economic expansion and sustain a growing population from the 1920s to the 1940s. The availability of immigrant labor was necessary to feed this growing metropolis. The United States was in a dilemma, however, since it already excluded Asians and other immigrants from its shores. Without a viable labor force, California, and San Diego in particular, looked south of the border and across the Pacific to meet those labor needs. It was Mexicans and Filipinos who became the major source of labor for San Diego. Their early migrations to San Diego illustrate both the shared and divergent experiences that influenced their move to the region, the early formations of their communities, and how they responded to the xenophobia and nativism that plagued the era of the Great Depression.

MEXICAN IMMIGRATION TO SAN DIEGO

San Diego was once part of Mexico, so there has always been a Mexican community within the city. They lived, worked, and traveled back and forth from Mexico to visit family and friends, and circular migration was common. Many of the families that came and settled in the region were part of familial and extended kinship networks; these networks fostered new arrivals who came to join relatives and friends in neighborhoods such as National City, Logan Heights, and Lemon Grove.[23]

Increased immigration of Mexicans to San Diego occurred during the first two decades of the twentieth century because of two events: the Mexican Revolution of 1910–1920 and World War I. The Mexican Revolution displaced and dispersed over a million of its citizens, with the majority of them fleeing to the United States. The ravages of war resulted in loss of land, poverty, starvation, and a devastated economic, social, and political structure. Mexican immigrants sought refuge and economic security in the United States. As political scientist Wayne Cornelius noted, "For the first (and probably the last) time in American history, tens of thousands of Mexicans were readily admitted to the United States … as economic refugees."[24] Most of these immigrants were ordinary workers and their families who wanted nothing more than a chance to survive. Political refugees, merchants, and other intellectuals formed this diaspora of Mexicans to the United States.[25]

During the Mexican Revolution, tens of thousands of Mexicans made their way into San Diego, not only from Tijuana/San Ysidro, but also from El Paso and other ports of entry. For example, longtime Logan Heights resident Consuelo Zuniga's mother's side of the family migrated to San Diego in 1912 to escape the political unrest that was going on in Mexico. They first ended up in Arizona, then made their way to San Diego, where they settled in Logan Heights. Her father's family migrated from Sonora to Douglas, Arizona. He traveled to the Imperial Valley, then also made his way to Logan Heights. Both her parents worked in the canneries. Connie's father eventually started working for Nelson Construction Company.[26]

The migration of Mexicans during the Mexican Revolution coincided with the onset of World War I (1914–1918), which created an acute labor shortage due to the loss of men who went to serve in the military. Rising industries such as factories, mines, construction, agriculture, fish canning, and transportation needed a labor supply to sustain the United States' involvement in the war effort. With the passage of the Immigration Acts of 1917 and 1924, which targeted both Asian and southern and eastern European immigrants, Mexicans were among the only immigrants from the Western Hemisphere who were exempt from these laws, and thus they were able to come in to the United States free of quota restrictions.[27] From 1918 to 1930, U.S. interests encouraged the influx of Mexican immigrants to fill labor needs. As one Mexican immigrant stated about the United States, "The country across the border promises new experience, excitement, adventure."[28] The chance to live free from war, earn a living, and provide their children with school was more than enough to entice many Mexicans to migrate north to the United States. Mexican immigrants found themselves in a position to fill the labor needs of California while sustaining their own economic livelihood. As such, the majority of Mexican immigrants who came to San Diego were laborers.

California was a key state that absorbed a great portion of the Mexican immigrants who came during the early twentieth century. According to Governor C. C. Young's Mexican Fact Finding Committee Report, *Mexicans in California*, the State of California saw an increase of 25,068 Mexican immigrants, or 316.0 percent, between 1900 and 1910, and another 55,077 immigrants from 1910 to 1920, or a 163.5 percent increase. Another 163.5 percent increase from 1920 to 1930 placed the total number of Mexicans in California at around 223,912.[29] Overall, 617,000 Mexican immigrants entered the United States legally, which was approximately one-half of the total legal Mexican population in the country.[30]

Although San Diego did have a much smaller Mexican population than its northern neighbor Los Angeles, its population also doubled every decade from 1900 to 1930, giving it the fifth highest percentage of Mexicans in the state of California.[31] Similarly, when looking at the Heller Committee Report, *How Mexicans Earn and Live*, which was a study based on the Mexican community of Logan Heights during the 1930s, census data was used to show that while Mexicans comprised 1.2 percent of the total population in the United States, they constituted 6.5 percent of the total population in California. San Diego was among the ten counties listed that had the highest percentage of Mexicans within the population. This number, however, can be misleading because the Heller Committee admitted that agricultural workers were not in included in their study due to the migratory nature of this particular group. This would have made the Mexican population much higher than listed in census and state reports, thus demonstrating San Diego's importance as a site of early Mexican community formation.[32]

By 1941, Mexicans comprised approximately 7.6 percent of San Diego's total 11.2 percent minority population. An economic and industrial report on San Diego, however, noted that the proportion of San Diego's Mexican population was small considering

Table 2.1 Estimated Number of Foreign-Born White Mexicans in California Counties
as of 1930

COUNTY	1910	1920	1930
Los Angeles	11,793	33,644	95,953
Imperial Valley	1,461	6,414	28,157
San Diego	2,224	4,104	7,572

Sources: Will J. French, dir., *Mexicans in California: Report of Governor C. C. Young's Fact-Finding Committee* (San Francisco: State of California Department of Industrial Relations, 1930), 46; and Paul S. Taylor, "Mexican Labor in the United States," *University of California Publications in Economics* 6, no. 1 (1928): 18.

that it shared a border with Tijuana, Mexico. State reports have documented that it was because there were not enough industries to keep Mexican workers.[33] Although there may be some truth to these statements, the fact that San Diego has historically been inundated by military personnel and retirees has created what Richard Griswold del Castillo calls "the basis of a conservative, Republican-dominated elite that has sought to develop San Diego as a tourist attraction with minimal attention to the needs of marginalized groups."[34] Indeed, this comment provides valuable insight to the racial mechanics that were working to ensure that the city's nonwhite population always remained minimal, at best. This will be further discussed in the following chapter.

One issue that is not discussed in state and federal reports when looking at San Diego's population statistics and industries is the fact that San Diego and the Imperial Valley are historically tied to each other with regards to Mexican migration. This can also be said of Filipino migration, which will be discussed in further detail later in this chapter. If we were to include those numbers from the Imperial Valley with San Diego's numbers, given the migration of Mexican agricultural workers between the two areas, there would be a tremendous increase in San Diego's population. Table 2.1 shows population statistics between Los Angeles, San Diego, and the Imperial Valley.

The reason for including the Imperial Valley is because it was once a part of San Diego County. It was not until 1907 that the Imperial Valley was made into a separate county. Both counties have been sites of historical migration, intimately tied together for both the Mexicans and their Filipino counterparts, who traveled the same roads together. In these mobile communities, workers circulated between the two counties as part of the larger migration circuit throughout the Pacific West Coast. For example, David Galbiso's Filipino-Mexican family, which included his parents and uncles, owned farmland in Niland, a small farming community located in the Imperial Valley. His uncle Geronimo first migrated to the United States from Hawai'i, where he worked for the Hawaiian Agriculture Company in 1924. After his contract was completed in 1926, he left for the continental United States. Geronimo worked in agriculture, traveling back and forth from Arizona to San Diego, primarily to Spring Valley during the

1940s, where an established network of Filipino laborers was present. While working in Spring Valley he was able to earn enough money to go into partnership with his brothers and purchase farmland in Niland in 1951. It was because of these experiences that Galbiso called San Diego the focal point for Filipinos who left the Imperial Valley to settle there. Family and friends who settled in both areas continue to maintain a network of familial and kinship relations over the years. In fact, every year there is a Niland reunion in San Diego that brings these families together.[35]

Early sociological studies of Mexican immigrants also showed that due to the seasonal nature of agricultural work in the Imperial Valley, ten thousand Mexican laborers out of a population of twenty-one thousand, or nearly one-half, were constantly migrating in and out of the area, making their way into San Diego, among other locations. Similarly, the cities of La Mesa and El Cajon, two other agricultural areas in San Diego County, are situated along the eastern route to the Imperial Valley. Given that they are linked by both Highway 80 and the Southern Pacific Railway, one scholar remarked, "San Diego was an important transit and shipping center for Imperial Valley fruit and truck stops."[36] These routes fed this connection of laborers and agricultural products. This coincided with the labor needs of neighboring San Diego, which also had a fluctuating Mexican population for the same reasons. In December of 1919 the newly built railroad connected San Diego to Imperial Valley to transport railroad, construction, and agricultural workers; it also provided a means to cement the link between both regions.[37] Thus, San Diego's Mexican population was much greater than what is portrayed by Governor Young's report. Including the Imperial Valley to some extent is reasonable, given its close relationship and proximity to San Diego. Although it still had a much smaller Mexican population, San Diego had an impressive increase in its numbers, reflecting the larger trends of population growth. Table 2.2 shows the increase per decade, from 1900 to 1970.

Early U.S. census data is notorious for being inaccurate based on fixed numbers for households interviewed. For one, census information cannot be accurate given the size of most Mexican families, which may not have been fully accounted for; the seasonal nature of agriculture and the mobile communities of workers who followed the crops; the fishing boats that had crews out to sea throughout the year; and the fact that many census takers may have underestimated the Mexican population based on recording only a few households in a given neighborhood. Census takers were known to undercount racial and ethnic populations in low-income communities. Griswold del Castillo also notes, for example, that "the 1930 census also did not count the American-born children of Mexican parents, a group that probably tripled the reported figures."[38] Moreover, the numbers may also be misleading because many Mexicans fluctuated between the San Diego–Tijuana border region, traveling to work or temporarily residing in San Diego. Indeed, Mexicans and Filipinos lived in transient, fluctuating communities. This is especially true for the period up until the 1920s because San Diego and

Table 2.2 Total Mexican Population in San Diego, 1900–1970

YEAR	TOTAL POPULATION	MEXICAN POPULATION
1900	17,700	638–893
1910	39,578	1,588–2,224
1920	74,683	3,563–4,104
1930	147, 995	9,266–20,000
1940	203,341	N/A
1950	334,387	15,490
1960	1,033,011	70,000
1970	1,357,387	150,000

Sources: U.S. Census Bureau, *Thirteenth–Twentieth Censuses, 1900–1970* (Washington, DC: U.S. Census Bureau, 1900–1970); and Alberto Camarillo, *Chicanos in a Changing Society: From Mexican Pueblos to American Barrios in Santa Barbara and Southern California, 1848–1930* (Cambridge, MA: Harvard University Press, 1996).

Note: Given the inaccuracy of census reporting on the Mexican community of San Diego due to the migratory nature of a segment of the population, I rely on Albert Camarillo's study, which utilized various variables in calculating the Mexican population of San Diego. See Camarillo, *Chicanos in a Changing Society*, 200–201. Other studies used to help determine population accounts include George B. Mangold, *Community Welfare in San Diego* (San Diego: San Diego County Welfare Commission and City of San Diego, 1929), 20; Lawrence Herzog, *Where North Meets South: Cities, Space, and Politics on the United States–Mexican Border* (Austin: University of Texas Press, 1990), 173; Philip R. Pryde, *San Diego: An Introduction to the Region* (San Diego, CA: Sunbelt Publications, 2004), 75–90; and San Diego Association of Governments (SANDAG), "Mapping the Census: Race and Ethnicity in the San Diego Region," *SANDAG Info 1* (April 2002), www.sandag.org/uploads/publicationid/publicationid_ 722_1120.pdf (accessed July 18, 2006).

Tijuana had an open border until the formal establishment of the Border Patrol in 1925. Even then, Mexicans continued to cross back and forth to work, shop, or visit family and friends in San Diego.[39] Repatriation drives in the 1930s, as well as Mexicans being lumped together under a white category in the 1940 census, have also made it difficult to estimate the population. As the geographer Phillip Pryde notes, "It is impossible to determine how many Spanish-speaking residents lived in the country during this time period because such information was not considered important enough to ask about in the census."[40] As Mexicans were making their transnational migration to settle and labor in San Diego, Filipinos were also making their transpacific migration.

FILIPINO IMMIGRATION TO SAN DIEGO

Like Mexican immigrants, the majority of Filipinos who came to the United States during the early twentieth century also initially came as "birds of passage." With economic conditions in the Philippines in shambles after its war with the United States, there were limited opportunities at home. As colonial subjects looking for a way to survive, thousands of Filipinos were first recruited by Hawai'i's sugar and pineapple plantations. Many moved on to the fish canneries and agricultural fields along the West Coast of the United States in order to come back home with some sort of financial success. They intended to buy land and live out their lives as property owners in the Philippines.

Although the majority of Filipinos left the Philippines for the United States out of necessity and economic survival for the families they left behind, many also came seeking adventure along the way. Ben Villarin, for example, was one of a group of young boxers who came to the United States to train with the famed Filipino fighter Speedy Dado in 1930. Although his career as a boxer never took off, Ben ended up living in Los Angeles, then moving to San Diego and settling in Logan Heights in the 1940s after he met and married his wife, Dorotea. She was a schoolteacher in the Philippines but did some work as an extra in war movies while in Los Angeles. Ben and Dorotea left the Philippines seeking adventure as well as an opportunity to work in the United States. Other occupations facilitated Filipino migration to the United States. According to historian Catherine Ceniza Choy, for example, Filipina nurses migrated to the United States in the early 1900s, an experience shaped by U.S. colonialism in the Philippines.[41]

As with their Mexican counterparts, economic motives, coupled with the thrill of adventure in a new land, were enticing enough to bring them to the United States. As colonial subjects who had the status of U.S. nationals, Filipinos had the freedom to move anywhere within the colonial empire of the United States. Filipinos' status as nationals, however, would come to haunt them later. As quasi-citizens they were neither citizen nor alien, thus they could not own or lease land, nor did they have ample political protection when they faced racial discrimination and violence.[42]

Because Filipinos came across the Pacific, their migration routes differed from those of Mexican immigrants. As early as 1906 Filipinos were sent to Hawai'i to work in the sugar and pineapple plantations. Sugar cane producers would be the main employers of Filipino immigrants to Hawai'i. As early as 1917, U.S. mainland agricultural interests were considering and even advocating for the importation of Filipinos, in addition to Mexicans, as a means to fill the labor shortages, most notably in California, during World War I.[43] Thus, the sugar planters of Hawai'i and the agricultural and fish-cannery employers of California and the Pacific West Coast turned to Filipinos to fill these positions. Filipinos, like Mexicans, were coming in by the thousands between 1920 and 1930 to labor in various industries. Laborers, however, were not the only ones who came from both Hawai'i and the Philippines. A key difference that distinguished the migration of Filipinos from the migration of their Mexican counterparts was that Filipinos came to the United States, and San Diego in particular, by way of the U.S. Navy. Given their colonial relationship with the United States, many Filipinos also came as government-sponsored students in the early 1900s. A brief look at the diversity of Filipino immigration to San Diego must be examined in order to understand the complex position Filipinos had as colonial subjects and settlers in the United States, as compared to Mexicans, who primarily came as laborers.

THE PENSIONADOS COME TO SAN DIEGO

Prior to their arrival as laborers and sailors to San Diego, Filipinos first came as government-sponsored students. After the Philippine-American War, a colonial government was established, which was ruled by Americans with a secondary level of Filipino administrators as part of the "Filipinization" of the country.[44] Part of this plan was to educate Filipinos in the United States and bring them back to the Philippines, where they would hold government posts. This was the beginning of the Pensionado Program, which lasted from 1903 to 1940. Under this program, five hundred *pensionados,* or "fountain pen boys," as they were also called, came to the United States.[45] The government supported most of the pensionados during the first phase of the program. In later years, two-thirds would be self-supporting students who worked in agriculture, domestic work, and service industries, while a smaller number were given partial support from the government or help from family and friends.[46] Documentation of this first group of pension-ados in San Diego was mentioned in various San Diego newspapers in 1903. They noted that "ninety-eight little brown men" were coming to San Diego County.[47] In all, ninety-six students actually arrived in California, landing in San Francisco aboard the steamer *Korea* on November 9, 1903. From there, a group went to Los Angeles by train; nineteen ended up in San Diego three days later. According to newspaper accounts, they were greeted by Mayor Frank P. Frary; W. L. Frevert, president of the San Diego Chamber of Commerce; Hugh J. Baldwin, county superintendent of schools; Frank P. Davidson, city superintendent; Thomas F. Branscome, superintendent in National City; and Miss Myers, principal at Coronado.[48] They spent the day with county superintendent of schools Hugh J. Baldwin at the schools where they were to be placed. From there, they were registered at the Horton House, where they signed in, and then proceeded to dine at the Manhattan in downtown San Diego.[49] They were given a reception at the home of Superintendent Baldwin, where they displayed their "rare musical ability, particularly on the guitar," which showed their hosts that they were "passionately fond of music."[50] While in San Diego the pensionados also amazed local residents, school administrators, and newspapers with their appearance. They were described as "neatly clad young men, well built, though slightly undersized, with well shaped heads."[51] Moreover, the fact that these Filipinos could speak English amazed their American hosts, who were not fully aware of the impact that U.S. colonialism had on the Philippines. Not only did they have some fluency in English, but most of them were also fluent in Spanish and their own local dialect.[52]

School officials also observed the similarity between Filipinos and Mexicans. A report to the Philippine Commission, for example, describes the area of southern California and its heavily Mexican-influenced region and, more notably, mentions that the Filipino pensionados attended the same school with Mexicans. It stated that "the Filipino in many respects is more like the Mexican than he is like any other race I know of."[53] This comment illustrates the shared cultural similarities these outsiders observed and foreshadows how both Filipinos and Mexicans would later be racialized and treated in the United States.

With regards to their other activities and how they fared in school, one newspaper reported that the initial group of Filipino students in San Diego completed their studies with an "honorable dismissal" and departed in June of 1904 back to the Philippines.[54] Though these were not really settled immigrants per se because they returned home, nonetheless, their presence marked the earliest documented arrival of Filipinos in San Diego as the county's first foreign exchange students. Another aspect of this colonial relationship was via the U.S. Navy, which was an avenue for Filipino migration to the continental United States that resonates to this day.

FILIPINOS IN THE U.S. NAVY

Like many of his countrymen in the Philippines, Ciriaco "Pablo" Poscablo dreamed of coming to America. The navy was one means to achieve this goal. In 1919, he left his hometown of Calasiao, Pangasinan, and traveled to Cavite, where he enlisted in the navy as a musician second-class. His other duties aboard the ship included working as a steward since his responsibilities went far beyond that of a musician in the navy. He was dispatched aboard the USS *Albany* in December of that year. He traveled to San Francisco, where he boarded the USS *Arizona* in 1922. He was discharged in San Pedro, California, in 1923. From there he traveled to San Diego aboard the USS *Melville*. In 1924 he was stationed at the San Diego Naval Training Center, where he received further training. Pablo remained in San Diego for the remainder of his life.[55]

Like Pablo, many Filipinos came to the United States via the navy to "see the world." Although Pablo enlisted as a musician, his duties aboard the ship included working as a steward like most Filipinos who joined the U.S. Navy. As with employment opportunities in the various industries on the West Coast, the navy proved to be another pipeline for Filipino migration to booming naval towns such as San Diego, Los Angeles, San Francisco, and Seattle in the early twentieth century.[56]

The Filipino presence in the navy was also a result of post-1898 U.S. colonialism and militarism in the Philippines. With U.S. control of the Philippines, the military established the practice of recruiting Filipinos since it was more costly to recruit and ship American soldiers from the United States back to the islands. Filipinos entered the U.S. Navy in 1901 as a result of General Order Number 40, which was signed by President William McKinley. This allowed approximately five hundred Filipinos into the navy. As historian Jocelyn Agustin Pacleb noted, "Thus began the Navy tradition of enlisting Filipinos outside of the U.S."[57] By World War I, the navy was the primary means by which Filipinos entered U.S. military service. They were, however, confined to the rank of steward. As stewards, Filipinos were essentially domestic servants for white naval officers. In order for them to obtain U.S. citizenship, they had to serve for at least three years in the military; otherwise, they were ineligible for this benefit.[58]

The recruitment of Filipinos into the U.S. Navy, as Pacleb also noted, "coincided with the migration of Filipina/os to the United States for educational and work opportunities prior to World War II."[59] By the end of World War I, approximately twenty-five thousand Filipinos came to U.S ports where they received their discharges and settled, finding employment in the naval yards as well as in a variety of other occupations.[60] This type of Filipino settlement in the early twentieth century differed from both Mexican immigration in general and the previous migration of pensionados who came in 1903. For one, while the pensionados received their education and went back to the Philippines, many of the early navy Filipinos settled in the United States, being among some of the first Filipino settlers. One of the earliest records of Filipinos landing in San Diego by way of the navy is in 1907, when the USS *Boston* anchored in the city's harbor. By then, only a small group of Filipinos resided in the city. According to Felix Budhi, who came to San Diego in 1908, there were a small number who lived around Market Street. As Budhi observed, "Around Market, Fifteenth, and Sixteenth, a small Filipino community is found … [and] a few of the Filipinos owned small restaurants combined with pool and gambling tables. Outside downtown there were only acres and acres of farms."[61]

This was one of the earliest cultural records of Filipino settlement in San Diego. Individuals such as Vicente Elequin and Tony Alcalde were among the small number of Filipinos who also came to San Diego between 1918 and 1919. Alcalde, for example, came to San Diego in 1919. He joined the navy to secure a steady income. As he recalled, the only work available in San Diego at the time was agricultural work or the navy.[62]

After their service in the U.S. Navy, Filipinos also worked in civil service jobs or agriculture.[63] Ricardo Romio, for example, was born in Logan Heights in 1937. His father, who was Filipino, and his mother, who was Mexican, both settled in Logan Heights in the early 1930s. His mother worked at the canneries and his father was in the navy. His father joined the navy in 1918 as a steward. After he got out of the navy, he went to work for civil service in North Island, then at the 32nd Street Naval Base, which bordered National City and Logan Heights. He served in both World Wars.[64] Freddie Ayap's Filipino father was also in the navy. He moved his family to Logan Heights in 1943 during World War II. After his retirement in 1949 he returned to farm work in the community of Encanto before he got a job in civil service as a custodian at North Island.[65]

As a naval center, San Diego has been home to one of the southernmost points of what Dorothy Fujita-Rony called the "colonial empire." Like Seattle, San Diego was a colonial metropolis where Filipinos arrived after traveling across the Pacific to come to the continental United States.[66] Many of them who came did not stay permanently, but left with the ships. Their voyages, however, allowed many Filipinos to set foot in San Diego. Indeed, the navy has been instrumental in the growth of the Filipino community in San Diego. Today, approximately half of the Filipino population in San Diego has some direct or indirect ties to the U.S. Navy.[67]

For many of the Filipino recruits, San Diego would be the first place they visited in the United States. They received training in Point Loma at the San Diego Naval Training Center. As sociologist Yen Le Espiritu notes, "Until 1998, San Diego was the site of the largest U.S. naval base and the Navy's primary West Coast training facility, the Naval Training Center (NTC)." Here, Filipinos came to receive training and spend their liberty on shore. Another study also documented that Filipinos were also employed in the naval yards. Given that they were only employed on a temporary basis, no records are available as to how many were engaged in this type of employment.[68] Although the U.S. Navy provided a means for Filipinos to earn a living and come to the continental United States, the majority of them made their way to labor in California agriculture and travel its migratory circuit.

MIGRATORY LABOR IN CALIFORNIA'S FIELDS

Like Mexicans, the majority of Filipinos who came to the continental United States from 1920 to 1934 were employed in agriculture. Indeed, as much as 59 percent of all Filipino workers were engaged in this industry.[69] Due to the number of Filipinos involved in agricultural work, chapter 4 will examine in detail the conditions in which they labored and their response to grower exploitation. What will be discussed in this chapter is the nature of the migratory labor circuit they worked along the West Coast and how San Diego was a part of this route despite its omission from the historical record.

San Diego was the southernmost tip of the West Coast migratory labor circuit, with a large agricultural industry to feed workers into this system, yet many state and independent studies in the 1930s, such as Bruno Lasker's *Filipino Immigration to the Continental United States and to Hawaii* and Will J. French's special bulletin, *Facts about Filipino Immigration into California,* fail to mention it as a locale for Filipino immigration.[70] San Diego did not register on the map despite the thousands of Filipino (and Mexican) migratory laborers who lived in or passed through San Diego to labor in the county's agricultural fields.

Given the nature of this type of invisible employment, census data is also inconsistent. Regarding actual numbers of Mexicans versus what was included by census takers, the same could be said about Filipinos. Because the majority of Filipinos were laborers in industries such as agriculture in San Diego and nearby Imperial Valley, their population fluctuated with the seasonal crops, creating a "portable community," a highly mobile population of migratory laborers that came in and out of San Diego. Indeed, as Linda España-Maram noted about these portable communities, "Because most Filipino laborers had to tailor a life in harmony with their migratory work patterns, they created a community that was versatile and, for them, functional. They took their communities with them."[71] Filipinos settled temporarily to harvest San Diego's many crops, only to leave and follow the migratory circuit that took them throughout the state of California, sometimes even as far as Alaska to work in the fish canneries.[72] This is also true for Mexican agricultural workers.

U.S. census data and other reports also do not account for the fluctuating navy population among Filipinos, who oftentimes went out to sea. This affected how communities were formed and, more importantly, how they sustained themselves as workers and sailors fluctuated in and out of San Diego. This created a sort of routine fluctuation of the Filipino community, which expanded when seasonal crops needed to be harvested and when the ships came into town and contracted when the naval vessels and migratory workers left. Table 2.3 provides some indication of San Diego's Filipino population from 1900 to 1970.

Given that state officials and researchers did not bother to include migratory laborers in studies on the Mexican community of San Diego, it is likely that they did not take into account Filipinos who also had similar employment, as well as those who were in the U.S. Navy. Census reports are also misleading given the fact that both Filipinos and Mexicans share many similar Spanish surnames. This could have led census reporters to assume that Filipinos were fewer in number if they were mistaken for Mexican and added to their population statistics. Since population counts do not document this,

Table 2.3 Filipino Population Statistics

YEAR	UNITED STATES	CALIFORNIA	SAN DIEGO
1900	–	–	–
1910	2,767	5	–
1920	26,634	2,674	48
1930	108,260	30,470	394
1940	98,535	31,408	799
1950	122,707	40,424	N/A
1960	181,614	67,134	5,123
1970	336,731	135,248	15,069

Source: Yen Le Espiritu, *Home Bound: Filipino American Lives across Culture, Communities, and Countries* (Berkeley: University of California Press, 2003), 101.

oral testimony is relied upon to give an idea of Filipino and Mexican presence since many of them were often overlooked in the residential areas where they rented homes. That, in addition to the census takers not even bothering to count Filipinos, could have led to a miscount on the actual numbers of them in San Diego.[73]

The memories and photographs of the workers, as well as some newspaper accounts, are among the only cultural records that exist which document how these fluctuating and sedentary communities affected the cultural landscape of San Diego. According to historian Adelaida Castillo-Tsuchida, for example, the earliest documentation of Filipinos who settled permanently in San Diego was in 1908.[74] The presence of these early immigrants would be the cement that held together the subsequent migrations of workers to the city. Porfirio S. Apostol, who arrived in San Diego in 1932 after traveling from Seattle, worked his way down through California. He observed that there were about one hundred Filipinos living in the city.[75] Even by the late 1950s, the Filipino community was considered small by population standards. Filipina resident Nena Amaguin also remarked on the Filipino community's size in San Diego when she settled there in 1958. She remarked that it was "very small. When we came here [there were] only a few Filipinos."[76] Although her statement does suggest that San Diego's Filipino community was small, again it may not take into account the portable communities or those that lived in other areas outside of her own in the downtown sector on J Street, where a small number of Filipino families resided. Filipino and Mexican communities, although small, managed to survive and steadily grow throughout the early twentieth century, being fed and then diminished by the fluctuating mobile communities that came with the crops or navy ships. There were always small, yet stable communities that lived in cities such as San Diego. A more detailed account of these community formations will be discussed in the following chapter.

GENDER IMBALANCE AMONG EARLY IMMIGRANTS

The makeup of the Mexican and Filipino immigrant communities differed in terms of their gender makeup. As previously mentioned, Mexicans who came to the United States during the years 1910 to 1920 to escape the Mexican Revolution were families as well as single men and women. Both men and women came to fill labor shortages during World War I and took advantage of the unrestricted access of immigration laws, resulting in a large, gender-balanced population. Men were not the only ones who came to labor in San Diego and other areas of the United States. Women also came on their own to work and earn a living in *el norte*.[77] Indeed, many Mexican women made the journey up north as widows, single mothers, and individuals. They, along with thousands of others, came to the United States to work and eventually settle in San Diego. Once there, some stayed in Logan Heights or National City, while other families

Table 2.4 Comparing the Mexican and Filipino Population in the United States, 1925–1929

GROUP	SINGLE (%)	MARRIED (%)	WIDOWED (%)	LESS THAN 30 YEARS OLD (%)
Mexican	55.1	40.6	4.2	71.0
Filipino	77.3	22.5*	0.2	84.3

Source: William J. French, dir., *Facts about Filipino Immigration into California, Special Bulletin No. 3* (San Francisco: California Department of Industrial Relations, 1930), 46.

*Most married Filipinos came without their wives.

traveled back and forth between communities because of the nature of their work. Irene Rivas, for example, grew up in Logan Heights during the 1920s. Her stepfather used to work for the Santa Fe Railroad and her mother was a housewife. Given the nature of his work on the railroads, her family had to move around a lot, to Campo, National City, and then back to Logan Heights.[78]

Although both Mexicans and Filipinos had a bachelor population in their communities, Filipinos had more of a gender imbalance. According to French's *Facts about Filipino Immigration into California*, the ratio of Filipino males to females was fourteen to one. Other studies rate this even higher, as much as twenty-three to one.[79] The majority of the bachelors who came to the United States were young as well, between the ages of sixteen and thirty. Those men who came to the United States did so without their wives. During the years 1920 to 1929, only 2,079 women came to California, compared to men who numbered 29,013, or 93.3 percent of those Filipinos who came to California. In all, between the years 1920 and 1929, approximately 31,092 Filipinos came to California.[80] A comparison of the Filipino and Mexican immigrant population can be seen in table 2.4.

ROUTES OF MIGRATION

The avenues of migration for both Filipinos and Mexicans to San Diego also tell a story. A sample of Mexican Immigration and Naturalization Records for the years 1935 to 1942, for example, provides an idea as to where they were coming from, their modes of transportation, and where they settled in San Diego. No one Mexican state produced a majority of immigrants coming to the United States; however, the Baja California region did supply a sizable number who settled in San Diego. The vast majority of those sampled came by way of border entries, such as San Ysidro or Calexico. This included walking, using a horse-drawn carriage, or driving an automobile through these border points. Some arrived through El Paso via the electric railway, railroad, and even by ships, which brought Mexican immigrants from Ensenada and other coastal ports along Baja California. The modes of transportation also varied according to the year the individual first came to San Diego, which ranged from the mid-1800s to the 1930s.[81] Although they came by different modes of transportation, those who settled in San Diego went to areas where already established communities were present, such as Logan Heights, National City, Chula Vista, and Lemon Grove.

The majority of Filipinos, however, came to the United States through the ports of Los Angeles and San Francisco. Some also came through the port of Seattle and even came by way of Mexico. Los Angeles and San Francisco had the greatest number of Filipino migrants to enter California. Of the total number of Filipinos in California who entered the state between 1920 and 1929 (31,092), approximately 17,425, or 56 percent, embarked from Honolulu, whereas 10,882, or 35 percent, embarked from the Philippines. The remaining 2,785, or 9 percent, arrived via foreign ports.[82] The reason the majority of those who immigrated embarked from Honolulu, Hawai'i, was the result of labor discontent and expanding opportunities in California and elsewhere along the Pacific West Coast. Many Filipino laborers were also blacklisted and deported to the continental United States. Thousands more left to try their luck with their families and friends who had migrated earlier.[83] In essence, Hawai'i became known as the halfway station between the Philippines and the continental United States, particularly California.[84] Once in San Diego, they had to settle and find a place to call home.

PLANTING ROOTS IN SAN DIEGO

For both Mexican and Filipino immigration to the continental United States, the discourse has been framed in terms of economic opportunity, but the role of family support was just as important, if not more so. Many immigrants came to establish a new home and be the anchor of community building for the subsequent family members and friends who would follow, while others sent money home to support their loved ones. For those family members who followed their loved ones, they began to build an extensive network and community that included family, friends, and extended kin. These relationships were strengthened by their commitment to each other and their cultural values. Anthropologist Roberto Alvarez Jr., who wrote about early Mexican immigration from Baja California to San Diego, observed how the practice of *parentesco,* which included kin ties between blood relations as well as non-kin ties among those who shared history and geographic locations, provided a means by which reciprocity and kinship solidarity were maintained among families and friends. That, along with the practices of *compadrazgo* (godparenthood) relationships, marriage, and, most importantly, *confianza,* or trust, was the basis by which all social relationships, networks, and institutions continued, including both familial and kinship ties among these migrants.[85] As Alvarez pointed out, "Most of the families that arrived were kin to the previous migrants. In a well-practiced pattern, they sought refuge and aid in the homes of close kin. Extended kindred, like hometown networks, continued to provide family bonds and new outlets for the growth of family interrelations … Incoming families and friends brought news of loved ones in the south and changes among kin in the homeland."[86]

If it were not for the role of already established families and kin that had set the foundation for others to join them, the experience would have been more difficult in an already alienating environment. This was also true for Filipinos, who relied on connecting with the few families that were present once they arrived in San Diego. Family and kinship ties were central for the survival of both Mexican and Filipino communities. Though the disbursement of families and friends occurred throughout San Diego County as they moved out of the original areas of settlement, they nonetheless continued to stay connected. They got together during religious, familial, and other social events such as weddings, baptisms, anniversary parties, family get-togethers, and funerals. These gatherings, though at times less frequent than in the past, illustrate how these ties have remained despite the geographical mobility and settlement of families.

Though some of these early communities have changed dramatically, such as Lemon Grove, Logan Heights, National City, and Chula Vista, some of these families or their descendents still remain, maintaining roots to the homes they once knew. Industries have changed, such as the closing of the local fish canneries in Logan Heights and surrounding areas, as well as the end of agriculture, specifically lemon orchards in Lemon Grove. These have given way to other wartime industries during the postwar era as well as technological industries. What has risen are the service-related industries that employ thousands of Mexicans and Filipinos. Yet for Filipinos, a mainstay in their own communities has been the navy, as more naval families arrived in San Diego, increasing existing communities or establishing new ones outside of the South Bay and Southeast sections of San Diego. But as more Mexicans and Filipinos continued to pour into the United States, local, state, and national officials began calling for their exclusion and, ultimately, their removal.

EXCLUSION AND REPATRIATION

Although Mexican immigration during the 1900s and 1910s was virtually ignored by immigration officers due to the labor needs of railroads, mining, and agriculture during World War I, by 1919 Mexicans were required to apply for admission when they entered a U.S. port of entry.[87] By the end of the 1920s and well into the dawn of 1930, the U.S. attitude toward its Mexican and Filipino populations went from one of necessity due to the labor shortages of World War I to one of disdain. Nativists and white labor accused both groups of taking away their jobs. Despite the need for both Mexican and

Filipino labor, by the late 1920s both groups were the targets of xenophobic whites who saw their numbers increasing too rapidly. Because the numbers of both Mexicans and Filipinos were rising prior to the years leading up to the Great Depression, politicians, conservative labor unions, and white labor saw them as a threat.[88] Of the estimated 45,208 Filipinos in the continental United States, approximately 30,470 came to California, which fueled the cry for their exclusion.[89]

Economic competition was the supposed reason behind the call for exclusion since Filipinos were allegedly displacing whites in various occupations, such as hotel, restaurant, and agricultural work.[90] This was absurd given the fact that service work and agricultural jobs were already racialized as "Filipino work" or "Mexican work." Nonetheless, white laborers still made these ridiculous claims even as they sought to avoid these jobs.[91] Mae Ngai notes that as the United States was shifting its relationship with the Philippines from a colonial to neocolonial model, the move to end Filipino immigration and exclude them from U.S. shores was a calculated "movement for decolonization and exclusion."[92] This was in response to the hysteria that was being drummed up by politicians and labor groups that saw the continuous flow of brown bodies from the Pacific and south of the border as a threat to the racial, moral, and economic livelihood of the country. Indeed, the unwarranted alarmist attitude was the cause for many editorials, commentaries, and even state reports on the "Filipino and Mexican problem." Such problems were the topic of many nativist groups, such as the Commonwealth Club, American Legion, Veterans of Foreign Wars, America for Americans Club, California Joint Immigration Committee, State Grange, Native Sons of the Golden West, the California State Federation of Labor, and the American Federation of Labor, many of which held conventions and passed resolutions calling for the exclusion of both Mexicans and Filipinos. Judge George J. Steiger of San Francisco, for example, also questioned their ability to assimilate, stating, "We all must agree that the Filipinos do not and cannot assimilate with our people."[93] By racially constructing Filipinos and Mexicans as outsiders and thus unable to assimilate with whites, momentum was gained in the public sphere for their exclusion and removal.

From the individual to the institutional level, workers, politicians, and organizations called for an end to both Mexican and Filipino immigration to the United States. What distinguished these groups from each other was the series of legislative measures targeting Filipinos specifically. The cause for alarm was made notably by individuals such as Congressman Richard Welch of California, who introduced a bill (H.R. 13900) on May 19, 1928, to the House of Representatives calling for the exclusion of Filipinos and classifying them as "aliens" in order to solve the so called "Philippine Problem." He, among others, helped fuel the flames for anti-Filipino sentiment by calling Filipino immigration "the third Asiatic invasion of the Pacific Coast."[94] He advocated for closing the doors on immigration, stating, "Filipinos are not our own people," despite the fact that they were still U.S. nationals. Congressman Charles Colden also proposed bill

H.R. 9281 in 1934, which would have restricted both Mexicans and Filipinos by placing quotas on "immigration from the Republic of Mexico and the Philippine Islands."[95]

Senator Samuel Shortridge proposed an amendment to the Harris immigration bill (S.51), stating that he was a "friend of the Philippine people and would give them independence at this very hour if I had the power." This statement showed that he was in favor of Philippine independence, not because he was a friend of Filipinos, but because he wanted to prohibit their entry into the United States. By granting Philippine independence, Filipinos would immediately have their status changed from national to immigrant, which in turn would allow for their exclusion.[96] This assumption can be gathered through a previous statement he made regarding his view of Chinese exclusion, where he stated, "We stopped the Chinese from coming to our shores not because we hated them, but because we loved our own."[97]

This statement is problematic for two reasons. First, exclusion of the Chinese and the subsequent targeting of Filipinos for exclusion were based on race, which was imbedded in the language of the exclusion and repatriation acts. Whites saw Filipinos as a threat, and they were not discreet in their motives. Second, the fact that racial violence toward Filipinos was so intense demonstrates the racial climate in which they were living. It was an intensity that surpassed even the animosity toward Mexicans during this time. If Shortridge was so concerned about "our people," he would have suggested that the United States did not need Filipino labor so long as there were Mexicans. In other words, he noted, "We do not have to look 6,000 miles across the Pacific to get this seasonal labor. It is overabundant in Mexico."[98] This shows that issues were far more complex than labor when dealing with Filipinos. Shortridge was successful in crafting his language to show an air of genuine concern, all the while distracting the public from his real intentions, which were anti-Filipino.

Eventually, the bills were defeated. Yet it did not stop its proponents, chiefly U.S. labor unions and politicians, from virtually ending both Filipino and Mexican immigration to the United States. As one individual noted in his address to the Commonwealth Club of California during a meeting on the issue of Filipino immigration, "If the presence of particular races is detrimental to our interests, that fact would seem ethically to justify action to control the evil."[99] Mexicans were also targeted, whether foreign or U.S. born. As one Americanization teacher noted, "He [the Mexican American] is really not part of the real America. Because of language and color he is foreign even to the so called 'hyphenated' American citizen; he may always be."[100] Filipinos and Mexicans were both demonized and dehumanized. Their presence was framed as an invasion that had to be curtailed. Thus the social, economic, moral, and health problems that they supposedly contributed to U.S. society needed to be dealt with by excluding them from the United States as well as calling for their repatriation or, rather, deportation.[101]

In response, both the Mexican and Filipino communities wrote their own editorials and commentaries attesting to their law-abiding ways, contributions to the city and state economy, and their desire to be a part of the United States.[102] Yet their presence came at a time when economic insecurity was at its height, with the collapse of the stock market in 1929 and the resultant Great Depression that lasted throughout the 1930s, leaving the United States in economic turmoil. It was during the 1930s that the treatment of both Mexicans and Filipinos was at its worst. For Filipinos, however, they faced greater violence than their Mexican counterparts. Filipinos were the victims of violent race riots, such as those that occurred in Exeter, Watsonville, and the Imperial Valley, among other areas of California and the West.[103] Because of the perceived economic and social competition that they had with white men over white women and "white jobs," Filipinos were beaten, stabbed, robbed, chased out of numerous towns, and even killed by bombings and shootings at the hands of white men in various cities throughout California. Mexicans were also viciously attacked. The Ku Klux Klan, for example, had an active chapter in San Diego and was responsible for many acts of violence against Mexican migrant workers. According to the civil rights and labor activist Robert Galvan, these violent acts of terror included migrant workers being hanged from trees in rural areas, buried alive, and lit on fire "to see them dance." The racism and terrorism against Filipinos was so intense that writer Carlos Bulosan noted, "I came to know afterward that in many ways it was a crime to be a Filipino in California."[104]

Despite the fact that numerically Filipinos were never a real threat to white labor, they were still the targets for exclusion, as was the case for both the Chinese and Japanese before them.[105] San Diego Assembly District candidate George B. Bowers, for example, argued that immigration from Japan, Mexico, and the Philippines was "not a problem of the future; it is a problem of today."[106] Ironically, this fear created an unholy alliance between those Filipinos pushing for independence and nativists who wanted to rid themselves of their "Filipino problem." Continued pressure by groups such as the American Federation of Labor, the Sons and Daughters of the Golden West, and the Commonwealth Club and efforts by Philippine officials resulted in the adoption and passing of the Tydings-McDuffie Act of 1934, which recognized Philippine independence but required it to be under U.S. rule until 1946.[107]

The passing of the Tydings-McDuffie Act was supposed to answer the problem of Philippine independence. This act did not solve the "Philippine problem." The act did not provide for either economic or national security of the Philippines, which still had complex economic and strategic interest for the United States.[108] With the stroke of a pen, Filipinos no longer possessed national status but were instead reclassified as immigrants. This virtually ended Filipino immigration to the United States from the thousands in previous years to a mere fifty Filipino immigrants per year after 1934. This was in essence an exclusion act.[109] This move proved to be devastating to the Filipino population, which immediately ceased to grow as it once had. The move to exclude Mexicans, however, failed.

Nativists such as Congressman Welch and Senator Hiram Johnson, among others, orchestrated the immediate repatriation of Filipinos, who were now seen as "indigents" leeching off welfare rolls, despite the fact that these claims were unsubstantiated. As nationals, Filipinos were ineligible for public relief despite paying taxes.[110] This fact was buried under the inflammatory rhetoric by public officials and conservative labor leaders, which further exacerbated public fear. A year later, the Filipino Repatriation Act passed, which was, in essence, a one-way ticket to the Philippines with the legal means to keep Filipinos from reentering the United States, despite the lofty excuse that it was for the benefit of Filipinos who wanted to go home. It was, in fact, as contemporary Filipino writer Manuel Buaken noted, a deportation and exclusion act.[111] The Immigration and Naturalization Service (INS) scheduled "deportation parties" to round up Filipinos across the United States. Many Filipinos carefully read the stipulations of the act, which stated, "No Filipino who received the benefit of this Act shall be entitled to return to the continental United States except as a quota immigrant under the provision of [the Tydings-McDuffie Act]."[112] They were well informed of the issue and thus were resistant to the hollow provisions of the Repatriation Act.

Despite the excuses that white politicians and city officials made that Filipinos were a burden on relief rolls, in fact, as a community, Filipinos pooled their resources together, rather than depending on welfare, for fear of being shamed and losing face.[113] Indeed, as Linda España-Maram notes regarding the Filipino community of Los Angeles, through the practice of *utang na loob* (mutual support) and other forms of mutual aid, Filipinos sustained each other through "a sense of responsibility for one another's welfare," which enabled them to avoid depending upon U.S. institutions for assistance. It was a sense of pride in not having to rely on outside support, but rather on each other.[114] This would be the same reason why they did not take advantage of the "voluntary" efforts for them to be repatriated at the onset of the Filipino Repatriation Act of 1935. In fact, only 2,190 took advantage of this act. Some left voluntarily due to their disillusionment because of their treatment in the United States. Of that number, 95 percent were men.[115]

In San Diego and the Imperial Valley, repatriation was also underway as newspapers advertised for the free transportation back to the Philippines.[116] Yet, by and large, the majority of Filipinos did not take advantage of this act because they did not want to go home as failures. To go back to the Philippines at the government's expense was shameful for many Filipinos. It was an admission of defeat for these young men, so, rather than be disgraced, they endured their treatment in the United States. As historian Adelaide Castillo-Tsuchida remarked, "To the average Filipino, it would have meant 'losing face' and suffering humiliation, or *mapapahiya,* to return home as a repatriate."[117] Rather, they stuck it out and used various survival mechanisms such as family, extended family, and community support to stay and endure the harsh years of the Great Depression. In the end, Filipino repatriation was a failure.

Their Mexican counterparts, on the other hand, fared a lot worse in terms of repatriation efforts. Mexicans, like the Filipinos, were blamed for the Great Depression, yet even more so because of their larger population in the United States. Immigration was virtually uninterrupted for two decades prior to the Great Depression, which enabled Mexican communities to grow at an escalating rate. Their substantially larger numbers made them a target for more forceful action. This included congressional legislation that was introduced in 1929 making unlawful entry into the United States a felony, along with a series of federal deportation campaigns also known as "repatriation."[118] As the historian Zaragosa Vargas notes, President Herbert Hoover mobilized public opinion against the Mexican population and "made Mexicans the prime targets for government persecution, regardless of whether or not they were citizens of the United States."[119] Mexicans were accused of burdening local economies through public relief and the taking of "American" jobs when they should be saved for white Americans.

In response to this allegation, Griswold del Castillo provides an important insight. As he notes, unlike what the popular imaginary constructed, which was that Mexicans were taking jobs and burdening welfare rolls, "Mexican nationals nationwide were among the least likely to rely on county welfare or charitable services, and the vast majority of them were already unemployed."[120] The majority of Mexicans did not want to go on relief rolls because it was an insult to be supported by the government. They would rather work several jobs or have multiple incomes from everyone in their family working rather than go on relief. This was true for Connie Zuniga's father during the Great Depression. He said he could never bring himself to collect welfare because it was a thing of pride. Instead, Connie's father worked numerous odd jobs in addition to his work in construction. Similar to the Zunigas, other Mexican families in San Diego also opted to work rather than go on relief during the Depression. Joe Lerma and his siblings, for example, helped contribute to the family income by working after school at the fish canneries or selling tacos and tamales.[121] Jesus Ochoa, who was the eldest of five children, helped his mother, who was the sole provider as a widow, by selling newspapers after school. His mother worked at Van Camp fish cannery. In 1940, he worked at the Civilian Conservation Corps camp in California, which was established by President Franklin Roosevelt during the Depression to provide work for unemployed men.[122]

Despite these facts, in Southern California as early as 1931, efforts were already being made to deport Mexicans. Memos were being circulated between the Los Angeles Chamber of Commerce and city officials, which stated: "By all means the Government should proceed to deport all undesirable aliens at this time, particularly those who are a burden to the community and if it can be speeded up I see no reason why it should not be done. ... The main thing however, is to keep from upsetting the whole Mexican population by wholesale raids and other methods which are misunderstood by the Mexican and set that Mexican afloat."[123] Despite their concerns over disrupting the Mexican population with wholesale raids, that is exactly what occurred. Studies on Mexican repatriation provide ample evidence of deportation raids as the immigration and police offi-cers rounded up Mexicans, both citizens and noncitizens, and sent them across the border. These agents of the state did not bother to distinguish the difference. Their racial uniform as "Mexican" was enough to subject them to deportation.[124]

Indeed, being Mexican became the physical marker that singled them out for racial profiling and, ultimately, deportation. As a result, entire families and large sectors of Mexican communities were deported through a concerted effort from national, state, local, and charitable agencies. As the mechanisms of repatriation, or deportation, targeted Mexican immigrants, U.S. citizens of Mexican descent were also affected. The deportation of U.S. citizens clearly violated their civil rights.[125]

Fear also facilitated their departure. As the historian George Sánchez notes regarding Los Angeles's Mexican community during the repatriation drives, fear resulted "in encouraging Mexicans of varying legal status—including American-born citizens of Mexican descent—to contemplate leaving." The involuntary roundups and coercion to leave was stressful. Many fled for fear of deportation.[126] Estimates vary, but contemporary studies suggest that up to one million persons of Mexican descent were repatriated back to Mexico during the years 1930 to 1935 in an effort to stabilize the country's economic woes by ridding itself of its "Mexican problem." Of this number, an estimated 60 percent were U.S. citizens by birth, a majority spoke English, and many had lived in the United States all their lives. This accounted for 20 percent of the Mexican population in the United States, a staggering number that fell victim to this forced removal.[127]

Although the size and growth of San Diego's Mexican communities were also affected, not all of San Diego's Mexican community was deported. Jose "Joe" Galvan, for example, worked the celery fields of the South Bay and did pick-and-shovel work on Works Progress Administration (WPA) projects during the Great Depression.[128] John Rubalcava's family was also one of the fortunate ones who had job security and was among those that were not deported. Most of John's family was either working or in school, which enabled them to be spared the humiliation and devastation of being repatriated. As John recalled, "I saw the ship down on Broadway, when we were sending them back, because I had some friends, and they were waving at me." He was around seven or eight at the time as he watched the ships depart from the marina on Broadway in San Diego.[129] Herb Ibarra also recalled the scene that took place during the repatriations in San Diego: "My mother knew that a relative of ours was on one of the boats, so she took me with her to San Diego Harbor. I won't ever forget the boats, the humanity packed onto the decks under armed guard. We saw our relative on the boat and we waved, but the guards wouldn't let us talk; wouldn't let anybody off the boat. I saw all of this, looking between the legs of adults."[130]

In San Diego County, the number of Mexicans and Mexican Americans who were formally repatriated was 1,913. According to historian Camille Guérin-Gonzales, this was twice the number of people who were on relief.[131] The number of Mexican families on relief in San Diego was relatively small, yet they were pressured by relief agencies to return to Mexico. Arthur Louch, who was head of the County Welfare Department, stated that between 400 and 500 Mexican families were on public assistance in San Diego. Although Louch also noted that 375 other alien nationalities were on public assistance, only Mexican families were targeted as being a burden on San Diego's economy. This does not even take into account U.S. citizens who were also on relief, which no doubt far surpassed any other group. Louch's goal was to deport Mexicans in San Diego before they became "spoiled by inactivity and public aid." Yet those who wanted to work and could find jobs in public works projects were thrown out for preference to U.S. citizens.[132]

Those who were persuaded to leave San Diego contacted Mexican consul Enrique Ferreira for financial assistance. They were transported by boat and railroad. Over half of San Diego's *repatriados* settled across the border in Baja California, such as Colonia Libertad in Tijuana. Overall, 70 percent settled along the Mexican border states of Baja California, Sonora, Sinaloa, Chihuahua, and Coahuila. Given the close proximity of these areas, it is highly likely that once they were able to, these same Mexican and Mexican American families returned to San Diego and other U.S. border cities because that is where they considered their home to be, especially for the majority of repatriates who were U.S. citizens.[133]

As a result of these mass deportation drives, whole communities were disrupted. Families and friends were torn apart and uprooted from their homes. Housing, businesses, and communities were lost, leaving behind the hopes, dreams, memories, and the lives that they once knew.[134] The economic insecurity of the U.S. public, as well as their fear, nativism, and lack of compassion toward Mexicans and Filipinos, put those Mexicans and Filipinos in a humiliating and unjust situation. With nearly 20 percent of the Mexican population and 7 percent of the Filipino population in the United States repatriated during the Great Depression, it was as Ngai noted, "a racial expulsion program."[135] These efforts, though a failure in many respects for both communities, show how, despite the move to exclude and remove both groups, they, in fact, continued to grow throughout the twentieth century. The demand for labor, especially during World War II, would be the catalyst for a renewed growth of both communities.

———

As Mexicans and Filipinos continued to immigrate to San Diego, they were coming into a city that had already decided where they could live. Although both groups came to live in areas where there were preexisting Mexican and Filipino populations in San Diego, they soon found out why. The politics and social implications of race had a strong hold over the city's nonwhite communities. The city was growing overall as more whites and nonwhites came into San Diego, which doubled the population every decade. What brought Mexicans and Filipinos to San Diego was primarily the need to fill the labor demands that the city required to continue its exponentially rapid growth. Yet as they came to labor for San Diego's economic development, they would not share in the freedom to live where they wanted or be able to move up the socioeconomic ladder. Their citizenship did not matter either. They were confined to barrios or "ghettos" in larger multiracial communities. As we will see in the following chapter, Mexicans and Filipinos were up against an unseen, albeit powerful force in their pursuit for economic, political, and social equality.

NOTES

1. Chuey's went out of business in 2009. Quoted from "Chuey's a Big Name over in Barrio Logan," *Currents*, August 23, 1978, D1, D3. See also "Jesus 'Chuey' Garcia, 1907–1995," *San Diego Union Tribune*, October 26, 1995, A1, A9, Folder: Obituaries, Box 1, Logan Heights Historical Society, San Diego.

2. Camille Guérin-Gonzales, *Mexican Workers and American Dreams: Immigration, Repatriation, and California Farm Labor, 1900–1939* (New Brunswick, NJ: Rutgers University Press, 1994), 24–25; Carey McWilliams, *Brothers under the Skin* (Boston: Little, Brown, 1943).

3. The terms *cultural record* and *cultural footprint* came out of conversations with my colleague and friend Robert Soza in July of 2009 while editing this book.

4. Gilbert G. González, *Guest Workers or Colonized Labor? Mexican Labor Migration to the United States* (Boulder, CO: Paradigm Publishers, 2006), 3.

5. See Renato Constantino, "The Miseducation of the Filipino," in *Vestiges of War: The Philippine-American War and the Aftermath of the Imperial Dream, 1899–1999*, ed. Angel Velasco Shaw and Luis H. Francia (New York: New York University Press, 2002), 177–92; Yen Le Espiritu, *Home Bound: Filipino American Lives across Cultures, Communities, and Countries* (Berkeley: University of California Press, 2003), 25–27; Dorothy Fujita-Rony, *American Workers, Colonial Power: Philippine Seattle and the Transpacific West, 1919–1941* (Berkeley: University of California Press, 2002), 51–61.

6. Fujita-Rony, *American Workers, Colonial Power,* 51–61.

7. Mae M. Ngai, *Impossible Subjects: Illegal Aliens and the Making of Modern America* (Princeton, NJ: Princeton University Press, 2004), 11–13, 94–95.

8 . Ronald Takaki, *Strangers from a Different Shore: A History of Asian Americans* (New York: Little, Brown, 1998); Sucheng Chan, *Asian Americans: An Interpretive History* (New York: Twayne Publishers, 1991).

9 . "Filipinos Displacing Japanese," *Philippine Republic*, March 1924, 18, Labor File, National Pinoy Archives, Filipino American National Historical Society, Seattle, Washington. All subsequent citations will be noted as FANHS, NPA. See also "Growers' Convention Votes to Import Filipino Labor," *Los Angeles Times,* May 17, 1917, II:1; Paul S. Taylor, *Mexican Labor in the United States* (New York: Arno Press, 1970); and Ngai, *Impossible Subjects,* 103.

10 . Ngai, *Impossible Subjects,* 94.

11 . California Department of Finance, *California Statistical Abstract—Population,* http://www.ca.gov/About/Facts/Population.html (accessed January 23, 2004); Philip R. Pryde, *San Diego: An Introduction to the Region*, 4th ed. (San Diego, CA: Sunbelt Publications, 2004), 75; Espiritu, *Home Bound,* 17.

12 . Richard Griswold del Castillo, ed., *Chicano San Diego: Cultural Space and the Struggle for Justice* (Tucson: University of Arizona Press, 2007), 2.

13 . U.S. Census Bureau, "2006–2008 American Community Survey, San Diego County, California," ACS Demographic and Housing Estimates: 2006–2008; San Diego Association of Governments (SANDAG), "Mapping the Census: Race and Ethnicity in the San Diego Region," *SANDAG Info 1* (April 2002), www.sandag.org/uploads/ publicationid/ publicationid_722_1120.pdf; Griswold del Castillo, *Chicano San Diego*, 2; and Espiritu, *Home Bound,* 17.

14 . For more on Horton, Kettner, Spreckels, and other "founding fathers" of San Diego, see Carl H. Heilbron, ed., *History of San Diego County* (San Diego: San Diego Press Club, 1936), 1–314; Iris H. W. Engstrand, *San Diego: Gateway to the Pacific* (Houston: Pioneer Publications, 1992), 29–41.

15 . "San Diego Headquarters Eleventh Naval District," *Standard Oil Bulletin* (April 1922), 7–12, Folder 18—Armed Forces, Navy, General #1, Lateral Files, San Diego Historical Society; and Rear Admiral Thomas J. Senn, "The History of the Navy in San Diego," in *History of San Diego County,* ed. Heilbron, 370–76.

16 . Richard Pourade, *The Glory Years: The Booms and Busts in the Land of the Sundown Sea* (San Diego, CA: Union Tribune Publishing Company, 1966), 120–21; and R. B. Davy, M.D., "The Climate of San Diego," in *San Diego: The City and the County,* ed. San Diego Chamber of Commerce (San Diego, CA: Gould and Hutton, 1888), 22–29. For more on population statistics, see *U.S. Census Reports, 1900–1960* (Washington: GPO, 1901, 1913, 1922, 1932, 1942, 1952, and 1961); San Diego

Chamber of Commerce, "Civilian Population," *San Diego Business* (February 1943), San Diego Historical Society.

17. Nicholas Mirkowich, "Urban Growth in the San Diego Region," *Economic Geography* 17, no. 3 (July 1941): 310; Clarence Alan McGrew, *City of San Diego and San Diego County: The Birthplace of California* (Chicago: American Historical Society, 1922), 347–75.

18. Roger W. Lotchin, *Fortress California, 1910–1961: From Warfare to Welfare* (Chicago: University of Illinois Press, 2002), 1–41; Kevin Starr, *The Dream Endures: California Enters the 1940s* (New York: Oxford University Press, 1997), 90–114; Norman W. Tolle, ed., "The Navy and San Diego: The Story of a Vital Link in the Nation's Defense Chain," *Union Title–Trust Topics* 2, no. 2 (March–April 1953): 2–19; Anthony W. Corso, "San Diego: The Anti-City," in *Sunbelt Cities: Politics and Growth Since World War II*, ed. Richard M. Bernard and Bradley R. Rice (Austin: University of Texas Press, 1983), 329–30; Bruce Linder, *San Diego's Navy: An Illustrated History* (Annapolis, MD: Naval Institute Press, 2001); Christine Killory, "Temporary Suburbs: The Lost Opportunity of San Diego's National Defense Housing Projects," *Journal of San Diego History* 39, no. 1–2 (Winter/Spring 1993): 34; Mary Taschner, "Boomerang Boom: San Diego 1941–1942," *Journal of San Diego History* 28, no. 1 (Winter 1982): 2.

19. Carey McWilliams, "The Boom Nobody Wanted," *New Republic*, June 30, 1941, 882; Taschner, "Boomerang Boom," 1–2; Lucinda Eddy, "War Comes to San Diego," *Journal of San Diego History* 39, no. 1–2 (Winter/Spring 1993): 51; Gerald Nash, *The American West Transformed: The Impact of the Second World War* (Lincoln: University of Nebraska Press, 1985), vii, 17, 56–59.

20. Starr, *The Dream Endures*, 90–91.

21. Abraham Shragge, "A New Federal City: San Diego during World War II," *Pacific Historical Review* 63, no. 3 (August 1994): 336–37.

22. Ibid., 355, 360–61; McWilliams, "The Boom Nobody Wanted," 882; Taschner, "Boomerang Boom," 1–2; Eddy, "War Comes to San Diego," 51; Nash, *The American West Transformed*, vii, 17, 56–59.

23. I also recognize that before the area which is now San Diego was a part of Mexico, it was inhabited by the Kumeyaay people, who are indigenous to the area. For more on this, see Griswold del Castillo, *Chicano San Diego*, 12–39; and Robert R. Alvarez Jr., *Familia: Migration and Adaptation in Baja and Alta California, 1800–1975* (Berkeley: University of California Press, 1991).

24 . Wayne Cornelius, quoted in Richard Louv, "U.S. Magnet Lures Mexican Migrants," *San Diego Union,* November 25, 1979, A14, Lateral File: Hispanic Heritage, Thelma Hollingsworth Local History Room, National City Public Library.

25 . See Michael J. Gonzales, *The Mexican Revolution, 1910–1940* (Albuquerque: University of New Mexico Press, 2002); Michael C. Meyer, William L. Sherman, and Susan M. Deeds, *The Course of Mexican History* (New York: Oxford University Press, 1999), 467–615; Matt S. Meier and Feliciano Ribera, *Mexican Americans/ American Mexicans: From Conquistadors to Chicanos* (New York: Hill and Wang, 1993), 108–10; Manuel G. Gonzales, *Mexicanos: A History of Mexicans in the United States* (Bloomington: Indiana University Press, 1999), 114–20.

26 . Consuelo "Connie" Zuniga, interview with author, San Diego, CA, August 20, 2001.

27 . Home Missions Council, *A Study of Social and Economic Factors Relating to Spanish-Speaking People in the United States,* 6, Untitled Folder, Box 63, George P. Clements Papers, Special Collections and University Archives, University of California, Los Angeles; Paul S. Taylor, "Some Aspects of Mexican Immigration," *Journal of Political Economy* 38, no. 5 (October 1930): 609–15, Folder: 1932–1933 Mexican Labor and Immigration, Box 80, George P. Clements Papers, Special Collections and University Archives, University of California, Los Angeles; Mary Catherine Miller, "Attitudes of the San Diego Labor Movement toward Mexicans, 1917–1936" (MA thesis, San Diego State University, 1974), 1; Guérin-Gonzales, *Mexican Workers and American Dreams,* 25–47; Manuel Gamio, *Mexican Immigration to the United States: A Study of Human Migration and Adjustment* (New York: Dover Publications, 1971); Lawrence A. Cardoso, *Mexican Emigration to the United States, 1897–1931* (Tucson: University of Arizona Press, 1980), 38–39; Max Sylvius Handman, "Economic Reasons for the Coming of the Mexican Immigrant," *American Journal of Sociology* 35, no. 1 (January 1930): 601–11.

28 . Mexican anthropologist Manuel Gamio documented it as another crucial time period of Mexican immigration to the United States. See Manuel Gamio, *The Life Story of the Mexican Immigrant: Autobiographical Documents* (New York: Dover Publications, 1971), 1; Gamio, *Mexican Immigration to the United States;* James L. Slayden, "Some Observations on Mexican Immigration," *Annals of the American Academy of Political and Social Science* 93 (January 1921): 123; Meier and Ribera, *Mexican Americans/American Mexicans,* 114–17; David G. Gutiérrez, ed., *Between Two Worlds: Mexican Immigrants in the United States* (Wilmington, DE: SR Books, 1996).

29 . Will J. French, dir., *Mexicans in California: Report of Governor C. C. Young's Fact-Finding Committee* (San Francisco: State of California Department of Industrial Relations, 1930), 35–45.

30. As Matt Meier and Felicano Ribera noted, an estimated one million Mexicans came to the United States as a result of the Mexican Revolution. See U.S. Bureau of the Census, *Population Census 1930* (Washington: GPO, 1933), 498; Meier and Ribera, *Mexican Americans/American Mexicans,* 109; Manuel P. Servín, "The Pre-World War II Mexican-American: An Interpretation," *California Historical Society Quarterly* (1966): 327.

31. French, *Mexicans in California,* 51; Taylor, "Some Aspects of Mexican Immigration," 609–15; Marion Towle, "Mexican Population in San Diego," Minority Survey, circa 1936, Folder 704: Mexicans, 1935 and 1938, Box 16, Federal Writers' Project Collection, Bancroft Library, University of California, Berkeley.

32. Constantine Panunzio, "How Mexicans Earn and Live: A Study of the Incomes and Expenditures of One Hundred Mexican Families in San Diego, California," *University of California Publications in Economics* 13, no. 1 (May 1933): 3–4. Both writer Carey McWilliams and historian Albert Camarillo noted that census data are just estimates, due to the fact that they only include Mexicans who are Spanish speaking. Actual populations are higher than what is reported. See "Mexican Population of California," Folder 3 (Mexicans—California), Box 27, Carey McWilliams Papers, Special Collections and University Archives, University of California, Los Angeles; Albert Camarillo, *Chicanos in a Changing Society: From Mexican Pueblos to American Barrios in Santa Barbara and Southern California, 1848–1930* (Cambridge, MA: Harvard University Press, 1996).

33. Arthur G. Coons and Arjay R. Miller, *An Economic and Industrial Survey of the Los Angeles and San Diego Areas Summary* (Sacramento: California State Planning Board, 1942), 314.

34. See Griswold del Castillo, *Chicano San Diego,* 3; and Mike Davis, Kelly Mayhew, and Jim Miller, *Under the Perfect Sun: The San Diego Tourists Never See* (New York: New Press, 2003).

35. I attended a family reunion in 2006, which enabled me to see the extent that Niland, the Imperial Valley, and San Diego are connected. See David Galbiso, interview with author, Chula Vista, CA, August 4, 2006; and David Galbiso, "Sakada in California's Imperial Valley," 1–5, Galbiso Family Collection, Filipino American National Historical Society (hereafter cited as FANHS), San Diego Chapter Archives.

36. Emory S. Bogardus, "The Mexican Immigrant," *Journal of Applied Sociology* 11 (1926): 471; Mirkowich, "Urban Growth in the San Diego Region," 308–9; and McGrew, *City of San Diego and San Diego County,* 372, 399, and 416–17.

37 . See Richard V. Dodge, "San Diego's 'Impossible Railroad,'" *Dispatcher,* no. 6, June 29, 1956, Railway Historical Society, http://www.sdrm.org/history/sda/history.html (accessed July 3, 2005).

38 . Griswold del Castillo, *Chicano San Diego,* 92.

39 . "U.S. Magnet Lures Mexican Migrants," *San Diego Union,* November 25, 1999, A14, Lateral File: Hispanic Heritage, Thelma Hollingsworth Local History Room, National City Public Library.

40 . Pryde, *San Diego,* 79.

41 . Lanny Villarin, interview with author, National City, CA, May 5, 2004. For more on the experiences of Filipina nurses, see Catherine Ceniza Choy, *Empire of Care: Nursing and Migration in Filipino American History* (Durham, NC: Duke University Press, 2003).

42 . Ngai, *Impossible Subjects,* 100.

43 . See "Fruit Interests Need More Abundant Labor," *Pacific Rural Press,* November 17, 1917, 498; "California's Labor Situation in a Nutshell," *Los Angeles Times,* May 27, 1917, 3; "Growers' Convention Votes to Import Filipino Labor," *Los Angeles Times,* May 17, 1917, 5.

44 . Filipinization was the compromising of U.S. colonialism with regards to Filipinos and how they fashioned democracy under U.S. rule while maintaining a sense of traditional Filipino customs and practices. See Teodoro A. Agoncillo, *History of the Filipino People* (Quezon City, Philippines: Garotech Publishing, 1990), 298–313.

45 . See McWilliams, *Brothers under the Skin,* 234; Takaki, *Strangers from a Different Shore,* 58.

46 . See William Alexander Sutherland, *Not by Might* (Las Cruces, NM: Southwest Publishing Company, 1953); Catherine Ceniza Pet, "Pioneers/Puppets: The Legacy of the Pensionado Program" (BA thesis, Pomona College, 1991); Fred Cordova, *Filipinos: Forgotten Asian Americans* (Seattle: Demonstration Project for Asian Americans, 1983), 125–26; Benicio T. Catapusan, "Problems of Filipino Students in America," *Sociology and Social Research* 26, no. 2 (November–December 1941): 146–53.

47 . "Filipino Students Will Arrive November 10th," *San Diego Union,* November 5, 1903, 3.

48 . See "Filipino Youths Have Arrived," *San Diego Union,* November 13, 1903; "Filipino Students Will Arrive November 10th," *San Diego Union,* November 5, 1903, 3;

"Filipinos Arrive to Be Educated," *Evening Tribune*, November 9, 1903, 1; "Filipino Boys: Nineteen of Them Here for an Education," *San Diego Sun*, November 13, 1903, 1; Sutherland, *Not by Might*, 148–49.

49. "Filipino Students Will Arrive November 10th," *San Diego Union*, November 5, 1903, 3; and "Filipino Boys Hard at Work," *San Diego Union*, November 17, 1903.

50. "Filipino Youths Have Arrived," *San Diego Union*, November 13, 1903.

51. Ibid.

52. "Our New Students," *National City News*, November 12, 1903, 1.

53. "Report of the Philippine Commission," source unknown, 926–27, Binder 2: San Diego County Pensionados—St. Louis World's Fair 1904—Non Pensionado Articles, Ron Buenaventura Collection, FANHS, San Diego Chapter Archives.

54. "Farewells Said by Filipino Students," *San Diego Union*, June 23, 1904, 6; and Adelaida Castillo-Tsuchida, "Filipino Migrants in San Diego, 1900–1946" (MA thesis, University of San Diego, 1979), 43.

55. Service Record of Ciriaco Poscablo, National Personnel Records Center, St. Louis, MO, record obtained December 24, 2004.

56. Leonard Dinnerstein and David M. Reimers, *Ethnic Americas: A History of Immigration* (New York: Columbia University Press, 1999), 88.

57. Riz A. Oades, *Beyond the Mask: Untold Stories of U.S. Navy Filipinos* (National City, CA: KCS Publishing, 2004); Jocelyn Agustin Pacleb, "Gender, Family Labor, and the United States Navy: The Post–World War II San Diego Filipina/o American Immigrant Navy Community" (PhD diss., University of California, Irvine, 2003), 47.

58. Cordova, *Filipinos*, 84–86.

59. Pacleb, "Gender, Family Labor, and the United States Navy," 52.

60. Statement of Brig. Gen. F. LeJ. Parker, Chief of the Bureau of Insular Affairs, before the House Committee on Immigration and Naturalization, *Hearings on H.R. 8708*, April 11, 1930, 88, taken from Bruno Lasker, *Filipino Immigration to Continental United States and Hawaii* (Chicago: University of Chicago Press, 1931), 25.

61. Felix Budhi, quoted in Castillo-Tsuchida, "Filipino Migrants in San Diego" (thesis), 41; and Adelaida Castillo-Tsuchida, "Filipino Migrants in San Diego, 1900–1946," *Journal of San Diego History* 22, no. 3 (Summer 1976): 31.

62. "U.S.S. Boston" (#230-A), San Diego, CA, March 6, 1907, Navy Folder, Photograph Collection, San Diego Historical Society; and Castillo-Tsuchida, "Filipino Migrants in San Diego," 43–46.

63. Judy Patacsil, Rudy Guevarra Jr., and Felix Tuyay, *Filipinos in San Diego* (San Francisco: Arcadia Publishing, 2010), 58, 67–69.

64. Ricardo Romio, interview with author, Lakeside, CA, May 4, 2004.

65. Freddie Ayap, interview with author, National City, CA, August 5, 2004.

66. Fujita-Rony, *American Workers, Colonial Power,* 35–36.

67. According to Yen Le Espiritu, of the one hundred Filipinos she interviewed for her study, approximately 50 percent settled in San Diego because of a parent or other relative who was in the navy. See Espiritu, *Home Bound,* 111; Oades, *Beyond the Mask,* 25.

68. Espiritu, *Home Bound,* 99; and Lasker, *Filipino Immigration to the Continental United States and to Hawaii,* 62–63.

69. Takaki, *Strangers from a Different Shore,* 318.

70. See Lasker, *Filipino Immigration to the Continental United States and to Hawaii,* and Will J. French, dir., *Facts about Filipino Immigration into California, Special Bulletin No. 3* (San Francisco: California Department of Industrial Relations, 1930).

71. Linda España-Maram, *Creating Masculinity in Los Angeles's Little Manila: Working-Class Filipinos and Popular Culture, 1920s–1950s* (New York: Columbia University Press, 2006), 39.

72. Linda Nueva España-Maram, "Negotiating Identity: Youth, Gender, and Popular Culture in Los Angeles's Little Manila, 1920s–1940s" (PhD diss., University of California, Los Angeles, 1996), 22; Fujita-Rony, *American Workers, Colonial Power,* 93–95; and Lasker, *Filipino Immigration to the Continental United States and to Hawaii,* 21.

73. See Castillo-Tsuchida, "Filipino Migrants in San Diego" (article), 28.

74. Castillo-Tsuchida, "Filipino Migrants in San Diego" (thesis), 27, 41. For more photo documentation of early Filipino settlement in San Diego, see Patacsil, Guevarra, and Tuyay, *Filipinos in San Diego,* 11–67.

75. In Ronald S. Buenaventura, "San Diego's Manongs of the 1920s and 1930s," *Filipino American National Historical Society Journal* 5 (1998): 30.

76 . Nena Amaguin, interview with author, San Diego, CA, July 6, 2004.

77 . Vicki L. Ruiz, *From Out of the Shadows: Mexican Women in Twentieth-Century America* (New York: Oxford University Press, 1998).

78 . Irene Rivas, interview with author, San Diego, CA, August 21, 2001.

79 . French, *Facts about Filipino Immigration into California,* 12.

80 . Ibid., 32, 42.This report also noted that both Mexicans and Filipinos had a large influx to the United States, which began in 1923.

81 . Immigration and Naturalization Records, Vols. 1–3, San Diego State University Special Collections. See also Alvarez, *Familia;* J. Blaine Gwin, "Immigration along Our Southwest Border," *Annuals of the American Academy of Political and Social Science* 93 (January 1921): 128.

82 . French, *Facts about Filipino Immigration into California,* 17, 23. For additional statistics, see Lasker, *Filipino Immigration to the Continental United States and to Hawaii,* 347–53.

83 . McWilliams, *Brothers under the Skin,* 235. One of the most famous Filipino labor leaders to come out of Hawai'i was Pablo Manlapit. He was deported to the U.S. mainland as a result of his labor activities in Hawai'i. For more on Pablo Manlapit, see Melinda Tria Kerkvliet, *Unbending Cane: Pablo Manlapit, a Filipino Labor Leader in Hawai'i* (Honolulu: University of Hawai'i Press, 2002).

84 . Paul Scharrenberg, "The Philippine Problem: Attitude of American Labor toward Filipino Immigration and Philippine Independence," *Pacific Affairs* 2, no. 2 (February 1929): 49.

85 . Alvarez, *Familia,* 57–59 and 95–98.

86 . Ibid., 110.

87 . Ngai, *Impossible Subjects,* 64.

88 . "Report to the Labor Council Mexican Immigration Committee," *San Diego Labor Leader,* February 14, 1930, 1, 8, San Diego–Imperial Counties Labor Council Collection, San Diego State University Special Collections.

89 . See H. Brett Melendy, "Filipinos in the United States," *Pacific Historical Review* 3, no. 4 (November 1974): 524; Espiritu, *Home Bound,* 101; Lasker, *Filipino Immigration to the Continental United States and to Hawaii,* 21–22; C. M. Goethe, "Filipino Immigration Viewed as a Peril," *Current History* 34 (June 1931): 353.

90 . Goethe, "Filipino Immigration Viewed as a Peril," 353.

91 . Michael Andrew Lewis, "Ethnic and Racial Violence in San Diego, 1880–1920" (MA thesis, San Diego State University, 1991), 51; and Ngai, *Impossible Subjects*, 108.

92 . Ngai, *Impossible Subjects*, 118–26.

93 . See *Commonwealth* 5, no. 45 (November 5, 1929): 306–79; Francisco E. Balderrama and Raymond Rodríguez, *Decade of Betrayal: Mexican Repatriation in the 1930s* (Albuquerque: University of New Mexico Press, 1996), 53–54; J. M. Saniel, ed., *The Filipino Exclusion Movement, 1927–1935*, Occasional Papers no. 1 (Quezon City, Philippines: Institute of Asian Studies, University of the Philippines, 1967), 9, 32–33; Judge George J. Steiger, "The Filipinos as I Meet Them," *Organized Labor*, March 8, 1930; Ngai, *Impossible Subjects*, 116–17; Melendy, "Filipinos in the United States," 543–45; and Castillo-Tsuchida, "Filipino Migrants in San Diego" (thesis), 90.

94 . See "Filipino Exclusion," *Wall Street Journal*, April 1, 1930, 17; Scharrenberg, "The Philippine Problem," 49–52; Melendy, "Filipinos in the United States," 543–45; Daniel R. Williams, "Philippine Exclusion," *Pacific Affairs* 2, no. 5 (May 1929): 281–83; and "Making Aliens of Citizens of the Filipinos," *Honolulu Advertiser*, January 22, 1929, File 2, Series 2, Box 1, RASL Clippings, Romanzo Adams Social Research Library, University Archives and Manuscripts, University of Hawai'i at Manoa. For more on the issues surrounding Philippine independence, see Fred C. Fisher, "The Moral Aspects of the Philippine Question," *Pacific Affairs* 3, no. 5 (May 1930): 460–69.

95 . "Comments on Filipino Exclusion Bill," *Filipino Nation*, May 1930, 43; and James D. Sobredo, "From American 'Nationals' to the 'Third Asiatic Invasion': Racial Transformation and Filipino Exclusion (1898–1934)" (PhD diss., University of California, Berkeley, 1998), 220.

96 . Samuel Shortridge, quoted in "How the United States Senate Stands on Filipino Exclusion," *Filipino Nation*, May 1930, 42.

97 . Ibid.; and Scharrenberg, "The Philippine Problem," 53.

98 . Shortridge, quoted in "How the United States Stands on Filipino Exclusion," 42.

99 . Aaron M. Sargent, "Survey of Filipino Immigration—Report of Immigration Section," *The Commonwealth* 5, no. 45 (November 5, 1929): 319.

100 . Helen W. Walker, "Mexican Immigrants and American Citizenship," *Sociology and Social Research* 13 (1929): 467.

101 . For more on the racialization of health, see Natalia Molina, *Fit to Be Citizens? Public Health and Race in Los Angeles, 1879–1939* (Berkeley: University of California Press, 2006).

102 . Filipino newspapers, such as the *Filipino Nation*, which was published by the Filipino Federation of America, Inc., had several editorials and commentary pieces attesting to their loyalty to the United States and their desire to be a part of America.

103 . See Howard DeWitt, *Anti-Filipino Movements in California: A History, Bibliography, and Study Guide* (San Francisco: R and E Research Associates, 1979); Howard DeWitt, *Violence in the Fields: California Filipino Farm Labor Unionization during the Great Depression* (San Francisco: Century Twenty-One Publishing, 1980); H. Brett Melendy, "California's Discrimination against Filipinos, 1927–1935," in *Racism in California: A Reader in the History of Oppression*, ed. Roger Daniels and Spencer Colin Jr. (New York: Macmillan, 1972), 147–48.

104 . Carlos Bulosan, *America Is in the Heart* (Seattle: University of Washington Press, 1990), 121; and Carlos Llaralde, "Roberto Galvan: A Latino Leader of the 1940s," *Journal of San Diego History* 52, no. 3 and 4 (Summer–Fall 2006): 154.

105 . Saniel, *The Filipino Exclusion Movement*, 4.

106 . "Candidate for Assembly District for Curtailment of Immigration," *San Diego Labor Leader*, March 14, 1930, 1, San Diego–Imperial Counties Labor Council Collection, Special Collections and University Archives, San Diego State University.

107 . For more on the Tydings-McDuffie Act, see B. Powell, "The Commonwealth of the Philippines," *Pacific Affairs* 9, no. 1 (March 1936): 33–43; Sobredo, "From American 'Nationals' to the 'Third Asiatic Invasion'"; Takaki, *Strangers from a Different Shore*, 331–32; Chan, *Asian Americans*, 55–56.

108 . See James S. Allen, "The Philippine Problem Enters a New Phase," *Pacific Affairs* 11, no. 2 (June 1938): 159–70.

109 . Between 1923 and 1929, an average of 4,177 Filipinos came per year. See French, *Facts about Filipino Immigration into California*, 11.

110 . Benicio T. Catapusan, "Filipino Immigrants and Public Relief in the United States," *Sociology and Social Research* 23, no. 4 (March 1939): 546–54.

111 . See Manuel Buaken, *I Have Lived with the American People* (Caldwell, ID: Caxton Printers, Ltd., 1948), 155–66; and "Filipino Repatriation Movement," 90–100, Repatriation File, NPA, FANHS, Seattle, Washington; and "Repatriation of Filipinos Offered," File 8:2, Carton 3, Federal Writers' Project on Migratory Labor, Bancroft Library, University of California, Berkeley.

112 . Ngai, *Impossible Subjects*, 121.

113 . John F. Wehman, dir., "Filipino Americans: Discovering Their Past for the Future," Filipino American National Historical Society Program Series, 1994.

114 . España-Maram, *Creating Masculinity in Los Angeles's Little Manila*, 42–43.

115 . Letter to Carey McWilliams from Henry B. Hazard, U.S. Department of Justice, Immigration and Naturalization Service, July 27, 1942, Folder 3, Box 8, Carey McWilliams Papers, Bancroft Library, University of California, Berkeley; Emory S. Bogardus, "Filipino Repatriation," *Sociology and Social Research* 21, no. 1 (September–October 1936): 67–71; "Petition to President Roosevelt," *Philippines Mail*, October 8, 1934, in *Asian Americans: Opposing Viewpoints*, ed. William Dudley (San Diego: Greenhaven Press, 1997), 131–34; Carey McWilliams, "Exit the Filipino," *The Nation*, September 4, 1935, 265, Folder 2–20 (Minorities—Filipino), Box 15, Carey McWilliams Papers, Special Collections and University Archives, University of California, Los Angeles; Luciano Mangiafico, *Contemporary Asian Immigrants: Patterns of Filipino, Korean, and Chinese Settlement in the United States* (New York: Praeger, 1988), 37; Melendy, "Filipinos in the United States," 543–45; Ngai, *Impossible Subjects*, 120–25.

116 . "Filipinos Expected to Be Repatriated," *San Diego Union*, March 8, 1936, 10.

117 . Castillo-Tsuchida, "Filipino Migrants in San Diego" (thesis), 24; Paul G. Cressey, *The Taxi-Dance Hall: A Sociological Study in Commercialized Recreation and City Life* (New York: Greenwood Press, 1968), 163; Ngai, *Impossible Subjects*, 122.

118 . Ngai, *Impossible Subjects*, 125; and Zaragosa Vargas, *Crucible of Struggle: A History of Mexican Americans from Colonial Times to the Present Era* (New York: Oxford University Press, 2011), 217.

119 . Vargas, *Crucible of Struggle*, 217.

120 . "Mexican Situation," Los Angeles Chamber of Commerce Interdepartmental Memo to Dr. Clements from Mr. Arnoll, June 16, 1931, Unnamed Folder, Box 80, George P. Clements Papers, Special Collections and University Archives, University of California, Los Angeles; "Mexicans Prefer United States to Free Trip Home," *San Diego Union*, April 22, 1934, 7; Guérin-Gonzales, *Mexican Workers and American Dreams*, 77–94; and Griswold del Castillo, *Chicano San Diego*, 94–95.

121 . Consuelo "Connie" Zuniga, interview with author; Joe Lerma, interview by Rene Zambrano, San Diego, CA, n.d., *U.S. Latinos and Latinas and World War II Oral History Project*, University of Texas at Austin, http://utopia.utexas.edu/explore/latino (accessed October 7, 2005).

122 . Jesus Ochoa, interview by Rene Zambrano, San Diego, CA, April 6, 2001, in *U.S. Latinos and Latinas and World War II Oral History Project,* University of Texas at Austin, http://www.lib.utexas.edu/voces/browse-locale.html?locale World+War+II (accessed October 7, 2005); Joe Lerma, interview by Rene Zambrano, San Diego, CA, n.d., in *U.S. Latinos and Latinas and World War II Oral History Project.*

123 . "Memo to C. P. Visel, Los Angeles Chamber of Commerce," January 8, 1931, Folder: 1932–33 (Mexican Labor and Immigration), Box 80, George P. Clements Papers, Special Collections and University Archives, University of California, Los Angeles.

124 . Vargas, *Crucible of Struggle,* 215–20; Balderrama and Rodríguez, *Decade of Betrayal,* 54–64; Abraham Hoffman, *Unwanted Mexican Americans in the Great Depression: Repatriation Pressures, 1929–1939* (Tucson: University of Arizona Press, 1976), 56–66; Rodolfo Acuña, *Occupied America: A History of Chicanos* (New York: HarperCollins, 1988), 202–6; Douglas Monroy, *Rebirth: Mexicans in Los Angeles from the Great Migration to the Great Depression* (Berkeley: University of California Press, 1999), 147–51; and Paul Spickard, *Almost All Aliens: Immigration, Race, and Colonialism in American History and Identity* (New York: Routledge, 2007), 301–2.

125 . Griswold del Castillo, *Chicano San Diego,* 95.

126 . "Memorandum Regarding Mexican Repatriation in California," n.d. (circa 1930s), Untitled Folder, Box 80, George P. Clements Papers, Special Collections and University Archives, University of California, Los Angeles; letter to Ortiz Rubio, President of Mexico, from J.A.H. Kerr, Los Angeles Chamber of Commerce, June 8, 1931, Folder: 1932–1933 (Mexican Labor and Immigration), Box 80, George P. Clements Papers, Special Collections and University Archives, University of California, Los Angeles; Emory S. Bogardus, "Mexican Repatriates," *Sociology and Social Research* 18, no. 2 (November– December 1933): 174–75, and George Sánchez, *Becoming Mexican American: Ethnicity, Culture, and Identity in Chicano Los Angeles, 1900–1945* (New York: Oxford University Press, 1993), 214.

127 . For more on these statistics, see Ngai, *Impossible Subjects,* 72–75; Griswold del Castillo *Chicano San Diego,* 94; Balderrama and Rodríguez, *Decade of Betrayal;* Paul Taylor, "Mexican Labor in the United States: Migration Statistics 4," *University of California Publications in Economics* 12, no. 3 (1934): 23–50; Hoffman, *Unwanted Mexican Americans in the Great Depression;* Guérin-Gonzales, *Mexican Workers and American Dreams.*

128 . "Jose 'Joe' Galvan Delgado, 89; Began Working Career at Age 12," *San Diego Union-Tribune,* August 23, 1998, B7, Lateral Files: Galvan, Thelma Hollingsworth Local History Room, National City Public Library.

129 . John Rubalcava, interview by Rene Zambrano, September 10, 2000, Chula Vista, CA, in *U.S. Latinos and Latinas and World War II Oral History Project.*

130 . Herb Ibarra, quoted in Richard Louv, "U.S. Magnet Lures Mexican Migrants," *San Diego Union,* November 25, 1979, A14, Lateral File: Hispanic Heritage, Thelma Hollingsworth Local History Room, National City Public Library.

131 . Letters and reports from Mexican consuls in Mexico City, Archivo de la Secretaria de Relaciones Exteriores (AREM), "Repatriation" files, courtesy of Camille Guérin-Gonzales, June 20, 2006. See also Guérin-Gonzales, *Mexican Workers and American Dreams,* 84, 145.

132 . "Indigent Aliens Cost S.D. $16,000 Monthly, Report," *San Diego Union,* July 27, 1934; "Survey of Alien Mexicans to Aid in Repatriation," *San Diego Union,* August 10, 1934; "City Asks U.S. to Provide Funds to Deport Aliens," *San Diego Union,* December 30, 1930, 7.

133 . Guérin-Gonzales, *Mexican Workers and American Dreams,* 84–89; and Griswold del Castillo *Chicano San Diego,* 95–96.

134 . Balderrama and Rodríguez, *Decade of Betrayal,* 105–6; Bogardus, "Mexican Repatriates," 169–76.

135 . Ngai, *Impossible Subjects,* 75 and 120–21.

You Ain't White! The Experience of Middle Eastern Americans

By Rita Stephan

Comedian Maz Jobrani recalls discovering when he was in high school that he was White. Jobrani told CNN that at first he "tried to deny it" (Blake 2010). Jobrani's skin was not white, and his parents spoke with an accent. "Strangers called him 'sheikh' and 'towel-head.' He was living in the San Francisco Bay area during the Iranian hostage crisis in the early 1980s and would occasionally hear, 'Go home, Iranian'" (2010). Jobrani recounts that when he discovered that he was supposed to check the box marked "White" on college applications, he protested to his high school counselor, saying, "What do you mean, white? I've been going through all this … ribbing and teasing for years, and I've been white all this time? You should have told me earlier" (2010). In 2010, Jobrani and other Middle Eastern activists launched the campaign "Check It Right; You Ain't White!"[1] to change how Middle Eastern Americans define themselves on the US census.

In December 2014, the Census Bureau announced its intention to explore creating a Middle Eastern and North African (MENA) category for inclusion in the 2020 census. This is a vitally important measure to correct the problematic undercount of the community. Although Americans of MENA origin share a complex linguistic and cultural heritage, they vary in their self-identification and how others identify them. Current estimate of the population with MENA origins reaches 3.2 million people (Factfinder.census.gov, 2014).

---

1. See "Iranian Census 2010 PSA with Maz Jobrani," www.youtube.com/watch?v=kgoLjFJ0rVg.

THE EMERGENCE OF THE MIDDLE EASTERN COMMUNITY IN THE UNITED STATES

The first North African to be known to have come to the United States was Estebanico Al Azemmouri (Estevanico) in 1527 (Agencia Islámica de Noicias 1998). Later accounts of Middle Easterners arriving from the former Ottoman Empire were mostly from Mount Lebanon, noting the first as Antonios Bishallany, a Maronite Christian, who arrived in Boston Harbor in 1854 ("Middle East," n.d.). Middle Easterners quickly became an integral part of the economic livelihood of the United States, working as peddlers, grocery store owners, and manual laborers. Some settled in major metropolitan areas; others explored the Midwest and the Wild West, paving peddling routes that later became trading networks between cities and small towns across the United States that had never previously seen manufactured products.

Figure 2.1 Photo of a Syrian immigrant named Abraham Swide, circa 1915. Swide was a dry goods peddler, a fairly common occupation for immigrants, many of whom aspired to one day establish their own stores. (Source: Fig. 2.1: Copyright in the Public Domain.)

In 1902, the Chinese Exclusion Act[2] threatened the Middle Eastern population in the United States with possible deportation for being Asiatic. Following directives by the Bureau of Immigration and Naturalization to crack down on the eligibility of certain immigrants for naturalization (which had previously been virtually automatic),

---

2. The Chinese Exclusion Act was the first law implemented to prevent a specific ethnic group from immigrating to the United States.

the courts began to question whether the Syrians' birthplace and racial appearance qualified them as White or, rather, as Asian, and therefore ineligible for citizenship. In several states, petitions of Syrian-born immigrants were challenged on the grounds that, having been born in the dominions of Turkey (Asia Minor) and therefore being of questionable racial stock, the Syrian was not a White person or a person of African descent or birth, as the 1870 statute required (Samhan 1999).

Starting in 1909, legal cases were fought in Georgia, Cincinnati, and St. Louis that brought to the forefront the identity of Middle Eastern Americans. A September 30, 1909, *New York Times* editorial asked, "Is the Turk a White Man?" Syrians, Armenians, and Lebanese sought to disassociate themselves from Asia and be classified as White in order to be recognized as American citizens. While race is no longer an applicable prerequisite to citizenship, all Americans of Middle Eastern or North African origins remain a White ethnic group—a racial identity to which they no longer subscribe.

MENA AMERICANS IN THE CENSUS

The Census Bureau and most other surveys consider MENA Americans as an ethnicity within the White race, but how and why did Middle Easterners become White? In 1910, 1920, and 1930, census takers checked off boxes that reflected official recognitions of linguistic communities residing in the United States. This included Arabic, Hebrew, Turkish, and Armenian, as well as "Near East Arabic dialects" in 1910. For immigrants from the Ottoman Empire before the 1930 census, Turkey was considered the country of "last residence" (for immigration) and "place of birth" (for naturalization); thus, linguistic codes acted as ethnic labels (Arabic, Jewish, Armenian, Assyrian, etc.) for former Ottoman subjects. When the Ottoman Empire officially collapsed, the new labels of Syrian, Lebanese, Iraqi, and Palestinian were used to denote "place of birth." Thus, the evolution and formation of linguistic and ancestry coding has led us to paths of enumeration that are complex on a number of levels.

In 1979, the Census Bureau introduced the ancestry question in response to the growing native-born population in the United States vis-à-vis immigrants. This move created groups based on personal identification with one or more ancestry group. The ancestry data provided demographic, social, economic, and health information on MENA Americans and other Americans. But because the MENA population was significantly undercounted, scholars, activists, and demographers began to claim that the MENA population is invisible and inaccurately counted in federal statistics of ethnic and racial groups in the United States.

In the early 1990s, the Arab American community led the battle over its invisible classification. However, the divergent opinions on the Whiteness of Middle Easterners, as well as disputes over the meaning and value of "Arab" vis-à-vis identifying with the colonial labeling of the region as the "Middle East," led to many contestations of changing the US federal classifications on race and ethnicity. Congressional hearings and negotiations with the Census Bureau highlighted the differences *between* Arab American organizations over self-definitions of community. The race and ethnic standards issued in the 1997 Office of Management and Budget's Statistical Policy Directive No. 15 explicitly classified "a person having origins in any of the original peoples of Europe, North Africa, or the Middle East" as "White."[3]

Although the MENA community was subject to injustice and harassment during the 1990s, the advent of the September 11, 2001, terrorist attacks not only brought undesired hypervisibility to the MENA community as the perceived enemies within, but also increased their insecurity. After the issuance of the PATRIOT Act in October 2001,[4] the community became subject to the targeting of the newly founded Department of Homeland Security (DHS), and the Census Bureau came into the mix by sharing data on Arab Americans with DHS. This incident revealed serious vulnerability in the community and shocked its faith in feeling as an integral part of the American society.

In the war on terrorism, these Americans of MENA origin were caught in a political system in which the United States became at odds with many Middle Eastern countries. MENA Americans who were awkwardly positioned as privileged White, and not recognized as a minority which denied them special rights allotted to minorities such as affirmative action were in fact subject to racial profiling and racist cultural stereotyping and excluded from the racial privileges of the White majority.

To reflect their new reality, the "Check It Right; You Ain't White" campaign spread widely during the 2010 decennial census among Arabs, Iranians, Assyrians, and other MENA groups. People who favored the creation of a separate classification for MENA were numerous. In 2011, a coalition was formed under the leadership of the Arab American Institute; it authored a historical letter to the Census Bureau requesting a MENA box on the census form. The bureau responded by publishing a notice in the *Federal Register*, which received an unprecedented number of favorable responses. In March 2012, and for the first time in the history of the United States, it was proposed that the 2020 census could have a MENA category. The recent move to test and possibly include a Middle Eastern or North African checkbox in the 2020 US Census would be a historic endeavor that would garner much controversy and comment in the media and in the field of race and ethnic studies.

---

3. https://www.whitehouse.gov/omb/fedreg_notice_15https://en.wikipedia.org/wiki/Race_and_ethnicity_in_the_United_States_Census

4. The PATRIOT Act grants US law enforcement and intelligence authorities unprecedented surveillance and investigative powers.

While these organic efforts were trying to gain recognition and visibility, the story changed for the MENA American community. The conflation between Muslims and Middle Easterners became widespread, confusing policymakers, scholars, and citizens alike. With the heating up of the international theater due to the rise of the Islamic State in Iraq and the Levant (ISIL) and its terrorist activities in Europe and the United States, a new theater opened up at home, creating a mélange between Muslim and MENA identities. In response to new policies aimed at protecting Americans from foreign threats, and limiting admission to the United States of immigrants from eight Muslim-majority MENA countries, many MENA American activists decided to shift their self-identification from Arab to Muslim; others began to use the two terms interchangeably; and a third group became marginalized for insisting to separate religion and ethnicity. While MENA is an ethnicity that can be counted, US laws made it illegal to officially track religious affiliations after the advent of the Holocaust in the 1940s. According to the Pew Research Center, about 3.5 million Americans are Muslims; one-quarter of this population consists of native-born African Americans (Mohamed 2016), and one-third of the immigrant Muslim population is Middle Eastern. The vast majority of American Muslims are of Asian heritage (Pew Research Center 2013).

WHO ARE THE MIDDLE EASTERN AMERICANS?

The Middle East, as defined in the coalition letter to the census, includes people with origins in the states of the Arab League, in addition to Turkey, Iran, and Israel. Established in 1945, the League of Arab States currently comprises twenty-two Arabic-speaking nations and enjoys a consultative status in the United Nations. Members of the League include Algeria, Bahrain, the Comoros Islands, Djibouti, Egypt, Iraq, Jordan, Kuwait, Lebanon, Libya, Mauritania, Morocco, Oman, Palestine, Qatar, Saudi Arabia, Somalia, Sudan, Syria, Tunisia, the United Arab Emirates, and Yemen (Suleiman 1999). Linguistic and religious ethnic groups—including the Kurds, Amazigh/Berbers, Assyrians, and Southern Sudanese—existed prior to the formation of the nation-state in many of these countries (Barakat 1993) and are also included as part of the Middle East, as are new ethnic groups that were introduced to the region as a result of historical and political global shifts, such as the Armenians, the Circassians, and the Turcomans (Haddad 2004).

In the 2014 American Community Survey (ACS), an estimated 3.3 MENA Americans lived in the United States, representing 1 percent of the total US population. The majority of this population reported being Arab (1,927,432), Armenian (461,076), Iranian (452,815), Turkish (206,911), Assyrian (107,056), and Israeli (148,514). The MENA American population was more likely than the total US population to have more males than females; the Arab population was 51 percent male and 40 percent female, compared with 49 percent male and 51 percent female for the total US population.

The high representation of males among MENA Americans is possibly reflective of the population's immigration patterns.

The MENA American population is also very young. The median age for this population in the 2014 ACS survey was 35.4 years, compared to the total US population median of 37.4 years. About 48 percent of the MENA American population was born in the United States, compared with 87 percent of the overall US population. Although many MENA Americans are native-born rather than foreign-born (e.g., Arabs and Armenians), their percentages are much lower than they are for other Whites and the total population.

MENA households were more likely than the rest of the US population to be family households, at 69 percent, compared to 66 percent for the overall US population. Likewise, female-headed family households, with no husband present, were more prevalent among Arab households (14 percent) than for all US households (13 percent). [5]

MENA American men and women were more likely to be married compared to the total population. Of the MENA American male population fifteen and older, 54 percent were married, compared to 50 percent of the total US population. MENA American women fifteen and older were also more likely to be married than were all women in the US population (51 percent and 47 percent, respectively). Additionally, the average family size was larger for MENA Americans (3.48), compared to the total US population (3.26).

Children occupy an important place in American society and among MENA Americans. A sign of children's well-being is reflected in the opportunities they have in regard to education. The MENA American population seems to have paid special attention to educating its children, especially girls. In regard to school enrollment, MENA American females are more likely to attend college or graduate school than are the rest of the US female population. About 38 percent of MENA American females are enrolled in college or graduate school, compared with 30 percent of females in the total population. Likewise, 38 percent of MENA American males are enrolled in college or graduate school, compared with 28 percent of males in the total population.

Educational attainments for MENA Americans are also remarkable.[6] Among MENA Americans eighteen years and older, 49 percent of males and 45 percent of

---

5. In the ACS, a *family* is defined as a householder and one or more people living in the same household who are related to the householder by birth, marriage, or adoption. All people in a household who are related to the householder are regarded as members of his or her family. Families are classified by type as either a "married-couple family" or an "other family," according to the sex of the householder and the presence of relatives. The data on family type are based on answers to questions on sex and relationship that were asked of all people (ACS Subject Definition 2010, 75).

6. The Census Bureau regards educational attainments as referring to the highest level of education completed, in terms of the highest degree or the highest level of schooling completed.

females hold a bachelor's degree or higher, compared with 29.9 percent of males and 30.2 percent of females in the total population. Again, due to immigration patterns, one would assume that most of these college degree holders are foreign-born, although the subject requires further statistical analysis.

Median MENA American family income was generally higher than it was for the rest of the US population, at $72,813, compared with $65,910 for the total US population. Alternatively, the poverty rate for MENA American families, at 14.62 percent, was higher than the poverty rate among families in the total population, which was 11.3 percent.[7]

CONTRIBUTIONS OF THE MENA COMMUNITY

MENA Americans have distinguished themselves in every aspect of American life (science and medicine, academia and sports, the arts and politics). In *Arab Americans: Making a Difference*, the late Arab American Casey Kasem (former host of *American Top 40*) lists a number of notable names in politics, such as Congressmen Nick Joe Rahall II (West Virginia), Ray LaHood (Illinois), Charles Boustany (Louisiana), Darrell Issa (California), and Senator John E. Sununu (New Hampshire). He also mentions the activists Ralph Nader, founder of the Green Party, and Candy Lightner, founder of Mothers Against Drunk Driving (MADD). Scientists on his list include the inventor of the heart pump, Dr. Michael DeBakey, and two Nobel Prize winners in chemistry, Dr. Ahmed H. Zewail and Dr. Elias Corey. Among the courageous but unfortunate astronauts on the *Challenger* was Arab American schoolteacher Christa McAuliffe. In business, noteworthy names include Jacques Nasser, the former president and CEO of Ford Motor Company, and Andrew Thomas, president and CEO of Heineken US. In fashion, brands like Haggar (creator of men's apparel), Joseph Abboud, and Reem Acra are worn by celebrities and many other Americans, while in entertainment, stars like Shakira, Tony Shalhoub, Jamie Farr, Marlo Thomas, and Kathy Najimy are among the many names of MENA Americans in the industry.

FINAL WORDS ON MENA IDENTITY

Middle Eastern Americans' construction of their collective identity as hyphenated Americans (just like Mexian-Americans, Asian-Americans) has been complex and full

---

7. Poverty rates, according to the US Census Bureau, reflect the percentage of families whose income in the twelve months prior to participating in the survey fell below the national poverty level, over a period of five years.

of challenges. The hyphenation between Middle Eastern and American is perceived as discordant. Historically, they had to go through a process of proving their Whiteness in order to gain entrance to American society and citizenship. Today, they have to go through a process of proving their patriotism and disassociating themselves from religion or politics in the Middle East in order to be accepted as American compatriots. As sociopolitical trends and forces have changed over the years, their collective identification has shifted from their quest for mere inclusion to a need for special recognition.

With the political awakening that compelled a number of MENA American leadership to mobilize along ethnic and national identities, the contemporary trends have given visibility to their ethnic identity as Middle Easterners and the religion of some as Muslims. The intensifying conflict in the Middle East has affected how they are identified or wish to be identified. While some have expressed a desire to gain recognition for their collective ethnicity, others have wanted to be embraced as Americans with their Islamic religious affiliation. Despite it all, MENA Americans, individually and within their communities, have had remarkable financial and political achievements that are worthy of recognition.

REFERENCES

Agencia Islámica de Noicias. 1998. *Se Confirma la Presencia de Musulmanes Hispanos en la América Precolombina.* www.webislam.com/noticias/41161-se_confirma_la_presencia_de_musulmanes_hispanos_en_la_america_precolombina.html.

American Community Survey. *Code Lists, Definitions, and Accuracy.* https://www.census.gov/programs surveys/acs/technical-documentation/code-lists.html

Barakat, Halim. 1993. *The Arab World: Society, Culture, and State.* Berkeley: University of California Press.

Blake, John. 2010. "Arab- and Persian-American Campaign: 'Check It Right' on Census." *CNN: Defining America*, May 14. www.cnn.com/2010/US/04/01/census.check.it.right.campaign.

Haddad, Yvonne Yazbek, 2004. *Not Quite American?: The Shaping of Arab and Muslim Identity in the United States.* Waco, TX: Baylor University Press.

"Middle East: Introduction." n.d. *Teaching Global Studies.* http://www.fas.harvard.edu/~gstudies/mideast/mecurr.htm.

Mohamed, Besheer. 2016. "A New Estimate of the U.S. Muslim Population." *Fact Tank*, January 6. www.pewresearch.org/fact-tank/2016/01/06/a-new-estimate-of-the-u-s-muslim-population.

Pew Research Center. 2013. *The Religious Affiliation of U.S. Immigrants: Majority Christian, Rising Share of Other Faiths.* www.pewforum.org/2013/05/17/the-religious-affiliation-of-us-immigrants/#muslim.

Samhan, Helen. 1999. "Not Quite White: Race Classification and the Arab-American Experience." In *Arabs in America: Building a New Future*, edited by Michael Suleiman. Philadelphia, PA: Temple University.

Suleiman, Michael, ed. 1999. *Arabs in America: Building a New Future.* Philadelphia, PA: Temple University Press.

PART III

SOCIAL INSTITUTIONS: MAINTAINING INEQUALITIES

UNTITLED
By Luis Xago Juárez de Baktun 12

BEYOND THE WHITE-AND-BLACK, HETERONORMATIVE BINARY: BLACK, LATINX, AND INDIGENOUS PARALLEL EXPERIENCES OF STATE-SANCTIONED POLICING
By Hortencia Jiménez

WHAT DOES IT MEAN TO RETURN HOME? NARRATIVES OF HOPE AND UNCERTAINTY
By Monica Lugo

THE POWER OF (MIS)REPRESENTATION: WHY RACIAL AND ETHNIC STEREOTYPES IN THE MEDIA MATTER
By Mari Castaneda

ALL THAT REFUSES TO CHANGE
By Eduardo Velasquez

UNDOCUMENTED WORKERS AND PRECARIOUS LABOR
By Shannon Gleeson

TRAPPED IN THE WORKING CLASS? LATINO YOUTH STRUGGLE TO ACHIEVE THE AMERICAN DREAM
By Karina Chavarria and Veronica Terriquez

RACE FRAMES AND THEIR IMPACT ON THE SENSE OF BELONGING OF BLACK STUDENTS IN A COLLEGE COMMUNITY
By Anita Davis, Angela Frederick, and Christopher Wetzel

NEPANTLERAS IN A COMMUNITY COLLEGE: STUDENT MOTHERS NEGOTIATING MOTHERING, SCHOOL, AND WORK
By Nereida Oliva and Hortencia Jiménez

Untitled

By Luis Xago Juárez de Baktun 12

Valle de Salinas
Believe us?
Action News Hate

does

"¡Eso y eso!"

Shhh …
Quiet

Con tu
Cuts of

Skin *y Hueso*

Nacidos
AFTER

19-Ninety-
Naaah-Thing

Ahora ya andan

Awarding

Al policía man

Con plaques and
Bass drums,
Acordeones

Y ya que our chiquillos continue to

Die

Mientras
los
States

Lie
Or?

Comply.

Mmm, pues … BREATHE

Beyond the White-and-Black, Heteronormative Binary: Black, Latinx, and Indigenous Parallel Experiences of State-Sanctioned Policing

By Hortencia Jiménez

INTRODUCTION

In the United States, we continue to have a White-and-Black binary that renders Native Americans and Latinxs invisible and contributes to the denial of historical and present-day policing.[1] It is important to bring policing of Latinxs and Native Americans to the forefront of analysis because of its colonial and historical roots. Latinxs are the second largest group killed by police after Blacks, and Native Americans are more likely to be killed by police than any another group in the United States (Males 2014; "The Counted" 2015). Violent policings of Latinxs and Native Americans are not anomalies or isolated cases but embedded in the fabric of US institutions such as the criminal justice system and immigration and customs enforcement, which racialize black, brown, and indigenous bodies. In this chapter, I provide a sociological historical-comparative and contemporary analysis of the parallel experiences of state-sanctioned and racial violence of Native Americans, African Americans, and Latinxs. Comparing the histories of these groups allows us to have a stronger understanding of mob and state violence of

---

1. In this chapter I use *Latinx* to refer to people of Latin American ancestry. Using Latinx, rather than Latino/a or Latin@, disrupts and acknowledges the vast spectrum of gender and sexual identities. The author recognizes that there is no single Latinx experience and that identity is fluid and dynamic.

both groups. This chapter is organized in three parts. The first part provides a snapshot of recent killings of African Americans, Latinxs, and Native Americans at the hands of law enforcement. In the second part, I examine the historical legacy of state violence, while in the third section, I examine immigration policing of both immigrants of color and LGBTQ immigrants. I end with final remarks.

CONTEMPORARY POLICE BRUTALITY AGAINST BLACK, LATINX, AND NATIVE AMERICANS

Abuse and killing by the police are common in Black, Latinx, Native American, and other minority communities (Embrick 2015; Males 2014; Nelson 2000). According to a 2014 report by the Center on Juvenile and Criminal Justice, Native Americans, who account for 0.8 percent of the population, comprise 1.9 percent of police killings. African Americans, who make up 13 percent of the population, are victims in 26 percent of police shootings. Law enforcement kills African Americans at 2.8 times the rate of White non-Latinos, and 4.3 times the rate of Asians (Males 2014). The use of smartphone devices that capture police shootings and then share the images on social networking sites has made it easier to capture, identify, and discuss aggressive policing in our country (Smiley and Fakunle 2016; Taylor 2016).

As of October 2016, there had been 266 killings of Black men. Black males between the ages of fifteen and thirty-four are nine times more likely to be killed by police officers than any other ethnic or racial group in the United States ("The Counted" 2015). The growing list of Black males being killed by police includes Oscar Grant, Eric Garner, Tamir Rice, Alfred Olango, Michael Brown, Trayvon Martin, and John Crawford, among many others. Included in the list of unarmed Black people killed by police are countless Black disabled/deaf victims, such as Darnell T. Wicker, Tanisha Anderson, Sandra Bland, Miriam Carey, Michelle Cusseaux, Ezell Ford, and many others. Darnell T. Wicker, for example, was a Black deaf veteran who was shot multiple times by police officers in Louisville, Kentucky, on August 8, 2016 (Burris 2016). According to the Harriet Tubman Collective (2016), people with disabilities are the largest minority group in the nation, with African Americans having the highest prevalence of disability. Yet the Black Lives Matter movement, in its August 2, 2016, groundbreaking policy platform, failed to mention "the intersection of ableism, audism, and anti-Black racism" (The Harriet Tubman Collective 2016). Black disabled and deaf people account for between 60 and 80 percent of the people murdered by police and are disproportionately impacted by state violence as a consequence of disability. The Harriet Tubman Collective comments that

> ableist social norms often criminalize the existence of dis-
> abilities such as schizophrenia, autism, oppositional-defiant

disorders, and developmental and intellectual disabilities. To be
sure, Black people with these and other disabilities are particularly vulnerable to unjust encounters with school officials, police
officers and the criminal legal system. (2016, para.7)

The Collective further adds that the "liberation will never come without the intentional
centering of Black Disabled/Deaf narratives and leadership. We know this because it
never has" (para. 8). Therefore, the Black Lives Matter movement "that seeks to end
police violence has no choice but to work to undo the racism *and* ableism and audism
which, together, make Black Disabled/Deaf people prime targets for police violence"
(para. 12).

Due to movements as Black Lives Matter, police brutality today is in media headlines. However, this has not been the case for Latinxs, who instead are barely heard
(Balthazar 2015). The national media largely ignores the stories of police shootings of
Latinxs, even when lethal force by police is an inescapable reality and an ongoing issue
in Latinx communities. In 2014, the Center for Juvenile and Criminal Justice noted
that the number of Latinx victims of police killings was 30 percent above the average,
and 1.9 times the rate for Whites (Males 2014). According to the *Guardian*, 306 Latinxs
were killed in 2015, making them the second largest group killed by the police after
blacks ("The Counted" 2015). Yet national news and protests of police brutality against
Latinxs do not spark the kind of outrage seen after the Garner and Brown cases. This
has been seen as early as 2013, with the death of thirteen-year-old Andy Lopez from
Santa Rosa, California, who was shot eight times by police. Immediately, this led to
outrage and protests in Santa Rosa and throughout California, but Lopez's tragedy
remained a local issue, while the killing of twelve-year-old Tamir Rice from Cleveland,
Ohio, received national news. Both of these cases involved children holding toy guns,
and both were declared justified shootings according to the police (Fountain 2016b).

Like African Americans, Latinx deaths are part of a growing list of brown bodies
killed by police—this includes the deaths of Andy Lopez, Anthony Nunez, Pedro
Villanueva, Ruben Garcia Villalpando, Amilcar Perez-Lopez, Jessica Hernandez, and
Antonio Zambrano-Montes, to name a few (Balthazar 2015; Turkewitz and Oppel
2015). According to *The Guardian's* "The Counted" database, as of October 2016,
Latinxs made up 133 of the 824 people killed by law enforcement—these deaths
remain lesser-known stories of police violence in Latinx communities and have not
received sustained and extensive media coverage, except for the Zambrano-Montes
death (Laughland 2015). In addition to analysis written elsewhere, I point to the role
of the Spanish networks such as Univision and Fusion and online digital publishers
such as Remezcla in bringing attention and coverage to Latinx deaths, but the national
mainstream media remains silent on the issue. Stories about Latinxs comprise less than
1 percent of all main news media coverage, and the majority of these stories feature

stereotypical stories of Latinxs as "illegal" immigrants and criminals (Planas 2015b). The mainstream media "can't think of [Latinxs] as victims of police brutality or anything else but immigrants," comments Gustavo Arellano, editor of *OC Weekly* (Planas 2015b, para. 10).

Latinx national leaders have been criticized for ignoring issues of police brutality and for not speaking up against mass incarceration. It is possible that some Latinx leaders ignore police brutality out of fear that concerns of Latinx communities will be associated with Black issues (Fountain 2016b) or that Latinxs will be dismissed as "illegal" in the United States and therefore criminal (Embrick 2015). It was not until October 2015 that the National Council of La Raza (NCLR), the largest Latinx civil rights organization, decided to examine police relations within Latinx communities (National Council of La Raza 2015).

Another group that is excluded and invisible in the discourse of police violence consists of Native Americans, Alaska Natives, and Native Hawaiians. Native Americans make up 0.8 percent of the population, yet they make up 1.9 percent of all police killings. Sociologist David Embrick writes that "2014 came to be silently known as one of the worst times in recent history for Native Americans, who have been subjugated historically to death and violence by a white supremacist state" (2015, 840). The continual marginalization and neglect of Native Americans, as Aaron G. Fountain (2016a) notes, must extend beyond police violence and include discussions of the overrepresentation of Native men and women in the prison system, victims of sexual violence, youth suicide, the murdering and kidnapping of a number of Native women in northern Minnesota, disproportionately high numbers of school suspensions and expulsions of Native youth, and high rates of poverty and unemployment. Native youth have the highest suicide rate of any United States ethnic group; Native adolescent women have a rate four times that of White women in the same age group (Millet 2015).

Native American issues with policing also include complaints about treatment while living and working on the reservation, such as the police targeting people while driving a vehicle that starts with a number 6, which is a marker of identification that the car is registered to a resident of a reservation (Amnesty International 2004; Loevy 2015). At the heart of these social problems is the legacy of colonialism and government policies and practices that have created and exacerbated economic, social, and political inequalities. In a 2015 speech prepared for the Generation Indigenous Convention, former first lady Michelle Obama called attention to the role of the US government and systemic discrimination in the origins of Native Americans' social problems:

> Let me offer just a few examples from our past, starting with
> how, back in 1830, we passed a law removing Native Americans
> from their homes and forcibly relocating them to barren lands
> out west. The Trail of Tears was part of this process. Then we

began separating children from their families and sending them to boarding schools designed to strip them of all traces of their culture, language and history. And then our government started issuing what were known as "Civilization Regulations"—regulations that outlawed Indian religions, ceremonies and practices—so we literally made their culture illegal. (Obama 2015, para. 20)

The Native Lives Matter movement was established in 2014 to bring attention to the aforementioned issues, but unfortunately many people in the United States are unsympathetic to the cause or unaware that it even exists (Fountain 2016a). The movement goes beyond inclusion of Native lives in the conversation of police violence against Blacks and Latinxs to one that acknowledges and situates the experiences of Native Americans within the history and legacy of colonialism, marginalization, and displacement. A recent report by the Lakota People's Law Project reveals that Native Americans' unfair treatment by law enforcement is not limited to isolated incidents but rather is "endemic of a deeply discriminatory justice system. Native American men are admitted to prison at four times the rate of white men and Native women at six-fold the rate of white women" (2015, 1). Additionally, Native Americans, in comparison with other racial groups, are more likely to be killed by police on a per capita basis (Males 2014). The report by the Lakota People's Law Project further accentuates that Native youth are disproportionately affected throughout the juvenile justice system as they suffer from two severe punishments, out-of-home placements and a transfer to the adult system (2015, 4). According to a 2007 report by the Centers for Disease Control and Prevention, children who are transferred to the adult criminal justice system have a 39 percent higher recidivism rate for violent crime, which contributes to the higher arrest and incarceration rate for Native adults.

According to a story by the *Last Real Indians*, an online media outlet, high rates of police violence directed toward the Native American community have not received the same level of attention as did the 2014 demonstrations in response to unarmed Black males being killed (Remle 2014). Within a span of two months in 2014, six Native Americans were killed by the police—Joy Ann Sherman (Lakota), Christina Tahhahwah (Comanche), Myles Roughsurface (Navajo), seven-year-old Hoopa tribal member Allen Locke (Lakota), and Naverone Christian Landon Woods (Gitxsan First Nation). In 2015, thirteen Native Americans were killed in officer-related incidents in the United States. As of October 2016, the tally of killings had already reached the yearly number for 2015. Out of one million people, 5.49 Native Americans are killed; this is a higher rate than the rate for Blacks, at approximately 5.03; for Latinxs, at 2.35; and for Whites, at 2.04 ("The Counted" 2016). While thirteen deaths may seem like a small number, Natives account for only 1 percent of the entire US population, making the small number rather significant (Roetman 2016). The following are some of the Native Americans we have lost because of violent policing: Jamie Lee Brave Heart, Hubert Burns, Loreal Tsingine, Patricia Kruger, and Phillip M. High Bear Sr., among many others. Two widely disturbing cases that received news coverage were the deaths of Paul Castaway, a Sicangu Lakota who was shot by Denver police four times in the torso, and John T. Williams, a homeless woodcarver of the Nuu-chah-nulth tribe who was shot four times by police within seconds of failing to drop a knife and a piece of cedar he was carrying (Millet 2015; Moya-Smith 2015). Castaway suffered from schizophrenia and was experiencing an episode the day he was killed. His mother, Lynn Castaway Eagle Feather, called 911 for help to get him back under control and told the operator that her son was mentally ill (Moya-Smith 2015). John T. Williams also had mental health problems and was deaf in one ear.

Apart from online media outlets such as *Indian Country Today*, major mainstream media outlets continue to neglect Native American issues, thus rendering them invisible, an unfortunate practice that occurs too often and "is not a relic of the distance past" (Fountain 2016a, para. 11); the media suffers from "willful blindness" (Millet 2015, para. 8). The Black-White binary "remains emblematic of the discourse on race relations," even though historical racial conflicts between Native Americans and non-Natives predates those of Blacks and Whites (Fountain 2016a). We "cannot achieve social and racial equality without the inclusion of [the country's] original inhabitants" (Fountain 2016a, para. 13). We must pay attention to Native American lives, as these are "the people who lived here for many thousands of years before this country was founded, and who also have an unalienable right to respect and justice" (Millet 2015, para. 13).

NATIVE AMERICANS, BLACKS, AND LATINXS: THE HISTORICAL LEGACY OF STATE-SANCTIONED VIOLENCE

In this section, I examine briefly the historical legacy of state violence and policing of Native American, Black, and Latinx bodies to jettison the White-Black binary that renders Latinxs and Native Americans invisible. In this chapter, I also accentuate the shared historical parallel experiences of contemporary immigration policing of black and brown immigrants.

NATIVE AMERICANS

It is well documented in the literature the brutal, inhumane, and violent treatment of indigenous peoples throughout the Americas. Before contact with European colonizers, the Americas were home to more than one hundred million indigenous people, but because of slavery, warfare, and diseases, about 95 percent of the population declined during the first two centuries of colonization (Golash-Boza 2015). The Native American way of life and their land were stripped through treaties, the breach of treaties, and force violent displacement on reservations (Olivera, 2009). Spanish explorers and conquistadores, such as Francisco Vásquez de Coronado, Hernando de Soto, and Juan de Oñate, committed massacres against Native Americans starting in the 1500s; this continued with the English explorers in the fifteenth through the nineteenth centuries. Violent massacres, such as Clear Lake (1850), Bridge Gulch (1852), Yontocket (1853), Blue River (1854), Wiyot (1860), Bear River (1863), Sand Creek (1864), Three Knolls (1865), 104 Washita River (1868), Marias (1870), Camp Grant (1871), Cypress Hills (1873), Sappa Creek (1875), Camp Robinson (1878), and Wounded Knee (1890), as well as countless others that took the lives of Native American women, men, and children constitute what is viewed by many Native Americans as genocide (Olivero 2009, 577). The Bear River Massacre is considered to be one of the "deadliest massacres of Native Americans in US history" and continues to remain obscured in history books because it occurred during the Civil War (Duisen 2016). The largest mass execution in US history was signed and ordered by President Abraham Lincoln on December 26, 1862: thirty-eight Dakota Indians were hanged in Mankato, Minnesota, for killing White settlers in the Santee Sioux uprising (Wiener 2012). The Battle of Kelley Creek of 1911, also known as the Last Massacre, is considered to be the last massacre in the twentieth century. *An American Genocide*, written by Benjamin Madley (2016), documents the systematic slaughter of California Indians, estimating that between nine thousand and sixteen thousand Native Americans were killed by vigilantes, state militiamen, and federal soldiers between 1846 and 1873. Recently, Autumn Depoe-Hughes, a descendant of survivors from the Sand Creek massacre in 1864, criticized the media for presenting the June 12, 2016, Orlando Pulse nightclub shooting as the deadliest mass shooting in US history without providing historical context and therefore dismissing the violent treatment of Native Americans at the hands of the US government. As she shared in an interview with *The Oregonian/OregonLive*, "It looked to me like a rewriting of history. I saw my family's history disappearing before my eyes" (Williams 2016, para. 4). She further added that

> presenting the events in Orlando without historical context does a disservice to us all ... especially Native Americans, whose brutal treatment at the hands of the U.S. government has often been given less attention than it deserves (Williams 2016, para. 14)

Violent killings and racial profiling in the United States are older than the contemporary "War on Terror" or the "War on Drugs." "Native Americans, even those who adopted and assimilated to European ways, have frequently been subject to disparate and violent treatment by law enforcement officials since the earliest days of the American colonies" (Amnesty International 2004, 2). In 1974, three Navajo men, Benjamin Benally, John Harvey, and David Ignacio, were murdered by white teenagers who exploded firecrackers on their bodies and tried to burn off their genitalia. David As Correia, associate professor of American Studies at the University of New Mexico, writes,

> The brutal murders were nothing new in Farmington, where white high school students had been known to sever the fingers of inebriated Navajo men and display them proudly in their lockers at school. Murdering and torturing Navajo men and women in the border towns that surround the reservation even has its own name: Indian Rolling. (2015, para. 2)

Correia comments that "Indian Rolling" is another word for lynching, and has been a part of everyday life in Indian Country. He notes that according to a 2004 report by the US Department of Justice, Native people experience violence at a rate twice that of the rest of the population. The vast majority of this violence, more than 70 percent, is committed by people of a different race. This is particularly true in New Mexico, where, according to a 2003 study by the New Mexico Advisory Committee to the US Commission on Civil Rights, Native people experience "acts of ethnic intimidation, threats of physical violence, assaults, and other potential hate crimes," as part of everyday life in border towns like Gallup, Farmington, and Albuquerque (Correia 2015, para. 2)

In 2014, three Albuquerque teenagers wandered in back alleys looking for homeless men, particularly Native homeless, to beat up. Allison Gorman and Kee Thompson were unable to escape and endured violence at the hand of the fifteen- and eighteen-year-olds, who admitted to police that they sought out Native homeless men to victimize (Correia 2015). It is estimated that twenty-five thousand Native Americans live in Albuquerque, New Mexico, accounting for 13 percent of the chronically homeless, who live in a part of town that Albuquerque police call the "War Zone." According to the homeless Native people who live in that part of town, "it's a war waged by police against Native people" (Correia 2015, para. 9). A homeless Native American man succinctly captures police harassment and brutality when he says, "You know I'm an alcoholic and I drink on the streets, and [the police] picked me up and they brought me all the way down to the Bio Park and they beat me up, while I was in handcuffs, and then they unhandcuffed me and let me go" (Correia 2015, para. 10).

The microaggressions are as devastating as the physical violence perpetrated on the bodies of Natives. Another Native man reported that officers would say, "Why don't you go back to the Rez? You're not welcome here in Albuquerque" (Correia 2015, para. 11). These incidents are not anomalies but are common in New Mexico, in towns that border the state's many Indian reservations, observes Correia. As of July 2013, in Gallup, a city in McKinley County, New Mexico, more than 170 Navajo citizens had died of unnatural causes (Correia 2015). In 2014, New Mexico had the highest rate of police killing in the United States, and among New Mexico's police departments, the Albuquerque Police Department had the highest rate of fatal police shootings—one of the highest in the country. More than 20 percent of homicides in Albuquerque in 2014 were committed by police officers.

Contemporary examples of racial profiling include Native Americans displaying tribal tags on their vehicles, as in the case of Louis Gray, former editor of the *Native American Times*; Mary Culley from the Creek Seminole Tribe being profiled coming and going from places where traditional ceremonies have been scheduled; and at airports, as in the case of Gerri McClelland of the Seneca tribe who was subjected to racial profiling. Gerri McClelland was carrying ceremonial turtle shells with her as she traveled to the Seneca reservation in Canada. Security officials insisted that she either take apart her ceremonial objects or check them into baggage where they could be damaged. Ms. McClelland was allowed to board but she chose to forgo her trip for fear that she would face the same racial profiling upon her connecting or return flight (Amnesty International 2004). A more recent act of violence against Native Americans was committed by security guards working for the Dakota Access Pipeline company on September 3, 2016, when at least six people were attacked by dogs, including a young child; dozens of others were pepper-sprayed for peacefully resisting the construction of the $3.8 billion oil pipeline since August 2016. Andy Rowell (2016), in an article written in *EcoWatch*, notes that the violence by the contractors is "state-sanctioned violence against peaceful protesters. The police stood idly by and did nothing" (2016, para. 17–18). The Standing Rock Sioux Tribe and one hundred more tribes from across the United States and Canada joined the efforts in the Camp of the Sacred Stones (Goodman 2016).

AFRICAN AMERICANS

Slave patrols and Night Watchers became the first funded and modern police departments in the American South that were designed to control and regulate the behaviors of slaves.[2] This included searching slave lodges, keeping slaves off roadways, breaking up slave-organized meetings, guarding against slave revolts, and catching runaway

---

2. Night Watchers were volunteer watchers that were assigned to control riots in cities throughout the North in the 1830s.

slaves (Durr 2015; Kappeler 2014).[3] This form of policing was institutionalized in the system of slavery, through laws such as the Fugitive Slave Laws. Virginia, for example, enacted more than 120 slave statues between 1689 and 1865 (Kappeler 2014). Branding was another common violent practice of policing. African and African Diaspora Studies professor Simone Browne, in her book *Dark Matters: On the Surveillance of Blackness*, writes that "branding was a practice of racializing surveillance that sought to deny black human life from being multiply experienced" (2015, 101). Lynching is the epitome of violence against Black bodies. There is a longstanding relationship between lynching and policing in Black communities. According to historical records, it was not uncommon for police officers to take part in the lynching ritual (Russell 2000).

This legacy of policing continued after the Civil War; it became a salient feature during the period of Reconstruction and Jim Crow. Marlese Durr writes that during Reconstruction, federal and state militia, as well as the Ku Klux Klan, emerged from disbanded slave patrols to "preserve individual and societal control over African American citizens" (2015, 875). The transition from slave patrols to publicly funded police departments is formally recognized as the first modern form of policing in the United States (Durr 2015).

Sociology professor David Embrick notes that the "legitimacy given to police agencies represents a rearticulation of slavery and Jim Crow era practices specifically designed to socially control people of color" (2015, 837). By the end of the 1930s, the problem of police violence became more evident as lynchings began to decline (Kelley 2000). Legal scholar Richard Delgado notes that after the Jim Crow era, the power elite turned to the "criminal justice system, mass incarceration, and heavy-handed policing," to "keep minority populations subjugated, afraid, and arrested" (as cited in Attanasio, 2015, para. 21).

Racist policing could not be ignored by the early to mid-1960s, as police violence and rioting escalated throughout US urban centers (Kelley 2000). Organizations such as the Black Panther Party, the Brown Berets, and the American Indian Movement centered their discourse around police repression, arguing that urban communities of color constituted "occupied zones" and/or functioned as "internal colonies" vis-à-vis the US nation-state (Kelley 2000, 38). The policing and criminalization of Black communities must be understood within the context of the decades of the War on Drugs and the effects of mass incarceration (Taylor 2016). The War on Drugs was launched by former president Richard Nixon in the 1970s and further expanded by the Reagan administration during the 1980s. Legal scholar Michelle Alexander calls mass incarceration the New Jim Crow, as the current system of mass incarceration

---

3. These systems of policing also targeted Native Americans; for example, New England settlers appointed Indian constables to police Native Americans, the St. Louis police organization was founded to protect residents from Native Americans in that frontier city (Kappeler 2014).

is a "system of racialized social control [that] purports to be colorblind" (Alexander 2012, 13). African Americans, among other minorities, are forced into what Alexander calls a caste-like system of formal social control, in which they are politically and economically disadvantaged because of their stigmatized label of felon. Alexander argues that the War on Drugs has had a devastating impact on the imprisonment of African Americans and other communities of color. The United States is the world's leader in incarceration with 2.2 million people in prison and jails. Over the last forty years there has been a 500% increase of the United States prison population (The Sentencing Project, 2015). This has led to the highest incarceration rates of all time. Currently, the United States accounts for 5 percent of the world's population but 25 percent of the world's prison population. Most of the prisoners are Black males, who are incarcerated at a rate of six times that of Whites (Alexander 2012; Taylor 2016).

Slave patrols were the forerunners to formal police forces, particularly in the South. This violent history of policing is helpful in contextualizing police brutality and state violence against Blacks, who are more likely than members of other racial groups to be harassed by police, stopped, and questioned and who continue to die at the hands of police. Similar to slave patrols, the Texas Rangers in the Southwest violently and brutally terrorized and policed Native Americans and Mexican Americans, a history that has too often been overlooked (Carrigan and Webb 2013 Gonzalez-Day 2006).[4] I accentuate this history in this chapter.

STATE-SANCTIONED VIOLENCE AGAINST PEOPLE OF MEXICAN DESCENT

One of the most egregious acts of violence against people of Mexican descent has been lynching. Lynching has long been thought of as a Black issue, and this has contributed to an absence of information on cases involving other non-White communities, such as Asians, American Indians, and Latinxs of Mexican and Latin American descent who were lynched in the West (Carrigan and Webb 2013; Gonzalez-Day 2006).[5] Even though the number of cases recorded in the West is considerably smaller than the number recorded in the South, these lynchings were no less dehumanizing, violent, and fatal. It is important to underscore that the story of Mexican lynching is not a "footnote in history but rather a critical chapter in the history of Anglo western expansion and

---

4. Other racial and ethnic minorities in the United States were also lynched, such as Italians, Chinese, Native Americans, and especially Mexicans, second only after African Americans (Carrigan and Webb 2013).

5. Lynching victims were divided into only two categories, Black and White. Included in the "White" category were Native Americans, Chinese immigrants, Italians, and Mexicans (Carrigan and Webb 2003).

conquest" (Carrigan 2003, 414). Between 1848 and 1928, mobs lynched at least 597 Mexicans in the Southwestern states of Texas, California, Arizona, and New Mexico, as well as in states far away from the border, such as Nebraska and Wyoming (Carrigan and Webb 2013).

Local authorities and deputized citizens played a role in mob violence against Mexicans. These included vigilantes, local law officers, and Texas Rangers who executed Mexicans without due process (Gonzalez-Day 2006). The most systematic abuse of legal authority was by the Texas Rangers, who targeted Mexican settlers and indigenous tribes, such as the Waco, Tonkawas, Lipan Apache, Karankawa, Kiowa, and Comanche nations (Carrigan and Webb 2003; Gonzales-Day 2006). Historian Monica Muñoz Martinez comments that the "Texas Rangers targeted the "Indian warrior" and the Mexican vaquero as enemies of White supremacy in the battle to control the region. In their efforts to secure Anglo settlement and a new racial hierarchy, the Rangers also policed Black bodies. They tracked and punished enslaved men and women trying to cross the Rio Grande river into Mexico to escape slavery in the US South, including Texas" (2014, 665).

The lynchings declined by the 1920s, largely because of pressure from the Mexican government. The culture of policing and state violence, however, did not end; it just evolved into what some scholars call "Juan Crow," de facto segregation of Mexican Americans during the 1940s, a period marked by social control (Attanasio 2015) and also mass deportations of the 1930s and 1950s. Chicanos became targets of racial violence and police repression in the decades of the 1930s and 1940s. The zoot suit riots revealed underlying tensions between a growing number of young *pachucos* and White servicemen and police officers in Los Angeles, California.[6] Tensions between the zoot suiters and servicemen escalated in June 1943, when White soldiers engaged in what amounted to a ritualized stripping of the zoot suit worn by Mexican Americans. More than six hundred Chicanos ended up in jail. Although the zoot suiters were victims of White racial violence, the police excused their behavior, explaining that the soldiers were simply "letting off steam" (Kelley 2000, 36). These riots were just the beginning; more followed in the wake of the Sleepy Lagoon case, in which police arrested some three hundred Chicano youths after Jose Dias was found dead near the Sleeping Lagoon, a water reservoir in East Los Angeles. In 1945, the US District Court of Appeals overturned the youths' convictions, acknowledging that they had been railroaded (Kelley 2000).

---

6. *Pachucos* were Mexican American youth who were referred to by the mainstream media as zoot suiters for their style of dress, speech, and countercultural activities. Working-class Mexican American *pachucos* represented defiance, resistance, and determination in creating an identity that was both American and Mexican in their own terms.

BORDER POLICING: FROM TEXAS RANGERS TO ANTI-IMMIGRANT VIGILANTE GROUPS

The Texas Rangers influenced the policing techniques during the expansion of the United States in the Caribbean and became models for the US Border Patrol, the Arizona Rangers, the Civilian Homeland Defense, the Ranch Rescue, and anti-vigilante groups such as the Minutemen (Martinez 2014; Vina, Nunez-Neto, and Weir 2006; Walsh 2008). In the last decade, anti-immigrant organizations have been created in attempts to police the border and to "take the law into their own hands" (Andreas 2006; Walker 2007; Walsh 2008, 20). In 2005, the Minuteman Project received international attention as hundreds of volunteers converged upon a narrow twenty-three-mile stretch of the Arizona-Mexico border to monitor the movements of suspected undocumented immigrants and to "assist" the US border patrol (Walsh 2008, 20). Since the project's founding, civilian patrols have extended to other border states in the Southwest and along the Canadian border (Walsh 2008).

The Minuteman Project is a grassroots vigilante movement dedicated to policing the nation's borders via "border watchers"; they are neither state actors nor state-sanctioned agents, but people who voluntarily enforce and extend many of the principles of governance and statecraft, whether surveillance, policing, security, or territoriality (Walsh 2008, 11). They have been sponsored by right-wing organizers, wealthy ranchers, businessmen, and politicians (Robinson 2006). Racist attacks, scapegoating, and state-sponsored repressive controls over immigrants are hallmarks of the Minutemen (Robinson 2006; Shapira 2013). The Minutemen present the "escalation" of border policing and surveillance following the North American Free Trade Agreement (NAFTA) and the economic liberalization of North America (Walsh 2008). In the 1990s, the United States witnessed a series of border enforcement strategies (i.e., Operation Hold-the-Line, Operation GateKeeper, Operation Safeguard) and expansion of the US-Mexico border via the 2006 Secure Fence Act that authorized the construction of at least seven hundred miles of fencing, including the installation of surveillance cameras (Andreas 2000; Salter 2004). There has also been an increase in budgets for law enforcement and surveillance technology, as well as in the establishment of the Department of Homeland Security (Salter 2004).

IMMIGRATION POLICING

Today, many unauthorized immigrants endure the same racial profiling and policing as native-born Blacks, Latinxs, and Native Americans have. Latin American and Caribbean men are disproportionately criminalized and more likely to be deported; about

88 percent are detained through the US criminal justice system (Golash-Boza 2015). The policing of deportation is seen at the national, regional, and local levels throughout the country (Capps et al. 2011; Hagan Leal, and Rodriguez 2015). Immigration scholars observe that since the mid-1990s, the United States has created laws that make it easier to arrest, detain, and deport immigrants, such as the 1996 Illegal Immigration Reform and Immigrant Responsibility Act (IIRIRA) and the Anti-terrorism and Effective Death Penalty Act (AEDPA), which were signed into law by former president Bill Clinton (Hagan, Leal, and Rodriguez 2015). Following the terrorist attacks of September 11, 2001, former president George W. Bush signed into law the USA PATRIOT Act, which furthered administrative authority to apprehend, detain, and deport immigrants who are perceived as a threat to national security (Salter 2004).

Each year, approximately four hundred thousand foreign-born people in the United States face formal deportation proceedings, which represents close to an eightfold increase since the mid-1990s (Golash-Boza 2015; Hagan, Leal, and Rodriguez 2015). According to Golash-Boza (2015, 6), this wave of immigration enforcement is referred as "mass deportation," as the number of deportees has been higher than in any other period in US history. Although the federal government claims that its deportation campaign is designed to target immigrants who have committed serious violent crimes, most of the removals are noncriminal and target Latinx undocumented workers from Mexico and Central America (Hagan, Castrol, and Rodriguez 2010) and the Caribbean (Golash-Boza 2015). Sociologist Tania Golash-Boza, in her book *Deported* (2015), notes that undocumented Mexicans, Hondurans, Guatemalans, and Salvadorans are more likely to be targeted in worksite and home raids than are undocumented Asians and Europeans, because of stereotypes about who is undocumented and also because there are high numbers of undocumented people among them (Golash-Boza and Hondagneu-Sotelo 2013).

The parallel experiences of African Americans, Latinxs, and Native Americans with the impact of mass incarceration is similar to the policing of immigrants that has been occurring for decades (Golash-Boza 2015). Racism in the criminal justice system has severe implications for Black and Latinx immigrants. For example, Jamaicans, Dominicans, and Haitians, who are phenotypically similar to African Americans, often experience the same racist ideologies and practices that lead to their incarceration (Golash-Boza 2015). Immigration policing is present in immigrant neighborhoods where immigrant men of color live. For example, immigrants from Latin American live in heavily policed Black or Latinx neighborhoods; hence, immigrants of African and Latin American descent get jailed and deported at higher rates than do immigrants of European and Asian descent (Golash-Boza 2015). It is therefore important to understand mass deportation alongside mass incarceration, because the "War on Drugs and the War on Terror work together" (Golash-Boza 2015, 145).

In the last few years, there has been a series of anti-immigrant laws that racially profile and discriminate immigrants, such as Arizona's SB 1070, which was passed in 2010, and Alabama's HB 56, passed in 2011. Immigrants are marked by their skin color and their language, and they experience routine instances of police abuse, such as traffic stops. Maldonado calls this the "hypervisiblity" of Latinxs in public spaces; it is even more noticeable in rural destinations, which makes it impossible for Latinxs to be anonymous (Maldonado 2014).

GENDER NON-CONFORMING IMMIGRANTS

Queer and transgender Latinxs have frequently experienced violence at the borders. According to Human Rights Watch, in the last few years, we have seen queer and transgender people fleeing Latin American countries because of violence. Under US immigration law, transgender women have a valid claim to asylum if they are fleeing their country due to persecution because of their gender identity or gender expression (Stauffer 2016). The US Court of Appeals for the Ninth Circuit ruled in *Avendano-Hernandez v. Lynch* in September 2015, that an undocumented transgender woman from Mexico who had a prior felony conviction could not be deported from the United States because of the high likelihood that she would experience future torture if she were returned to Mexico. In June 2015, Immigration and Customs Enforcement (ICE) provided a new set of transgender detention guidelines that recognizes the vulnerability of transgender people in detention; however, these guidelines lack an independent oversight to ensure their implementation in nearly 250 facilities throughout the United States (Stauffer 2016).

A recent report by Human Rights Watch notes that transgender women, most of them from Mexico, Guatemala, El Salvador, and Honduras, are held in immigration detention centers. ICE officials estimate that on a given day, among a nationally detained population of about thirty thousand migrants and asylum seekers, about sixty-five are transgender women. They have fled their home countries because of torture, sexual violence, and other forms of persecution related to their gender identity or gender expression (Stauffer 2016). In 2016, the US government appeared to move away from holding transgender women in men's facilities and began transferring many to a segregated unit at the Santa Ana city jail in Santa Ana, California, that exclusively houses transgender women (Stauffer 2016). Still, under ICE policy, immigration officials can house transgender women in men's facilities. Many are traumatized because while in detention, they experience humiliating and abusive strip searches by male guards, sexual assault, and unreasonable use of solitary confinement, and are denied access to Medicare treatment, such as hormone replacement therapy and HIV-related care (Stauffer 2016).

Over the years, transgender immigrant activists and allies have led local and national advocacy efforts to improve treatment of transgender women and to advocate for their release from detention. Organizations such as Familia: Trans Queer Liberation Movement (Familia TQLM) and the Transgender Law Center have organized public demonstrations and online social media efforts, including the #FreeMarichuy, #FreeNicoll, and #FreeChristina campaigns, which have brought attention to the plight of detained transgender immigrants (Frankel 2015; Rivas 2014; Stack, 2015). Jennicet Gutiérrez, a transgender woman who is undocumented and a founding member of Familia TQLM, interrupted former president Barack Obama during the White House pride celebration on July 21, 2014, shouting, "There is no pride in how LGBTQ and transgender immigrants are treated in this country," and said that "if the President wants to celebrate with us, he should release the LGBTQ immigrants locked up in detention centers immediately" ("Undocumented Transgender Woman" 2015).

FINAL REMARKS

Since 1492 for indigenous peoples, and since 1619 for people of African descent, communities of color have endured centuries of violence and brutality at the hands of European colonizers, settlers, and later US citizens. "From mass rapes, torture, lynchings, murder, and enslavement to the restricting of movement, employment, and racial classifications, Native peoples and peoples of African descent have endured a constant state of being looked, and acted, upon as being less than" (Remle 2015, para. 10). State violence of the past is very much alive today, from the Minuteman to policing deportations and anti-immigrant legislation. Examining the historical roots of violent policing and current policing perpetuated by the criminal justice system and immigration and customs enforcement allows us to move beyond the White-and-Black binary and see the shared parallel experiences of Natives, Blacks, and Latinxs. Their experiences and struggles are connected, from prison sentences to drug convictions to immigration policing (Alexander 2012; Golash-Boza 2015).

For Latinxs, the conversation needs to address Latinx anti-Blackness, and take a stand against racism, criminalization, state violence, and racial justice. Anti-Black racism needs to be challenged in Latinx communities and unpacked in classroom conversations around race, racism, and systemic oppression. The June 2017 court acquittal of Latinx police officer Yanez who shot and killed Philando Castile in the summer of 2016 while he wore his seatbelt calls for non-Black Latinxs to stand for Black Lives Matter because justice "begins by making Black Lives Matter" (Franco 2017). Amanda Alcantara (2015), journalist and community organizer, calls on Latinxs to join the struggle to dismantle racist systems that incarcerate Black men because this will help in the struggle against detention centers that disproportionately affect Latinx immigrant families. She further notes that just as the Civil Rights Movement benefited Latinxs, the Black Lives Matter movement has the potential to do the same. This is also echoed by Raquel Reichard, politics and culture editor at *Latina* magazine. Reichard writes that "saying black lives matter isn't code for 'all other lives are worthless.' Latino lives are important, but instead of erasing the black struggle through problematic offshoots like 'all lives matter,' we should be supporting the Black Lives Matter movement" (2015). She further adds that when activists declare that Black lives matter, they are saying that all Black people, including Afro-Latinos, are valuable, important, and deserving of justice. Supporting the Black Lives Matter movement facilitates Latinxs' ability to underscore and place at the center of analyses important, nuanced conversations about racial justice and work together with Blacks because their respective "destinies are intertwined" (Garza 2014, para. 12; Reichard 2015).

Suffering police violence and racism is also a lived experience for Native American communities. Gyasi Ross, member of the Blackfeet Indian Nation and Suquamish Nation, calls on national organizations such as the NCAI, NIGA, NARF, and NIEA to get involved with and support Black Lives Matter "while taking care of business within our own Native communities. It's not either/or" (Ross 2015, para. 13). In an article entitled "Indigenous Solidarity with #BlackLivesMatter," Matt Remle, a Hunkpapa Lakota who is a contributing writer to *Last Real Indians*, comments that Native American communities have been able to draw attention to the high rates at which Native peoples have been killed by the police, in part due to the efforts of the Black Lives Matter movement in bringing national attention to the issue of police violence. As he writes, "the message that 'Black Lives Matter' is one which resonates within Native communities, in that we understand the pain, anger and frustration that comes with feeling our lives are somehow less than others, especially when [it comes] to being victims of both state sanctioned and white supremacist violence" (Remle 2015). Native, Latinx, and Black people's lives have historically not mattered "in the eyes of the colonial settler society" (Remle 2015, para. 11). State and police violence have been common features in the lives of Native Americans, African Americans, and Latinxs. The intertwined parallel experiences of Native Americans, Blacks, and Latinxs have the potential to move us beyond differences and recognize commonalities and work toward dismantling systems of oppression that place Latinxs and their families in detention centers and African Americans and Native Americans in the prison system.

DISCUSSION QUESTIONS

1. How does the Black-and-White binary render policing of Native Americans and Latinxs as invisible?

2. Explain the parallel experiences of state-sanctioned and racial violence against Native Americans, African Americans, and Latinxs.

3. Describe immigration policing. What are the similarities and differences between racial profiling and immigration policing? Who is affected, and why?

WEBSITE LINKS

Black Lives Matter: http://blacklivesmatter.com

The Counted: www.theguardian.com/us-news/ng-interactive/2015/jun/01/the-counted-police-killings-us-database

Equal Justice Initiative: www.eji.org

Familia: Trans Queer Liberation Movement: http://familiatqlm.org

Indian Country Today: http://indiancountrytodaymedianetwork.com

Last Real Indians: http://lastrealindians.com

The Sentencing Project: www.sentencingproject.org

Transgender Law Center: http://transgenderlawcenter.org/about/mission

AUDIOVISUAL MATERIALS

Dakota 38, Smooth Feather Productions: http://smoothfeather.com/dakota38

Lost in Detention, PBS: www.pbs.org/wgbh/frontline/film/lost-in-detention

Immigrants for Sale, Brave New Films: www.youtube.com/watch?v=gF12SgkQKKk

Slavery to Mass Incarceration, Equal Justice Initiative: www.youtube.com/watch?v=r4e_djVSag4

We Shall Remain—An American Experience, PBS: www.pbs.org/wgbh/amex/weshallremain

SUGGESTIONS FOR FURTHER READING

Alexander. M. 2012. *The New Jim Crow: Mass Incarceration in the Age of Colorblindness.* New York: The New Press.

Carrigan, W. D., and C. Webb. 2013. *Forgotten Dead: Mob Violence Against Mexicans in the United States, 1848–1928.* Oxford: Oxford University Press.

Golash-Boza, T. 2015. *Deported: Immigrant Policing, Disposable Labor and Global Capitalism*. New York: New York University Press.

Mogul, J., A. Ritchie, and K. Whitlock. 2011. *Queer (In)Justice: The Criminalization of LGBT People in the United States*. Boston: Beacon Press.

Olivero, M. J. 1990. "Native American Massacres." In *Encyclopedia of Race and Crime*, edited by H. T. Greene and S. L. Gabbidon, 577–580. Thousand Oaks, CA: SAGE Publications.

REFERENCES

Alcantara, A. 2015. "#BlackLivesMatter and Anti-Blackness Among Latinxs." *Feministing*. http://feministing.com/2015/01/06/blacklivesmatter-and-anti-blackness-among-latinxs.

Alexander. M. 2012. *The New Jim Crow: Mass Incarceration in the Age of Colorblindness*. New York: The New Press.

Amnesty International. 2004. *Threat and Humiliation: Racial Profiling, Domestic Security, and Human Rights in the United States*. www.amnestyusa.org/pdfs/rp_report.pdf.

Andreas, P. 2006. "Politics on Edge: Managing the US-Mexico Border." *Current History* 105(688): 64–68.

Attanasio, C. 2015. "Latino Lynchings, Police Brutality, and the Challenges of Minority Law-Enforcement." *Latin Times News*.

Balthazar, C. 2015. "Police Brutality Toward Latinos Is Up but Fails to Get Coverage, Undocumented Immigrants Have 'Fear' of Contacting Authorities." *Latin Post*. www.latinpost.com/articles/58930/20150610/police-brutality-latino-community.htm.

Browne, S. 2015. *Dark Matters: On the Surveillance of Blackness*. Durham and London: Duke University Press.

Burris, S. K. 2016. "Kentucky Cops Never Gave Black Man a Chance to Drop His Saw before Shooting Him to Death: Witnesses." *Raw Story*. www.rawstory.com/2016/08/kentucky-cops-never-gave-black-man-a-chance-to-drop-his-saw-before-shooting-him-to-death-witnesses.

Capps, R., M. R. Rosenblum, C. Rodriguez, and M. Chishti. 2011. *Delegation and Divergence: A Study of 287(g) State and Local Immigration Enforcement*. Washington, DC: Migration Policy Institute.

Carrigan, W., and C. Webb. 2003. "The Lynching of Persons of Mexican Origin or Descent in the United States, 1848 to 1928." *Journal of Social History* 37(2): 411–438.

Carrigan, W. D., and C. Webb. 2013. *Forgotten Dead: Mob Violence Against Mexicans in the United States, 1848–1928*. Oxford: Oxford University Press.

Centers for Disease Control and Prevention. 2007. "Effects on Violence of Laws and Policies Facilitating the Transfer of Youth from the Juvenile to the Adult Justice System: A Report on Recommendations of the Task Force on Community Preventive Services." *Morbidity and Mortality Weekly Report (MMWR)* 56(RR-9). www.cdc.gov/mmwr/pdf/rr/rr5609.pdf.

Correia, D. 2015. "Police Violence Against Native People." *CounterPunch*. www.counterpunch.org/2015/06/09/police-violence-against-native-people.

"The Counted: People Killed by Police in the U.S." 2015. *The Guardian*. www.theguardian.com/us-news/ng-interactive/2015/jun/01/the-counted-police-killings-us-database.

"The Counted: People killed by police in the U.S." 2016. Retrieved from www.theguardian.com/us-news/ng-interactive/2015/jun/01/the-counted-police-killings-us-database.

Duisen, M. V. 2016. *10 Horrific Native American Massacres*. http://listverse. com/2016/07/19/10-horrific-native-american-massacres.

Durr, M. 2015. "What Is the Difference between Slave Patrols and Modern Day Policing? Institutional Violence in a Community of Color." *Critical Sociology* 41(6): 873–879.

Embrick, D. G. 2015. "Two Nations, Revisited: The Lynching of Black and Brown Bodies, Police Brutality, and Racial Control in 'Post-Racial' Amerikkka." *Critical Sociology* 41(6): 835–843.

Fountain, A. 2016a. "Native Lives Matter Goes beyond Police Brutality." *Aljazeera America*. http://america.aljazeera.com/opinions/2016/2/native-lives-matter-goes-beyond-police-brutality.html.

Fountain, A. 2016b. "Stop Ignoring the Police Killings of Latinos." *Aljazeera America*. htttp://america.aljazeera.com/opinions/2016/2/stop-ignoring-the-police-killings-of-latinos.html.

Franco, M. 2017. Latinx Anti-Blackness Killed Philando Castile. *Mijennte*. Retrieved on June 16, 2017 from https://mijente.net/2017/06/16/latinx-anti-blackness-killed-philando-castille/.

Frankel, A. 2015. "Dispatches: Fighting to Be Free in the U.S.—Nicoll's Story." *Human Rights Watch*. www.hrw.org/news/2015/03/18/dispatches-fighting-be-free-us-nicolls-story.

Garza, A. 2014. "A Herstory of the #BlackLivesMatter Movement." *The Feminist Wire*. http://www.thefeministwire.com/2014/10/blacklivesmatter-2/.

Golash-Boza, T. 2015. *Deported: Immigrant Policing, Disposable Labor and Global Capitalism*. New York: New York University Press.

Golash-Boza, T., and P. Hondagneu-Sotelo. 2013. "Latino Migrant Men and the Deportation Crisis: A Gendered Racial Removal Program." *Latino Studies* 11(3): 271–292.

Gonzalez-Day, K. 2006. *Lynching in the West: 1850–1935*. Durham, NC: Duke University Press.

Goodman, A. 2016. "FULL Exclusive Report: Dakota Access Pipeline Co. Attacks Native Americans with Dogs & Pepper Spray." *Democracy Now*. www.democracy-now.org/2016/9/6/full_exclusive_report_dakota_access_pipeline.

Hagan, J., B. Castro, and N. Rodriguez. 2010. "The Effects of U.S. Deportation Policies on Immigrant Families and Communities: Cross-Border Perspectives." *North Carolina Law Review* 88: 1800–1822.

Hagan, J., D. Leal, and N. Rodriguez. 2015. "Deporting Social Capital: Implication for Immigrant Communities in the United States." *Migration Studies* 3(3): 370–392.

Laughland, O. 2015. *Pasco Police officers who shot Antonio Zambrano-Montes not questioned for months*. The Guardian. Retrieved from https://www.theguardian.com/us-news/2015/jul/02/pasco-police-officers-who-shot-antonio-zambrano-montes-not-questioned-for-months

The Harriet Tubman Collective. 2016. *Disability Solidarity: Completing the "Vision for Black Lives."* http://harriettubmancollective.tumblr.com/post/150072319030/htcvision4blacklives

Kappeler, V. E. 2014. *A Brief History of Slavery and the Origins of American Policing*. http://plsonline.eku.edu/insidelook/brief-history-slavery-and-origins-american-policing.

Kelley R. D. G. 2000. "Slangin' Rocks ... Palestinian Style: Dispatches from the Occupied Zones of North America." In *Police Brutality: An Anthology*, edited by J. Nelson. New York: W. W. Norton & Company. Pp.21–59.

Lakota People's Law Project. 2015. *Native Lives Matter*. www.docs.lakotalaw.org/reports/Native%20Lives%20Matter%20PDF.pdf.

Loevy, D. 2015. "Do Indian Lives Matter? Police Violence Against Native Americans." *Counter Punch*. www.counterpunch.org/2015/10/29/do-indian-lives-matter-police-violence-against-native-americans.

Madley, B. 2016. *An American Genocide: The United States and the California Indian Catastrophe, 1846–1873*. New Haven and London: Yale University Press.

Maldonado, M. M. 2014. "Latino Incorporation and Racialized Border Politics in the Heartland: Interior Enforcement and Policeability in an English-Only State." *American Behavioral Scientist* 58(14): 28–63.

Males, M. 2014. "Who Are Police Killing?" *Center on Juvenile and Criminal Justice Blog*. www.cjcj.org/news/8113.

Martinez, M. M. 2014. "Recuperating Histories of Violence in the Americas: Vernacular History-Making on the U.S.-Mexico Border." *American Quarterly* 66(3): 661–689.

Millet, L. 2015. "Native Lives Matter, Too." *The New York Times*. www.nytimes.com/2015/10/13/opinion/native-lives-matter-too.html?_r=0.

Moya-Smith, S. 2015. "Police Shoot, Kill Mentally Ill Native American Man; Family Demands Justice." *Indian Country Today*. http://indiancountrytodaymedianetwork.com/2015/07/15/police-shoot-kill-mentally-ill-native-american-man-family-demands-justice-161082.

National Council La Raza. 2015. *And Justice for All: An NCLR Blog Series on Latinos and Policing Practices*. Retrieved from http://blog.nclr.org/2015/09/30/and-justice-for-all-an-nclr-blog-series-on-latinos-and-policing-practices/

Nelson, J. 2000. *Police Brutality: An Anthology*. New York: W. W. Norton & Company.

Obama, M. 2015. Prepared Remarks of First Lady Michelle Obama for White House Convening on Creating Opportunity for Native Youth. The White House, Office of the First Lady. www.whitehouse.gov/the-press-office/2015/04/08/prepared-remarks-first-lady-michelle-obama-white-house-convening-creatin.

Olivero, M. J. 2009. "Native American Massacres." In *Encyclopedia of Race and Crime*, edited by H. T. Greene and S. L. Gabbidon, 577–580. Thousand Oaks, CA: SAGE Publications.

Planas R. 2015a. "Antonio Zambrano-Montes' Death Isn't The First 'Ferguson Moment' for Latinos." *The Huffington Post* 20 February. http://www.huffingtonpost.com/2015/02/20/antonio-zambrano-montes_n_6714466.html

Planas R. 2015b. "Why the media pays less attention to police killings of Latinos." *The Huffington Post*, 24 February. http://www.huffingtonpost.com/2015/02/24/police-killings-latinos_n_6739448.html

Reichard, R. 2015. "5 Reasons Latinos Should Support Black Lives Matter." *Latina*. www.latina.com/lifestyle/our-issues/latinos-should-support-black-lives-matter#5.

Remle, M. 2014. "Six Native Americans Killed by Police in Last Two Months of 2014." *Last Real Indians*. http://lastrealindians.com/six-native-americans-killed-by-police-in-last-two-months-of-2014.

Remle, M. 2015. "Indigenous Solidarity with #BlackLivesMatter." *Last Real Indians*. http://lastrealindians.com/indigenous-solidarity-with-blacklivesmatter-by-matt-remle.

Rivas, J. 2014. "LGBT Activists Protest Abuses Suffered by Transgender Detainee." *Fusion*. http://fusion.net/story/6237/lgbt-activists-protest-abuses-suffered-by-transgender-detaine

Robinson, W. 2006. "Aqui Estamos y No Nos Vamos! Global Capital and Immigrant Rights." *Race and Class* 48(2): 77–91.

Roetman, S. L. 2016. "Number of Native Americans Killed by Police Could Double by End of 2016." *Indian Country Today*. http://indiancountrytodaymedianetwork.com/2016/08/04/native-americans-killed-police-could-double-end-2016-165372.

Ross, G. 2015. "Massacre at Charleston: #BlackLivesMatter for Native People Because History." *Indian Country Today.* http://indiancountrytodaymedianetwork.com/2015/06 /21/massacre-charleston-blacklivesmatter-native-people-because-history-160807.

Rowell, A. 2016. "Dakota Access Pipeline Company Attacks Native American Protesters With Dogs and Mace." *EcoWatch.* www.ecowatch.com/dakota-access-pipeline-dog-attack-1998191259.html.

Russell K 2000. "What Did I Do to Be So Black and Blue?" : Police Violence and the Black Community. In *Police Brutality: An Anthology,* edited by J. Nelson. New York: W. W. Norton & Company. pp. 135–148.

Salter, M. B. 2004. "Passports, Mobility, and Security: How Smart Can the Border Be?" *International Studies Perspectives* 5(1): 71–91.

Shapira. H. 2013. *Waiting for José: The Minutemen's Pursuit of America.* Princeton, NJ: Princeton University Press.

Smiley, C. J., and D. Fakunle. 2016. "From 'Brute' to 'Thug': The Demonization and Criminalization of Unarmed Black Male victims in America." *Journal of Human Behavior in the Social Environment* 26(3–4): 350–366.

Stack, L. 2015. "Activist Removed After Heckling Obama at L.G.B.T. Event at White House." *New York Times.* www.nytimes.com/2015/06/25/us/politics/activist-removed-after-heckling-obama-at-lgbt-event.html?_r=0.

Stauffer, B. 2016. "'Do You See How Much I'm Suffering Here?': Abuse against Transgender Women in US Immigration Detention." *Human Rights Watch.*

Sullivan, L. 2011. "Native Foster Care: Lost Children, Shattered Families." *NPR.* www.npr.org/2011/10/25/141672992/native-foster-care-lost-children-shattered-families.

Taylor, K. Y. 2016. *From #BlackLivesMatter to Black Liberation.* Chicago. Haymarket Books.

The Sentencing Project. "*Fact Sheet: Trends in U.S Corrections.*" http://sentencingproject.org/wp-content/uploads/2016/01/Trends-in-US-Corrections.pdf

Turkewitz, J, & Oppel, R. 2015. *Killings in Washington State Offers 'Ferguson' Moment for Hispanics.* The New York Times. Retrieved from https://www.nytimes.com/2015/02/17/us/killing-in-washington-state-offers-ferguson-moment-for-hispanics.html.

"Undocumented Transgender Woman Who Interrupted President at White House Pride Event Calls to End Deportation." 2015. *#Not1More.* www.notonemoredeportation.com/2015/06/24/whpride.

Vina, S., B. Nunez-Neto, and A. Weir. 2006. "Civilian Patrols along the Border: Legal and Policy Issues." *Congressional Research Service Report,* Library of Congress, September 28.

Walker, C. 2007. "Border Vigilantism and Comprehensive Immigration Reform." *Harvard Latino Law Review* 10: 135–174.

Walsh, J. 2008. "The Case of the Minuteman Project. Surveillance and Governance: Crime Control and Beyond." *Sociology of Crime, Law, and Deviance* 10: 11–34.

Wiener, J. 2012. "Largest Mass Execution in US History: 150 Years Ago Today." *The Nation.* www.thenation.com/article/largest-mass-execution-us-history-150-years-ago-today.

Williams, K. 2016. "Orlando Shooting Headlines Gloss over Native American Massacres." *The Oregonian/OregonLive.* www.oregonlive.com/today/index.ssf/2016/06/orlando_shooting_headlines_glo.html.

What Does It Mean to Return Home? Narratives of Hope and Uncertainty

By Monica Lugo

As she worked on the colorful paper flags she had volunteered to make for the international festival at her son's school, Lucy described how she felt a few years ago, when her husband announced that he was going to Mexico to see his mother one last time. She spoke of feeling great anxiety at that time. For the first time, Lucy confronted the possibility that her husband could not return to Dallas. If that happened, how was she going to pay the monthly rent of their mobile home, cover all their expenses, and care for their two young children all on her own? Despite the uncertainty and anxiety caused by her husband's impending departure, Lucy was clear about one thing: "I think, I think that I won't ... of my own accord I will not return ... (I: You will not return?) Mm, I am telling you, I, of my own free will, I will not return! I will stay here as long as I possibly can!"

Being deported, or deciding to go back to Mexico when life has become intolerable in the United States (Serwer 2012), is perhaps the ultimate consequence of being undocumented in the United States (Abrego 2013). Yet, as the preceding excerpt suggests, for many immigrants who have built their lives in the United States, the experience of leaving may be just as painful as the experience of staying.

In the wake of the September 11 terrorist attacks of 2001, legal changes leading to the criminalization of undocumented immigrants accelerated, and the threat of deportation grew even more pervasive (De Genova 2002). In light of the rapidly evolving legal context, a number of scholars of migration have shifted their focus from studying undocumented immigrants specifically to a systematic examination of the mechanisms by which migrant illegality is produced and sustained (Coutin 2000; De Genova 2002, 2004; Ngai 2004). Several other scholars have focused on the ways in which the increasingly restrictive immigration laws deeply affect the external structure of immigrants' lives (Abrego 2011, 2013; Abrego and Menjivar 2011; Gonzales 2011; Willen 2007). But how do Mexican immigrant women understand and feel about the possibility of leaving? Beyond the frightening realities associated with living in the United States without papers, in what ways would returning to Mexico affect these women's present lives and their imagined futures? These are particularly salient questions within the context of both the current US immigration regime and the economic restructuring of the Mexican state that have resulted in the massive defunding of public health care and public education systems (Galvez 2011).

In this chapter, I examine what it means to return to Mexico for Mexican mothers living in the Dallas metropolitan area without papers. Using data collected from in-depth interviews, I analyze the factors that shape Mexican women's subjective concerns about returning to Mexico. While I examine data from forty-three study participants, for this chapter I focus on the lived experiences of two women to illustrate the interaction between the legally produced condition of illegality (De Genova 2002) and the women's aspirational longings as they shape their desire to remain in the United States. An examination of the narratives reveals that the fear and distress caused by the threat of deportation are significantly shaped by the women's desire to provide and secure educational opportunities for their children.

THE CONTEXT

EDUCATION IN MEXICO

While Mexican public education has been guaranteed by the Constitution of 1917 to be secular, free, and accessible to all (Murillo 1999), the quality of education is poor. According to the director of the National Institute of Educational Assessment (INEE), Sylvia Schmelkes, the average school level in Mexico is secondary education (Brito and Mercado 2014). On average, a Mexican student receives eight years of schooling, compared with about thirteen years in Canada and the United States (Agren 2012). In 2014, Schmelkes made the case that Mexican public schools are failing Mexicans by offering them antiquated and irrelevant curriculum content, which leaves them utterly ill prepared for the challenges of the twenty-first century.

For much of the twentieth century, the provision of social services in Mexico had developed rapidly (Murillo 1999). As part of this development, there was a massive expansion of schooling that was predicated in part on the national post-revolutionary state-building project and in part on the strengthening power of the Mexican state over the power of the Roman Catholic Church. However, since the 1980s and responding to the debt crisis and economic recession, Mexico has aimed at controlling its fiscal deficits through adjustment measures and fiscal restraint. In this context, public education emerged as a sector where the federal government sought to increase efficiencies and reduce expenditures (Murillo 1999). As Schmelkes (2012) observes, one consequence of the fiscal restructuring is that Mexico's public education system has lost its priority in the national social policy agenda. According to the Organisation for Economic Co-operation and Development, an international economic advisory group based in Paris, the state of Mexico's education has put the country at a disadvantage in an increasingly globalized world.

ILLEGALITY, DEPORTABILITY, AND SELF-DEPORTATION IN THE UNITED STATES

Ironically, while globalization has facilitated the circulation of goods, including drugs and weapons, the transnational circulation of persons has become increasingly restrictive (Bauman 1998). Efforts to deal with undocumented Mexican immigrants in recent years have relied on a variety of measures, including an increasingly militarized border (Cornelius 2001 Fassin 2011), the expansion of bureaucratic apparatuses and technologies of surveillance of the borders and the territory (Coutin 1998 Menjivar and Abrego 2012), the promise of a wall that will span the entire US-Mexico border, the widening of legal grounds for deporting individuals (Hagan et al. 2008; Ngai 2004), and the removal of legal barriers that protect undocumented and documented immigrants from deportation (Golash-Boza 2014; Hagan et al. 2008; Ngai 2004). In his analysis of immigrant "illegality," De Genova (2002) contends that in the current US immigration regime, the most effective strategy used in the control of undocumented immigrants is *deportability*, not actual deportation (see also Ngai 2004), even as fears and concerns have grown considerably among immigrants amid the nationwide raids taking place in the wake of the 2016 election. De Genova argues that in the process of rendering Mexicans as "illegal"—and thus deportable—aliens, their illegality "has to be recreated more often than on the occasions of crossing the border" (2002, 437). For instance, immigrants' inability to obtain various forms of state-issued documents; the policing of public spaces, including the places where they work, where they buy food, and where they live; their ineligibility for housing loans, public assistance programs, and health care; and the requirement that they demonstrate their eligibility for employment have had the effect of "transforming even mundane activities into illicit acts" (Coutin 2000; De Genova 2002, 427).

Riding the most recent tide of anti-immigrant sentiment, politicians and legal scholars[1] have pushed for state immigration laws intended to "encourage" undocumented

---

1. Kris Kobach, former secretary of state of Kansas and former law professor, has masterminded a set of controversial anti-immigration laws, such as Arizona's SB 1070 and Alabama's HB 56, as part of what is commonly referred to as the *attrition through enforcement* movement. This legal framework advances the

immigrants to "make the decision" to return home—that is, to self-deport. Referred to as *attrition through enforcement*—or self-deportation—the strategy is built on the notion that local and state officials have the "inherent authority" to dramatically increase the probability of enforcement (Kobach 2007). Up until 2016 many of the proposed policies of attrition had either not passed legislative approval in state legislatures or were declared unconstitutional by the Supreme Court. However, by early 2017 in an effort to crack down on "sanctuary cities," the state of Texas finally succeeded in passing SB4, a measure that among other things penalizes sheriffs and police chiefs who prevent rank-and-file officers from asking about immigration status. While other states, e.g. Florida, North Carolina, etc., have also managed to pass laws designed "to discourage the settlement of illegal aliens and to make it more difficult for illegal aliens to conceal their status" (Kobach 2007; Vaughan 2006), Texas's SB4 is particularly severe in that it will likely result in the racial profiling of individuals by officers who might indiscriminately ask for any individual's immigration status (Alvarez 2017).

DESCRIPTION OF RESEARCH

The data for this chapter come from in-depth, tape-recorded interviews with forty-three Mexican women living and working in the Dallas metropolitan area. The study participants migrated from both rural and urban centers in Mexico. All the study participants migrated to the United States after 1990 and were undocumented at the time of the interviews. All the women had worked as or were employed as domestic workers at the time of the interviews. They were diverse in terms of demographic characteristics (e.g., level of education, age, civil status, number of children), occupational characteristics prior to migration, length of time in the United States, and English-language skills. The Mexican women in this study ranged from twenty-nine to forty-eight years of age. Out of forty-three study participants, only three did not have any formal schooling.

CHILDREN'S EDUCATIONAL OPPORTUNITIES

Studies of family and migration have identified that one of the most important motivations to migrate to the United States is having children (Boehm 2008; Hondagneu-Sotelo and Avila 1997; Salazar-Parreñas 2005). In my study, however, I found that

---

notion that local and state officials have the "inherent authority" to enforce federal immigration laws. The movement's driving principle states that attrition is effectively achieved through raising the probability of enforcement. Kobach currently serves as vice-chair of the "Presidential Advisory Committee on Election Integrity" in the Trump administration.

for the Mexican immigrant women I interviewed, many of whom migrated without children, their children became a motivation to stay (see Hondagneu-Sotelo 1994). For Gisela and Karen, their ability to provide their children with superior educational opportunities compared to their options in Mexico was a particularly strong reason to remain in the United States. Yet, as I listened to their narratives, it soon became clear that the decision to stay in the United States for their children's education was not a particularly easy one to make.

Gisela

Gisela, a forty-two-year-old woman from Cd. Juarez, Chihuahua, described how difficult it was for her to finally make the decision to move to Dallas permanently. While her parents and most of her siblings had migrated to the United States starting in the 1980s, it was not until 2002 that she decided to join them. As a result of the 1986 immigration laws that allowed undocumented immigrants to regularize their immigration status, everyone in her family was either a naturalized US citizen or a legal permanent resident, except Gisela. She explained that she refused to stay permanently in the United States because "I had half my life in Juarez, and if they had petitioned me, it would have meant that my trips to Juarez would have stopped, and I just couldn't do that." At the time, Gisela was a young, single woman who was happy to be striking out on her own. She had her own apartment and owned a small business selling cell phones. After the September 11 terrorist attacks, she recalled, "I began to struggle financially; I couldn't pay the rent." Seeing her struggling for money, her family intensified the pressure for her to migrate, until she finally gave in. In many important respects, life in Dallas was not as easy for her as her siblings had made it out to be. Migrating to Dallas was certainly better for her financially, but it was a blow to her rich social life and her self-esteem. Going out on the weekends with her group of long-time friends was "part of my life! That is what I miss the most about living in Juarez—sitting with my friends over coffee to laugh, and converse." For Gisela, equally challenging as not having a group of longtime friends who were her social equals was the fact that as an undocumented immigrant, her best option for work was domestic service. When asked about this transition, Gisela said, "In Mexico, I was the boss! ... And then you come to the United States, and all you can do is domestic service. ... I can adapt to whatever, as long as ... as long as I have an income to meet my needs, but it is difficult to go down in rank so much!"

A few years after Gisela settled in Dallas permanently, she met a man and became the mother of two girls. At the time of the interview, Gisela had separated from her husband and her daughters were three and five. Listening to Gisela's narrative, you can recognize how her aspirational framework had gradually changed since she first arrived in Dallas. While working as a housekeeper could never be her "dream job," and the meaning she associates with the work had not changed, she had learned to see it as the medium through which she could ensure that her daughters could go to college. When I asked Gisela if she would consider going back to Mexico to raise her daughters, she said, "If I could ... that all of us would go to Mexico, I would do it!" and after thinking for a moment, she added, "but, also, here the museums! The parks! Umm, so much to teach them! That's the difference, the world that can be taught to them here, which we don't have there, unless you live in Mexico City! And you have money, but in Chihuahua, well, what do we have?"

Karen

For Karen, a thirty-three-year-old single mother of a twelve-year-old girl, the decision to stay in the United States was not one she made alone. In 2006, Karen and her then-six-year-old daughter migrated to Dallas, where a few of Karen's siblings already lived. As in Gisela's case, Karen also experienced the far-reaching economic consequences of the terrorist attacks of September 11, as the *maquiladora* where she worked as a human resource specialist went bankrupt. The closing of the *maquiladora* not only affected Karen but her entire hometown of Villa de Arriaga in San Luis Potosi. Without a job, Karen accepted her father's financial support, but soon she realized that her father was determined to control every aspect of her life. For Karen, her migration to Dallas was motivated not so much by economic reasons but more by a desire for autonomy and independence. Yet, as Karen came to find out, in the United States, a job as a nanny/housecleaner would hardly lead her to the independent life she desperately wanted to find.

As the years passed, Karen, however, has grown deeply ambivalent about staying in the United States. On the hand, she sees her prospects in the United States as bleak. Her job caring for other people's children is so dreadful that Karen "prays to God that she doesn't have to do this for the rest of her life." But, with current legal restrictions on employment and the omnipresent threat of deportation, domestic service is for Karen the only available and practical option. On the other, she sees her daughter's future in the United States as "bright" and full of promises. Speaking of such ambivalence, Karen shared:

> Right now, I don't know; I am between a rock and a hard place, because I feel like leaving, but I, here in particular, I see a great future for my daughter, since she is very intelligent; school is going super well, things like that, but for me, outside of working on this, I don't see any future; I don't see anything! ... And now suddenly I get these feelings of leaving, but, aghh, now my daughter says that she won't leave for any reason! Now she won't! ... And I'm like, "What am I going to do?!" ... I mean, yes, I am afraid. ... What if I am? I mean, what if I am limiting

her? I mean, because, obviously, the schools here—she is in the Longfellow; it is an academy—I mean, in Mexico I would have to pay for a private school, because public schools are not good; it necessarily has to be a private school.

This excerpt illustrates that there are several sources to Karen's ambivalence. On the one hand, Karen feels that Mexico's public school system is not equipped to meet her daughter's academic potential. But she is not sure that she can afford a private school in Mexico that would be as good as the Longfellow Academy where her daughter currently attends and which is part of the public independent school district of Dallas. On the other hand, her growing daughter is exerting increasing pressure to be included in her mother's decisions, highlighting the interactive aspect of carework (Kurz 2002, 749). Tellingly, Karen's physical feeling of being tied (*"estoy atada"*) emerges from believing that if she decides to go home, she is harming her daughter's bright future, but if she stays, the violent legal environment (Menjivar and Abrego 2012), one that has criminalized and dehumanized immigrants like her, will hinder hers.

For many Mexican women, to migrate to or to remain in the United States has become a means to deal with the consequences of the economic restructuring of the Mexican state. As part of larger modernization projects, Mexico has adopted neoliberal policies that have resulted in the massive defunding of public education systems (Galvez 2011). Hence, many Mexican women with children have come to see the private school as the only route to a quality education, which most women could not afford if they were to return to Mexico.

CONCLUSION

For Gisela and Karen, two Mexican women living their lives in Mexico, the terrorist attacks of September 11th had a powerful and disruptive effect. While neither of these women ever planned to migrate to the United States, their lives were dramatically altered as their economic prospects in Mexico became severely diminished. Looking for emotional and financial independence they migrated north, only to find that over the years, the decision to stay in the United States and endure the punitive legal environment was as complicated as the decision to return to Mexico. This chapter contributes to the literature on gender, migration, and family ties by illustrating how concern for their children motivates Mexican women to stay in the United States, despite the uncertainty and ambivalence they experience as undocumented workers. Previous research has shown that children are a key motivation for people to migrate to the United States (Boehm 2008; Hondagneu-Sotelo and Avila 1997; Salazar-Parreñas 2005), and my research adds to this literature by revealing how children are a key motivation for immigrants to *remain* in the United States. This chapter sheds light on how concern about their children's educational future is shaped by women's intersecting identities as women, mothers, and undocumented immigrants. In particular, their narratives are imbued with norms about womanhood and motherly sacrifice.

DISCUSSION QUESTIONS

1 . To what extent do the experiences of Lucy, Gisela, and Karen support or contradict the image of the undocumented immigrant as the "criminal alien"?

2 . What is the effect of "deportability" in everyday life? Is it the same for immigrant men as it is for immigrant women?

3 . What does it mean when we say that "illegality" is not a fixed status or the consequence of violating an immigration law but a sociopolitical condition that is constantly produced and maintained?

WEBSITE LINKS/AUDIOVISUAL MATERIALS

Immigration Battle, by Shari Robertson and Michael Camerini (2015): www.pbs.org/independentlens/videos/immigration-battle

"Immigrants in the United States: How Well Are They Integrating into Society?" by T. Jimenez (2011): www.wilsoncenter.org/sites/default/files/integration-Jimenez.pdf

"On Immigration Policy, Partisan Differences but Also Some Common Ground," Pew Research Center, U.S. Politics and Policy (2016): www.people-press.org/2016/08/25/on-immigration-policy-partisan-differences-but-also-some-common-ground

SUGGESTIONS FOR FURTHER READING

Abrego, Leisy. 2014. *Sacrificing Families: Navigating Laws, Labor and Love Across Borders*. Palo Alto, CA: Stanford University Press.
Dreby, Joanna. 2010. *Divided by Borders: Mexican Migrants and Their Children*. Berkeley: University of California Press.
Boehm, Deborah A. 2012. *Intimate Migrations: Gender, Family, and Illegality among Transnational Mexicans*. New York: New York University Press.
Cornelius, Wayne. A. 1992. "From Sojourners to Settlers: The Changing Profile of Mexican Immigration to the United States." In *U.S.-Mexico Relations: Labor Market Interdependence*, edited by J. A. Bustamante, C. W. Reynolds, and R. A. Hinojosa Orjeda, 155–195. Palo Alto, CA: Stanford University Press.

REFERENCES

Abrego, L. J. 2011. "Legal Consciousness of Undocumented Latinos: Fear and Stigma as Barriers to Claims Making for First and 1.5 Generation Immigrants." *Law and Society Review* 45: 337–369.

Abrego, L. J. 2013. *Latino Immigrants' Diverse Experiences of Illegality*. Cambridge, UK: Cambridge University Press.

Abrego L. J., and C. Menjivar. 2011. "Immigrant Latina Mothers as Targets of Legal Violence." *International Journal of Sociology of the Family* 37: 9–26.

Agren, D. 2012. "Education System: Holding Mexico Back, Critics Say." *USA Today*, March 30. http://usatoday30.usatoday.com/news/world/story/2012-03-21/mexico-education/53872544/1.

Alvarez, P. 2017. "Will Texas's Crackdown on Sanctuary Cities Hurt Law Enforcement? *The Atlantic*, June 6. https://www.theatlantic.com/politics/archive/2017/06/texas-sb4.../529194/.

Bauman, Z. 1998. *Globalization: The Human Consequences*. New York: Columbia University Press.

Boehm, Deborah A. 2008. " 'For My Children:' Constructing Family and Navigating the State in the U.S.–Mexico Transnation." *Anthropological Quarterly* 81: 777–802

Brito, O., and A. Mercado. 2014. "Desercion, el Mayor Problema Educativo en Mexico: INEE." *Política*, April 29. www.milenio.com/politica/Desercion-problema-educativo-Mexico-INEE-crimen-falta_de_recursos-politicas_educativas-Sylvia_Shmelkes_0_289771266.html.

Cornelius, W. A. 2001. "Death at the Border: Efficacy and Unintended Consequences of U.S. Immigration Control Policy." *Population and Development Review* 27: 661–685

Coutin, S. B. 2000. *Legalizing Moves: Salvadoran Immigrants' Struggles for U.S. Residency*. Ann Arbor: University of Michigan Press.

Coutin, S. B. 1998. "From Refugees to Immigrants: The Legalization Strategies of Salvadoran Immigrants and Activists." *International Migration Review* 32: 901–25

De Genova, N. P. 2002. "Migrant 'Illegality' and Deportability in Everyday Life." *Annual Review of Anthropology* 31: 419–447.

De Genova, N. P. 2004. "The Legal Production of Mexican/Migrant 'Illegality.'" *Latino Studies* 2: 160–185.

Fassin, D. 2011. "Policing Borders, Producing Boundaries: The Governmentality of Immigration in Dark Times." *Annual Review of Anthropology* 40: 213–226.

Galvez, A. 2011. *Patient Citizens, Immigrant Mothers: Mexican Women, Public Prenatal Care, and the Birth Weight Paradox*. New Brunswick, NJ: Rutgers University Press.

Golash-Boza, T. 2014. "From Legal to 'Illegal': The Deportation of Legal Permanent Residents from the United States." Pp. 203–222 in *Constructing Immigrant "Illegality," Critiques, Experiences, and Responses,* edited by C. Menjivar and D. Kanstroom. Cambridge: Cambridge University Press.

Gonzales, R. G. 2011. "Learning to Be Illegal: Undocumented Youth and Shifting Legal Contexts in the Transition to Adulthood." *American Sociological Review* 76: 602–619.

Hagan, J., K. Eschbach and N. Rodriguez. 2008. "U.S. Deportation Policy, Family Separation, and Circular Migration." *International Migration Review* 42:64–88.

Hondagneu-Sotelo, Pierrette. 1994. *Gendered Transitions: Mexican Experiences of Immigration*. Berkeley: University of California Press.

Hondagneu-Sotelo, P. and E. Avila. 1997. " 'I'm Here, but I'm There': The Meanings of Latina Transnational Motherhood." Pp. 388–414 in *Women and Migration in the*

U.S.-Mexico Borderlands: A Reader, edited by D.A. Segura and P. Zavella. Durham, NC: Duke University Press.

Kobach, K. 2007. "Attrition through Enforcement: A Rational Approach to Illegal Immigration." *Tulsa Journal of Comparative and International Law* 15: 155–163.

Kurz, D. 2002. "Caring for Teenage Children." *Journal of Family Issues* 23: 748–767.

Menjivar, Cecilia and Leisy J. Abrego. 2012. "Legal Violence: Immigration Law and the Lives of Central American Immigrants." *American Journal of Sociology* 117: 1380–1421.

Murillo, M. V. 1999. "Recovering Political Dynamics: Teachers' Unions and the Decentralization of Education in Argentina and Mexico." *Journal of Interamerican Studies and World Affairs* 41: 31–57.

Ngai, M. M. 2004. *Impossible Subjects: Illegal Aliens and the Making of Modern America.* Princeton, NJ: Princeton University Press.

Salazar-Parreñas, R. 2005. *Children of Global Migration: Transnational Families and Gendered Woes.* Palo Alto, CA: Stanford University Press.

Schmelkes, S. 2012. "Los Grandes Problemas de la Educacion Basica en Mexico." *EL INIDE*, January 4. www.inidedelauia.org/2012/01/los-grandes-problemas-de-la-educacion.html.

Serwer, A. 2012. "Self-Deportation: It's a Real Thing and It Isn't Pretty." *Mother Jones*, January 23. www.motherjones.com/mojo/2012/ 01/romneys-self-deporta-tion-just-another-term-alabama-style-immigration-enforcement.

Vaughan, J. 2006. "Attrition through Enforcement: A Cost-Effective Strategy to Shrink the Illegal Population." *Center for Immigration Studies. Accessed May 16, 2015 at http://cis.org/Enforcement-IllegalPopulation.*

Willen, S. S. 2007. "Toward a Critical Phenomenology of 'Illegality': State Power, Criminality and Abjectivity among Undocumented Migrant Workers in Tel Aviv, Israel." *International Migration* 45: 8–36.

The Power of (Mis) Representation: Why Racial and Ethnic Stereotypes in the Media Matter

By Mari Castañeda

As communication systems reach nearly every corner of the world, the mass media matter more than ever, because they influence how people see and understand themselves and others in the world. As a powerful social force that makes the most of visual, audio, and textual techniques, the media have the capacity to shape civil society, its discourses, its policies, and the built environment all around us (Schiller 2014). Therefore, media are not insignificant audiovisual outlets that merely entertain and inform; they are culturally expressive conduits that have the power to transform the popular imaginary into real-world practices of love and hate, peace and violence. Certainly, audiences are not passive robots who merely accept everything that is broadcast to them, but given our societal context in which media images drive so much of the narrative in politics, culture, and economics, it is deeply important to acknowledge the mass media's power, so that we may develop the critical agency necessary to make informed decisions and take appropriate actions. Furthermore, understanding the role of media as a communicative stimulus becomes especially necessary when it comes to deconstructing the media (mis)representation of racial and ethnic populations and the stereotypes that are perpetuated.

This essay examines why racial and ethnic stereotypes in the media matter and their implications. It does so through four sections as an effort to clearly articulate the media's importance, even as digital technologies promise to upend the status quo. The first section lays out the ways in which media representations and misrepresentations have the power to incite cognitive and social impact. The second section discusses the most dominant ethnic and racial stereotypes in the media, and the section thereafter aims to engage with the issue as to how media representations justify racial inequality and discrimination. The final section shows the different ways in which organizations, activists, and young people are working to change the circulation of narratives, because media matter, and it matters how we engage with the media.

THE POWER OF MEDIA (MIS)REPRESENTATION

A few years ago, the founder and director of the National Hispanic Media Coalition, Alex Nogales, argued that the lack of favorable images of Latinos in the United States and the nearly nonexistent access to the airwaves by communities of color placed the US Latino community at significant risk. The risk Mr. Nogales was referring to included the very real threats that Latinos face through physical assaults and deportations, as well as the symbolic violence that permeates across the media landscape, which became especially evident during the 2016 US presidential primaries and in the aftermath of the presidential election, in which the 45th US president attempted to install a Muslim ban and approved executive orders specifically targeting undocumented people. Unfortunately, the lack of diversity across the US media landscape and the racialized caricatures that are often broadcast on the airwaves create a cultural context in which people of color are particularly viewed through a stereotypical lens. In the summer of 2015, for instance, an arts and culture reporter for the New York Times reviewed the television programming created by the prolific cultural audiovisual artist Shonda Rhimes, one of the few African American television writers and producers in Hollywood. In the newspaper review, the reporter asserted that Ms. Rhimes's success and the popularity of her television work was due to its foundation in the "angry Black woman" trope. The stereotypical characterization of this artist and her abundant body of work demonstrated that even historically and culturally sensitive popular culture writers are not impervious to institutional and cultural racism. Additionally, despite Ms. Rhimes's momentous success, the racial stereotypes of Black, Latino, and multiracial people still govern media discourses, even when these people achieve the status of highly regarded media interlocutors.

A larger issue has to do with the fact that racial minorities are not adequately represented in the traditional mainstream media (Castañeda, Fuentes-Bautista, and Baruch 2015). The limited media diversity not only creates limited understanding of the social world, but can also produce real violence—thus the "significant risk" that was noted previously. The anti-immigrant discursive and physical attacks as well as the nonstop Immigration and Customs Enforcement (ICE) deportations authorized by President Barack Obama during his administration have emboldened a plethora of hate speech on the radio dial and hate crimes, particularly against people of color. Although industry representatives argue that media themselves, including popular culture, have little to no power to create material effects in the world, they fail to recognize the data amassed over the years (see Bryant and Oliver 2009). Multiple studies have demonstrated the cognitive and social impact that the media have on everyday people, especially children (Dohnt and Tiggemann 2006; Greenberg and Mastro 2008; Rivadeneyra, Ward, and Gordon 2007). Over time, these children become adults whose values are in part shaped by a media system that in the United States is based on a capitalist, racist, and sexist framework in its content and regulatory processes. For instance, the rise of virulent racist taunts at K–12 schools during the 2016 presidential primaries, especially at sporting events, is the direct result of a political media landscape that utilizes the persuasiveness and pervasiveness of communication systems to espouse a White supremacist ideology that aspires to diminish people of color as legitimate social and political actors.

It is important to acknowledge that the capacity of the media to stereotypically (mis)represent minorities is tied to the history of colonialism and exploitative labor in the United States (Castañeda 2015). Consequently, by marginalizing non-White communities, dominant structures can write these communities out of history as well as hinder their capacity for political-economic agency. This is one of the reasons why so many people of color, Latinos and African Americans in particular, have historically fought ardently for media access. In *Broadcasting Freedom: Radio, War, and the Politics of Race, 1938–1948*, Barbara Savage (1999) argues that black leaders understood the importance of media images and the need to exert influence on their representation. The media are not merely entertainment and information venues, but powerful social forces that impact our material, social, and political realities. She notes that the "highly capitalized white-controlled national media of film and radio" left very few opportunities for African Americans and Latinos to influence the popular images of ethnic communities, and "radio broadcasting remained an inaccessible political medium for the expression of dissident views, especially on race" (1999, 44). Thus, despite the liberal democratic principles of free speech, Savage and other scholars have shown that the media, especially broadcasting, have utilized policy processes to protect the entrenched political and racialized status quo as represented through communication content. Nowhere is this more evident than in the racial and ethnic stereotypes that have permeated the airwaves and print culture, although today such stereotypes are reproduced through specific media practices, such as publicizing the names and faces of criminals of color but not necessarily those of criminals who are White.

RACIAL AND ETHNIC STEREOTYPES IN THE MEDIA

The media are persuasive and pervasive, which is why racial and ethnic stereotypes continue to persist. Digital technology has deepened the omnipresence of and transformed access to media content into a commodity that is available 24/7. Additionally, through individual mobile equipment and spectrum frequency accessibility, individuals can consume audiovisual images virtually, anytime and anywhere. The rise of "reality television" has also transformed popular cultural images from being merely fiction into possible reflections of society. Audiences view the broadcast of racial and ethnic stereotypes as simply reflecting how things (and people) "truly are"; hence, these images are perceived as potentially real and unquestionable. The mainstream reproduction of racial and ethnic stereotypes, and the ways in which they intersect with class, gender, and sexuality in the media, therefore creates the conditions that maintain the status quo and reinforce racist, classist, sexist, and homophobic hegemony. By reinforcing a White supremacist and pro-capitalist ideology in news and entertainment programming, forms of social control can be sustained in which people of color are perceived as largely embodying negative racial and ethnic stereotypes and, consequently, are deemed unworthy of upward mobility or educational resources. Consequently, the subtle (and sometimes not so subtle) message becomes that the places where people of color best belong are prisons, agricultural fields, kitchens, and homeless shelters, but not in positions of power.

In the case of Latinos, regardless of citizenship status, the continuously marketed narrative of deportation to Mexico or somewhere else in Latin America becomes viewed as a political and economic (and apparently not racist) action that bolsters the idea that Mexicans and Mexican-Americans in particular do not belong in the United States, and are unworthy of its resources (Castañeda 2008). Media images create meaning, and as the demographics in the United States, and across the Americas, continue to shift toward more people of color, those images will mean the difference between intersectional inclusion and violent exclusion. By analyzing the discourse and visual iconography of minority stereotypes constructed through mass media, including digital platforms, we can specify the cultural politics of how race, gender, sexuality, and class are segregated and represented as silos by the regime of neoliberal communications. People's lived experiences in fact intersect across these and various other axes, but the mainstream media aim to veil the intersectionality of racial, gender, sexuality, and class realities while continuously reproducing minority stereotypes that reinforce oppressive conditions on and off the airwaves. The symbolic violence of racial formation across US media platforms is especially insidious because it helps define who is and who is not worthy of (cultural) citizenship and access to resources, such as education.

How do the media illustrate the embodiment of sexist, racist stereotypes, and how does this in turn affect how people of color are treated? According to Michael Omi and Howard Winant (1994), racial formations are the result of processes in which multiple forces (political, economic, social, and communicative) influence the significance and substance of racial categories, which then influence notions of racial meanings. Because race is such an enduring category in the United States, even changes to the social context or symbols of stereotypes or racial myths are not enough to eradicate what Chandra Mohanty notes as the underlying presence of racial meaning systems that anchor American culture. Thus, "stereotypes contribute to the racist definitions people of color must ensure vis-à-vis a dominant white, middle-class, professional culture" (Mohanty 2006, 55).

HOW DO MEDIA REPRESENTATIONS JUSTIFY RACIAL INEQUALITY AND DISCRIMINATION?

Racial minority stereotypes in the media vary across ethnic/racial groups, but at their core, there are similarities that cut across all of them. Mass media stereotypes of Latinos, African Americans, Native Americans, and Asian Americans tend to highlight racialized, classed, and sexist notions regarding their sexuality, sociability, intelligence, trustworthiness, and socioeconomic standing. This means that these racial/ethnic groups are consistently represented in the media as hypersexual, violent, unintelligent, dishonest, and consistently poor. The characterization of these groups in these ways creates images and perceptions of who deserves cultural citizenship, to be part of the nation, to be counted as valuable, and to merit recognition as a noteworthy contributor to society (Entman and Rojecki 2001). By representing racial minorities through negative stereotypes, it raises the question as to whether "these people" have a right to the societal resources available to those who are part of a productive populace. With too few media representations that challenge negative characterizations, especially of Latinos, African Americans, and Native Americans, these populations are then granted limited privileges in civil society. The result then becomes that they need to be controlled, managed, subdued, and perhaps even incarcerated or unwelcome in everyday society. The impact is felt not only interpersonally, such as when a young Latina enters a high-end store and is followed throughout, or an African American male is targeted by the police, but also in the kinds of biased policies and practices that are instituted by educational, economic, or political institutions, which ultimately hurt not only minorities in the long run, but White populations as well (Ross and Lester 2011).

The following are some of the more common racial stereotypes that are promulgated by the media, especially about Latinos and African Americans. Latinas are sexualized maids or anchor baby mamas, that is, undocumented women whose sole purpose is to birth children on US soil. Latinos are passive garden workers or alcoholics. African American men are gang members or drug dealers. African American women are prostitutes or junkies. These are just a handful of stereotypes, and others can just as well be listed for Asians and Native Americans. It is important to note that these problematic stereotypes work to subvert the human agency of racialized groups because media representations become transformed into seemingly "real knowledge" and produce the deeply hurtful notion that these racial/ethnic populations deserve to be somewhat outcast (Yosso 2002). Consequently, such media representations create the belief that minority groups lack the capacity to cultivate the fertile political, social, and cultural land of the United States and only White communities have the knowledge and power to deserve the bountiful resources of the nation. Given this history, is there a way to challenge the current context and change the course of the media's future? Yes, there is! As social actors, we the people must care about and actively engage in countering the negative media stereotypes of racial minorities in our everyday discourses, behaviors, and beliefs.

WORKING TO CHANGE THE NARRATIVE, BECAUSE MEDIA MATTER

The fact that minority populations are nearly nonexistent and/or stereotyped in the US media is not inconsequential. The media and the material conditions they embody communicate the importance or lack of importance of racial/ethnic communities, especially with regard to their intellectual and political power. These communities are valued differentially according to the needs of the media sector, the imperatives of the global economy, and the cultural politics of the United States (Castañeda 2015). Media matter, and these issues, especially with regard to stereotypes, must be critically investigated if all people are to be full participants in our social world and in the eradication of media exploitation. Organizations such as the National Hispanic Media Coalition, the Media Action Grassroots Network, and the Center for Media Justice and Free Press are examples of how coalitions can be formed to develop media activist movements that aim to transform our communicative system in the twenty-first century.

The rise of digital technologies is also providing a slew of possibilities, especially for developing counternarratives that challenge the mainstream and create alternative images of racial/ethnic communities. There is a great need to increase positive Latina/o and Latinx media representation, and many immigrant rights activists, media justice advocates, and critical scholars are increasingly understanding how mass communications can work as powerful tools that have the potential to reshape the negative stereotypes and misinformation about people of color and low-income communities that circulate in the mainstream entertainment and news environments, and sometimes create dangerous situations for marginalized communities. It is ironic that Latinos are disproportionately absent from mainstream English-language media sectors, while at the same time young Latinos continue to be the most coveted consumer demographic of the near future (Castañeda 2008). Given the present contradictions in which Latinos are both celebrated as the next top consumers and reviled as the least-wanted citizens, it is more crucial then ever to understand the ways in which the media uses their capitalist practices of representation to divide and conquer communities. We are at a moment when the sociocultural and political milieu is changing once again, and with increasing access to digital media, now is the time to shift the power of representation, to develop more expansive narratives about the rich complexity of race and ethnicity in the United States and beyond.

DISCUSSION QUESTIONS

1. If the media are powerful in creating and sustaining racial/ethnic stereotypes, how can that same power be utilized to challenge stereotypical images?

2. US society has a long history of promulgating particular notions of race, class, gender, and sexuality, but what is at stake for mass media in reproducing those narratives?

3. How can the widespread use of digital technologies and social media both reinforce as well as disrupt problematic narratives about communities of color?

WEBSITE LINKS

Center for Media Literacy: www.medialit.org/reading-room/how-break-stereotype

Media Action Grassroots Network: http://mag-net.org

Media for Social Justice: http://proof.org

National Hispanic Media Coalition: www.nhmc.org

AUDIOVISUAL MATERIALS

Latinos Beyond Reel (educational film documentary), Media Education Foundation

Miss Representation (commercial documentary film), The Representation Project

White Like Me (educational film documentary), Media Education Foundation

SUGGESTIONS FOR FURTHER READING

Behnken, B. D., and G. D. Smithers. 2015. *Racism in American Popular Media: From Aunt Jemima to the Frito Bandito*. Santa Barbara, CA: Praeger.

Dines, G., and J. M. M. Humez. 2011. *Gender, Race, and Class in Media: A Critical Reader*. Thousand Oaks, CA: SAGE Publications.

Pickering, M. 2001. *Stereotyping: The Politics of Representation*. Basingstoke, UK: Palgrave.

Rosenthal, A., D. Bindman, and A. W. B. Randolph. 2016. *No Laughing Matter: Visual Humor in Ideas of Race, Nationality, and Ethnicity*. Hanover, NH: Dartmouth College Press.

REFERENCES

Bryant, J., and M. B. Oliver, eds. 2009. *Media Effects: Advances in Theory and Research*. New York: Routledge.

Castañeda, M. 2008. "The Importance of Spanish-Language and Latino Media." In *Latina/o Communication Studies Today*, edited by Angarhard N. Valdivia. New York: Peter Lang.

Castañeda, M. 2015. "La Lucha Sigue: Latina and Latino Labor in the US Media Industries." *Kalfou* 1(2).

Castañeda, M., M. Fuentes-Bautista, and F. Baruch. 2015. "Racial and Ethnic Inclusion in the Digital Era: Shifting Discourses in Communications Public Policy." *Journal of Social Issues* 71(1): 139–154.

Dohnt, H., and M. Tiggemann. 2006. "The Contribution of Peer and Media Influences to the Development of Body Satisfaction and Self-Esteem in Young Girls: A Prospective Study." *Developmental Psychology* 42(5): 929.

Entman, R. M., and A. Rojecki. 2001. *The Black Image in the White Mind: Media and Race in America*. Chicago: University of Chicago Press.

Greenberg, B. S., and D. E. Mastro. 2008. "Children, Race, Ethnicity, and Media." In *Handbook of Children, Media, and Development*, edited by S. L. Calvert and B. J. Wilson, 74–97. Malden, MA: Wiley-Blackwell.

Mohanty, C. T. 2006. *Feminism without Borders: Decolonizing Theory, Practicing Solidarity*. Durham, NC: Duke University Press.

Omi, M., and H. Winant. 1994. *Racial Formation in the United States: From the 1960s to the 1990s*. New York: Routledge.

Rivadeneyra, R., L. M. Ward, and M. Gordon. 2007. "Distorted Reflections: Media Exposure and Latino Adolescents' Conceptions of Self." *Media Psychology* 9(2): 261–290.

Ross, S. D., and P. M. Lester. 2011. *Images That Injure: Pictorial Stereotypes in the Media*. Santa Barbara, CA: Praeger.

Savage, B. D. 1999. *Broadcasting Freedom: Radio, War, and the Politics of Race, 1938–1948*. Chapel Hill: University of North Carolina Press.

Schiller, D. 2014. *Digital Depression: Information Technology and Economic Crisis*. Urbana: University of Illinois Press.

Yosso, T. J. 2002. "Critical Race Media Literacy: Challenging Deficit Discourse about Chicanas/os." *Journal of Popular Film and Television* 30(1): 52–62.

All That Refuses to Change

By Eduardo Velasquez

Channeling the spirit of Howard Beale,
I refuse to leave you alone
free without a care.

Do you know that the Revolution will not be televised?
There are things going on that three networks won't certify.

When younger generations speak,
Why is it they're stereotyped as obnoxious, weak?

Clamoring for progressive strides,
All that refuses to change eventually dies.

Regarding youth, race, and ethnicity,
Why are politicians, who never took a course in sociology, leading me?

What is the reason for police and school shootings?
The rabbit hole is deep, and to dig deeper yet, I am doing.

I refuse to leave you alone to your living room,
To your TV, your dinner, your domestic worries,
And I will move

Only when you understand the message sent;
      Are you listening?
Your presence is required; we have much to amend.

Undocumented Workers and Precarious Labor

By Shannon Gleeson

According to the International Organization for Migration, an estimated 10 to 15 percent of the 214 million international migrants across the world are undocumented (United Nations 2013). In the United States, approximately 5.4 percent of the civilian workforce is undocumented (Passel and Cohn 2009). This is a global phenomenon fueled by an increase in economic and political insecurity, a continually growing immigration enforcement apparatus, and expanding communication and transportation technology. Since the 2008 recession, the flow of undocumented migrants has slowed somewhat, but has stabilized in the United States (Passel and Cohn 2015).

The 1986 Immigration Reform and Control Act requires employers to verify employee work authorization, or face employer sanctions, which go largely unenforced. Various mechanisms such as I-9 audits, Social Security No-Match letters, the use of the federal e-Verify database, and large-scale workplace raids have been used to ensure compliance, with devastating consequences for affected workers (Kerwin and McCabe 2011). Undocumented workers are overrepresented in industries in the informal economy, such as day labor, where the misclassification of independent contractors abounds. They also often work in industries where the use of temporary agencies and other subcontracted arrangements is common, in order to shift the responsibility of complying with employment authorization and worker protection requirements. Despite their lack of work authorization, it is precisely their vulnerability that often makes them desirable to employers. Undocumented status, conversely, can deter workers from coming forward to complain about poor workplace conditions (Gleeson 2010).

In the United States, undocumented workers face a paradoxical circumstance whereby—despite federal laws that render them deportable—workers are often eligible for federal, state, and sometimes local workplace protections, regardless of their immigration status. This is the case in most all arenas of US labor standards enforcement, with the exception of the contested arena of collective bargaining. In a 2002 Supreme Court decision, *Hoffman Plastics v. National Labor Relations Board*, the majority opinion found that undocumented workers are indeed employees who have the right to engage in collective, concerted activity. However, in the event that they are unlawfully fired for organizing, their lack of workplace authorization means that they are ineligible for backpay. Though limited to the National Labor Relations Act, this decision has had ripple effects across other arenas of rights (Griffith 2012). Meanwhile, labor advocates have fought for agreements that create a firewall between key labor standards enforcement agencies and immigration officials. Yet these memoranda of understanding have been found to be largely ineffective (National Employment Law Project 2016). At the time of this writing, the new administration of Donald Trump has proposed changes to labor and immigration policy that will heighten the precarious position of immigrant workers. The promise to hire fifteen thousand additional immigration agents (Naylor 2017) and remove priorities set by former president Barack Obama will, advocates argue, "reduce willingness to report workplace rights violations" (Francis 2017).

Local context matters for the lives of undocumented immigrants. California, for example, has recently passed added protections for undocumented workers (National Employment Law Project 2013) and prohibitions against collaboration with federal immigration officials under the Trust Act (Ramakrishnan and Colbern 2015). In others states, such as Arizona, undocumented workers face further legal barriers to fair employment, such as the mandatory use of the otherwise voluntary federal e-Verify system. While there is evidence that these restrictions are correlated with a decline in the noncitizen Hispanic population in the state (Bohn, Lofstrom, and Raphael 2013), the data reveal no consistent improved labor market outcomes for other workers (Bohn, Lofstrom, and Raphael 2015). Other local policies, such as higher minimum and living wage standards, provisions to combat wage theft, and even the creation of municipal identification cards, can all benefit the lives of undocumented immigrants.

Though it is often assumed that immigrants take jobs, labor economists have found that they in fact fulfill a largely complementary role in the US labor force (Peri 2010). However, studies such as the three-city 2008 Unregulated Work Survey find that undocumented workers are more likely to earn less, face higher rates of workplace violations, and confront additional obstacles to filing formal claims (Bernhardt et al. 2009). Research also finds that undocumented workers are more likely to work in more hazardous conditions, without earning a premium that other workers often do (Hall and Greenman 2014). Undocumented workers in the United States are eligible to pay taxes through an Individual Taxpayer Identification Number (ITIN). However, despite paying into key benefit systems such as Social Security, Medicare, and unemployment, there is largely no legal way for undocumented workers to later draw on these sources of support (Gardner, Johnson, and Wiehe 2015).

Though they enjoy a whole host of protections, undocumented workers must nonetheless confront an era of mass deportation, which intensified in the mid-1990s following the Antiterrorism and Effective Death Penalty Act and the Illegal Immigration Reform and Immigrant Responsibility Act. Despite his stated priorities to the contrary, from 2009 to 2015, more than half of the immigrants removed during Barack Obama's presidency had no criminal convictions (Department of Homeland Security 2015). Deportation trends are both gendered and racialized. Men and immigrants from Latin America are far more likely to be deported (Golash-Boza and Hondagneu-Sotelo 2013). Golash-Boza attributes this to the "neoliberal cycle," which creates the low-wage jobs that rely on undocumented workers, who are ineligible for most all public benefits, while confronting an enhanced immigration enforcement apparatus that increasingly relies on private actors to uncover and deport workers (Golash-Boza 2015).

The local context for undocumented workers can be critical to determining their opportunity for legalization, other forms of deportation relief and work authorization, and the rights afforded to them at work. The free trade policies in the United States differ from those in Europe, which has largely tied the free flow of labor to the free flow of capital. However, even in Europe, workers can often fall in and out of authorized status, depending on the economic climate in which they find themselves, because migration visas are tied to an immigrant's ability to find work (McKay, Markova, and Paraskevopoulou 2012). In the United States, too, migrants can lose their status quickly if their employer no longer requires their services or their temporary status lapses (Abrego and Lakhani 2015). Though a great deal of migrants arrive under clandestine circumstances, many others also simply fall out of status in this way, or by simply overstaying a tourist or student visa. For the most part, there is no simply way to easily transition into legal status when this happens.

In the United States, three decades have transpired since the last mass legalization program. The 2012 Deferred Action for Childhood Arrival program provided work authorization and deportation relief for more than 750,000 young people (Krogstad 2017), though Obama's 2014 proposal to do the same for parents of US-born and legal permanent-resident children was challenged in the courts and failed. Before leaving office, President Obama also removed the "wet-foot, dry-foot" policy that Cubans so long enjoyed. The current focus in the Trump administration has overwhelmingly been on deportation, building a wall on the border with Mexico, and a xenophobic travel ban, which is currently being contested in the courts.

However, in other countries, such as Spain and Italy, there has been a history of periodic legalizations (Calavita 2005). In places throughout the Global South, where countries often lack the bureaucratic capacity to regulate unauthorized work effectively, workers may also rely on an elaborate underground economy to produce work documents, effectively rendering them what Kamal Sadiq refers to as "paper citizens" (Sadiq 2009). Though often considered a phenomenon limited to international migrants, the experiences of many internal migrants who have circumvented the hukou system, which ties the individual's ability to work and receive key social benefits in China, are also instructive (Friedman and Kuruvilla 2015).

Despite the challenges they face, undocumented workers have been critical to organizing efforts, such as the iconic Justice for Janitors campaign, the current Global Hyatt Boycott, and the ongoing Fight for $15. Many labor unions have also become a central ally for promoting the rights of undocumented workers. While the AFL-CIO—the major labor federation for US unions—has openly embraced the rights of undocumented workers only since 2000 (AFL-CIO 2001), several labor unions today have championed inclusive policies and provided resources for helping undocumented workers access key rights and benefits, such as the 2012 Deferred Action for Childhood Arrivals program and the still-pending 2014 Deferred Action for Parental Accountability proposed policy. "Immigrant unions" (Hamlin 2008), such as the United Food and Commercial Workers, the Service Employees International Union, and UNITE HERE!, have also been critical to turning out voters, and mobilizing even nonvoters to campaign in favor of elected allies and policies that promote the well-being of immigrant workers (Francia and Orr 2014; Kerrissey and Schofer 2013) .

Aside from traditional labor unions, worker centers (including 501(c)3 nonprofit organizations) have provided key legal services to help workers seeking immigration relief and help with contesting workplace violations (Fine 2006). These groups often work in coalition to promote national and international policies that strengthen the rights of undocumented workers. While undocumented workers the world over face many limits to their agency at work and beyond, through the help of civic organizations, they have been successful in winning key victories, such as the right to obtain a drivers' license, the Domestic Worker Bill of Rights, and language in collective bargaining contracts that protects undocumented workers. These nonprofits are critical to what Els de Graauw describes as the process of "making immigrant rights real," helping create new rights and implement existing ones (2016).

DISCUSSION QUESTIONS

1 . In what way does immigration law shape workers' ability to get a job, as well as the protections they have at work?

2 . In what ways do social networks shape labor market experiences for undocumented workers?

3. Despite the challenges that undocumented workers face, how do they exert agency on the job and beyond?

4. How does place and local context shape the experiences of undocumented workers?

WEBSITE LINKS

Migration Policy Institute: www.migrationpolicy.org

Mobilizing Against Inequality: www.ilr.cornell.edu/mobilizing-against-inequality

National Day Labor Organizing Network: www.ndlon.org/en

National Domestic Workers Alliance: www.domesticworkers.org

National Guestworker Alliance: www.guestworkeralliance.org

AUDIOVISUAL MATERIALS

AbUSed: The Postville Raid (2010): www.imdb.com/title/tt1737082

De Nadie (2005): www.imdb.com/title/tt0451698

The Hand That Feeds (2014): www.imdb.com/title/tt2812712

Made in LA (2007): www.imdb.com/title/tt1091814

Sleep Dealer (2008): www.sleepdealer.com

SUGGESTIONS FOR FURTHER READING

Donato, K. M., and A. Armenta. 2011. "What We Know About Unauthorized Migration." *Annual Review of Sociology* 37: 529–543.
Goldring, L., and P. Landolt. 2011. "Caught in the Work–Citizenship Matrix: The Lasting Effects of Precarious Legal Status on Work for Toronto Immigrants." *Globalizations* 8(3): 325–341.
Gomberg-Muñoz, R. 2011. *Labor and Legality: An Ethnography of a Mexican Immigrant Network*. New York: Oxford University Press.
Paret, M., and S. Gleeson. 2016. "Precarity and Agency Through a Migration Lens." *Citizenship Studies* 20(3–4): 277–294.

REFERENCES

Abrego, Leisy J., and Sarah M. Lakhani. 2015. "Incomplete Inclusion: Legal Violence and Immigrants in Liminal Legal Statuses." *Law & Policy* 37(4): 265–293.

AFL-CIO, American Federation of Labor and Congress of Industrial Organizations. 2001. "A Nation of Immigrants (Presented at the AFL-CIO 24th Biennial Convention: Conventions, Revolutions, and Executive Council Statements, Las Vegas, NV, December 2–6)." Washington, DC. www.aflcio.org/aboutus/thisistheafl-cio/convention/2001/resolutions/upload/res5.pdf.

Bernhardt, Annette, Ruth Milkman, Nik Theodore, Douglas Heckathorn, Mirabai Auer, James DeFilippis, Ana Luz González, et al. 2009. "Broken Laws, Unprotected Workers: Violations of Employment and Labor Laws in America's Cities." Center for Urban Economic Development, National Employment Law Project, and the UCLA Institute for Research on Labor and Employment. http://nelp.3cdn.net/319982941a5496c741_9qm6b92kg.pdf.

Bohn, Sarah, Magnus Lofstrom, and Steven Raphael. 2013. "Did the 2007 Legal Arizona Workers Act Reduce the State's Unauthorized Immigrant Population?" *Review of Economics and Statistics* 96(2): 258–269.

Bohn, Sarah, Magnus Lofstrom, and Steven Raphael. 2015. "Do E-Verify Mandates Improve Labor Market Outcomes of Low-Skilled Native and Legal Immigrant Workers?" *Southern Economic Journal* 81(4): 960–979. doi:10.1002/soej.12019.

Calavita, Kitty. 2005. *Immigrants at the Margins: Law, Race, and Exclusion in Southern Europe*. Cambridge: Cambridge University Press.

de Graauw, Els. 2016. *Making Immigrant Rights Real: Nonprofits and the Politics of Integration in San Francisco*. Ithaca, NY: Cornell University Press.

Department of Homeland Security. 2015. "Yearbook of Immigration Statistics 2015." www.dhs.gov/immigration-statistics/yearbook/2015.

Fine, Janice. 2006. *Worker Centers: Organizing Communities at the Edge of the Dream*. Ithaca, NY: ILR Press.

Francia, Peter L., and Susan Orr. 2014. "Labor Unions and the Mobilization of Latino Voters: Can the Dinosaur Awaken the Sleeping Giant?" *Political Research Quarterly* 67(4): 943–956. doi:10.1177/1065912914544036.

Francis, Laura D. 2017. "Fear of Immigration Raids May Harm Workplace Rights." *Bloomberg BNA*.

Friedman, Eli, and Sarosh Kuruvilla. 2015. "Experimentation and Decentralization in China's Labor Relations." *Human Relations* 68(2): 181–195. doi:10.1177/0018726714552087.

Gardner, Matthew, Sebastian Johnson, and Meg Wiehe. 2015. "Undocumented Immigrants' State & Local Tax Contributions." The Institute on Taxation & Economic Policy. www.itepnet.org/pdf/undocumentedtaxes2015.pdf.

Gleeson, Shannon. 2010. "Labor Rights for All? The Role of Undocumented Immigrant Status for Worker Claims-Making." *Law and Social Inquiry* 35(3): 561–602.

Golash-Boza, Tanya. 2015. *Deported: Policing Immigrants, Disposable Labor and Global Capitalism*. New York: NYU Press.

Golash-Boza, Tanya, and Pierrette Hondagneu-Sotelo. 2013. "Latino Immigrant Men and the Deportation Crisis: A Gendered Racial Removal Program." *Latino Studies* 11(3): 271–292.

Griffith, Kati L. 2012. "Undocumented Workers: Crossing the Borders of Immigration and Workplace Law." *Cornell Journal of Law and Public Policy* 21: 611–697.

Hall, Matthew, and Emily Greenman. 2014. "The Occupational Cost of Being Illegal in the United States: Legal Status, Job Hazards, and Compensating Differentials." *International Migration Review*, April, 1–37.

Hamlin, Rebecca. 2008. "Immigrants at Work: Labor Unions and Non-Citizen Members." In *Civic Hopes and Political Realities: Immigrants, Community Organizations, and Political Engagement*, edited by S. Karthick Ramakrishnan and Irene Bloemraad, 300–322. New York: Russell Sage Foundation Press.

Kerrissey, Jasmine, and Evan Schofer. 2013. "Union Membership and Political Participation in the United States." *Social Forces* 91: 895–928. doi:10.1093/sf/sos187.

Kerwin, Donald M, and Kristen McCabe. 2011. "Labor Standards Enforcement and Low-Wage Immigrants: Creating an Effective Enforcement System." Washington, DC: Migration Policy Institute. http://www.migrationpolicy.org/pubs/laborstandards-2011.pdf.

Krogstad, Jens Manuel. 2017. "Unauthorized Immigrants Covered by DACA Face Uncertain Future." Washington, DC: Pew Research Center. http://www.pewresearch.org/fact-tank/2017/01/05/unauthorized-immigrants-covered-by-daca-face-uncertain-future.

McKay, Sonia, Eugenia Markova, and Anna Paraskevopoulou. 2012. *Undocumented Workers' Transitions: Legal Status, Migration, and Work in Europe*. New York: Routledge.

National Employment Law Project. 2013. "California's New Worker Protections Against Retaliation." www.nelp.org/page/-/Justice/2013/ca-worker-protections-against-retaliation.pdf.

National Employment Law Project. 2016. "Immigration and Labor Enforcement in the Workplace: The Revised Labor Agency-DHS Memorandum of Understanding." *Fact Sheet*, May 23. www.nelp.org/publication/immigration-and-labor-enforcement-in-the-workplace.

Naylor, Brian. 2017. "Trump's Plan To Hire 15,000 Border Patrol And ICE Agents Won't Be Easy." *NPR.org*. www.npr.org/2017/02/23/516712980/trumps-plan-to-hire-15-000-border-patrol-and-ice-agents-wont-be-easy-to-fulfill.

Passel, Jeffrey S., and D'Vera Cohn. 2009. "A Portrait of the Unauthorized Migrants in the United States." http://pewhispanic.org/files/reports/107.pdf.

Passel, Jeffrey S., and D'Vera Cohn. 2015. "Unauthorized Immigrant Population Stable for Half a Decade." www.pewresearch.org/fact-tank/2015/07/22/unauthorized-immigrant-population-stable-for-half-a-decade.

Peri, Giovanni. 2010. "The Effect of Immigrants on U.S. Employment and Productivity." *Federal Reserve Bank of San Francisco*, August 30. www.frbsf.org/economic-research/publications/economic-letter/2010/august/effect-immigrants-us-employment-productivity.

Ramakrishnan, Karthick, and Allan Colbern. 2015. "The 'California Package' of Immigrant Integration and the Evolving Nature of State Citizenship." https://escholarship.org/uc/item/99w6b4kd.pdf.

Sadiq, Kamal. 2009. *Paper Citizens: How Illegal Immigrants Acquire Citizenship in Developing Countries*. New York: Oxford University Press.

United Nations. 2013. "Irregular Migration, Human Trafficking, and Refugees." In *International Migration Policies Report: Government Views and Priorities*. ST/ESA/SER.A/342. Department of Economic and Social Affairs: Population Division. www.un.org/en/development/desa/population/publications/pdf/policy/InternationalMigrationPolicies2013/Report%20PDFs/k_Ch_5.pdf.

Trapped in the Working Class? Latino Youth Struggle to Achieve the American Dream

By Karina Chavarria and Veronica Terriquez

Changes in the economy and the rising costs of higher education have limited opportunities for upward mobility for young people from modest economic backgrounds. Keeping in mind this economic context, this study examines the economic prospects for Latino young adults ages eighteen to twenty-six. Using surveys collected from a representative sample of California youth in 2011, this study focuses on college and employment patterns. Results show that social class inequality largely contributes to differences in college enrollment among Latinos, based on how long they and their families have lived in the United States. It also compares their college enrollment and employment patterns to those of Whites. However, racial inequality persists in enrollment to selective universities, regardless of young adults' socioeconomic origins. At the same time, Latino youth experience similar job participation rates as do their White peers. This study also shows no differences in the mobility paths among Latino youth, regardless of how long their families have lived in the United States. This study suggests that a contemporary group of Latino youth may face *working-class stagnation* across immigrant generations, and that racial inequalities in access to positions of power in the economy and public sphere will continue as a result of Latinos' comparatively low enrollment rates in four-year colleges in general, but in prestigious universities in particular.

COMPETING THEORIES ON LATINO IMMIGRANT INCORPORATION

Most Latinos in the United States today are immigrants who were born abroad and migrated to the United States, or they belong to the second generation—that is, they are the children of immigrants. Yet a minority—mostly of Mexican origin—have lived in this country for a few generations or longer, making them part of the third-plus generation. Notably, the lower socioeconomic background of many first-generation Latino immigrants has consequences for the group as a whole. Scholars often agree that low levels of education and high rates of working poverty among first-generation immigrant Latino parents mean that their children may face difficulties with incorporating. This is because many Latino immigrant parents lack the social networks, financial resources, and educational background needed to help their children succeed academically and to access high-quality jobs when they get older (Alba and Nee 2003; Portes and Rumbaut 2006; Waters and Jimenez 2005). Yet scholars offer competing explanations of how Latinos may progress as their families spend more time in the United States. Some scholars offer a cautiously optimistic prediction of Latino descendants' trajectories, suggesting that each generation after migration will experience some level of economic advancement (Alba and Nee 2003; Bean et al. 2011; Vallejo 2012; Waldinger, Lim, and Cort 2007). Yet recent evidence suggests that Latinos' economic incorporation seems to be taking longer as a result of the uncertain legal status of many first-generation immigrant parents, particularly Mexicans (Bean et al. 2011). Additionally, a precarious legal status has limited the success of 1.5-generation youths who remain undocumented and lack a path to permanent legalization and citizenship (Abrego 2006; Gonzales 2011). However, prior studies mostly use information collected from earlier or older groups of Latinos, and thus cannot fully consider current demographic, economic, and social contexts in which a contemporary group of Latino youth is coming of age.

Offering a somewhat different viewpoint, Telles and Ortiz (2008) focus on how racial discrimination limits opportunities for educational and economic success. Telles and Ortiz's work reminds us that Latino socioeconomic advancement cannot be understood without looking at how Latinos are doing compared to Whites. Only by comparing across ethnic/racial groups can we understand Latinos' economic prospects.

CONTEMPORARY CONTEXTS IN YOUTH TRANSITIONS TO ADULTHOOD

The historical, social, and economic conditions in which youth become adults strongly impact their life paths (Shanahan 2000). Today's youth are coming of age after four decades of continuous and large-scale migration from Mexico, Central America, the Caribbean, and other parts of Latin America. In some regions, like California, a century of migration, mostly from Mexico, allows Latinos to interact with new immigrants, even when they have lived in the United States for various generations. As Jiménez (2010) shows, third-plus-generation Latinos can keep their ties to ethnic culture, and this replenishment of the Latino population may lead to similarities in Latino youths' experiences across immigrant generations, including how they are treated by out-group members (Fernández-Kelley and Konczal 2005; Rumbaut 2004). Therefore, Latinos' ethnic/racial background cannot be ignored as a possible factor that might unify Latino youths' experiences, regardless of how long their families have lived in the United States (Massey 2009).

Further, it is important to consider how the current economic context affects opportunities for a current group of Latino youth to improve over previous generations. Today's youth are becoming adults in a time defined by increasing income inequality and a shrinking middle class (Duncan and Murnane 2011). Along with this growing economic inequality has been the decrease in educational achievement across generations. Whereas in the past it was common for children to obtain more education than their parents, now the proportion of youth receiving less education than their parents is increasing (Janus and Hout 2011). Likely adding to such changes are the rising costs of four-year college tuition (Ma and Baum, 2016; Grapevine 2012). As such, Latino youth pursuing a college education may not be as fortunate as were earlier generations of Latinos who grew up when higher education was more affordable. We might expect the current economic context to limit the educational attainment of Latinos, contributing to similar rates of Latinos' college enrollment across immigrant generations.

We also might expect differences in family socioeconomic background to affect racial inequalities in the educational and labor outcomes between Latino and White youth (Sewell 1971; Sewell and Hauser 1975; Deil-Amen and Turley 2007). Because first-generation Latino immigrant parents are mostly working-class, 1.5- and second-generation Latino youth are at a disadvantage in terms of their college and job prospects compared to White youth. Because studies suggest that older generations of US-born Latinos did not achieve equality with Whites (Brown 2007; Telles and Ortiz 2008; Vallejo 2012; Waldinger and Cort 2007), such inequality may affect the third-plus generation as well. The opportunities for Latino youth to "catch up" to White youth may be seriously restricted by their low socioeconomic origins.

PRESENT STUDY

This study compares the postsecondary enrollment and employment of 1.5-, second-, and third-generation Latino youth ages eighteen to twenty-six, and the rates of Latinos to those of Whites of the same age group. We are interested in understanding how well Latinos are faring based on how long they and their families have lived in the United States, and we want to explore the extent to which their economic prospects differ from those of Whites. We focus on youth from California, a state where Latino youth outnumber White youth, and where more than 75 percent are of Mexican or Central American descent (based on author tabulations of the 2010 American Community Survey). While Mexicans have a longer history in the state than do Central Americans, evidence points to Central Americans facing similar experiences and treatment by out-group members, as well as similar social conditions, because most Central Americans live among Mexicans (Davenport, Castañeda, and Manz 2002).

For the analysis, we use telephone survey information from the California Young Adult Study (CYAS), which includes college enrollment, employment, and civic partici-pation of eighteen- to twenty-six-year-old youth. CYAS survey information comes from landline and cell phone interviews collected in 2011 with 2,200 randomly selected youth who attended school in California at any point before age seventeen. Youth living in high-poverty areas were oversampled (Terriquez 2014). For this study, youth who were in high school during the survey or who had just graduated in 2011 were excluded. The youth left in the study are 861 Latinos, including 133 who are 1.5 generation, 527 who are second generation and have at least one immigrant parent, and 201 who are third-plus generation with US-born parents. Latinos are those who claim a Latino, Hispanic, or Chicano iden-tity, aside from other racial identifications. The 1.5-generation group are youth who were born outside of the country but attended school in California before the age of seventeen.

The outcomes we look at—education and employment—can give us an idea of the future well-being of young Latinas/os. For education, we use college enrollment because few have completed their postsecondary education, and it contains four categories: (1) never enrolled in college; (2) enrolled in a community college (but never in a four-year college); (3) enrolled in a four-year state university or similarly ranked four-year private school; and (4) enrolled in a selective four-year college, such as an Ivy League school, a University of California school, or other similarly ranked school.[1] We distinguish between the last two types of colleges because those who attend selective schools tend to have more job options than those at state colleges do. Next, we examine patterns of youth employment, distinguishing between those who reported having a paid job at the time of the survey and those who did not. Working during early adulthood matters for understanding Latinos' future experiences with poverty, creating families, and health. The third outcome examined is youths' disconnection from both school and work. For this study, disconnected youth are those who lack a bachelor's degree and are not enrolled in any type of educational program (including adult school or vocational program), and are not working. Disconnected youth are at risk of not receiving the educational and career training necessary for their future well-being, with some possibly being on paths toward future poverty and downward mobility.

---

1. Youth who enrolled in a vocational program, but never enrolled in college, were placed in the "were placed group. Youth who attended a community college and transferred to a four-year college were placed in the "state college"tor "selective college" group, depending on the college last attended. Because of students' complex enrollment patterns, this outcome variable does not differentiate among current students, those who have taken a break from their studies and are "stopped out," and those who have already received their intended degree.

In this chapter, we review descriptive information that captures the experiences of Latino and White young adults. We also summarize the results of regression analysis that consider non-ethnic factors, including legal status and class status, which typically affect youths' transitions to adulthood.

FINDINGS

Table 3.1 presents information describing outcome and control factors that are separated by immigrant generation and race/ethnicity. Results demonstrate that Latino youths' class background improves considerably with each generation after migration, with parents' education and homeownership increasing from the 1.5 to the third generation, while the number of youth who describe coming from a low-income background decreases. That is, Latinos experience a gradual increase in four-year college enrollment across Latino immigrant generations. Yet these encouraging within-group social mobility prospects pale in comparison to those for Whites. When compared to Whites, Latinos are less likely to enroll in state universities and about one-third as likely to enroll in selective four-year colleges, demonstrating large racial/ethnic differences in four-year college enrollment. Latinos, then, continue to experience struggles in attaining a middle-class status, given their lower levels of college enrollment. Meanwhile, job participation patterns point to little differences across Latino generations, with 22 percent of 1.5-generation youth not in school or employed, compared to 18 percent for later generations. When compared to Whites, 18 percent of Latinos were out of both work and school, compared to 10 percent for Whites. That is, no racial/ethnic differences in youths' job participation were evident.

Additional analyses, published elsewhere (Terriquez 2014), point to very little difference in Latino youth mobility by immigrant generation. We find no differences in college enrollment across the 1.5, second, and third generations after considering youths' family socioeconomic background. Specifically, most Latino youth are unlikely to enroll in a four-year college if their parents did not obtain a bachelor's degree, no matter how long their families have lived in the United States. In other words, most Latino youth who come from working-class family backgrounds are likely to stay in the working class. At the same time, a small minority of Latino youth who are raised by parents with a bachelor's degree are more likely to enroll in a four-year college, including a more selective school. This suggests that the small Latino middle class is reproducing its privilege across generations.

Interestingly, White and Latino youth raised by parents with similar levels of education have fairly similar chances of enrolling in community colleges or less selective four-year state schools. Yet, regardless of socioeconomic origins, Whites have higher rates of enrolling in selective four-year universities that offer the greatest social economic

Table 3.1 Descriptive statistics for Latino and White 18-26 year olds

California Young Adult Study (Weighted Results)

Latino immigrant generation

Dependent variables	1.5	2	3+	all Latinos	Whites
Postsecondary educational enrollment					
Never enrolled in college	43%	34%	27%	35%	18
Enrolled in Community College (but not 4 YR)	37%	43%	42%	41%	35%
Enrolled in a state or similar 4 year college	15%	18%	23%	18%	28%
Enrolled in a top-tier college or university	5%	6%	8%	6%	19%
Currently working for pay	59%	62%	58%	61%	63%
Out of school, out of work, & no BA	22%	17%	18%	18%	10%
Sample characteristics					
Average age	22.3	21.1	21.8	21.6	21.9
Gender					
Male	57%	51%	43%	51%	53%
Female	43%	49%	57%	49%	47%
Socio-economic background					
Parents lack high school degree	48%	35%	9%	32%	2%
Raised by parent(s) with a college degree	10%	13%	24%	15%	52%
Low-Income background	75%	61%	32%	58%	16%
Parents owned home	39%	56%	63%	54%	78%
Raised in single-parent household	16%	27%	37%	27%	33%
Immigrant generation					
1.5 generation	100%	0%	0%	24%	4%
2nd generation	0%	100%	0%	54%	14%
3rd generation+	0%	0%	100%	22%	82%
Legal Status					
Citizen	69%	100%	100%	93%	100%
Legal permanent resident	38%	0%	0%	9%	0%
Undocumented/other	31%	0%	0%	7%	0%
Unweighted sample size	**133**	**527**	**201**	**861**	**561**

opportunities. That is, Latinos experience a racial disadvantage that can be attributed to discrimination and unequal opportunity due to their racial/ethnic minority status.

It is important to note that Latino young adults have similar employment rates to those of Whites. In other words, they are not necessarily experiencing downward economic mobility and disproportionately high unemployment rates. However, as other research has shown, Latinos tend to obtain much lower-paying jobs than Whites do, and they are less likely than their White counterparts to obtain jobs with health insurance and other benefits (Semyonov, Lewin-Epstein, and Bridges 2011).

Finally, additional analysis indicates that young adults who lack legal documentation experience great disadvantages when compared to their counterparts with papers. Those who lack any permission to live and work in the United States enroll in four-year colleges at extremely low rates and have higher rates of unemployment. This finding highlights the need for a pathway to citizenship for young people who experience blocked mobility.

DISCUSSION

Overall, this study highlights similarities in the social mobility paths of Latino 1.5, second, and third generations. The findings do not contradict earlier studies, but describe the mobility trajectories of a contemporary group of youth. Findings suggest very little, if any, improvement in the economic prospects of Latinos based on how long their families have lived in the United States. Results also support previous research that suggests undocumented youth from the 1.5 generation face different challenges to their educational or workforce incorporation (Abrego 2006; Gonzales 2011). However, the recent implementation of former president Barack Obama's Deferred Action for Childhood Arrivals mandate, which allows this population to work legally, and the California Dream Act, which helps undocumented youth get state financial aid, will likely improve the future opportunities of this segment of the Latino population.

This study also demonstrates how race continues to matter in the future social standing of Latino youth. Results show significant racial inequality in Latino youths' enrollment in selective colleges and universities. Even after including their class status, the racial differences remain. Because selective universities channel graduates into higher-status jobs and into public leadership positions, these findings suggest that Latino youth will face problems in accessing such positions of power in the economy and public fields. This study signals a need to continue addressing both socioeconomic and class inequalities in order to provide today's youth with a fair chance at achieving the American Dream. Further research is needed to assess the degree to which this large population is incorporating into US educational and labor market institutions across the nation and over time.

DISCUSSION QUESTIONS

1. Even though discrimination by class status does not often appear in news headlines, in what ways can class discrimination limit opportunities for people to improve their economic position?

2. How can examining race and class together help us better understand the inequality being reproduced generation after generation?

3. Consider contemporary social movements, such as Black Lives Matter. How can looking at racial discrimination and a lack of jobs help us understand the creation of groups focused on social justice?

SUGGESTIONS FOR FURTHER READING

Crowley, S. 2003. "The Affordable Housing Crisis: Residential Mobility of Poor Families and School Mobility of Poor Children." *Journal of Negro Education* 72(1): 22–38.

Rogers, J., M. Bertrand, R. Felon, and S. Fanelli. 2011. *Free Fall: Educational Opportunities in 2011*. Los Angeles: UCLA IDEA, UC/ACCORD.

Rumberger, R. W. 2010. "Education and the Reproduction of Economic Inequality in the United States: An Empirical Investigation." *Economics of Education Review* 29: 246–254.

Schaefer, R. T. 2001. *Race and Ethnicity in the United States*. 2nd ed. Upper Saddle River, NJ: Prentice Hall.

REFERENCES

Abrego, Leisy J. 2006. "'I Can't Go to College Because I Don't Have Papers': Incorporation Patterns of Latino Undocumented Youth." *Latino Studies* 4: 212–231.

Alba, Richard, and Victor Nee. 2003. *Remaking the American Mainstream: Assimilation and the Contemporary Immigration*. Cambridge: Harvard University Press.

2010 American Community Survey. U.S. Census Bureau. https://www.census.gov/programs-surveys/acs.

Bean, Frank, Mark A. Leach, Susan K. Brown, James D. Bachmeier, and John R. Hipp. 2011. "The Educational Legacy of Unauthorized Migration: Comparisons Across U.S.-Immigrant Groups in How Parents' Status Affects Their Offspring." *International Migration Review* 45(2): 348–385.

Brown, Susan K. "Delayed Spatial Assimilation: Multigenerational Incorporation of the Mexican-Origin Population in Los Angeles." *City & Community* 6(3): 193–209.

Davenport, Allison, Xochitl Castañeda, and Beatriz Manz. 2002. "Mexicanization: A Survival Strategy for Guatemalan Mayans in the San Francisco Bay Area." *Migraciones Internacionales* 1(3): 102–123.

Deil-Amen, Regina, and Ruth Lopez Turley. 2007. "A review of the transition to college literature in sociology." *Teachers College Record* 109(10): 2324–2366.

Duncan, Greg J. and Richard J. Murnane (Eds.). 2011. *Whither opportunity?: Rising inequality, schools, and children's life chances*. Russell Sage Foundation.

Fernández-Kelley, Patricia and Lisa Konczal. 2005. "'Murdering the Alphabet' Identity and entrepreneurship among second-generation Cubans, West Indians, and Central Americans." *Ethnic and Racial Studies* 28(6): 1153–1181.

Gonzales, Roberto G. 2011. "Learning to Be Illegal: Undocumented Youth and Shifting Legal Contexts in the Transition to Adulthood." *American Sociological Review* 76(4): 602–619.

Grapevine. 2012. "One-Year (FY11–FY12), Two-Year (FY10–FY12), and Five-Year (FY07– FY12) Percent Changes in State Fiscal Support for Higher Education, by State and by Source of Fiscal Support." Illinois State University's Center for the Study of Education Policy.

Hout, Michael and Alexander Janus. 2011. "Educational Mobility in the United States since the 1930s." In Greg J. Duncan and Richard J. Murnane(eds.), *Wither Opportunity*. Russell Sage. Pp. 165–186.

Jiménez, Tomas R. 2010. *Replenished Ethnicity: Mexican-Americans, Immigration, and Identity*. Berkeley: University of California Press.

Lee, Jennifer, and Frank D. Bean. 2010. *The Diversity Paradox: Immigration and the Color Line in 21st Century America*. New York: Russell Sage Foundation.

Ma, Jennifer, and Sandy Baum. 2016. "Trends in community colleges: Enrollment, prices, student debt, and completion." *College Board Research Brief*.

Massey, Douglas S. 2009. "Racial Formation in Theory and Practice: The Case of Mexicans in the United States." *Race and Social Problems* 1: 12–26.

Portes, Alejandro and Rubén G. Rumbaut. 2006. *Immigrant America: a portrait*. University of California Press.

Rumbaut, Rubén G. 2004. "Ages, Life Stages, and Generational Cohorts: Decomposing the Immigrant First and Second Generations in the United States." *International Migration Review* 38(3): 1160–1205.

Semyonov, Moshe, Noah Lewin-Epstein, and William P. Bridges. 2011. "Explaining Racial Disparities in Access to Employment Benefits." *Ethnic and Racial Studies* 34(12): 2069–2095.

Sewell, William H. 1971. "Inequality of opportunity for higher education." *American Sociological Review* 36(5); 793–809.

Sewell, William H., and Robert M. Hauser. 1975. *Education, Occupation, and Earnings: Achievement in the Early Career*. Academic Press.

Shanahan, Michael J. 2000. "Pathways to Adulthood in Changing Societies: Variability and Mechanisms in Life Course Perspective." *Annual Review of Sociology* 26.

Telles, Edward, and Vilma Ortiz. 2008. *Generations of Exclusion: Mexican Americans, Assimilation, and Race*. New York: Russell Sage Foundation.

Terriquez, Veronica. 2014. "Trapped in the working class? Prospects for the intergenerational (im) mobility of Latino youth." *Sociological Inquiry* 84(3): 382–411.

Vallejo, Jody A. 2012. *Barrios to the Burbs: The Making of the Mexican American Middle-Class*. Palo Alto, CA: Stanford University Press.

Waldinger, Roger, Nelson Lim, and David Cort. 2007. "Bad jobs, good jobs, no jobs? The employment experience of the Mexican American second generation." *Journal of ethnic and migration studies* 33(1): 1–35.

Waters, Mary C., and Tomás R. Jiménez. 2005. "Assessing Immigrant Assimilation: New Empirical and Theoretical Challenges." *Annual Review of Sociology* 31: 105–125.

Race Frames and Their Impact on the Sense of Belonging of Black Students in a College Community

By Anita Davis, Angela Frederick, and Christopher Wetzel

INTRODUCTION

Americans commonly understand racism to be a pathological problem of a few individuals. Thus, our discussions of racism are often reduced to debates over whether specific perpetrators truly harbor prejudice in their hearts. Social scientists, by contrast, recognize racism as a system of race-based group privilege that is interwoven into the daily operation and cultural life of our institutions. As Bonilla-Silva, Lewis, and Embrick (2004) explain, "Racism springs not from the hearts of 'racists,' but from the fact that dominant actors in a racialized social system receive benefits at all levels … whereas subordinate actors do not."

Racial inequality is maintained in part through race frames, or the value systems and stories we tell about race (Warikoo and de Novais 2015). These frames serve as the glue that holds the entire system of race-based group privilege together. They make the pervasive racial inequalities we live with appear natural, fair, or altogether invisible (Bonilla-Silva 2017). Americans are found to hold multiple, and often conflicting, race frames, including the color-blind ideology, backstage racist values, and diversity and social justice frames.

While research has documented the race frames held by White college students (Smith, Senter, and Strachan 2013; Warikoo and de Novais 2015), scholars have devoted less attention to exploring how these race frames shape Black students' experiences and sense of belonging on college campuses. Drawing from a campus climate survey administered to students at a small, predominantly White liberal arts college, we explore common experiences that Black students have shared. As we demonstrate, Black students' lived experience with prevailing race frames contribute to their alienation, as they report feeling both invisible and hypervisible in multiple facets of campus life.

METHODS

The data presented here are drawn from a campus climate survey completed by students at Little Southern College,[1] a liberal arts college nestled in an urban city in the American South. All students were invited to participate in the online survey, which asked both closed- and open-ended questions about their sense of belonging on the college campus.

About half of the student body (53%) participated in the survey. The majority of participants (78.2%) self-identified as White, non-Hispanic. Other participants self-identified as Asian (7.1%), Black/African American (6.6%), multiracial (4.3%), and Hispanic/Latino/a (3.6%). A substantial proportion of the students (61%) reported being of upper-middle-class status.

FINDINGS

Of all the racial and ethnic identities represented in the student body, Black students are the least likely to report feeling a sense of belonging in the campus community. Thus, their experiences can tell us much about racial dynamics on college campuses. In the following sections, we explore how encounters with four race frames shape Black students' experiences at Little Southern. All narratives included in the chapter were written by students who self-identified as Black/African American.

THE COLOR-BLIND IDEOLOGY

Researchers have documented the rise of a new belief system among White Americans, which Eduardo Bonilla-Silva (2017) terms "the color-blind ideology." Those who subscribe to this frame believe that the United States has entered a post-racial era in which racial oppression is a relic of the past. Working from this premise, many White Americans believe that discussing race only serves to keep us tied to the racist history

---

1. All proper names are pseudonyms.

that we could otherwise leave behind. The color-blind ideology compels many Whites to try to demonstrate that they are not racist by shying away from discussing race or by taking on an "innocent until you prove it's racism" stance. Thus, this racial frame inhibits important conversations about systematic racial inequality and the privileges that accompany Whiteness. In fact, new racial resentments have arisen in tandem with the color-blind ideology, including the belief that Whites are the new victims of racism through affirmative action programs (Bonilla-Silva 2017).

Our data suggest that the classroom is an important site where the color-blind ideology is reinforced and, consequently, where racial microaggressions are frequently perpetuated. *Microaggressions* are brief, everyday exchanges that send denigrating messages to certain individuals because of their group membership (Sue 2010). April shared a classroom experience that poignantly illustrates how the color-blind ideology operates at multiple levels to shape classroom dynamics. April's class was discussing Betty Friedan's *The Feminine Mystique*, which described the lack of fulfillment that college-educated White housewives were experiencing in the 1950s. April described a moment when she challenged the unspoken assumption that the experiences of middle-class White housewives were a universal experience for women.

> The major part of the discussion was how the female White students … could relate to the women in the book. … I said that I could not relate to these women. Rather than not being able to fulfill their personal needs in regards to having a job … women of color will work two or three part-time jobs and not be able to provide adequately for their families. Some lower-class women will never have the ability or privilege to go to college. … The students in the class were silent and just looked at me. The professor broke the silence by saying, "That was very articulate." I could not believe this is how the students of the Little Southern community responded to my critique.

In this moment, April experienced a profound sense of invisibility, as White women in the class bonded over a book in which she could not see herself or the experiences of persons whom she knows. The color-blind frame contributes to these moments of invisibility in college classrooms, as curricula often include predominantly White authors who represent predominantly White experiences, all presented as if race is irrelevant to the conversation.

When April spoke up, she was met with both silence and stares from her White classmates, being rendered both hypervisible and invisible in the same moment. What are we to make of the White students' silence? Is it a reflection of the apathy, anger, or lack of empathy found to be generated by the color-blind frame? Perhaps. But something more is likely also at play. Because White students are often socialized to believe that race and racism are topics that should not be openly discussed, in public at least, they often feel disconcerted when race and racism are explicitly addressed. The color-blind frame leaves them without a road map for discussing race in open, healthy ways. In fact, they often feel more comfortable denying the centrality of racism than they do saying, "I hear you," or "I want to understand." This silence can feel like a manifestation of apathy and resentment when received by students of color. The professor's response also contributed to these injuries. "Articulate" is a backhanded compliment frequently given to African Americans, which sets them up as an exception while reinforcing the stereotype that Blacks are generally not "well spoken."

BACKSTAGE RACISM

Despite claims of colorblindness, evidence suggests that White Americans often engage race quite differently in the company of other Whites. In their 2007 book, *Two-Faced Racism*, Leslie Picca and Joe Feagin analyzed the journal entries of college students who were asked to write about "racial events," or moments when race became salient in their interactions with others. They found that White students frequently engage in racist performances "backstage," that is, when they are in the company of other Whites. These performances include using racial epitaphs, mocking racial and ethnic minorities, and engaging in storytelling that increases racial resentment. Some individuals do challenge these practices and opt out of spaces where these racial events are perpetuated. Picca and Feagin demonstrate, however, that racism is still part of a shared culture among Whites. Many White college students are still teaching, learning, practicing, and normalizing racism on their campuses.

As undergraduates at residential colleges live, study, and party in close proximity to one another, the racism that Whites often reserve for backstage is revealed to students of color. Michael described such a moment. One evening, as Michael approached a group of fraternity houses with a White friend, a fraternity member greeted his friend using the "N" word. As Michael explained,

> I assume he didn't see me. … However, from the look on his
> face, he knew I heard him. I was made uncomfortable, because
> he chose to ignore me and not to apologize or even ask if I was
> offended. I felt invisible.

Like other college campuses, Little Southern has recently been rocked by controversy surrounding racial epitaphs and other dehumanizing comments that were posted anonymously to several social media platforms associated with the college. Twenty-one percent of the Black students who completed our survey named these incidents as contributing to their diminished sense of belonging. Taylor explained:

> It took a toll on me mentally, emotionally, socially, and academically. … I'm still dealing with these wounds that I was left with, but I am better managing myself. I still don't feel as if I completely belong here, though.

The backstage conditioning of Whites to dehumanize people of color also likely contributes to patterns of microaggressions that Black students report experiencing. These students shared stories of being held to higher scrutiny by campus security, being made to feel unwelcome at fraternity parties, feeling isolated when White students avoid taking a seat next to them, and feeling invisible when common courtesies such as holding the door are not extended to them. These microaggressions reflect broader patterns of Whites' social distancing from Blacks (Lee and Bean 2010).

THE DIVERSITY FRAME

The *diversity frame* touts the benefits to be gained in diverse communities. Though often competing with the color-blind ideology, the diversity frame is a prominent system of meaning in higher education and is shown to offer some positive benefits for both White students and students of color (Berrey 2011; Smith, Senter, and Strachan 2013). This frame has its limitations, however, as it tends to deemphasize structural inequalities. Bell and Hartmann (2007) call this dynamic the "happy talk" of diversity. They find that while we often espouse the rewards of diversity, these commitments quickly break down as we confront the tensions that arise in diverse communities.

Though college campuses are regarded as bastions of diversity, our survey results reveal that White and Black students can have strikingly different cross-racial experiences. For example, White students at Little Southern are significantly more likely than Black students to participate in fraternities and sororities (66 percent vs. 20 percent, respectively), and Black students are significantly more likely than White students to participate in multicultural organizations (72 percent vs. 12 percent, respectively). For White students, both fraternities and sororities are found to be almost completely White environments (Park 2014). The high level of segregation in Greek life can severely limit White students' opportunities for interracial engagement, as participation in sororities and fraternities is associated with less cross-racial interaction and fewer interracial friendships, especially on less racially/ethnically diverse campuses (Kim, Park, and Koo 2015; Park and Kim 2013). Indeed, while Black students are often singled out for "all sitting together in the cafeteria" (Tatum 2003), the self-segregation of White students in sororities and fraternities is frequently overlooked.

Black students at Little Southern are significantly more likely than White students to participate in multicultural organizations, which also tend to be racially homogenous. Research suggests, however, that participating in ethnic student organizations does not impede the cultivation of interracial friendships for students of color (Park and Kim 2013). For example, Park (2014) found that 74.3 percent of African American students reported that they had at least one close friend of another race out of their four closest friends, compared to only 48.5% of White students.

In addition, the diversity frame can often mask inequalities, even as differences are celebrated. "Diversity talk" can lead White students to believe that their campus is free from racial injustice. This danger is particularly salient on campuses like Little Southern, where White students still have limited cross-racial friendships and where students of color often feel like classrooms are unsafe spaces to share their perspectives. Consider a classroom experience that Erica shared:

> One of my classmates said that discrimination and racism didn't exist on our campus, but … if you were to go to specific places, then you'd just have to know that people wouldn't be as accepting. I already didn't feel wholly accepted in my class … but it was so wild to me that he thought that we were. … Furthermore, no one in my class truly refuted his statement, and some offered similar ones.

Reflecting the diversity frame, the White students in Erica's class were confident that their campus was a welcoming place free from racial inequality. As our data indicate, this is a perception not shared by the majority of Black students. In addition, words like "accepting" and "tolerant," often used in tandem with the diversity frame, allow dominant actors to perceive their community as inclusive while rendering invisible patterns of privilege and inequality. As Meghan Burke (2013) argues, acceptance and tolerance are not synonymous with justice.

Finally, consider the "you" and the implied "we" in the White student's declaration. This exemplifies what Bell and Hartmann (2007) call "Whites as hosts" thinking, in which White Americans still assume they are the "we," the hosts with a "normal," nonracial identity, and people of color are the "you," the guests who spice up the community by bringing "diversity" and "culture" to the table. Thus, the diversity frame can contribute to dynamics in which people of color are expected to be others' teachers, to share parts of themselves on demand, and to adhere to dominant norms defined by the majority population.

THE SOCIAL JUSTICE FRAME

Like the diversity frame, a social justice perspective regards human differences as valuable. Yet, the social justice frame also requires recognition of both privilege and inequality and calls on us to work together to address injustices in our community. The narratives shared by Black students suggest they often enfold the social justice and diversity frames together. They expect that addressing inequality should be part of the college's espoused commitment to diversity.

Over the past ten years, Black students have asked, and received permission, to interrupt a scheduled meeting of the faculty to express concerns about the need for more inclusive classroom environments. Black students, in coalition with others, have played a pivotal role in organizing campus events to highlight the need for more education and accountability around issues of diversity and inclusion on the campus. And while the social justice frame appears to be the weakest paradigm on the Little Southern campus, in moments when a social justice frame has emerged, Black students' sense of belonging appears to increase. For example, Black students were active in organizing and participating in campuswide conversations to address the racist social media posts previously discussed, and 20 percent of Black students taking the survey named these campuswide conversations as a time when they felt like they belonged in the community. As Marcus described:

> While the initial response was a sense of betrayal, I soon felt a sense of camaraderie with the other students who were attempting to make a change within the campus. … In our attempts to think of ways to remedy the issue and heal the wounds that this incident had caused, we slowly began to rebuild the bonds that had been broken, and dissolve the seeds of distrust that the … incident had sowed.

This example is particularly instructive for two reasons. First, it highlights how Black students' social justice work can increase their own sense of belonging. Second, it illustrates the powerful message White students send when they also engage in social justice work on their campuses. Whether by employing a social justice frame in a conversation, or by showing up to events addressing inequities on campus, White students can communicate to Black students that they are not invisible, that they are not alone in feeling that such behaviors are unacceptable, and that they are not alone in the desire to take action. These messages counter other race frames that diminish Black students' sense of belonging on campus.

Nikki also described her complex reactions to a public gathering to address the social media incident:

The turnout from professors, students, and faculty to address issues that I feel are often ignored on campus was so great. The fact that my community was so willing to gather in solidarity for that really affirmed my belief that Little Southern was the place for me. Of course, after the event I felt as if a lot of students … still didn't believe that the issues were worth putting in effort to address … which left me feeling upset and confused.

Here we see an important place of contradiction. Employing a social justice frame can help increase Black students' sense of belonging and offer spaces where they feel truly seen. Yet, the social justice frame can initially cause discomfort for some White students, as it can challenge the color-blind frame and backstage racism, and expose the limits of diversity happy talk.

DISCUSSION

Findings from our study underscore the interconnected roles that students, faculty, and the institution play in reinforcing race frames on college campuses. In this final section, we consider what we all might do to create a more welcoming environment on our campuses.

KNOW THAT YOUR WORDS AND ACTIONS MATTER

Each story shared previously has an *actor*, someone whose actions caused another student to feel unwelcome or alienated in the community. The examples shared previously also illustrate how our small gestures can send powerful messages to others.

1.   Identify a time when you employed one of the race frames discussed in this article. Why do you think you employed that race frame? How has your perspective changed?

2.   What small change can you take in your daily routine to make your campus community more welcoming? Consider small but powerful gestures, such as where you choose to sit, how you might generate social connections with others, and to whom you offer a smile.

DON'T BE A BYSTANDER

The narratives shared previously reveal that the silence of bystanders sends a powerful message. Challenging instances of othering takes courage, and it takes practice. Remember, you don't have to be funny or brilliant or perfect to interrupt these dynamics. All it takes is someone willing to begin the conversation by saying, "This troubles me." Be that someone!

1 . Identify a common racial narrative you hear on your campus. How does this narrative reinforce the color-blind ideology, backstage racism, or the diversity frame? How might you interject a social justice perspective into the conversation the next time you hear this narrative?

BUILD COALITIONS

Racially homogenous student organizations likely strengthen different race frames. Yet these organizations also present ideal opportunities for interracial dialogue and social interactions.

1 . How might the student organizations to which you belong engage in regular activities with groups made up of students from different racial/ethnic backgrounds?

2 . Students also experience marginalization based on other identities (social class, LGBTQ, disability, etc.). How might your student groups build coalitions with each other? How might you act as an ally for students who belong to multiple groups?

WEBSITE LINKS

Compilation of college student demands to end racial injustice on their campuses: http://www.thedemands.org

Diversity section of *Inside Higher Ed*: www.insidehighered.com/news/focus/diversity

Racism Review: www.racismreview.com/blog/2016/03/01/race-in-the-academy-ubc

The Society Pages on race: https://thesocietypages.org/#/race

Students' section of *The Chronicle of Higher Education*: http://chronicle.com/section/Students/19?cid=UCHESIDENAV2

Understanding Race: www.understandingrace.org

AUDIOVISUAL MATERIALS

"How to Tell Someone They Sound Racist," Jay Smooth: www.youtube.com/watch?v=b0Ti-gkJiXc

"If Microaggressions Happened to White People," MTV: www.youtube.com/watch?v=KPRA4g-3yEk

"A SocImages Collection: Race-Themed College Parties," Sociological Images, https://thesocietypages.org/socimages/2015/10/12/individual-racism-alive-and-well/

SUGGESTIONS FOR FURTHER READING

Burke, M. A. 2013. "Colorblindness vs. Race Consciousness: An American Ambivalence." *The Society Pages*, July 24. https://thesocietypages.org/specials/colorblindness-vs-race-consciousness.

Lee, J., and F. D. Bean. 2010. *The Diversity Paradox: Immigration and the Color Line in 21st Century America*. New York: Russell Sage Foundation.

Picca, L. H., and J. Feagin. 2007. *Two-Faced Racism: Whites in the Frontstage and Backstage*. New York: Routledge.

REFERENCES

Bell, J. M., and D. Hartmann. 2007. "Diversity in Everyday Discourse: The Cultural Ambiguities and Consequences of 'Happy Talk.'" *American Sociological Review* 72: 895–914.

Berrey, E. C. 2011. "Why Diversity Became Orthodox in Higher Education, and How It Changed the Meaning of Race on Campus." *Critical Sociology* 37(5): 573–596.

Bonilla-Silva, E. 2017. *Racism without Racists: Color-Blind Racism and the Persistence of Racial Inequality in America*. 5th ed. Lanham, MD: Rowman & Littlefield.

Bonilla-Silva,E., A. Lewis, and D. G. Embrick. 2004. "'I Did Not Get That Job Because of a Black Man...': The Story Lines and Testimonies of Color-Blind Racism." *Sociological Forum* 19(4): 555–581.

Burke, M. A. 2013. "Colorblindness vs. Race Consciousness: An American Ambivalence." *The Society Pages*, July 24: https://thesocietypages.org/specials/colorblindness-vs-race-consciousness.

Kim, Y. K, J. J. Park, and K. K. Koo. 2015. "Testing Self-Segregation: Multiple-Group Structural Modeling of College Students' Interracial Friendship by Race." *Research in Higher Education* 56: 57–77.

Lee, J., and F. D. Bean. 2010. *The Diversity Paradox: Immigration and the Color Line in 21st Century America*. New York: Russell Sage Foundation.

Park, J. J. 2014. "Clubs and the Campus Racial Climate: Student Organizations and Interracial Friendship in College." *Journal of College Student Development* 55(7): 641–660.

Park, J. J., and Y. K. Kim. 2013. "Interracial Friendship, Structural Diversity, and Peer Groups: Patterns in Greek, Religious and Ethnic Student Organizations." *The Review of Higher Education* 37(1): 1–24.

Picca, L. H., and J. Feagin. 2007. *Two-Faced Racism: Whites in the Frontstage and Backstage*. New York: Routledge.

Smith, J. M., M. Senter, and J. C. Strachan. 2013. "Gender and White College Students' Racial Attitudes." *Sociological Inquiry* 83(4): 570–590.

Sue, D. W. 2010. *Microaggressions in Everyday Life: Race, Gender, and Sexual Orientation*. Hoboken, NJ: John Wiley & Sons.

Tatum, B. D. 2003. *Why Are All the Black Kids Sitting Together in the Cafeteria? And Other Conversations about Race*. New York: Basic Books.

Warikoo, N. K., and J. de Novais. 2015. "Color-Blindness and Diversity: Race Frames and Their Consequences for White Undergraduates at Elite U.S. Universities." *Ethnic and Racial Studies* 38(6): 860–876.

AUTHOR NOTE

1. Anita A. Davis, Department of Psychology, Rhodes College; Angela H. Frederick, Department of Anthropology and Sociology, Rhodes College; Christopher G. Wetzel, Department of Psychology, Rhodes College. Angela Frederick is now at the Department of Sociology and Anthropology, University of Texas at El Paso.

We wish to thank the students at Little Southern College who shared their stories with us. We hope their courage will help us all identify ways to create campuses that are welcoming for not only Black students, but for all students. We also want to thank Tamara Brown, Darlene Loprete, and Dwain Pruitt for helpful feedback on the chapter.

Correspondence concerning this chapter should be addressed to Angela Frederick, Department of Sociology and Anthropology, University of Texas at El Paso, El Paso, TX 79968. Email: ahfrederick2@utep.edu.

Nepantleras in a Community College: Student Mothers Negotiating Mothering, School, and Work

By Nereida Oliva and Hortencia Jiménez

INTRODUCTION

As first-generation college graduates from working-class and immigrant backgrounds, we are the first in our families to be faculty members in academia while parenting. We experience the everyday challenges and realities of parenting, housework duties, childcare, and paid work outside the home. The community college student mothers on our campus mirror similar experiences, as they, too, are juggling parenting, family obligations, jobs, and school commitments. As such, we have a personal interest and investment in examining and honoring the experiences, knowledge, and realities of community college mothers—a group that is highly invisible in educational research as well as in other disciplines. While the number of students enrolling in community colleges across the nation has increased over the years, little is known about their experiences (Zarate and Burciaga 2010). As female faculty of color in the community college system, we recognize that there is a lack of scholarly research that centers on the experience of community college student mothers (with the notable exception of Duquaine-Watson 2007, 2017).

While we recognize that the higher education field has shifted its focus to community college students because of an increase in enrollment, the focus has neglected to include the experiences and realities of student mothers (Flores, Horn, and Crisp 2006). Nonetheless, we have found new and emerging research on faculty of color (Gutiérrez y Muhs, Flores Niemann, González, and Harris 2012; Tellez 2013), mothering and education (Ochoa 2011), mothers in academia (Castaneda and Isgro 2013), and graduate student mothers (Mercado Lopez 2011) that emphasizes the interconnection between motherhood and education.

Building on this recent scholarship, we employ an intersectional analysis that centers on community college student mothers and further complicates existing discourses on mothering and education to accentuate that motherhood and education are not mutually exclusive. This study incorporates a grounded theory and Chicana feminist framework approach that allows us to examine and understand the experiences and lived realities of community college mothers. Our endeavor is to avoid the common pitfall of presenting women as docile and self-sacrificing mothers.

This chapter is organized in three parts. First, we offer an analysis of the existing literature on student parents in higher education, with a focus on student mothers. Second, we discuss the methodology and results, which center on two themes: (1) the bad mother narrative and (2) the notion of "it won't be like this for long." Last, we engage the study's findings with Gloria Anzaldúa's concept of *nepantla*, a space where expectations and ideas collide and create new meaning and new perspectives to set forth a more extensive and thorough understanding of the experiences and realities of community college student mothers.

LITERATURE REVIEW

In the last year, student parents' needs, such as parent centers and subsidized on-campus childcare, have made headway in national mainstream newspapers and magazines, such as the *Washington Post*, *Time*, *The Hill*, and *The Atlantic*, to name a few (Freeman 2015; Merisotis 2015; Miller 2015; Paquette 2015). According to a 2014 study from the Institute for Women's Policy Research, there were 4.8 million college student parents of dependent children in 2011 (about 26 percent of all college undergraduates), and the majority (about 71 percent) are women. About 2 million students (or 43 percent of the total student parent population) are single mothers (Gault, Reichlin, Reynolds, and Froehner 2014a). Nearly half (45 percent) of all student parents attend public two-year institutions, while 16 percent attend public four-year schools (Gault, Reichlin, Reynolds, and Froehner 2014b). Most of the student parents at community colleges are mothers of color—Black mothers comprise 53.7 percent, Latina mothers 40 percent, and American Indian mothers 40.1 percent. They also happen to be low-income, work full-time, lack childcare, and graduate with high debt (Reichlin 2015). Childcare on campus declined from 53 percent in 2003–2004 to 46 percent in 2013; the decrease has been most dramatically felt at community colleges, with fewer than half of all two-year campuses offering campus childcare services as of 2013 (Gault, Reichlin, Reynolds, and Froehner 2014b). Childcare access impacts student mothers' educational pursuits.

A report published in 2013 by the American Association of University Women (AAUW) found that millions of women attend community colleges, but many do not reach their goals, due to limited availability of on-campus childcare. Given the challenges that community student parents face, particularly with childcare, only 26 percent of two-year student parents attain a degree or certificate in six years (Reichlin 2015).

Little has been published in the academic literature on the experiences of student mothers in community colleges; they are underexplored and as such are an unacknowledged population. The only study to date is "'Pretty Darned Cold': Single Mother Students and the Community College Climate in Post-Welfare Reform America," published in 2007 by Julian M. Duquaine-Watson in the journal *Equity & Excellence in Education*. Duquaine-Watson's ethnographic study on single mothers attending a community college in a Midwestern state in the United States found that community college single mothers are significantly more vulnerable to unwelcoming attitudes, practices, and policies encountered in their everyday interactions with faculty, staff, and students—what she terms the "chilly climate" (2007, 229).

Similar accounts have been reported by graduate student mothers who felt that professors had lower expectations of them, felt discriminated against because of their gender, and felt out of place in graduate school (Solorzano 1998). Lynch (2008) found connections between structural environment and sociocultural identities and graduate student mother potential attrition rates. Graduate student mothers in Lynch's study lacked financial support from their home department and university, and had limited options for affordable childcare. Lynch's findings also point to the importance of creating and fostering positive relationships and interactions between faculty and graduate student mothers to ensure students' graduate school success and sense of satisfaction. Although most study participants reported feeling intellectually supported, the majority did not feel emotionally supported by advisors and faculty members. One graduate student mother in Lynch's study noted that when she informed her advisor that she was pregnant, he responded, "Why did you do that for?"—implying that having a child would impact her future professional opportunities and that she "blew it" (2008, 600). Additionally, this study also shed light on how graduate student mothers negotiate being a "good mother" and a "good student" and the central role support systems play in the overall experiences of graduate student mothers.

Few institutions have tailored policies and practices that meet the needs of graduate student parents, and many faculty also lack an awareness of the types of support and resources available to graduate student parents (Springer, Parker, and Leviten-Reid 2009). Fewer than 15 percent offer any of the following: family-friendly space, dissertation support groups, childcare subsidies, or faculty training on the issues faced by graduate student parents (2009, 441). Findings from Springer and colleagues' study nonetheless suggest that departments do accommodate graduate student parents on a case-by-case basis.

The aforementioned studies provide a foundation for furthering the analysis of women in higher education. We build on this literature by focusing on community college student mothers, an increasing student population that is understudied and undertheorized. As former student mothers and current faculty members at a community college, we feel the need and urgency to examine and understand the lived experiences and realities of our students to better meet and address their needs inside and outside of the classroom.

METHODOLOGY

We conducted four focus groups, which included a total of thirteen college student mothers at Pacific Coast Community College[1], a community college located in Salinas, California. The participants represent a diverse group based on age, social class, education, career aspirations, and ethnic and racial background. At the time of the interview, they were between the ages of twenty-one and forty-six. All were enrolled either part-time or full-time at Pacific Coast Community College; they were more likely to be married (six participants) or single (four participants) than divorced. Each mother had an average of two children. Most participants earned less than $26,000 per year, with one making between $41,000 and $60,000.

Focus groups were conducted on campus in a private room located inside the Office of Student Life; four or five student mothers participated in each focus group. The focus groups lasted one to two hours and were conducted by one or both professors, Nereida Oliva and Hortencia Jiménez. Questions were open ended, which allowed student mothers to speak freely in their native language. Both researchers are bilingual and bi-literate, and interviews were transcribed in Spanish and English. At the end of each focus group, each participant was given a meal voucher for $50, courtesy of the division of Student Affairs. Pseudonyms are used for the participants who requested their anonymity.

Qualitative research of a small sample provides an opportunity to capture the particulars and complexities of student mothers' lives, which we would otherwise not be able to access and about which little is known in the academic literature. This study does not attempt to generalize the experiences of other community college student mothers, but rather offers a micro analysis of a single group of student mothers at a community college. This research is informed by grounded theory, a qualitative approach developed by Glaser and Strauss (1967) that involves the construction of theory through the analysis of qualitative data. Grounded theory is an approach that

---

1. Pacific Coast Community College is a pseudonym. It is a public two-year community college designated as a Hispanic-Serving Institution (HSI) with an enrollment of at least 25% Latinx students (Excelencia in Education, 2017).

sets out to *discover* theory from data (Glaser & Strauss 1967, 1) instead of collecting data to verify theory.

In addition, our methodology is also informed by a Chicana feminist epistemological perspective. A Chicana feminist perspective allows us to be culturally sensitive and responsive to the everyday life experience and realities of community college student mothers. A Chicana feminist perspective also means acknowledging that many student mothers have different intersections of identity, so their experiences must be viewed through an intersectional lens. This is important because the majority of student mothers attending community colleges are first-generation, low-income students of color (Reichlin 2015). Furthermore, a Chicana feminist perspective allows us to use what Delgado Bernal (1998) refers to as "cultural intuition." Our cultural intuition "informs how we develop and enact the research process" (Calderon, Delgado Bernal, Perez Huber, Malagon, and Velez 2012, 515) and allows us to take a closer look at what usually goes overlooked or misinterpreted under traditional qualitative research paradigms (Tijerina Revilla 2004).

For us, our cultural intuition is very much informed by our own experiences as mothers in academia—as students and now as scholars. What we present is not the common narrative of the docile, self-sacrificing mother but one that is unapologetic for the sacrifices that the mother is making for her children and family.

FINDINGS

Our findings are organized around two common themes: the "bad mother" narrative and the idea that "it won't be like this for long."

THE BAD MOTHER NARRATIVE: "I'M SPENDING A LOT OF TIME DISCIPLINING HIM"

This section is organized around two student mothers who demonstrate the dynamics of the "bad" mother narrative as they pursue their college education. Western discourses and definitions of mother socially construct the "good" versus "bad" mother. This dichotomy is problematic, as it obscures the myriad ways in which mothers do mothering. As Guerra, Rios, and Stokes (2011, 216) point out, "good mothers can be found in many forms—single mothers, lesbian mothers, working mothers." The bad mother narrative emerges when student mothers feel that they are spending more time disciplining their children than spending time with them. Rosa, a thirty-one-year-old Mexican American mother of a five-year-old girl described it this way:

My challenge is discipline, 'cause I'm a single mom, so it's kinda like I have to be the mom and dad, and it's hard because I like want to be the good parent all the time, and it's hard when I have to put down my foot, and then I get the sad face. And it's hard, too, because I live at home with my mom, and my mom wants to be the good parent all the time.

Rosa is a single mother who lives with her parents, and although they are supportive and take care of her daughter while she is in school, Rosa feels that her mother undermines her parenting when it comes to disciplining her daughter. Rosa spends most of her day at school attending classes and doing her coursework as well as working. Rosa feels bad that the time that she has with her daughter revolves around discipline. As she says, "It sucks, because sometimes in that limited time, I have to be punishing her." She recalls one time when she spanked her daughter and "felt bad doing that" but "wanted to spank her" because her parents "have a lot of empty threats," and she doesn't want her daughter growing up and seeing her as "an empty threat," because, as she said, "I'm not an empty threat." Rosa has no choice but to be the disciplinarian, even though she doesn't "want to," because if she doesn't discipline her daughter, her "parents let her get away with everything," and this is "definitely really hard."

Lola, a thirty-year-old biracial mother of a three-year-old boy, does not have support from extended family members. She feels that she is "spending a lot of time disciplining" her son, and it makes her "feel really bad"; she expresses feeling "guilty all the time." She articulates it this way:

I feel like I'm spending a lot of time disciplining him, and it makes me feel really bad. I just feel guilty all the time; instead of us enjoying our time, it's just like … I just get tired; I run out of patience.

Lola articulates a common sentiment that many mothers—in particular single student mothers—feel when they are with their children after they spend their day at school and/or work. When they arrive home, they have to tend to domestic chores and prepare meals for their children. Their parental responsibilities do not wait, because as single moms they "have to do everything" on their own, and as Lola put it, "it's hard to go to school, and work, and be a single mom."

The bad mother narrative can be understood through the intersections of their identity as single mothers, workers, and college students who are dealing with everyday educational stressors and childrearing struggles. They have to "work a lot" to be able to afford to live on their own and "come to school full-time," as Lola comments. Rosa's and Lola's narratives indicate that mothering and education are not mutually exclusive but constitutive of one another.

IT WON'T BE LIKE THIS FOR LONG

Darius Rucker, an American country music artist and lead vocalist of the rock band Hootie & the Blowfish, cowrote the song "It Won't Be Like This for Long," which was released in November 2008 in honor of his daughters. The song chronicles how the lives of a couple change from the arrival of their infant, who keeps both parents awake for most of the night, to when the daughter turns four and is taken to preschool and holds onto her father's leg because she does not want to go, to the father observing his daughter and realizing that she will eventually be a teenager who may walk down the aisle one day. His daughter will soon grow, and he will not be able to observe her much longer.

Like many college students, the student mothers in this study expressed feeling overwhelmed balancing the everyday realities and responsibilities of motherhood, student life, and work. Yet they realize that this challenging phase will soon pass and "it won't be like this for long," as Krystal, a single mother of two noted. Krystal is in the nursing program at Hartnell College, known to be rigorous, demanding, and taxing in terms of students' time and energy, both intellectually and physically. Krystal feels exhausted and stressed, but when it comes to her children's bedtime routine and seeing them fall asleep, she feels like crying. As she comments:

> You're just like, it won't be like this for long, so it helps me; it helps to center me and bring me back, "Oh my God, they are driving me up …" I want to run away, and then I have to be like, but then I'm going to miss this. … I have to just play [the song] to remind myself that they're going to be grown soon.

Knowing that "it won't be like his for long" can be understood as the underlying force for student mothers' dedication and commitment in achieving and completing their academic and professional goals. The student mothers demonstrate high aspirations for themselves but also high levels of investment in their education while negotiating their role and responsibilities as mothers. Consequently, the student mothers also illustrate their resiliency through their everyday negotiation of the challenges, triumphs, and nuances of being a student mother.

Karla, a twenty-one-year-old single mother of a one-year-old and pregnant with her second child, is focused and clear on her education and career aspirations. As she says,

[I] want to first complete my AA in 2017 and then go on with my BA, and I want to do that before 2019. And career goals—I want to do something like case work or social work in the prison system.

Karla works full-time with an organization that helps individuals who were previously incarcerated transition to the community. Karla notes that her current job position has influenced her academic and professional goals. Being a mother, working full-time, and attending school full-time is not easy. Karla shared, "There's days where I just want to give up, and there's days where I'm just fully motivated, but I don't know how to get through the day."

Martina is a twenty-six-year-old mother of three children. She began her educational journey years prior to becoming a mother and took "a class here and a class there." She confessed that schoolwork was not as much of a priority as her employment was. Once she obtained a full-time job, she dropped her courses to focus on her job. After her second pregnancy, she decided to return to school because she felt that she "had to do something, more than just go back to work." Martina "kind of jumped into it" and enrolled in college courses. Martina shared that this time she was no longer worried about her physical appearance or what others thought about her. Rather, Martina's focus was on her academic performance and doing her work and going home to her family. As she said, "I'm just here to listen to my teacher and get my work in, and then I need to go home to my children." Like Karla, Martina also wants to "hopefully transfer" to a four-year university to continue her education. Martina went on to share, "As a woman they [her three daughters] need to know that their mom is going to college, and we've got to get through this together and go to school, and I feel that like—I don't want to say I owe it to them, because I owe it to myself, but I just want them to have that good role model in their life."

Martina is a role model for her children, and her educational journey is a collective process that includes her daughters, who motivate and inspire her. Martina recognizes that the sacrifices she is making for herself and her family will benefit everyone. However, obtaining an education is a personal endeavor, something that she owes to herself. Karla and Martina's resiliency is intricately woven into their everyday actions that move them closer to their academic and professional goals. Balancing and negotiating multiple roles is not easy, but because they know it won't be like this for long, Karla and Martina are fully invested in achieving their academic and professional goals every step of the way. Their resiliency allows them to look beyond the everyday struggles and challenges and focus on the bigger picture—a college degree.

DISCUSSION

The goal of this chapter was to provide a more in-depth examination and understanding of the experiences of community college student mothers. Our analysis reveals that the mothers are in constant physical and emotional movement between their roles as student mothers and workers. This movement causes student mothers tension and stress in their daily lives. Despite facing daily challenges and obstacles, the student mothers hold high aspirations for themselves in achieving a college education for the benefit of themselves and their families.

We argue that community college student mothers are articulating an awareness and state of being that point to a state of contradiction and complexity, what Gloria Anzaldúa refers to as *nepantla*. According to Anzaldúa (2000), 548–549),

> *Nepantla* is the site of transformation, the place where different perspectives come into conflict and where you question the basic ideas, tenets, and identities inherited from your family, your education, and your different cultures. *Nepantla* is a zone between changes where you struggle to find equilibrium between the outer expression of change and your inner relationship to it.

Drawing on Gloria Anzaldúa's framework, we suggest that the lives and experiences of community college mothers must be understood, validated, honored, and recognized in this state of *nepantla* that allows them to participate in multiple realities that often lead to uneasiness and contradiction. Chicana feminist scholars have used Anzaldúa's notion of *nepantla* to document and understand the experiences of youth of color (Mendoza 2015), teacher education classrooms (Gutierrez 2008; Prieto and Villenas 2012), Chicanas in higher education (Burciaga, 2007), and grassroots organizers (Blackwell, 2010). These authors highlight the multidimensionality of being and having to negotiate the in-between spaces, a kind of "third space" that embodies "everywhere" and "nowhere" at the same time (Gutierrez 2008).

For the student mothers in this study, being in *nepantla* can be understood by how the student mothers negotiate and straddle the good mother/bad mother dichotomy. Social constructs regarding mothering and motherhood often determine what is a "good mother" and what is a "bad mother." A "good mother" is someone who is selfless, is married, and had a planned pregnancy at an "appropriate age," whereas a "bad mother" is stereotyped to be a teen mother, a "welfare queen," or a mother with a career who has no time for her kids.

Due to school demands, the student mothers often feel "guilty" about not being able to spend quality time with their children and instead spend more time disciplining them when they do spend time with them. Even though we highlighted how Rosa and

Lola, both of whom are single mothers, demonstrate the "bad mother" narrative, all the mothers in this study, regardless of marital status, shared feelings and thoughts that mirrored the experiences of Rosa and Lola. The daily negotiation of roles and responsibilities as mothers and students thrusts the student mothers in this study into a space where they reject the good mother/bad mother dichotomy and forge mothering practices that are best suited for their everyday realities and needs. Furthermore, being in *nepantla* enables each mother to imagine and work toward her and her children's future, as the state of *nepantla* reassures the student mothers that "it won't be like this for long."

As educators, it is important to see the multidimensionality of community college student mothers. Although we are not the first scholars to theorize on *nepantla* and its usefulness in higher education and Chicana studies, we are making an important intervention—we are uniquely contributing to a literature that has historically ignored the experiences of community college student mothers. Anzaldúa's theory of *nepantla* offers an asset-based approach to understanding the experiences of student mothers. Through a *nepantla* perspective, we humanize, validate, and honor their struggles, pain, and sacrifices as sources of strength, resilience, and wisdom. As *nepantleras*, the student mothers are able to do two things at once—mothering while learning. As the data for this study demonstrated, mothering while learning is not an easy task, but one that the student mothers do fiercely.

DISCUSSION QUESTIONS

1. The chapter is organized around what key findings about community college student mothers?

2. How do student mothers articulate their educational aspirations and goals?

3. What could we learn from more research on community college student mothers?

4. How do the authors draw on Gloria Anzaldúa's framework of *nepantla* to understand community student mothers?

WEBSITE LINKS

American Association of University Women: www.aauw.org/resource/women-in-community-colleges

Chicana Motherwork: http://chicanamotherwork.wix.com/mysite

Institute for Women's Policy Research: www.iwpr.org

Motherhood Initiative for Research and Community Involvement: http://motherhoo-dinitiative.org

AUDIOVISUAL MATERIALS

Maid in America, PBS Independent Lens (educational film documentary): www.pbs.org/independentlens/maidinamerica

Chicana Motherwork Podcast: http://chicanamotherwork.wix.com/mysite#!podcast/c8k2

SUGGESTIONS FOR FURTHER READING

Collins, P. H. 1994. "Shifting the Center: Race, Class, and Feminist Theorizing about Motherhood." In *Mothering: Ideology, Experience, and Agency*, edited by E. Glenn, G. Chang, and L. Forcey. New York: Routledge.

Gumb, A. P, C. Martens, M. Williams, and L. J. Ross. 2016. *Revolutionary Mothering: Love on the Front Lines*. Oakland, CA: PM Press.

Hays, S. 1996. *The Cultural Contradictions of Motherhood*. New Haven, CT: Yale University Press.

Smith Silva, D. 2011. *Latina/Chicana Mothering*. Bradford, Ontario, Canada: Demeter Press.

St. Rose, Andresse, and Catherine Hill. 2013. *Women in Community Colleges: Access to Success*. Washington, DC: American Association of University Women (AAUW).

Téllez, Michelle. 2013. "Lectures, Evaluations, and Diapers: Navigating the Terrains of Chicana Single Motherhood in the Academy." *Feminist Formations* 25(3): 79–97.

Villalobos, Ana. 2014. *Motherload: Making It All Better in Insecure Times*. Berkeley: University of California Press.

REFERENCES

Blackwell, M. 2010. "Líderes Campesinas: Nepantla Strategies and Grassroots Organizing at the Intersection of Gender and Globalization." *Aztlan* 1: 13–47.

Burciaga, R. 2007. "Chicana PhD Students Living in *Nepantla: Educacion* and Aspirations beyond the Doctorate." PhD diss., UCLA.

Castañeda, M., and K.Isgro. 2013. *Mothers in Academia*. New York: Columbia University Press.

Calderón, D., D. Delgado Bernal, L.Pérez Huber, M.C., Malagón, and V.N. Vélez, V. N. 2012. "A Chicana feminist epistemology revisited: Cultivating ideas a generation later." *Harvard Educational Review*, 82:513–539

Collins, P. H. 2000. *Black Feminist Thought: Knowledge, Consciousness, and the Politics of Empowerment*. 2nd ed. New York: Routledge.

Delgado Bernal, D. 1998. "Using a Chicana Feminist Epistemology in Educational Research." *Harvard Educational Review* 68(4): 555–582.

Duquaine-Watson, J. M. 2007. "'Pretty Darned Cold': Single Mother Students and the Community College Climate in Post-Welfare Reform America." *Equity & Excellence in Education* 40(3): 229–240.

Duquaine-Watson, J. M. 2017. *Mothering by Degrees: Single Mothers and the Pursuit of Postsecondary Educuation*. Rutgers University Press. New Brunswick, NJ.

Flores, S.M., C. L. Horn, and G. Crisp. 2006. "Community Colleges, Public Policy, and Latino Student Opportunity." *New Directions for Community Colleges* 133: 71–80.

Freeman, A. 2015. "Single Moms and Welfare Woes: A Higher-Education Dilemma." *The Atlantic*. www.theatlantic.com/education/archive/2015/08/why-single-moms-struggle-with-college/401582.

Gault, B., L. Reichlin, E. Reynolds, and M. Froehner. 2014a. "4.8 Million College Students Are Raising Children." *Institute for Women's Policy Research*, November 17. https://iwpr.org/publications/4-8-million-college-students-are-raising-children.

Gault, B., L. Reichlin, E. Reynolds, and M. Froehner. 2014b. "Campus Child Care Declining Even as Growing Numbers of Parents Attend College." *Institute for Women's Policy Research*, November 17. https://iwpr.org/publications/campus-child-care-declining-even-as-growing-numbers-of-parents-attend-college.

Gault, B., L. Reichlin, E. Reynolds, and M. Froehner. 2014c. "Campus Child Care Declining Even as Growing Numbers of Parents Attend College." *Institute for Women's Policy Research*, November 17. https://iwpr.org/publications/campus-child-care-declining-even-as-growing-numbers-of-parents-attend-college.

Glaser, B., and A. Strauss. 1967. *The Discovery of Grounded Theory: Strategies for Qualitative Research*. London: Aldine Transaction.

Guerra, P., D. Rios, and M. Stokes. 2011. "The Telenovela Alborada: Constructions of the Latina Mother in an Internationally Successful Soap Opera." In *Latina/Chicana Mothering*, edited by D. Smith-Silva. Toronto: Demeter Press.

Gutierrez, R. 2008. "What Is 'Nepantla' and How Can It Help Physics Education Researchers Conceptualize Knowledge for Teaching?" *PER Conference Invited Paper Series* 1064: 23–25.

Gutierrez, R. 2012. "Embracing *Nepantla*: Rethinking 'Knowledge' and Its Use in Mathematics Teaching." *Journal of Research in Mathematics Education*1(1): 29–56.

Gutiérrez y Muhs, G., Y. Flores Niemann, C. González, and A. Harris, eds. 2012. *Presumed Incompetent: The Intersections of Race and Class for Women in Academia*. Boulder: University Press of Colorado.

Hochschild, A. 1997. *The Time Bind: When Work Becomes Home and Home Becomes Work*. New York: Metropolitan Books.

Lamphere, L., P. Zavella, F. Gonzales, and P. B. Evan. 1993. *Sunbelt Working Mothers: Reconciling Family and Factory*. Ithaca, NY: Cornell University Press.

Lynch, K. D. 2008. "Gender Roles and the American Academe: A Case Study of Graduate Student Mothers." *Gender and Education* 20(6): 585–605.

Mendoza, S. 2015. "Reimagining Education with Nepantlera/o Elementary-Aged Youth through Anzaldua and Critical Youth Studies." PhD diss., University of Utah.

Mercado Lopez, M. 2011. "I Feel a Revolution Occur in My Womb: Mapping Cognitive and Somatic Transformation through Readings of *mestiza* Maternal *facultad*." PhD diss., University of Texas at San Antonio.

Merisotis, J. 2015. "America's College Students Have Changed: Will Federal Policy Keep Pace?" *The Hill*. http://thehill.com/blogs/congress-blog/education/254517-americas-college-students-have-changed-will-federal-policy-keep.

Miller, Z. 2015. "Hillary Clinton Outlines College Plan for Students with Children." *Time*. http://time.com/3999036/hillary-clinton-college-children.

Paquette, D. 2015. "This Simple Addition to College Campuses Could Cut Costs for a Quarter of Undergrads." *Washington Post*. www.washingtonpost.com/news/wonk/wp/2015/08/11/this-simple-addition-to-college-campuses-could-cut-costs-for-a-quarter-of-undergrads.

Prieto, L., and S. Villenas. 2012. "Pedagogies from Nepantla: Testimonio, Chicana. Latina Feminisms and Teacher Education Classrooms." *Equity and Excellence in Education* 45(3): 411–429.

Reichlin, L. 2015. "Supporting Student Parent Success in Community Colleges." *Institute for Women's Policy Research*, October 8. https://iwpr.org/publications/supporting-student-parent-success-in-community-colleges.

Segura, D. 1994. "Working at Motherhood: Chicana and Mexican Immigrant Mothers and Employment." In *Mothering: Ideology, Experience, and Agency*, edited by E. Glenn, G. Chang, and L. Forcey. New York: Routledge.

Solorzano, D. 1998. "Critical Race Theory, Racial and Gender Microaggressions, and the Experiences of Chicana and Chicano Scholars." *International Journal of Qualitative Studies in Education* 11:121–136.

Springer, K. W., B. K. Parker, and C. Leviten-Reid. 2009. "Making Space for Graduate Student Parents: Practice and Politics." *Journal of Family Issues* 30(4): 435–457.

Tellez, M. 2013. "Lectures, Evaluations, and Diapers: Navigating the Terrains of Chicana Single Motherhood in the Academy." *Feminist Formations* 25(3): 79–97.

Tijerina Revilla, A. 2004. "Muxerista Pedagogy: Raza Womyn Teaching Social Justice through Activism." *The High School Journal* 87(4): 80–94.

Zarate, M. E., and R. Burciaga .2010. "Latinos and College Access: Trends and Future Directions." *Journal of College Admission*, 209 :24–29.

PART IV

OLD AND NEW CHALLENGES: LOOKING INTO THE FUTURE

ALL IN THE NAME OF ASSIMILATION
    By Celeste Torres

WATER PROTECTORS: STORIES OF INHABITED TERRITORIES
    By Gilliam Jackson, Trey Adcock, and Juan G. Sánchez Martínez

BLACK AND LATINX MILLENNIAL STUDENTS AND RACIAL JUSTICE ACTIVISM IN
THE AGE OF BLACK LIVES MATTER
    By María Joaquina Villaseñor

WHITE PRIVILEGE: MOVING BEYOND GUILT INTO RESPONSIBILITY AND ACTION
    By Debra Busman

SEMILLAS Y CULTURAS: FOODWAYS IN ETHNIC STUDIES
    By Melissa M. Moreno

FROM MEXICO TO THE UNITED STATES: DISCOVERING AND ADVOCATING FOR
SOCIAL JUSTICE
    By Cristobal Salinas Jr.

INDIGENOUS IMMIGRANTS FROM THE MEXICAN STATE OF OAXACA RESIDING IN
MONTEREY COUNTY, CALIFORNIA: THE SEARCH FOR MEANING AND AGENCY
    By Renata Funke

REINCARNATION
    By Gloria Anzaldúa

All in the Name of Assimilation

By Celeste Torres

For years I compromised, especially on My Name.
I'd introduce myself with the name my mother hand-wove for me
But what was repeated back came watered down and tasted mild in my mouth.
I realized my name, too flavorful for untrained palettes,
Was much too warm to swallow.

The English pronunciation silences, strips, and replaces sounds
From the symphony my father conducted, bringing my name to life.
In Spanish, no letter remains silent;
Each demands its presence;
Each stands alone with dignity.

I've learned my culture is too much to stomach.
Like my name, too hard to swallow,
A mouthful to those unknowing of its flavors,
Too demanding for those lacking willingness and effort.

I've compromised on my name.
I've adopted the flat, meek pronunciation,
All in the name of assimilation.

But like the letters of my name,
I've learned to demand my presence,

To take up space where I'd been silenced,
And challenged those who watered me down.

Because Like My Culture,
I Am Too Much For Those Unwilling
To Stomach.

Water Protectors: Stories of Inhabited Territories

•••

By Gilliam Jackson, Trey Adcock, and Juan G. Sánchez Martínez

Since the colonial period of the Americas, treaties, constitutions, and laws have used a specific "language of domination" to ignore and erase American Indian and indigenous knowledge of ancestral territory. Underlying five centuries of genocide, displacement, and cultural appropriation is a colonial belief that ancestral territories are "wasteland" or "empty lands" (*terra nullius*), based on a social contract in which humans buy and sell "natural resources" as if they were owners of Mother Earth. That is not the case in the stories that follow. In this chapter, we will discuss the doctrine of discovery as a legal and structural foundation for colonial practices that continue into the present day. To highlight five hundred years of indigenous resistance, two contemporary testimonies of activism and advocacy in protecting water will be provided: the Cherokee resistance against the Tennessee Valley Authority (TVA) in western North Carolina during the 1970s, and the recent struggle against the development of the Dakota Access Pipeline (DAPL) on the Standing Rock Sioux reservation. These stories feature the belief that activist research is a form of ceremony.

THIS STORY DIDN'T START IN 2016

The DAPL, developed by Energy Transfer Partners, is an approximately 1,200-mile project running from the Bakken region of North Dakota southeast into Illinois. The almost $4 billion project will utilize a pipe, 30 inches in diameter, to transport 470,000 gallons of fracked oil daily. The original route was to run slightly northeast near the North Dakota state capital of Bismarck, which is approximately 92 percent White. This route was ultimately rejected because of environmental concerns. Plans for the pipeline were subsequently rerouted through the treaty lands of the Standing Rock Sioux, just north of the current reservation border and under Lake Oahe, thereby jeopardizing sacred sites and the primary water reservoir of the tribe.

On April 1, 2016, the Standing Rock Sioux tribe established the Sacred Stone Camp to peacefully protect the Missouri River (*Mni Soce*, or "Churning Waters"), the Cannonball River, and the treaty lands in which the Dakota/Lakota ancestors remain. Almost four hundred archeological sites face desecration along DAPL, and twenty-six are at the confluence of these two rivers (Brave Bull). In only few months, the Oceti Sakowin Camp became the largest indigenous mobilization on Turtle Island since the 1970s, as well as a paradigmatic demonstration for all nations.

This story, however, did not start in 2016. Since the Treaty of Fort Laramie of 1851, the US Congress has moved the borderlines of the original treaty several times (in 1861, 1868, 1877, 1889, and 1958), breaking its commitments to the old chiefs, and displacing communities (see the legal history summary by Kiana Herold [2016]). Thus, this is a story of indigenous resilience and remembrance beyond nation-state narratives and borderlands. On December 4, 2016, under President Barack Obama's administration, the Army Corps of Engineers denied the easement through Lake Oahe and began "undertaking an environmental impact statement to look at possible alternative routes."

Figure 4.1 (Oceti Sakowin Camp. Solidarity with Standing Rock. Friday, September 2, 2016.)

POWER OF PLACE

BIO: Trey Adcock (Cherokee Nation) obtained his PhD from the University of North Carolina at Chapel Hill, where he was awarded a Sequoyah Dissertation Fellowship in the Royster Society of Fellows. Currently, he is an assistant professor in education and director of American Indian outreach at the University of North Carolina, Asheville. At UNC Asheville, he works directly with the American Indian student population as the faculty advisor for the Native American Student Association and serves on the Diversity Action Council for the university. He resides on a small farm in the mountains of western North Carolina with his wife and two kids.

> Follow the sky
>
> Into the blue
>
> You are part sky
>
> Sky is part you

—John Trudell, from *What It Means to Be a Human Being* (2001)

On a cold, windy overcast morning, we approached the front lines of the fight against DAPL. Thirty to forty people milled around, many huddled together for warmth, engaged in intense-looking conversation. As we drew closer, someone quickly moved toward us and rapidly instructed the three of us in nonviolent tactics, employing us to not lash out and to stay calm. As we adjourned, another one of the Red Warriors moved like a shadow in front of us and opened his clenched fist to reveal traditional paint to apply to our faces as protection, and as a reminder of the historical continuum of resistance that we were part of. Silently, we each applied the paint under our eyes and entered into the circle that was forming around what appeared to be the leader of the group, carrying a briefcase by his side. Standing there, the cold and wind felt like they were cutting against the bone. It was late summer, and for a moment my mind drifted to what the dead of winter would be like for the water protectors. After an initial prayer, various people moved into the circle to provide updates on the bulldozers, helicopters, and dog-wielding mercenaries who had been hired by Energy Transfer Partners.

Out of the corner of my eye, a young woman moved through the crowd and into the center of the circle with a tightened jaw and pursed lips. Wearing weathered boots, sweatpants, and a heavy brown and black coat, she carried herself with the presence of a mother, a daughter, a warrior. She was short in stature, and red paint was barely visible below her eyes as she began to talk. "We must remember that this is both a physical movement of resistance but also a mental one. Some of you can return home when the battle ends. … I, however, am *of* here. These hills, these rocks, this water … ." She paused, underscoring the intensity of the moment. "I am of this place and will always be of this place. I will never leave. I will raise my kids here, my grandkids here. … I will die here." Her eyes connected, seemingly, with every individual there.

Her point made, she slowly turned and moved back into the crowd, leaving the weight of her words in the center. A renewed sense of purpose and strength could be felt as quiet anxiousness set in.

Figure 4.2 (Oceti Sakowin Camp. Friday, September 2, 2016.)

This portrait from the front lines of Standing Rock was one of the many sacred stories we held as we returned home to *Tsalagi Uweti*, the "Old Cherokee" lands in western North Carolina. I came back to this moment, to the woman's words, in the coming weeks. During our time in North Dakota, there were other instances that reinforced and underscored the connection between place and sacredness, the relationship between community and geography, and the sovereignty and ceremony of relationships. John Trudell reminded us of these connections:

We're human beings. And the DNA of the human being—my bone, flesh, and blood—is literally made up of the metals, minerals, and liquids of the Earth. We are literally shapes and forms of the Earth. That's who we are. And we have being.

> Our being comes from our relationship to the Sun, and to the universe. (2001)

The power and sacredness of *place* is a central aspect of the Standing Rock fight against DAPL. Vine Deloria Jr. describes an indigenous worldview where reciprocal relationships form the foundation of all life—relationships that are both biological and spiritual, inherently personal:

> The vast majority of Indian tribal religions, therefore, have a sacred center at a particular place, be it a river, a mountain, a plateau, valley, or other natural feature. This center enables the people to look out along the four dimensions and locate their lands, to relate all historical events within the confines of this particular land, and to accept responsibility for it. (1994, 67)

Place is deeply engrained into every relationship, a sacred bond. As a Cherokee Nation citizen, I am aware that Cherokee people, too, have many sacred places. In my mind, however, there is one that stands out: *Kituwah*. I have been taught that this word translates to "of this dirt." Our sacred stories, ceremonies, language, song, prayers, and identity are deeply interwoven into a sacred relationship with *Kituwah*. This sense of place cuts directly into identity, sovereignty, and ceremony. It speaks to who we are as a people—*Anigiduwagi*, the people of *Kituwah*.

One of the more sinister aspects of the colonial projects is the disconnecting of people from place. Attempting to break the umbilical cord between the sacred place and nationhood. A significant way in which this was done and continues to be done is through what legal scholars refer to as the doctrine of discovery.

This doctrine is essentially a series of papal bulls written in the fifteenth century to provide international legal justification for Christian nations to wage war on indigenous lands and their inhabitants. Christian explorers were basically given the right, by various popes, to claim lands they "discovered" in the name of their Christian monarchs. Any land that was not inhabited by Christians was available to be "discovered," claimed, and exploited. If the "pagan" inhabitants could be converted, they might be spared. If not, they could be enslaved or killed (Newcomb 1992). The Catholic pope laid the foundation for the doctrine of discovery in 1452 by issuing the papal bull *Dum Diversas*, which instructed the Portuguese in Western Africa "to invade, capture, vanquish, and subdue all Saracens, pagans, and other enemies of Christ, to put them into perpetual slavery, and to take away all their possessions and property." Thus, the foundation for the brutal system of colonization is the intentional dehumanization and dislocation of indigenous populations from their lands, as they were considered heathens and savages.

In 1823, Supreme Court Chief Justice John Marshall brought the doctrine of discovery into US law through his ruling in the *Johnson v. McIntosh* case. Writing for a unanimous court, Chief Justice Marshall stated that Christian European nations had assumed "ultimate dominion" over the lands of America during the Age of Discovery, and that—upon "discovery"—the Indians had lost "their rights to complete sovereignty, as independent nations," and retained only a right of "occupancy" in their lands (Newcomb 1992). Indian nations were thus subjugated to the authority of the US court system and ultimately to congressional plenary power, under which the "Christian" US government could claim possession of indigenous lands.

This ruling continues to have impact in the present day, as the doctrine of discovery is a foundation on which the United States is assuming sovereignty and dominion over the territory of the *Oceti Sakowin* ("Great Sioux Nation") in a coercive manner (Newcomb 2016). Thus, Western legal systems continue to favor the extraction of resources on indigenous lands to benefit the formerly Christian, European colonial powers that "discovered" those lands (Newcomb 2016). The truly insidious part of the struggle in the Dakotas today is not just that governments continue to dispossess indigenous people of their land, but that, backed by the legal jargon of the "law of Christendom," multinational corporations and banks are able to threaten the sacred spaces and territory of indigenous people in the name of profit.

Figure 4.3 (Resistance Art/Sign. Treaty Land, Standing Rock Sioux Tribe.)

POWER OF RESISTANCE

BIO: Gilliam (Gil) Jackson (Eastern Band of Cherokee Indian) grew up in the Snowbird community, where he resides today. He is a former administrator of the *Atse Kituwah* Cherokee-language immersion school and is currently an adjunct professor of Cherokee language at UNC Asheville. He continues to be an activist for indigenous issues, especially in regard to environmental issues. Gil holds a BS in secondary education from the University of Georgia and a master's degree in administration and planning from the University of Tennessee.

> We have a right to know who we are, but it comes with a responsibility … nationhood is a commitment, not just an inheritance.
> —Margaret Kovach (2009)

On a chilly, overcast day on the Snowbird reservation, Gil is sitting in his well-worn recliner, reflecting on his experiences almost forty years ago in the fight against the Tellico Dam project in western North Carolina. This topic has been brought up a couple of times since the three of us left the front lines of the Standing Rock movement.

When presenting at the campus of UNC Asheville on our collective experience during the dog attacks at Standing Rock, one of the first questions from audience members was "were you afraid?" Gil replied, "I wasn't afraid on the front lines of DAPL. … This isn't the first [time] I have taken action!"

His response was reminiscent of the time we were driving into Bismarck, North Dakota, and began discussing the route into camp. Gil was riding in the backseat with the supplies we were bringing hugged in tight all around him, when he leaned forward and matter-of-factly stated, "I have one more thing to say. I don't care if they try and stop me! If it takes me walking into camp with supplies, that's what I am gonna do, and ain't nobody gonna stop me." Defiance in the face of force and intimidation. Defiance within a five-hundred-year continuum of American Indian resistance to colonial forces. Defiance that is alive and well today.

Now, as we sit in Gil's one-room cabin in the foothills of Snowbird Mountain, not far from the land that he grew up on and that most of his family still resides on, Gil begins to talk of his time fighting for the preservation of ancestral Cherokee towns in the face of developers. Gil exhales, leans back, and speaks slowly and steadily as he tells the story of the TVA's desire to build a dam in Loudon County, Tennessee, in the late 1970s. The project was designed to enact eminent domain to sixteen thousand acres of land, then create a huge lake by damming a portion of the Tennessee River known as the "Little T," the last free-flowing body of water in the state and one of the most sacred areas for the Cherokee people. Only two centuries prior, the area to be dammed and flooded was considered by many to be the sacred center of the Cherokee Nation.

For the TVA, the purpose of the dam was not to produce electricity but rather to create a lake that could be used for recreation and for developers to bring more business into the area. Environmentalists, farmers, and the Eastern Band of Cherokee Indians, of which Gil is a member, all protested, albeit for different reasons. For Gil and his family, it was about the preservation of Cherokee mounds, historical towns, and other sacred sites. One of these sites, *Chota*, was particularly important. Gil doesn't waste his words when describing what the site means to him and other Cherokee people:

> *Echota* in our language means *e tso ta*, "where your fire is," and that's where I firmly believe the location of our sacred fire was in the beginning. It is one of the most sacred places for Cherokee … and they flooded it. *Echota* is where people had to go to ask permission to get fire so that they could take it back to their own village, so that they would have a part of the sacred fire. … *Echota* is also an area where a lot of sacred medicine grew, and grew nowhere else. And according to one of the medicine men, A_____ Sequoyah, that is where he used to go to get some of the medicine that he could not find anywhere else. But in addition to that—it's very similar to what is happening to farmers in Iowa with DAPL. Similar to what is happening out in Standing Rock … it just continues. Rich corporations, rich people get what they want, and the whole point is that the government can just come over and take your land, take your river, and without really any regard for who you are, who your people are, and, um, they have no respect … bottom line.

His voice deepens as he recalls being a graduate student at the University of Tennessee, when he first heard about the project, and then going home to participate in the resistance movement:

> We organized and eventually filed a class-action suit against the TVA, the Tennessee Valley Authority. There was [sic] three of us that were plaintiffs: myself, A Sequoyah, and Richard Crowe. A___ Sequoyah was a very well-known medicine man, and Richard was like a cultural ambassador, so to speak. He taught a lot of songs and dances, many of which would not have been known without his teaching 'em. We filed suit on the basis of the Native American Freedom of Religious Act, which was completely ignored. It's a federal law, and they said, 'The heck with the federal law. The need to develop the last free-flowing body

of water in Tennessee supersedes the need for you Indians' ... is basically what they said."

Reflecting back on those times, Gil describes the threats that came with being at the forefront of the campaign to block the dam:

> We were getting threats with bombs. The road we were traveling to get to our meetings and our organization gatherings—it was littered with tacks, so our tires would go flat. People who are invested in those kind of projects ... will do anything for money. But I wasn't scared. That's just not in my nature.

Despite the protestors' efforts, the project was eventually approved by President Jimmy Carter. The dam was built, and the Cherokee sacred sites were flooded. As he adjusts in his recliner, Gil continues:

> Archaeologically, Carter's decision was very impactful, negatively, but more important than that is [the fact that] the water is now dead. It has no value other than recreation. Its dead. It's not free-flowing. They killed the river. You can kill the river several ways. You can pollute it, dam it, and. ..."

Gil's voice trails off as his sips coffee and looks out the window. The frustration and anger from those times are coming back and filling the space. He takes a deep breath, and his voice becomes more concentrated:

> If you look at Native American belief, then water is life, in my opinion. Our people said water is alive, and therefore it also gives life. Therefore, when you dam a portion or pollute a portion, you kill it. You kill life. Not only are we trying to protect life, which encompasses animals, fish, birds, but also other humans. Unfortunately, this story happens over and over again. Now, look, there is also a pipeline coming through the East Coast of North Carolina; there are pipelines everywhere. They have no regard for people who consider water as sacred, who need water. Kids today have to get out in nature, have to be in the woods, need to smell the flowers, and everyone has to hear water flowing. Just sit and play next to free-flowing water. It's good medicine. People need to understand—we have got to have water. We as Cherokee understand [that] water is critical

Figure 4.4 (Horse Race, Oceti Sakowin Camp, Saturday, September 3, 2016.)

to life. I have gone for days without food but only hours without water. We have to relearn to appreciate what our Creator has given us. We collectively have to nurture what the river gives us. Water is life.

POWER OF STORIES

They aren't just entertainment.
Don't be fooled.
They are all we have, you see,
all we have to fight off
illness and death.
You don't have anything
if you don't have the stories.
—Leslie Marmon Silko, from *Ceremony* (2006)

My name is Juan Guillermo Sánchez Martínez. When people ask me where I am from, I prefer to answer in this borrowed language: I am from the Andes. I prefer to avoid using citizenships, or labels based on race, ethnicity, or immigration status. I simply grew up in an Andean city of almost ten million people, surrounded by lagoons, hot springs, and waterfalls. In July 2016, I moved to *Antokiasdiyi* (the Place Where They Race, what the Cherokee call the French Broad River) to teach at the University of North Carolina, Asheville. Wherever I go, I am conscious that I am a visitor, and that I carry my family history and the Andean dark soil, where salty corn grows and potatoes bloom as fast as the fog spreads through the peaks of the mountains.

I started this brief story about our visit to the Oceti Sakowin (the Sacred Stone Camp) with my own coordinates, because these words are rooted in the Andes, and are woven with pieces from both the South and the North. Like many others of my generation, I have been decolonizing my own history for decades, and traveling has been a part of this exercise of "forgetting and remembrance" (Roncalla 2000). Indigenous poets, elders, medicine men and women, and friends have guided me on this journey. As an immigrant, I have understood my work as a bridge (or *chaca*, in Quechua).

On February 5, 2016, I met Trey Adcock, Cherokee Nation Oklahoma member, professor at UNCA, and *anejodi* (stickball) player. Ama (Cherokee for "water") guided our conversation. He told me about a Cherokee language class that was being offered for the first time at UNCA. Seven months later, I was attending said class. Gilliam Jackson, Eastern Band of Cherokee, and Barbara Duncan, director of the Museum of the Cherokee Indian, were the instructors. On Tuesday, August 30, 2016, Gil showed the class the first nonindigenous report about the Standing Rock struggle: "Rewrite: The Protests at Standing Rock" by Lawrence O'Donnell (of MSNBC). At that point, I did *not* know much about DAPL. At the end of class, Gil told me that he and Trey were thinking about bringing some supplies to the camp. "Why don't you come with us?" he asked. I didn't think twice about it. I felt honored.

We left on September 1 from *Antokiasdiyi*. Twenty-five hours of nonstop driving to North Dakota was enough time to read, watch videos, and discuss indigenous sovereignty, treaties, transnational mining, and the fossil fuel industry (see the documentary *One Million People* about our trip). As advocates, we know that the first action in solidarity with other communities is to be informed. While we were crossing half of the turtle's shell, I kept thinking about the 2012 victory of the Sarayaku nation in protecting the Amazon against the Ecuadorian government, a battle that lasted two decades in international courts (see the documentary *Children of Jaguar*). I also kept thinking about the Mapuche nation and their struggle to protect their springs and aquifer against the Chilean pine and eucalyptus industries (see Deutsche Welle's documentary *The Mapuche of Chile*), and the Mikmak women who protected the aquifer from the fracking industry in Elsipogtog, New Brunswick, Canada, in 2014 (see the documentary *Elsipogtog: The Fire over Water*). All these stories are about water protectors. As Sacred Stone Camp founder LaDonna Brave Bull Allard explains:

Where the Cannonball River joins the Missouri River, at the site of our camp today to stop the Dakota Access Pipeline, there used to be a whirlpool that created large, spherical sandstone formations. The river's true name is *Inyan Wakangapi Wakpa*, River That Makes the Sacred Stones, and we have named the site of our resistance on my family's land the Sacred Stone Camp. The stones are not created anymore, ever since the US Army Corps of Engineers dredged the mouth of the Cannonball River and flooded the area in the late 1950s as they finished the Oahe dam. They killed a portion of our sacred river. (2016)

We all know that oil spills from pipelines are inevitable, and energy based on fossil fuels is unsustainable. The Oahe Dam, the Missouri River, the Mississippi River, and the Gulf of Mexico are all interconnected. If water is food, medicine, memory, and the veins of Mother Earth, what are we going to do to protect it?

We finally arrived at the Oceti Sakowin Camp on Friday, September 2. The prairie winds, the white sage, and the sweet grass were singing in the afternoon. The camp had prayer circles, medicine songs, children playing around the tipis, prayerful and peaceful people reflecting on forgiveness, speeches on history, and visitors from all over the world expressing solidarity around the fire. There was no doubt: this movement was about all nations coming together to protect water—the youth and the elderly, scholars and artists, indigenous and nonindigenous people who believe that *Mni Wiconi* (Water Is Life) needs to be protected for generations to come.

On Saturday, September 3, we woke up to the medicine songs from the council tipi. At the same time, a group of thirty women were walking back from the river, singing a powerful song. Later that day, conflicting emotions emerged after a confrontation between the DAPL private security guards and the unarmed water protectors. Vicious dogs were protagonists, as though time had regressed to the Christopher Columbus invasion, when Spanish mastiffs were sent to attack the inhabitants of this continent. Despite these events, the Oceti Sakowin faith keepers called for calm and forgiveness— yet, on that weekend and the weeks to follow, the national and international media focused only on the violence, anger, and fear, and most outlets failed to explain what the Dakota Access Pipeline had done, which was to desecrate ancient sites in treaty lands based on the map that the Standing Rock Historical Preservation Office had provided on Friday, September 2, to the US Army Corps of Engineers in Washington, DC (see the video by Tim Mentz [2016]).

That Saturday afternoon, we went to the site of the confrontation and listened to the testimonies of Chairman Dave Archambault II, elder Tim Mentz, and Gracey Claymore, the youth representative. Their deep words brought tears to the eyes of those who recorded the videos and messages. Tim Mentz's explanation went beyond our

Figure 4.5 (Tim Mentz. Standing Rock Historical Preservation Office.)

understanding: these sacred sites have been hidden for centuries, and now it was the time to expose them, paradoxically, in order to protect them. Connected to specific constellations, such as the council of the seven buffalos (the Pleiades), and the fasting ceremonies of the medicine men, these places create a balance for all the nations.

Since then, many news, videos, and opinion pieces have been posted, but the spirit of the Oceti Sakowin Camp remained the same. In addition to the solidarity shown by the many Native American and First Nations, other indigenous nations visited the camp, such as Sarayaku, Mayans, Maori, and Hawaiians. Despite the pepper-spray, water cannons, massive arrests, rubber bullets, and tear gas, this story remains about water and peace, not about fire or anger. As scholars and advocates, we understand that there are moments to read and write, and there are moments to act. We envision the same balance for academia and education: science, art, and spirituality as the foundations for research.

Today, our challenge is to facilitate an intercultural dialogue between opposing mind-sets: while the CEO of the DAPL is worried about the company's profit margins, the Standing Rock Sioux tribe and their allies are willing to die to protect the water for thousands of citizens. Vine Deloria Jr.'s *God Is Red* helps us understand this crossroads: "Developing a sense of ourselves that would properly balance history and nature and space and time is a more difficult task than we would suspect and involves a radical reevaluation of the way we look at the world around us. Do we continue to exploit the earth or do we preserve it and preserve life?" (1994, 61).

In the current intersection between environmental and pan-indigenous movements, this radical reevaluation is necessary: a balance between time and space. Rather than overestimating logic, evolution, and progress in linear time, in which mind/body, subject/object, and nature/culture are disconnected, what if we focus on the present, and take responsibility for the land that we inhabit? Two decades ago, French philosopher Michel Serres also thought about this possibility:

> We must therefore carry out a harrowing revision of modern natural law, which presupposes the unformulated proposition that only man, individually or in groups, can become a legal subject. … Objects themselves are legal subjects and no longer mere material for appropriation, even collective appropriation. Law tries to limit abusive parasitism among men but does not speak of this same action on things. If objects themselves become legal subjects, then all scales will tend toward an equilibrium. (1998, 37)

Serres's proposal probably sounded naïve in the 1990s. However, today we know that Mother Earth has rights in Bolivia and Ecuador, and that a Maori river in Te Urewera Park has the same rights as any other citizen in *Aotearoa* (New Zealand). It is not too late for the United States to get in tune with the new era of our blue planet. The water protectors of Oceti Sakowin can guide us in this new endeavor.

When we were driving back on Sunday, September 4, after we passed Bismarck, North Dakota, everything looked different on the freeway. We did not want to leave the prairies, but we had to work on Tuesday. After only two and a half days in the Oceti Sakowin Camp, we felt that we had a responsibility to the ancestors of the Great Plains, and to the Missouri and Cannonball rivers. We also believed that this journey was meant to be. A few months have passed since returning to *Antokiasdiyi*, and we have been giving talks about our experience, presenting our video, creating awareness among students and local communities of western North Carolina, as well as internationally through virtual magazines such as Hawansuyo.com, and conferences such as the Action Research Network meeting 2017 in Cartagena, Colombia.

WHERE ARE YOUR STORIES?

We would like this story to be a bridge between two different mind-sets—the starting point for a conversation. The title of Edward Chamberlin's 2004 book—*If This Is Your*

Figure 4.6 (From left to right: Gilliam Jackson, Juan Sánchez, Chairman Dave Archambault II, and Trey Adcock.)

Land, Where Are Your Stories?—provides a seed for said discussion. Native stories about the land must be taken seriously by indigenous and nonindigenous politicians and lawyers who are responsible for writing the upcoming nation-state's stories (i.e., constitutions, laws, bills). In weaving diverse narratives, we will create balanced policies. Therefore, in order to protect water and nature for future generations, we need a radical change in our social contract, and our understanding of legal subjects. It is a time for neither guilt nor anger; rather, it is a time for desire and hope. In the information era, new generations have a key role in pointing out the untruthful stories, and the narratives that benefit the few. Video, music, poetry, civil disobedience, and ceremony can make a difference!

EPILOGUE

After eleven months of spiritual resistance in the Oceti Sakowin camp, Governor Doug Burgum of North Dakota, supported by the Trump administration in the White House, signed an emergency evacuation order on February 15, 2017, reaffirming a February

22 deadline for protestors to leave the treaty land. While we write this epilogue, federal and local law enforcement agents are surrounding the protectors of water, preparing to forcefully remove them. We truly believe, however, that even if the pipeline passes through these sacred lands, the Standing Rock movement has raised consciousness about the power of prayerful and peaceful civil disobedience. There is not fear nor anger in our hearts. This is not the first or the last battle. Right now, indigenous peoples around the world are guiding parallel mobilizations, and despite uncertainty and disappointments about this specific issue, water binds us all. *Mni Wiconi!* Meanwhile, let's reflect on water with this offering/poem:

DIGGING IN THE UNDERGROUND'S NIGHT

By Juan G. Sánchez Martínez

We're not gonna change the world
           we're gonna hug it with all its thorns
we're gonna accept it, yeah
as we accept our wino father
                     singing
                             broken
                                     at the edge of the night

we're not gonna change our neighbor
           we're gonna hug him with all his knives
we're gonna say to him hello, like that
as deer say hello to each other
                        in the middle
                           of the hunt

we're not gonna change the world
           we're gonna listen to it with all its moles
we're gonna let it talk
as we allow the kid to draw himself with crayons

we're not gonna change our neighbor
           we're gonna dress him with all his wounds
we're gonna deeply sing for him
as we sing from
               the
                      cliff

                    to the
                              empty space

we're not gonna change the world
          we're gonna smile at it with all its worms
we're gonna give it five
as the frogs give five to each other
                              in the dense
                              wetland

we're not gonna change the world
          the thing is that we're not gonna change
we're not gonna change the business
          for a few old *ceibas*
                    not our gold or *niquel*
                              for the capybara's smile or the tapir
                              we're not gonna change the *soya* or the palm tree
                                        for the stream songs where the idle tiger bathes
                              how can you think that we're gonna change the black gold
                    for some messy buffalo
          grazing on the sweet great plains
          the thing is that we're not gonna change
and the *athabasca* hole will be deeper
          and the *Cerrejon* crack will be darker
                    and the void of *Yanacocha* and the scar of *Chuquicamata*
                    will continue bleeding
                              why should we change
                              if anyway the thirst and the hunger will know how to kiss us
                    sooner than later
          the grandchildren will behead us with the turbines' propellers
          and they'll burn us alive in the refineries' ovens
and our voices will become smoke
blind smoke
          they'll burn us with shoes and tires
          and the rubber sap will finally become
                                        ash
                                             injury
                                             upon
                                             injury
                                             on the

bark tree

and the blood will forget the men's and women's humming

digging the underground

the night will forget

the water

will continue

flowing

DISCUSSION QUESTION

1. How do you understand time? How do you understand space? Why is important to discuss these things if we want to create an intercultural dialogue?

WEBSITE LINKS

History and culture of the Standing Rock Oyate: www.ndstudies.org/resources/IndianStudies/standingrock/historical_gs_reservation.html

Indigenous Environmental Network: www.ienearth.org

NYC Stands for Standing Rock committee syllabus for teaching about DAPL: https://nycstandswithstandingrock.wordpress.com

Standing Rock Sioux tribe website: http://standwithstandingrock.net/oceti-sakowin

AUDIOVISUAL MATERIALS

Aljazeera. 2015. *Elsipogtog: The Fire over Water—Fault Lines*. https://www.youtube.com/watch?v=9fleh95UWGo.

Deutsche Welle. 2015. *The Mapuche of Chile—Struggle for Territorial Rights and Justice*. www.youtube.com/watch?v=41pnfq27Oak.

Gualinga, Eriberto. 2012. *Children of Jaguar*. www.youtube.com/watch?v=bJdQinKAyqA.

Mentz, Tim. 2016. *Standing Rock Sioux Tribe Culturally Significant Sites*. www.youtube.com/watch?v=w6NapCXUjU0.

O'Donnell, Lawrence. 2016. *Rewrite: The Protest at Standing Rock*. www.msnbc.com/the-last-word/watch/rewrite-the-protests-at-standing-rock-751440963846.

Sánchez Martínez, Juan Guillermo, Trey Adcock, and Gilliam Jackson. 2016. *One Million People: Standing Rock*. https://vimeo.com/190289221.

SUGGESTIONS FOR FURTHER READING

Chamberlin, Edward. 2004. *If This Is Your Land, Where Are Your Stories?* Toronto, Vintage.

Dunbar-Ortiz, Roxanne. 2014. "Introduction" and "Doctrine of Discovery." *An Indigenous People's History of the United States*. New York: Beacon Press.

REFERENCES

Brave Bull Allard, LaDonna. 2016. "Why the Founder of Standing Rock Sioux Camp Can't Forget the Whitestone Massacre." *Yes Magazine!*

Deloria Jr., Vine. 1994. *God Is Red: A Native View of Religion*. Golden, CO: Fulcrum Publishing.

Herold, Kiana. 2016. "*Terra Nullius* and the History of Broken Treaties at Standing Rock." *Intercontinental Cry: A Publication for the Center for World Indigenous Studies*.

Kovach, Margaret. 2009. *Indigenous Methodologies: Characteristics, Conversations, and Contexts*. Toronto: University of Toronto Press.

Newcomb, Steve. 1992. "Five Hundred Years of Injustice." *Shaman's Drum* Fall:18–20.

Newcomb, Steve. 2016. "The Dakota Access Pipeline and the 'Law of Christendom.'" *Indian Country Today*. https://indiancountrymedianetwork.com/news/opinions/the-dakota-access-pipeline-and-the-law-of-christendom.

Roncalla, Fredy Amilcar. 2000. "Fragments for a Story of Forgetting and Remembrance." *Hawansuyo*.

Serres, Michel. 1998. *The Natural Contract*. Ann Arbor: University of Michigan Press.

Silko, Leslie M. 2006. *Ceremony*. New York: Penguin Books.

Trudell, John. 2001. *What It Means to Be a Human Being*. https://ratical.org/many_worlds/JohnTrudell/HumanBeing.html.

Black and Latinx[1] Millennial Students and Racial Justice Activism in the Age of Black Lives Matter

By María Joaquina Villaseñor

In 2014, the Pew Research Center published findings of a survey that revealed that the Millennial generation, those between the ages of eighteen and thirty-three at the time of the study, "are relatively unattached to organized politics and religion, linked by social media, burdened by debt, distrustful of people, in no rush to marry—and optimistic about the future." The Pew study noted that this is the first generation of "digital natives" who did not have to adapt to the Internet, social media, and changes in mobile technology. That same year, the *New York Times* published an editorial describing Millennials as the "Self(ie) Generation" (Blow 2014) and the term has been emblematic of accusations against this generation writ large—that they are narcissistic and self-absorbed. Indeed, Ruth Milkman notes, "The dominant narrative about the 'Millennial' generation (roughly those born between 1980 and 2000) portrays its members as lazy, narcissistic, entitled, and politically disengaged" (2014, 55). The creation and perpetuation of generational labels and stereotypes naturally result from the uneven power dynamics of an older generation with access to platforms of expression who make critical generalizations of younger generations (i.e., "Those darn kids!" … but in the *New York Times*). Even so, Millennials seem to have gotten a particularly bad rap.

---

1. In keeping with contemporary usage practices, I use the term "Black" to refer to people of the African diaspora who reside in the United States. I use "Latinx" in keeping with the current practice of using the gender-inclusive term for people of Latin American origin and/or descent in the United States.

Millennials are also the most racially diverse generation in US history, with "some 43% of Millennial adults" identifying as non-White, and this group, non-white Millennials, also expresses "low levels of social trust" (Pew Research Center 2014). Despite stereotypes and generalizations that say Millennials are self-absorbed and politically apathetic, Millennials of color have already made a mark on our nation as agents of change in the ongoing struggle for social justice, particularly in regard to issues of racial justice, and also in struggles for justice for immigrant rights, and LGBTQ+ rights and liberation; indeed, Millennials of color have excelled in linking these struggles and recognizing intersections of social identities. Millennials of color are taking their "low levels of social trust" and their largely progressive political ideologies and using them to advance social justice agendas across the United States in bold and visionary ways. Importantly, college campuses have served as crucial sites in these struggles, and college students, high school students, and other youth have been instrumental in these social justice movements.

Black student activism in the twenty-first century has been characterized by its deep grounding in and engagement with community issues. Perhaps the most critical of these issues has been the problem of deadly police and vigilante violence against Black people across the United States. In a particularly infamous case, Trayvon Martin was killed in February 2012, three weeks before his eighteenth birthday. In *Who We Be: The Colorization of America*, Jeff Chang recounts that Martin was killed by George Zimmerman, a neighborhood watch vigilante who told a 911 dispatcher that Martin looked like he was up to "no good" (2014, 304). Significantly, Chang notes that Martin's death went unnoticed nationally until the Reuters wire service picked up the story nine days later, after "lawyers Benjamin Crump and Natalie Jackson took the case, and communications expert Ryan Julison began telling the story to the media" (2014, 306). According to a story by Dani McClain in *The Nation*, hundreds of Florida high school students staged walkouts in protest one month later, in March 2012, when Zimmerman had still not been arrested and charged (2014, 18). McClain's story highlights the crucial role played by young activists who sought to hold Zimmerman accountable for Martin's killing:

> A group of current and former Florida college activists knew that they had to do something … the group planned a 40-mile march from Daytona Beach to the headquarters of the Sanford Police Department—40 miles symbolizing the 40 days that Zimmerman had remained free. … The march culminated in a five-hour blockade of the Sanford PD's doors on Easter Monday. The marchers demanded Zimmerman's arrest and the police chief's firing. Within two days, both demands had been met (2014, 18)

Although Zimmerman was eventually acquitted of Martin's murder, the work of high school and college activists was crucial in igniting the movement that aimed to hold Zimmerman accountable, pushing the legal system to enact a process to bring justice. Still, Zimmerman's acquittal was yet another blow to the collective psyche of Black Americans, dogged by the extraordinary pain of loss, as well as the constant fear of danger, violence, and even death at the hands of law enforcement and vigilantes.

In the aftermath of the verdict acquitting Zimmerman, a flurry of youth activism took place—some within colleges and universities, some within governmental spaces, and some within the digital realm of social media. Describing an immediate action taken by activists, Chang writes, "Three days after the verdict. ... Hundreds of people—Black, Latino, and white, mostly young but some with graying hair ... start[ed] what would become a monthlong, around-the-clock occupation [of the office of Florida governor Rick Scott]," (2014, 312). Calling themselves the Dream Defenders, the group urged the passage of a piece of legislation "they called the Trayvon Martin Civil Rights Act. It would repeal Stand Your Ground laws and school zero-tolerance policies; require law enforcement agencies to define, prohibit, and train their officers around racial profiling; and promote youth restorative justice programs" (2014, 312).

At the same time that young activists were pressuring Florida's state government to enact changes, across the country college students staged countless protests expressing their outrage not only in the aftermath of the death of Trayvon Martin, but also following the vast number of African Americans who died (and continue to die) in police custody. The nature and sheer number of these deaths—the deaths of Michael Brown, another unarmed youth, Eric Garner, Walter Scott, Sandra Bland, Philando Castile, and Alton Sterling, to name but a few—have maintained the intensity of the outrage of the public, an outrage that has fueled unrest in the streets, such as in the well-known case of Ferguson, Missouri, where in response to the killing of Michael Brown, and the acquittal of the officer who shot him, many protests were held, both organized and spontaneous. Indeed, according to the website Mapping Police Violence (2016; mappingpoliceviolence.org), there were more than one hundred deaths of unarmed African Americans at the hands of law enforcement in 2015 alone.[2]

In the aftermath of the death of Trayvon Martin (and beginning with the highly publicized death of Oscar Grant, another unarmed young African American man in Oakland, California), countless college students on hundreds of college campuses across the country have responded with numerous forms of activism on their campuses as well. After Trayvon Martin was said to have looked threatening because of the hoodie sweatshirt he was wearing at the time of his fatal altercation with George Zimmerman,

---

2. Police and state-sanctioned violence has also been devastating to Latinx communities. See "Beyond the White-and-Black, Heteronormative Binary: Black, Latinx, and Indigenous Parallel Experiences of State-Sanctioned Policing," by Hortencia Jiménez, in this volume.

students across the country marched in protest wearing hoodie sweatshirts in the spring of 2012. In the summer of 2016, a Google search for the terms "Trayvon Martin hoodie march college campuses" yielded more than 180,000 results, and the articles published described marches everywhere, from Miami to Maine, Minnesota, Texas, Connecticut, California, and beyond.

After the death of Michael Brown, while Ferguson, Missouri, burned with the anger of its primarily Black residents,[3] college students all over the United States staged "die-ins." In these demonstrations within marches and rallies, all participants would lay down silently, in unison, often holding signs with expressions of outrage and fear at the loss of Black and Brown lives at the hands of law enforcement, such as HANDS UP; DON'T SHOOT, the phrase that Michael Brown was reported to have said just before being fatally shot by police.[4]

Social media has been an indispensable tool in contemporary racial justice activist movements. The phrase "Black Lives Matter" is perhaps the most well-known expression to emerge from social media in the context of the activist movements I have described. Three Black Millennial women—Alicia Garza, Patrisse Cullors, and Opal Tometi—were the activists who first used this term on social media in the wake of the killing of Trayvon Martin and the subsequent acquittal of George Zimmerman, and thus are thought to be key founding figures in the movement. Garza explains, "Black Lives Matter is an ideological and political intervention in a world where Black lives are systematically and intentionally targeted for demise. It is an affirmation of Black folks' contributions to this society, our humanity, and our resilience in the face of deadly oppression" (Black Lives Matter 2015).

Politically engaged Millennials who use social media have been disparaged by terms such as "slacktivist," which suggests that their use of social media platforms like Twitter is a self-indulgent means to engage in pretending to be part of a social movement (Gladwell 2010). However, Black Lives Matter leaders have been vocal in their assertions that the phrase and the hashtag are intended to be means for connecting people to the movement to end the "deadly oppression" against the Black community, and "to celebra[te] and humaniz[e] ... Black lives," not merely in the digital sphere, but, more crucially, "in the streets" (Black Lives Matter 2015). Furthermore,

---

3. In 2015, the US Justice Department released a report concluding that "[their] investigation revealed ... [that] disparities [disproportionate number of arrests, tickets, and use of force] occur, at least in part, because of unlawful bias against and stereotypes about African Americans" (Berman and Lowery 2015). Thus, it's clear that the protests and outrage in Ferguson, Missouri, that were ostensibly prompted by the death of Michael Brown and the lack of law enforcement accountability and official culpability for his death had a considerably broader and deeper basis and context.

4. Cross-racial coalition building has been another critical part of this movement. For example, there is a very active group in the San Francisco Bay Area called "#AsiansforBlackLives" (https://a4bl.wordpress.com).

the protests in Ferguson, Missouri, after the death of Michael Brown highlight the way in which the highly interactive social media platform of Twitter was a tool for immediate communication and engagement. Twitter also facilitated more traditional "in-the-streets," "bodies-on-the-line" protests, as "protestors from around the nation flocked to Ferguson to participate in demonstrations calling for the arrest of the officer responsible for the fatal shooting." Twitter users posted more than 3.6 million posts regarding Michael Brown and his death using the organizing term #ferguson in the first week of the protests alone (Bonilla and Rosa 2015, 4).

In light of the dominant representations of young activists of color and their demonstrations in the mass media, social media has provided a much-needed vehicle for constructing narratives and counterstories, in addition to helping activists show solidarity and organize. Bonilla and Rosa point out that "it is surely not coincidental that the groups most likely to experience police brutality, to have their protests disparaged as acts of 'rioting' or 'looting,' and to be misrepresented in the media are precisely those turning to digital activism at the highest rates" (2015, 6). Moreover, Bonilla and Rosa emphasize the importance of recognizing that the phenomenon of using technology and media as tools of social movements is not unique to the current moment, citing a number of historical examples, including the way in which "transistor radios allowed Cuban guerrilla fighters to transmit from the Sierra Maestra" and "television coverage transformed the riots in Selma, Alabama, into a national event" (2015, 7).

As the Black Lives Matter movement on and off college campuses continues to challenge police brutality and state-sanctioned violence against Black communities, Black students and other students of color continue to engage in racial justice struggles regarding the circumstances of their lives on campus and the racism, exclusion, alienation, and/or lack of belonging they may experience therein. In 2015, at the University of Missouri, a student group called Concerned Student 1950 (referencing the year when the University of Missouri first accepted Black students) was formed in response to a slew of racist incidents, including a swastika smeared on a wall in feces and students saying they had been subjected to racial slurs, with inadequate response from university administration (Elignon 2015). In response to the incidents and what the students perceived as a lack of responsiveness from the administration, students organized a number of protests, culminating in a hunger strike; the University of Missouri's football team also vowed to boycott all football-related activities until then president of the university system, Tim Wolfe, stepped down. After weeks of organized actions, student activists were successful in pressuring Tim Wolfe to resign from his position. During this same time period, Ithaca College, Claremont McKenna College, and Virginia Commonwealth University were but a few of the other schools where students of color across the nation decried racial biases that they face on campus and learning conditions that they experience as hostile and unwelcoming (Smith and Thrasher 2015). In an online news article, Smith and Thrasher highlighted the links being made by scholars between student activism in the past and the present: "At least one academic proclaimed the birth of a new social movement, echoing the student activism of the 1960s and drawing on the Black Lives Matter groundswell of the present. Where it is headed is hard to discern, but the cause is clear: chronic lack of racial transformation in US higher education" (Smith and Thrasher 2015). Through their bold and committed actions, today's college student activists for racial justice are attending to the unfinished business and the unfulfilled promise of the 1960s and 1970s. While there are more students of color attending colleges and universities now than in the past, and institutions of higher learning have changed considerably in the last fifty years, it is clear that institutions of higher education have more work to do in terms of "fundamentally redefin[ing] higher education" against centuries-old White supremacy in order to be truly inclusive of all students (Biondi 2012, 43).

Before Concerned Student 1950, Black Lives Matter, and Dream Defenders, there were "DREAMers"—youth activists, mostly Latinx, who have been organizing for immigrant rights, particularly for undocumented immigrants since 2006, when the House of Representatives passed the Border Protection, Antiterrorism, and Illegal Immigration Control Act, HR 4437 (Valdivia Ordorica and Clark-Ibáñez 2015, 165). The bill sought to increase the number of border patrol agents policing the US-Mexico border, to further criminalize undocumented immigrants by increasing prison penalties for them, and to impose penalties on anyone who would help undocumented immigrants (Valdivia Ordorica and Clark-Ibáñez 2015, 165). While HR 4437 passed in the House of Representatives, it ultimately failed to pass in the Senate, but it succeeded in igniting a "political fuse" in immigrant rights activism, much of which had young people at its center as youth protests exploded across the United States (Barbarena, Jiménez, and Young 2014, 43). Citing the work of several other scholars, Hinda Seif notes that of the "three and a half to five million people [who] marched throughout the United States against [the] congressional proposal ... more than half ... may [have been] under 28" (2011, 60). The defeat of HR 4437 in the Senate marked a victory for activists, and the organized efforts to defeat the bill were foundational for the mostly youth immigrant rights activism of the DREAMers, who are so called because of the Development, Relief, and Education for Alien Minors (DREAM) Act that would create a pathway to citizenship for undocumented immigrants who were brought to the United States as children "who have completed at least two years of college or military service," a law for which activists have organized and advocated since 2006 (Milkman 2014, 55). The DREAM Act was first proposed by Senator Richard Durbin (D-IL) and Representative Howard Berman (D-CA) in 2001 (Valdivia Ordorica and Clark-Ibáñez 2015, 165).

Colleges and universities have been critical sites for the organizing of undocumented youth activists and their allies, and the struggle for access to affordable higher education for undocumented immigrant students has been a cornerstone in their immigrant rights movements. Challenges related to college affordability for undocumented immigrant students are multiple, as policies requiring undocumented immigrant students to pay out-of-state and/or international student tuition make the cost of tuition prohibitive for many of them. Yet, due in large part to immigrant rights activists, eighteen states have passed in-state tuition laws since 2001, and five states now allow undocumented immigrant students to receive state financial aid (National Conference on State Legislatures 2015). As a result of a change in these laws, college has become more affordable for undocumented immigrant students, and more of them are attending college now than in the past. Access to college has increased the likelihood that undocumented immigrant youth would "remain active in civic life" (Seif 2011, 68), and, indeed, this has created opportunities for students to find organizations that offer community, support, and opportunities for student activism and engagement. California is especially noteworthy in the number of active student organizations comprised of students who call themselves "DREAMers" or "AB 540 students" (AB 540 is the law about in-state tuition for undocumented immigrant students in California). The University of California, Los Angeles; the University of California, Santa Cruz; California State University, Dominguez Hills; and California State University, San Marcos are but a few of the schools in California that have active student organizations engaging undocumented immigrant students and their allies (Seif 2011; Valdivia Ordorica and Clark-Ibáñez 2015).

Within the walls of colleges and universities and outside of them, DREAMer activism has taken various forms. Veronica Vélez, Lindsay Perez Huber, Corina Benavides Lopez, Ariana de la Luz, and Daniel G. Solórzano make a helpful distinction between two primary types of activism in which youth immigrant rights activists have engaged. They use the term "direct activism" to refer to "overt political acts of protest that often involve the physical body as a vehicle for protest, including walkouts, sit-ins, or wearing clothing with political slogans that represent the movement"; they use "indirect activism" to refer to "political acts that express critical concern, but do not focus on attempting to physically challenge public institutions and/or their actors" (2008, 16). Both of these kinds of activism have been powerful and effective in raising the social and political awareness of the public, gaining support for immigrant rights causes from key lawmakers, and ultimately concretely impacting the laws and policies that affect immigrants. This is despite the fact that undocumented student organizers face numerous obstacles to their participation in rallies, sit-ins, phone banks, and other forms of in-person activism because of their status, including the fact that they are "unable to legally drive," they "often work long hours in low-paying jobs … or [are] working in the informal economy," and they also face a "constant risk and fear of deportation" (Valdivia Ordorica and Clark-Ibáñez 2015, 171).

While the use of social media and online activism has been an important part of the other examples of Millennial racial justice activism discussed earlier, the unique challenges faced by undocumented immigrant activists are an additional reason why social media and online activism have been a crucial part of their movements. Online tools such as Google+, Facebook, Twitter, and Tumblr have been critical to undocumented student organizing, and are used extensively for virtual meetings, to exchange information, and to "make connections with activists across the nation"; the national organization United We Dream is an example of a youth-led organization that employs these and other online tools and platforms to communicate virtually, as well as to organize in-person events (Valdivia Ordorica and Clark-Ibáñez 2015, 168, 171). A number of websites also serve as hubs that provide information and connect activists. One example is DreamACTivist.org, which posts updates related to immigration rights, and also connects online users to resources and other immigrant youth. As in the case of young Black racial justice activists, these social media and online platforms are not providing substitutes for in-person organizing and actions, but facilitating the processes necessary to make effective online actions happen. Additionally, they are providing the means for Latinx youth activists to tell their own stories, often providing important counternarratives to mainstream media that have sometimes portrayed them as "'truants' and 'troublemakers'" (Vélez et al. 2008, 8).

Although the DREAM Act has not passed, DREAMers saw a victory in 2012 when "President Barack Obama took executive action on immigration and announced the Deferred Action for Childhood Arrivals (DACA) federal program … [which] provides an opportunity for eligible undocumented immigrant youth to receive temporary work authorization and relief from deportation" (Valdivia Ordorica and Clark-Ibáñez 2015, 165). President Obama further sought to expand the federal program to support DACA and extend some protections to affected undocumented immigrant parents under a Deferred Action for Parents of Americans and Lawful Permanent Residents (DAPA) program, but that program encountered extreme opposition, and in 2014, Texas and twenty-five other states filed a lawsuit attempting to block it. A June 2016 Supreme Court decision with a 4–4 split effectively blocked the plan proposed by President Obama, including DAPA (Park and Parlapiano 2016). Thus, as Valdivia Ordorica and Clark-Ibáñez remind us, "Because DACA is not enough, organizers, networks, and campaigns continue to fight regarding issues affecting undocumented communities across the United States" (2015, 178).

Black and Latinx Millennial activists have been successful in furthering their agendas in a way that surfaces the complexity of people's lived experiences, given that all people inhabit multiple social identities. For example, a signature event for DREAMers in recent years has been "Coming Out of the Shadows Days," in which undocumented immigrant students "come out" as undocumented. This discursive parallel to LGBTQ+ discourse is not coincidental, as many of the undocumented immigrant student activists identify as queer. One of their slogans, "Undocumented, Queer, and Unafraid," speaks to an identification with the LGBTQ+ movement, as well as to their "refus[al] to apologize either for their lack of legal status or their sexuality" (Milkman 2014, 58). In another important example of the propensity of young activists of color to recognize and articulate intersectional concerns, more than sixty organizations related to the Black Lives Matter movement (referring to itself as the Movement for Black Lives) have recently issued a set of demands and related policy briefs, which includes "end[ing] … the war on black immigrants," and "end[ing] … the war on Black trans, queer, and gender nonconforming people" (Movement for Black Lives 2016). While the demands were issued in the midst of the 2016 US presidential election season, Black Lives Matter activists have long articulated these kinds of concerns, as well as advocating for Black women's rights, the rights of Black people with disabilities, and others.

In assessing the activism of the DREAMers, Seif writes, "Some of the most creative, courageous, and effective organizing in the contemporary United States has been conducted by undocumented youth in support of the DREAM Act" (2011, 69). Agreeing with and borrowing from Seif's assertion, I suggest that Black Millennial activists have engaged and are engaging in similarly extraordinary "creative, courageous, and effective" modes, instances, and ongoing projects in racial justice activism. Consider, for example, the memorable and iconic action taken by activist Bree Newsome, who in 2015 climbed the flagpole in front of the state capitol building in Columbia, South Carolina, to take down the Confederate flag as lawmakers began to debate whether it should remain there in the aftermath of a Charleston massacre fueled by racial hatred, in which nine Black people were murdered. Newsome scaled the thirty-foot flagpole and took the flag in her hand, exclaiming, "I come against you in the name of God. This flag comes down today!" (Democracy Now 2015). Newsome's bold symbolic action was seen all over the world in a video shared widely on social media and celebrated by many who saw her action as a challenge to racially oppressive ideologies and their current perpetuation in the name of history and heritage. While in this social media age of "clicks" and "likes," these stories may seem ephemeral, a story like Newsome's highlights the fierce commitment, energy, and fresh vision of racial justice and activism held by Millennials of color.

There is, unfortunately, a dark side to the intense activism in which many Millennials of color have engaged. Many of these young people have articulated high levels of stress, and even mental health challenges, as a cost of bearing the burden of witnessing and/or directly experiencing violence, hostility, and isolation because of race, sexuality, class, gender, citizenship status, or other social factors and, beyond that, working to combat those hardships. In an online editorial in *AfroPunk* magazine, Alie Jones, a self-described "Millennial blacktivist," writes,

> This year during Black History Month, a 23-year-old Black Lives
> Matter activist, MarShawn M. McCarrell, committed suicide on
> the steps of the Ohio State House. Hours before he took his life,

MarShawn posted on his Facebook, saying, "My demons won today, I'm sorry." ... As millennial blacktivists we're constantly throwing ourselves on the line for our causes, not realizing the emotional impact. I would like to challenge and encourage more young black people like myself to practice the revolutionary art of self-care. (2016)

Jones's essay goes on to cite and echo Audre Lorde's well-known statement: "Caring for myself is not self-indulgence; it is self-preservation, and that is an act of political warfare." Jones's and Lorde's words are valuable reminders to young activists of color that they must care for themselves deeply, and that personal care has important political implications. However, these words also have value for those of us who are activists and educators from the older generations. We must recognize that the racial justice activist work in which many Millennials of color are engaging have multi- and intergenerational implications, and just as the older generations stand to benefit from the societal and educational changes for which Millennials of color are advocating, so must we recognize that the responsibility to care for them is a shared responsibility. Yes, Millennials of color must care for themselves. But their well-being is the responsibility of older generations, too, and we must be skeptical of and resistant to the critiques—of their so-called self-absorption, of their narcissism, for example—that erase the complexity of their identities, their humanity, and their considerable contributions to struggles for social justice in the present moment.

DISCUSSION QUESTIONS

1. How do the mainstream media portray Millennials and their racial justice activism, and how does the author's view of Millennials of color differ from mainstream stereotypes about Millennials?

2. What are the strategies and characteristics of the racial activism in which Millennials of color have engaged in recent years?

3. Why and how has social media been an indispensable tool in the racial justice movements of Millennials of color? What are the unique challenges faced by undocumented immigrant student activists, and how do social media and online tools help them engage in activism, despite those challenges?

WEBSITE LINKS AND AUDIOVISUAL MATERIALS

Black Lives Matter: http://blacklivesmatter.com

The Center for Racial Justice Innovation: www.raceforward.org

New York Times interactive timeline: "Black Activism on Campus" (February 2016): www.nytimes.com/interactive/2016/02/07/education/edlife/Black-HIstory-Activism-on-Campus-Timeline.html?_r=0#/#time393_11363

Pew Research Center, reports and articles on Millennials: www.pewresearch.org/topics/millennials

"Reporter's Notebook: The 'Post-Racial Generation' that Wasn't": www.youtube.com/watch?v=Qvl5CIZvsSE

United We Dream: Immigrant Youth Building a Movement for Justice: http://unitedwedream.org

SUGGESTIONS FOR FURTHER READING

Clark-Ibáñez, Marisol. 2015. *Undocumented Latino Youth: Navigating Their Worlds.* Boulder, CO: Lynne Rienner Publishers.

Delgado Bernal, Dolores, C. Alejandra Elenes, Francisca E. Godinez, and Sofia Villenas, eds. 2006. *Chicana/Latina Education in Everyday Life: Feminista Perspectives on Pedagogy and Epistemology.* Albany: State University of New York Press.

Ward, Jesmyn, ed. 2016. *The Fire This Time: A New Generation Speaks about Race.* New York: Scribner.

REFERENCES

Barbarena, Laura, Hortencia Jiménez, and Michael P. Young. 2014. "'It Just Happened': Telescoping Anxiety, Defiance, and Emergent Collective Behavior in the Student Walkouts of 2006." *Social Problems* 61(1): 42–60.

Berman, Mark, and Wesley Lowery. 2015. "The 12 Key Highlights from the DOJ's Scathing Ferguson Report." *Washington Post.* www.washingtonpost.com/news/post-nation/wp/2015/03/04/the-12-key-highlights-from-the-dojs-scathing-ferguson-report/?utm_term=.59a38fc44b34.

Biondi, Martha. 2012. *The Black Revolution on Campus.* Berkeley: University of California Press.

Bonilla, Yarimar, and Jonathan Rosa. 2015. "#ferguson: Digital Protest, Hashtag Ethnography, and the Racial Politics of Social Media in the United States." *American Ethnologist* 42(1): 4–17.

Black Lives Matter. 2015. "The Creation of a Movement." http://blacklivesmatter.com/herstory.

Blow, Charles M. 2014. "The Self(ie) Generation." *New York Times.* www.nytimes.com/2014/03/08/opinion/blow-the-self-ie-generation.html?_r=0.

Chang, Jeff. 2014. *Who We Be: The Colorization of America*. New York: St. Martin's Press.

Democracy Now. 2015. "Bree Newsome: As SC Lawmakers Debate Removing Confederate Flag, Meet the Activist Who Took It Down." www.democracynow.org/2015/7/6/bree_newsome_as_sc_lawmakers_debate

Elignon, John. 2015 "At University of Missouri, Black Students See a Campus Riven by Race." *New York Times*. www.nytimes.com/2015/11/12/us/university-of-missouri-protests.html.

Gladwell, Malcolm. 2010. "Small Change: Why the Revolution Will Not Be Tweeted." *The New Yorker*. www.newyorker.com/magazine/2010/10/04/small-change-malcolm-gladwell.

Jiménez, Hortencia. 2016. "Beyond the White-and-Black, Heteronormative Binary: Black, Latinx, and Indigenous Parallel Experiences of State-Sanctioned Policing." In *Readings in Race, Ethnicity, and Immigration*, edited by Hortencia Jiménez [this volume]. San Diego, CA: Cognella.

Jones, Alie. 2016. "How Revolutionary Self-Care Becomes an Act of Radical Activism." *AfroPunk*. www.afropunk.com/m/blogpost?id=2059274:BlogPost:1402098.

Mapping Police Violence. 2016. "Police Violence Map and Data." http://mappingpoliceviolence.org.

McClain, Dani. 2016. "The Black Lives Matter Movement Is Most Visible on Twitter: Its True Home Is Elsewhere." *The Nation*. www.thenation.com/article/black-lives-matter-was-born-on-twitter-will-it-die-there.

Milkman, Ruth. 2014. "Millennial Movements: Occupy Wall Street and the Dreamers." *Dissent* 61(3): 55–59.

Movement for Black Lives. 2016. "End the War on Black People." https://policy.m4bl.org/end-war-on-black-people.

National Conference on State Legislatures. 2016. "Undocumented Student Tuition: Overview." www.ncsl.org/research/education/undocumented-student-tuition-overview.aspx.

Park, Haeyoun, and Alicia Parlapiano. 2016. "Supreme Court's Decision on Immigration Case Affects Millions of Unauthorized Immigrants." *New York Times*. www.nytimes.com/interactive/2016/06/22/us/who-is-affected-by-supreme-court-decision-on-immigration.html.

Pew Research Center. 2014. *Millennials in Adulthood*. www.pewsocialtrends.org/2014/03/07/millennials-in-adulthood.

Seif, Hinda. 2011. "'Unapologetic and Unafraid': Immigrant Youth Come Out from the Shadows." *New Directions for Child and Adolescent Development* 134: 59–75.

Smith, David, and Steven Thrasher. 2015. "Student Activists Nationwide Challenge Racism—and Get Results." *The Guardian*. www.theguardian.com/us-news/2015/nov/13/student-activism-university-of-missouri-racism-universities-colleges.

Valdivia Ordorica, Carolina, and Marisol Clark-Ibáñez. 2015. "DREAMer Activism: Challenges and Opportunities." In *Undocumented Latino Youth: Navigating Their Worlds*, by M. Clark-Ibáñez, 163–178. Boulder, CO: Lynne Rienner Publishers.

Vélez, Veronica, Lindsey Perez Huber, Corina Benavides Lopez, Ariana de la Luz, and Daniel G. Solórzano. 2008. "Battling for Human Rights and Social Justice: A Latina/o Critical Race Media Analysis of Latina/o Student Youth Activism in the Wake of 2006 Anti-immigrant Sentiment." *Social Justice* 35, 7–27.

White Privilege: Moving Beyond Guilt into Responsibility and Action

By Debra Busman

WHITE PRIVILEGE: A STORY

It's a warm summer day at the Sand City shopping center, and I am walking out of Target when my cart triggers the store's security alarm. Two young red-shirted employees approach me with smiles and say, "We're so sorry, Ma'am." I show them my receipt, everything checks out, they apologize for the error and inconvenience, and I am on my way in less than a minute. Nothing much to note, and I wouldn't have thought any more about it, except that two doors down, a young Black man had also been exiting the store at the same time the alarm went off. He, however, was not greeted by young smiling clerks, but instead by two bulky mall "rent-a-cops" who backed him up against the wall, physically blocking his exit. It all was over quickly, as the clerks who found the error in my receipt signaled to the rent-a-cops that my cart was indeed the culprit. The security guards stepped aside, and the young Black man left the store, shaking his head. Just another day.

As White folks, we move through the world in radically differing ways from people of color, and sometimes White privilege can be as "simple" as who gets smiled at, called "Ma'am," and apologized to for being inconvenienced while exiting a department store, and who is criminalized, presumed guilty, and backed against a wall. Or worse. In her groundbreaking essay, "White Privilege and Male Privilege: A Personal Account of Coming to See Correspondence through Work in Women's Studies," feminist scholar Peggy McIntosh (1988) attempted to make visible the daily personal workings of racial privilege in her own life. As a woman, she noted how easy it was for her to notice the ways in which men carried gender dominance and privilege, and therefore posited that there was "most likely a phenomenon of White privilege that was similarly denied and protected." However, she found the workings of racial privilege to be much more elusive. "As a White person," she observed, "I realized I had been taught about racism as something that puts others at a disadvantage, but had been taught not to see one of its corollary aspects, White privilege, which puts me at an advantage" (McIntosh 1988).

To counter this socially conditioned "not-seeing" of racial advantage, McIntosh made a list, coming up with fifty ways in which her life was impacted by White privilege on an everyday basis. For example:

> I can, if I wish, arrange to be in the company of people of my race most of the time; I can be sure that my children will be given curricular materials that testify to the existence of their race; If a traffic cop pulls me over, or if the IRS audits my tax return, I can be sure I haven't been singled out because of my race; When I am told about our national heritage or about "civilization," I am shown that people of my color made it what it is; I can be sure that if I need legal or medical help my race will not work against me; I can easily buy posters, postcards, picture books, greeting cards, dolls, toys, and children's magazines featuring people of my race; I can choose blemish cover or bandages in "flesh" color that more or less match my skin.

This painstaking list rendering visible the racial advantages of White privilege is a large reason why McIntosh's essay, later renamed "White Privilege: Unpacking the Invisible Knapsack," is still widely anthologized and taught as an important foundational text in colleges and antiracism workshops across the country almost three decades years later. In this chapter, I will examine a few of the key issues that antiracist theorists and educators have explored since McIntosh's work and suggest possible "action plans" for future study and implementation.

WORKING DEFINITIONS: WHAT WHITE PRIVILEGE IS, AND IS NOT

McIntosh describes White privilege as "an invisible package of unearned assets that I can count on cashing in each day, but about which I was 'meant' to remain oblivious" (1988). Antiracist educators Jon Greenberg and Tim Wise provide further working definitions:

> What is White Privilege? The reality that a White person's whiteness has come—and continues to come—with a vast

array of benefits and advantages not shared by many people of Color (POC). It doesn't mean that I, as a White person, don't work hard (I do) or that I haven't suffered (well, I have known struggle), but simply that I receive help, often unacknowledged assistance, because I am White. (Greenberg 2015)

White privilege refers to any advantage, opportunity, benefit, head start, or general protection from negative societal mistreatment that people deemed White will typically enjoy, but that others will generally not enjoy. These benefits can be material (greater opportunity in the labor market, or greater net worth, due to a history in which Whites had the ability to accumulate wealth to a greater extent than persons of color), social (presumptions of competence, creditworthiness, law-abidingness, intelligence, etc.), or psychological (not having to worry about triggering negative stereotypes, rarely having to feel out of place, not having to worry about racial profiling, etc.). Operationally, White privilege is simply the flip side of discrimination against people of color (Wise 2014).

Having White privilege does not mean having everything good and easy in life. It does not deny individual hardship, nor does it mean that one hasn't faced other forms of discrimination and struggle. It means being advantaged in mostly invisible and unacknowledged ways that pass as "normal," and it means not being directly impeded by one's racial identity. Having White privilege does not mean that one is a bad person and/or a racist, but it does mean that we are all thoroughly enmeshed within unjust societal/institutional systems of racism and White supremacy. It does not mean that those of us who are White are somehow guilty or to blame for the racism in this world. While White people are not responsible for the systems of racial oppression we were born into, we have benefited and continue to benefit from them. I do believe that if we care about justice and equality, we are responsible for unpacking these "invisible knap-sacks" of White privilege and doing what we can to create a more just and equitable world.

THE WORKINGS OF INTERSECTIONALITY

McIntosh's listing of White privilege has been critiqued for its mostly unacknowledged middle-class standpoint and positionality. White students raised in poor and work-ing-class environments, in particular, have bristled at items on the list such as "If I should need to move, I can be pretty sure of renting or purchasing housing in an area which I can afford and in which I would want to live," feeling this to be an advantage coming out of class privilege and not necessarily available to them as working-class Whites. LGBTQ folks, often facing violent homophobia, point out that White privilege alone does not ensure that they, like McIntosh, "can travel alone or with my spouse without expecting embarrassment or hostility in those who deal with us." Coined by law professor and critical race theorist Kimberlé Crenshaw, the term *intersectionality* describes how multiple forms of discrimination function simultaneously to shape social inequalities and impact the ways in which we all move through the world with complex interacting and overlapping sets of social identities—race, class, gender identity, nationality, ability.

As I walked out of Target and set off the alarm that summer day, there is no doubt that racial privilege was the dominant force at play in determining how I was treated. I also carried multiple other identities and privileges, moving through the world as an able-bodied, middle-aged, middle-class-appearing person, all of which served to protect and set me apart from the hyper-criminalized and racially targeted identities of the young Black man two doors down. Other carried identities and experiences—being lesbian, formerly homeless, an incest survivor, a less-than-law-abiding adolescent, a teen street survivor who had been brutally targeted by police violence—may have shaped how I felt and operated in the world, but it was White privilege that got me through those doors that day with a smile and apology.

While intersectionality can be helpful for White folks navigating possible other marginalized identities regarding economic class, ability, or gender identity, it's critical that it not be used as a way for those of us who are White to avoid dealing with our own racism and White privilege. Rather, it provides a powerful theoretical understanding of how people of color often face multiple forms of discrimination in addition to racism, and how social justice movements must include a critical examination of all intersecting forms of discrimination. "People of color within LGBTQ movements; girls of color in the fight against the school-to-prison pipeline; women within immigration movements; trans women within feminist movements; and people with disabilities fighting police abuse—all face vulnerabilities that reflect the intersections of racism, sexism, class oppression, transphobia, able-ism and more" (Crenshaw 2015).

WHITE FRAGILITY

Acknowledging racial privilege is fraught territory for those of us who are White and challenges deeply held belief systems. In reflecting on the difficulties she experienced in coming to terms with her own White privilege, McIntosh said, "The pressure to avoid it is great, for in facing it I must give up the myth of meritocracy ... the myth that democratic choice is equally available to all" (1988). Many of us continue to hold onto the belief that when we succeed, it is only because we have earned that success with our hard work and our intelligence and that any other person who works hard enough and is intelligent enough can do the same. As White people, we have been conditioned to see race as something affecting people of color and racism as somehow external to our lives. We may vigorously condemn racism, yet lack the awareness and skills to examine the impact that White supremacy has had on ourselves and the ways in which we benefit from systems of unequal institutionalized racial power. This avoidance allows White people to move through the world without bearing the "social burden" of racial discrimination, yet renders us "racially illiterate" and woefully unprepared to engage in meaningful conversations about race (DiAngelo 2015; Sleeter 1996).

White people in North America live in a social environment that protects and insulates them from race-based stress. This insulated environment of racial protection builds White expectations for racial comfort while at the same time lowering the ability to tolerate racial stress, leading to what I refer to as *White fragility*. White fragility is a state in which even a minimum amount of racial stress becomes intolerable, triggering a range of defensive moves. These moves include the outward display of emotions such as anger, fear, and guilt, and behaviors such as argumentation, silence, and leaving the stress-inducing situation (DiAngelo 2011).

We can see these defensive moves at play in virtually every college classroom and antiracism workshop in which racism, and especially White privilege, is directly addressed. For many White people, these encounters may be the first time we have received a direct and sustained challenge to our racial understandings. Our education and socialization have not given us the tools, modeling, and experience necessary to have these conversations. In her essay, "White Fragility: Why It's So Hard to Talk to White People about Racism" (2015), Dr. Robin DiAngelo breaks down some key patterns of White socialization that contribute to White people's difficulty in understanding the systemic workings of racism. For example:

1. **Segregation:** Most Whites live, grow, play, learn, love, work, and die primarily in social and geographic racial segregation. Yet our society does not teach us to see this as a loss.

2. **The good/bad binary:** The most effective adaptation of racism over time is the idea that racism is a conscious bias held by mean people. If we are not aware of having negative thoughts about people of color, don't tell racist jokes, are nice people, and even have friends of color, then we cannot be racist. Thus, a person is either racist or not racist—if a person is racist, that person is bad; if a person is not racist, that person is good.

3. **Individualism:** Whites are taught to see themselves as individuals, rather than as part of a racial group. Individualism enables us to deny that racism is structured into the fabric of society. This erases our history and allows us to distance ourselves from the history and actions of our group (DiAngelo 2015).

DiAngelo goes on to list several other patterns that contribute to White privilege and White fragility—entitlement to racial comfort, racial arrogance, racial belonging, psychic freedom, and constant messages that we are more valuable—and reminds us that "the antidote to White fragility is ongoing, and includes sustained engagement, humility, and education" (DiAngelo 2015).

MOVING INTO ACTION

McIntosh concludes her essay by asking how, once we have raised our awareness of racial privilege, we can then turn such knowledge and advantage into actions that create systemic change.

I could have walked out of Target that summer day and thought nothing more about the experience, completely oblivious to the disparate treatment the young man of color was receiving two doors down. I could have walked out the door, which is in fact what I did, acutely aware of the White privilege at work as I was treated with deference, respect, and smiling apology. I noticed what was happening, fully understood the inequity, and noted that the young man was released and was okay; we exchanged knowing glances, head shakes, and eye rolls as we walked to our cars. But did my awareness and understanding of White privilege alone do anything to challenge racial injustice? Did my knowledge of history, racism, the school-to-prison pipeline, and the criminalization of youth of color do anything to protect Tamir Rice, a twelve-year-old boy killed by police as he played with a toy gun in a local park? Did my awareness do anything to help prevent the killing of Michael Brown, John Crawford, Eric Garner, Walter Scott, or Philando Castile, or the shooting of Charles Kinsey, a Miami social worker who was shot while laying on the ground, arms in the air, pleading with officers not to shoot him or the young autistic man in his care, sitting on the sidewalk, playing with a toy truck? In this post-election flurry of Islamophobia and racialized and anti-immigrant rhetoric and hate crimes, did individual awareness alone do anything to protect Indian aviation engineer Srinivas Kuchibhotla, shot dead by a White man yelling, "Get out of my country!" before opening fire in a Kansas City bar? On a smaller, local level, did my consciousness of White privilege do anything to impact policy, practice, and customer relations at the local Target store?

Clearly, awareness alone is not enough. Drawing on DiAngelo's "antidote to White fragility," here are some possible suggestions for ways in which we can continue this important work of challenging racial injustice:

Education

Read poems, stories, and novels; study history; check out videos, TED Talks, and films by people of color and Whites working for racial justice. Read Ta-Nehisi Choates, bell hooks, and Tim Wise. Read Howard Zinn's *The People's History of the United States*, Rudolfo Acuña's *Occupied America*, and other books that share the histories and struggles of people of color but are not taught in mainstream education. Learn stories not only of racial injustice, but also of social movements of resistance, including stories of resistance by White allies that are often rendered invisible in the school curriculum. A great place to start is with the eighty-four books banned by the Tucson Unified School District in 2012, when it voted to close down the Social Justice Education Program (Romero 2012; see www.librotraficante.com/Banned.html).

Diversify your news sources, and explore alternative media—check out Colorlines. com; *Native News Online*; *Huffington Post's* Black Voices, Asian Americans, Middle East, and Latino Voices sections; *Al Jazeera English*; and *The Root*. Read works by White antiracist activists and educators, such as Paul Kivel, Robin DiAngelo, Frances Kendell, Christine Sleeter, Beverly Tatum, and Tim Wise. Form a book club and read works by diverse writers. Learn about the issues facing communities of color in your area and get involved in groups organizing for change.

Sustained Engagement

White privilege and racial justice work is challenging and requires ongoing commitment and perseverance. It is hard to do this work in isolation, and for White folks it is especially important to connect with other White folks. Groups like Standing Up for Racial Justice (SURJ) have started chapters all over the country to organize White people committed to fighting racial injustice.

Through community organizing, mobilizing, and education, SURJ moves White people to act as part of a multiracial majority for justice with passion and accountability. The group works to connect people across the country while supporting and collaborating with local and national racial justice organizing efforts (SURJ Mission Statement 2016).

Groups like SURJ understand the need for Whites to do our own work around racial privilege, and also to step up as allies (or, as Native organizer Klee Benally notes, "accomplices") in racial justice movements, following the leadership of communities of color while also understanding the need to "challenge the narrative of White supremacy by breaking White silence" (SURJ 2016). Check out the SURJ website (www.showingupforracialjustice.org) and see if there is an affiliated group in your area. If not, consider starting one!

The National Coalition Building Institute (NCBI) is a diverse organization dedicated to the elimination of racism and other forms of oppression, including ethnicity, gender, class, age, sexual orientation, religion, disability, and job and life circumstance. It offers welcoming diversity/prejudice reduction workshops, constituency caucus programs, and trainings in controversial issues process, all in a supportive environment. NCBI is a great place to do ongoing work around intersectionality, and heal in the areas in which you have been privileged and marginalized by oppression. Check out the NCBI website at http://ncbi.org to find an affiliate chapter in your area.

Find out what communities of color are doing in your area and join the struggle. Folks are doing great work, organizing around racial justice, the school-to-prison pipeline, immigration, citizenship, environmental racism, public policy, LGBTQ rights, Islamophobia, economic justice, voting rights, criminal justice, employment, restorative justice, and more. Sustained racial justice work means going back and forth between personal, internal healing work and "action" work out in the community, countering the systemic inequities of racism. Blogger J. B. W. Tucker (2016) has put together a comprehensive listing of data demonstrating the impact of institutionalized racism in eleven categories—police, the war on drugs, prison (mass incarceration), criminal justice/the courts, education, employment, wealth, the workplace, voting, the media, and housing—gathering statistics that show what he calls the "evidence-based policies" of discrimination and White privilege. Explore his website at www.jbwtucker.com/ultimate-white-privilege-statistics and see if there are areas that might spark you into action.

Humility

Countering ongoing socialization designed to render White privilege invisible is tremendous work and requires not only strength and perseverance, but also great humility. White folks must step out of personal and societal comfort zones, knowing that we will inevitably make mistakes. As DiAngelo notes, "'Getting it' when it comes to race and racism challenges our very identities as good White people. It's an ongoing and often painful process of seeking to uncover our socialization at its very roots" (DiAngelo 2015). In doing antiracism work, White people will be placed in the uncomfortable situation where, at times, folks of color will be more "expert" about our White privilege than we are. We will definitely make mistakes. A quote that has proven helpful to me is from a meme on the SURJ website, in which Maurice Mitchell says, "Your individual anxiety about possibly getting things wrong has nothing to do with my liberation." For me, this is a nice reminder that the work is always more important than the fear.

Increasingly, antiracist workers are examining the ways in which racism has also damaged the humanity of Whites. In their recent book, *Combined Destinies: Whites Sharing Grief about Racism*, authors Ann Todd Jealous and Caroline Haskell write:

> The degrading and relentlessly dehumanizing evil called "racism" is an institutionalized system of economic and social oppression of one group of people by another. Such oppression is not possible without causing harm to the perpetrators. ... We cause psychological and spiritual damage to ourselves whenever we are hurtful to others. (2013)

Whites engaged in this work are examining the ways in which our own dignity, humanity, and liberation are inextricably interwoven, caught up, as Dr. Martin Luther King Jr. reminds us, "in an inescapable network of mutuality, tied into a single garment of destiny" (Elliott 2016; King 1963). SURJ describes this as follows:

> We use the term mutual interest to help us move from the idea of helping others, or just thinking about what is good for us, to understanding that our own liberation as White people, our own humanity, is inextricably linked to racial justice. Mutual interest means we cannot overcome the challenges we face unless we work for racial justice. It means our own freedom is bound up in the freedom of people of color. (SURJ 2016)

Let the work begin.

DISCUSSION QUESTIONS

1. In his essay, "10 Examples That Prove White Privilege Protects White People in Every Aspect Imaginable," Jon Greenberg creates his own White privilege list of ten things he has learned about racial privilege from people of color. Go online, check out his list (http://everydayfeminism.com/2015/11/lessons-white-privilege-poc), and come up with your own list of the top ten privileges you believe White people carry in today's society.

2. Read Dr. DiAngelo's entire article on "White Fragility" (https://goodmenproject.com/featured-content/white-fragility-why-its-so-hard-to-talk-to-white-people-about-racism-twlm) and reflect on your own experiences in having conversations about race and racial privilege. For those who are White, what emotions do you notice coming up for you during discussions around race? Do you notice any of the racial stress triggers DiAngelo describes? For those who are students of color, what have been the most challenging responses you've received from White people during discussions of race? Do you notice these racial stressors at play for White folks? What would be the most important thing you wish White people would "get" about race and privilege?

3. Which of the "action" items suggested for White people wanting to understand White privilege and work toward racial justice would be most productive? What role do you believe White people have in ending racism? What are other actions White folks can take that would be helpful in creating racial justice?

WEBSITE LINKS

Cracking the Codes: The System of Racial Inequity (World Trust Films): http://racialequitytools.org/curricula

Curriculum for White Americans to Educate Themselves on Race and Racism—from Ferguson to Charleston (Citizenship & Social Justice): http://citizenshipandsocialjustice.com/2015/07/10/curriculum-for-white-americans-to-educate-themselves-on-race-and-racism

Everyday Feminism: http://everydayfeminism.com

List of books banned in the Tucson School District (Librotraficante): www.librotraficante.com/annotatedBibliography.pdf

Racial Equity Tools: www.racialequitytools.org/home

Showing up for Racial Justice (SURJ): www.showingupforracialjustice.org

SUGGESTIONS FOR FURTHER READING

Coates, T. 2015. *Between the World and Me*. New York: Spiegel & Grau.
Collins, P.H. and Bilge, S. 2016. *Intersectionality*. Malden, MA: Polity Press.
DiAngelo, R. 2012. *What Does It Mean to Be White? Developing White Racial Literacy*. New York: Peter Lang.
DiAngelo, R. 2015. "White Fragility: Why It's So Hard to Talk to White People about Racism." https://goodmenproject.com/featured-content/white-fragility-why-its-so-hard-to-talk-to-white-people-about-racism-twlm.
Elliott, G. 2016. "10 Ways White Supremacy Wounds White People: A Tale of Mutuality." American Friends Service Committee. http://afsc.org/blogs/acting-in-faith/10-ways-white-supremacy-wounds-white-people-tale-mutuality.
Hooks, B. 2000. *Where We Stand: Class Matters*. New York: Routledge.
Kendall, F. 2012. *Understanding White Privilege: Creating Pathways to Authentic Relationships Across Race*. New York: Routledge.
Kivel, P. 2011. *Uprooting Racism: How White People Can Work for Racial Justice*. Gabriola Island, British Columbia, Canada: New Society Publishers.
Rankine, C. 2014. *Citizen: An American Lyric*. Minneapolis, MN: Graywolf Press.
Wise, T. 2010. *Colorblind: The Rise of Post-racial Politics and the Retreat from Racial Equity*. San Francisco, CA: City Lights Books.
Zinn, H. 2003. *A People's History of the United States*. New York: HarperCollins.

REFERENCES

Crenshaw, K. 2015. "Why Intersectionality Cannot Wait." *Washington Post*. www.washingtonpost.com/news/in-theory/wp/2015/09/24/why-intersectionality-cant-wait/?utm_term=.c65ea1076e7a.

DiAngelo, R. 2011. "White Fragility." *International Journal of Critical Pedagogy* 3(3). http://libjournal.uncg.edu/ijcp/article/viewFile/249/116.

DiAngelo, R. 2015. "White Fragility: Why It's So Hard to Talk to White People about Racism." https://goodmenproject.com/featured-content/white-fragility-why-its-so-hard-to-talk-to-white-people-about-racism-twlm.

Elliott, G. 2016. "10 Ways White Supremacy Wounds White People: A Tale of Mutuality." American Friends Service Committee. http://afsc.org/blogs/acting-in-faith/10-ways-white-supremacy-wounds-white-people-tale-mutuality.

Greenberg, J. 2015. "10 Examples That Prove White Privilege Protects White People in Every Aspect Imaginable." *Everyday Feminism.* http://everydayfeminism.com/2015/11/lessons-white-privilege-poc.

Jealous, A. T., and C. T. Haskell, eds. 2013. *Combined Destinies: Whites Sharing Grief about Racism.* Dulles, VA: Potomac Books.

King, M. L., Jr. 1963. "Letter from a Birmingham Jail." www.thekingcenter.org/archive/document/letter-birmingham-city-jail-0.

McIntosh, P. 1988. "White Privilege and Male Privilege: A Personal Account of Coming to See Correspondence through Work in Women's Studies." In *Race, Class, and Gender: An Anthology*, edited by M. Anderson and P. Hill Collins, 94–105. Belmont, CA: Wadsworth.

Romero, E. 2012. "The Battleground for America's Narrative: An Annotated Bibliography of the 84 Banned Books in Arizona." www.librotraficante.com/annotatedBibliography.pdf.

Showing up for Racial Justice (SURJ): http://www.showingupforracialjustice.org/

Sleeter, C. 1996. "White Silence, White Solidarity." In *Race Traitors*, edited by N. Ignatiev and J. Garvey. New York: Routledge.

Tucker, J. B. W. 2016. "The Ultimate White Privilege Statistics & Data Post." www.jbwtucker.com/ultimate-white-privilege-statistics.

Wise, T. 2014. "Frequently Asked Questions: Tim Wise, Antiracist Essayist, Author and Educator." http://www.timwise.org/f-a-q-s/.

Semillas y Culturas: Foodways in Ethnic Studies

By Melissa M. Moreno

It's a fall day in the middle of a fall community college semester at a semi-rural Hispanic Serving Institution (HSI) with more than 45 percent Chicana/o and Latina/o student enrollment. It is the opening of the *Semillas y Culturas* (Seeds and Cultures) Conference on the college campus, and the sounds of *ayoyotes*, the seed-filled rattles on the ankles of Mexica-Aztec dancers, remind us of rain. We have not heard the sound of rain during the harsh drought in several years. *Maestra de danza* (teacher of dance) Adelita Serena speaks to a group of more than two hundred students and community members about the interconnection among water, land, seeds, food, and culture at this conference co-hosted by the school's Ethnic Studies program and the Center for Families—a local community non-profit organization. Local Native community member Mike Duncan also speaks and acknowledges that we stand on Wintun homeland, and that the land has a history. He offers a song with a hand drum and recognizes the ancestors of the California region who served as first stewards and tended to the land before colonial settlers arrived. Both Serena and Duncan encourage everyone attending this one-day conference to value knowledge about native food, cultural traditions, and an indigenous peoples' history from the keynote speakers, panel, workshops, and cultural sharing.

Throughout the day, there are participants of various generations engaging in dialogues and discussions in and outside of workshop sessions. Some participants talk about how healthy food is not a priority because there is only time for working, trying to do well in school, and maybe engaging in local politics. Others describe that young people learn in society to distance themselves from their traditional foods (i.e., corn, beans, squash, etc.) and to consume only the standard U.S. American diet, especially unhealthy processed fast food, leading to diabetes. Some, like the youth members of the Pueblo Unido organization, talk about how their farmworker families surrounded by agricultural fields are living in a "food desert." This means that it is difficult to find affordable and good-quality or healthy fresh foods nearby their local community. Yet others describe how historically Native, Mexican American, Mexican immigrant, and indigenous migrant families have experienced colonial and labor oppression in the large-scale agricultural industry that feeds the nation. For this reason their children often do not want to have anything to do with the study of agriculture or food systems. Throughout the day, several participants express interest in learning more about the history of the land, indigenous agriculture, food heritage, and traditional native cuisine.

In other words, these participants are interested in learning what social science calls *foodways*—intersecting practices having to do with food in culture, traditions, and history. More specifically, they are interested in learning about practices associated with the California, Southwest, and Mesoamerican regions, because many of their ancestors were (or are still) rooted to these areas at one point or another in time. They call for cultivating *semillas y culturas* (seeds and cultures), which means preparing the new generation to develop the sensibilities to acquire relevant foodways literacy that could be used to participate in cultural exchanges in the future.

This chapter focuses on how I, as an ethnic studies educator trained in sociology, used sociological imagination—awareness of the relationship between personal experience and wider society. With it I created a space for a community to engage in foodways literacy within a network of relationships centered on Native and Chicana/o Studies. This means working collectively toward understanding why and how it is important to access healthy traditional food in culture and society (Loo 2014). My hope is that readers will be introduced to a context of working toward foodways literacy and praxis.

EFFORTS ON THE GROUND

"Get out of the fields!" This message about removing myself from doing work in agriculture fields was communicated to me early in my life (Turner 2015). There seemed to be generational trauma associated with the land because of the various displacements and oppressive agricultural labor my family had personally experienced. As a granddaughter of farmworkers originally from the Southwest and Mesoamerican regions and a daughter of farmworkers in Central California, I heard this message many times. For my parents, the land was a priority only when they resisted that our community housing be demolished by county board of supervisors in the late 1970s because it was a sign of poverty in what is now called the San Joaquin Valley, also known as Yokut homeland (Moreno 1997). Mostly there was time only for working in the fields, engaging in bilingual education school politics, and getting us kids to do well in school.

Even though we went hungry when the agricultural landowners did not pay my father, foodways did not seem to be the main focus in the household or community. With some institutional opportunities, offered through Head Start, Migrant Education, and then later affirmative action programs, I became the first of my family to graduate from primary and secondary schooling and then the first to earn college degrees.

In college, I began to understand the relationship among culture, society, and ecology. I learned that sociologists familiar with conflict theory (the idea that groups in society are in constant conflict about power) understand that colonial dominant institutions had negatively impacted the social status of indigenous people and their descendants, as well as women (Childs 1998). In this subordinate status, indigenous people and women's knowledge, specifically about culture and ecology, have been made less significant compared to patriarchal Western ways of knowing (Childs 1993; Collins 1990; Jacob 2013). Some sociologists have offered historical ways of understanding the global perspectives of indigenous people and non-elites, which go beyond a new world order, about power structures that have negatively impacted our global environment (Brecher, Childs, and Cutler 1993; Burawoy et al. 1991; Childs 2002). Others have specifically studied the contemporary implications of toxic pollutants spread by global institutions and corporations in our society, and the social movements calling for environmental justice (Szasz 1994). Given that our environment has an impact on our food supply, sociologists who are aware of environmental justice concepts and movements are now investigating food justice concepts and activism (Alkon and Norgaard 2009; Loo 2014). These sociologists have recognized that environmental and food justice struggles take place within the contexts of institutional racism, racial formations, and racialized geographies in our society. In other words, they are conscious that low-income communities of color struggle with accessing affordable, healthy, and fresh foods more than any other groups in society. Some Native sociology scholars, such as Jacob (2013) and others, have explained the significance of indigenous cultural revitalization, activism, and healing from colonization to restore and sustain land, foodways, traditional culture, and water resources. As descendants of indigenous and migrant peoples of this hemisphere (Anzaldúa 1987; Forbes 1973; Perez 1999), Chicanas/os and Latinas/os, as well as Central American and Mexican indigenous migrants, have historically contended with issues related to land displacement, labor, health, education, and foodways struggles (Chabrán 2015; Deeb-Sossa and Moreno 2015; Fox and Rivera-Salgado 2004; Noriega et al. 2001; Peña 1998, 2005; Peña, Calvo, McFarland and Valle 2017; Rodriguez 2014; Zavella 2016).

With structural support, I got out of the agricultural field, and into the ethnic studies field. In and outside of academic institutions, I was trained by many caring interdisciplinary scholars in sociology, women's studies, and education. But it is in the ethnic studies field where I, like other Native, Chicana/o, and Latina/o faculty at other college campuses, became aware of sociological imagination and came to practice being an "organic intellectual" (Gramsci 1971). We have created a space for lifelong learning about a wide range of sociological understandings about cultures, ecology, and politics with students in courses and the communities we serve. In essence, ethnic studies is where we have come to perform our public sociology, where doing sociology has meant teaching. This is where we have facilitated life-long learning about our relationship to land and traditional food that at times we abandoned while going through the educational pipeline and eating mostly a standard U.S. American diet (Calvo and Esquibel 2015; Jiménez 2006; Luna 2011; Solis, 2017). Like many others, we have been inspired by the early American Indian Movement, which was among the first to bring to our attention the serious impacts of land depletion and toxic pollutants in our environment. Also the early United Farm Workers Movement, which was the first to focus on agricultural workers, helped us become aware of food pesticides in the dominant food system (Pulido 1996). Many of us had access to free breakfast through the programs that the Black Panthers conceptualized, advocating that food is one of the first needs in poor communities of color. In addition the efforts of the South Central Los Angeles Farm mobilization, one of the largest organic urban farms in the history of the nation created by mostly Chicana/o, Latina/o, and American Indian people to address food justice, has been imprinted in our contemporary collective memory as well (Irazabal and Punja 2009; Peña 2005). Also some of us have been moved by the work of Native food justice organizations and farms, such as the Acequia Institute, Almunyah de las Dos Acequias, Denfensa de Maiz, Intertribal Agriculture Council, Mujeres de Maiz, Native Culinary Association, Native Seed Search, Pueblo Food Project, Slow Food Turtle Island Association, Traditional Native American Farmers Association, White Earth Land Recovery Project, among others. Non-native food justice organizations and farms that have also been inspirational include the Bayer Farm, Beacon Food Forest, Cultural Conservancy, Gill Tract Farm, LandPaths, Occidental Arts and Ecology Center, Soil Born Farms, Slow Food Movement, Spiral Gardens Community Food Security Project, Yisrael Farms, UC Santa Cruz Farm and Alan Chadwick Garden, Veggielutions, UC Davis Student Farm and Ecology Garden, West Oakland Farmers Market, and others.

As an educator in a web of relationships, I have learned firsthand that culture, ecology, and politics are all deeply intertwined. Peña (1998) explains that to focus solely on the "politics of culture" or the "politics of ecology" is a dominant worldview that members of racial ethnic minority communities cannot afford to hold, especially given the direct effects of colonialism on the conditions and health of Chicano/Latino communities in the United States. The next frontier of colonization, according to Calvo and Esquibel (2015), is the human body, through the imposition of the evolving standard U.S. American diet on Native, Chicano, and Latino communities. Several researchers have pointed out that the food we consume is already having various negative health effects on our current and next generation of students, faculty, and community members

(Algert, Agrawal, and Lewis 2006; Calvo and Esquibel 2015; Chabram-Dernersesian and de la Torre 2008; Peña 2010, Peña, Calvo, McFarland and Valle 2017).

With awareness of the negative impacts of the standard U.S. American food on our health, some faculty and scholars across colleges have begun teaching courses related to foodways and food justice, with an emphasis on indigenous food of this hemisphere. Specific classes include "Decolonize Your Diet: Food Justice in Communities of Color" by Luz Calvo (Murphy 2016), "Decolonizing the Diet Towards an Indigenous Veganism" by Claudia Serrato, "Anthropology of Food, Culture, and Society" by Guillermina Gina Nunez-Mchiri and others. With an emphasis on land, Devon Peña has taught "Food Justice Movements in Mexico and the US," "Agroecology," as well as "Sociology of Sustainable Agriculture" and Liza Grandia has taught "Native Foods and Farming in the Americas." Other college professors have created units within courses (i.e., anthropology, Chicana/o studies, ecology, English, ethnic studies, gender, health, Native studies, sociology, etc.) about foodways, food justice, or decolonizing diets. For example, at the Merced College Los Banos Campus, English professor Susan Kimoto has taught students to read, write, and research representations of climate debates and about the standard U.S. American diet (S. Kimoto, personal communication, August 25, 2016); also the campus is creating a food forest as a teaching lab for all disciplines (Witte 2014). At University of Texas, El Paso (UTEP), another English course taught by Meredith Abarca has focused on food narratives. In Chicana/o Studies health courses on their own campuses, Jennie Luna and Clarisa Rojas teach about the significance of Mesoamerican foodways. Also in the Chicana/o Studies course called "Introduction to Chicana/o Culture" at University of California, Davis, Angie Chabram requires her students to research one or more cultural food dishes, research the ingredients, and conduct interviews with people who cook the food to understand the multiple (and sometimes conflicting) discourses and practices associated with cultural food (A. Chabram, personal communication, August 26, 2016). In a similar way, at UTEP, Faculty Nunez-Mchiri also asks students to research a cuisine that has been passed down through generations in their family, document the recipe and preparation, interview family members about the cuisine and its meaning, discuss the ingredients, and also trace the origins of the ingredients as well (G. G. Nunez-Mchiri, personal communication, August 17, 2016). All these courses shed light on foodways, food justice, and health crisis in this hemisphere, especially among the Native, Chicana/o, and Latina/o community members.

CONTEXT AND PRAXIS ON THE GROUND

With an awareness of foodways and food justice, Native and Chicana/o Studies classes hosted and helped organize the *Semillas y Culturas* Conference in 2014 and 2015 at a community college ("Seeds and Cultures Conference at College" 2015). Global and historical awareness of the Native Wintun region where the *Semillas y Culturas* Conference took place was initially unfamiliar to the students and community members. Given the Indian Gaming Regulatory Act, the local Native tribe currently has a strong economic and cultural base. However, in the past, they experienced oppression during the mission and gold rush eras, which included Indian slave and anti-Indian land policies that negatively impacted their status, natural resources, and foodways (Anderson 2013; Bauer 2016; Dadigan 2015; Middleton 2011). Similar to what happened with other nations, the destruction of the Wintun homeland medicinal plants, and foodways led to diabetes and other illnesses (Anderson 2013; LaDuke 1999; Wildcat 2009). Today, they focus on sustainability, responsible stewardship, and the removal of degrading Indian logos.

The historical and contemporary multicultural history and educational inequalities of this region and the town where the conference was held have been documented and analyzed by Trueba, Rodriguez, Zou, and Cintron (1993). They found that past institutional racist policies negatively impacted today's educational, economic, and political opportunities and disparities experienced by the different racial ethnic groups in the area, in particular Mexican Americans and immigrants. As in other rural and semi-rural towns in California, the Mexican population significantly increased its demographic with changes in labor and immigration policies (e.g., the Bracero Program, IRCA; Gonzalez 2000; Guerin-Gonzales 1994; Hayes-Bautista 2004). The Bracero Program, a guest-worker policy initiated by the US government, called for the importation of Mexican laborers, who were used to develop the large-scale agricultural industry from 1942 to 1964 (Hayes-Bautista 2004; Takaki 1993). Currently, the local town has 55,468 people, and 47 percent or more identify as Chicano/Latino. Today, this community remains surrounded by large-scale agricultural fields, in what some see as a heartland of Monsanto.

As a way of addressing social justice and educational inequality in schools and society caused by institutional racism, Ethnic Studies courses were developed after 1968. In the community where the conference took place, one of the local high schools has offered Mexican American History and Chicano Studies courses (on and off) since the 1970s. As of 2016, the local school district passed a resolution requiring one year of Ethnic Studies education. Also, Ethnic Studies course offerings were expanded at the local community college, which now offers an associate's degree in Chicana/o Studies. In 2006, community college students, including Eric Alfaro, Steven Payan, Octavio Melchor, Carlos Ramirez, Irvin Orozco, Olga Chavez, and Judy Rios, with the support of staff, protested and demanded a full-time Chicana/o faculty, a degree in Chicana/o Studies, and also a multicultural center (S. Payan, personal communication, August 24, 2016). The local newspaper documented this history. In 2008, an Ethnic Studies full-time position was created. The job description emphasized teaching and developing

Chicano and Native Studies courses and degrees, as well as others as needed. Since 2008, I have been the only full-time instructional Chicana professor at the college serving and developing the next generation of leaders across the disciplines. My students are mostly Chicana/o and Latina/o, who are also the largest racial ethnic population in the college. In my ethnic studies teaching, I introduce students to concepts about social inequality, social justice, and foodways.

In 2008, there were several goals and objectives developed for the Ethnic Studies program at the community college. They included developing the social awareness of students and stimulating their leadership and community service potential. As many educators know, social awareness and altruism can be developed through various topics, including social justice and food justice. With this approach, ethnic leadership and community service potential can arise from understanding issues related to institutions and food systems as well. Also, another goal and objective is to provide students with a solid academic understanding of their socioeconomic, political, and historical realities. To address this goal, ethnic studies educators provide an understanding of the socioeconomic, political, and historical realities that have been shaped by the history of land and labor. Yet another goal and objective is the development of students' ability to think critically and express themselves in an organized, logical, and critical manner. This goal can be addressed and practiced through interdisciplinary research regarding the conditions of ethnic communities addressing issues of social justice or even food justice.

To support the classroom curriculum, and in addition to offering courses, the Ethnic Studies program organized more than one hundred events (i.e., workshops, panels, exhibitions, and conferences) and also created a Three Sisters Garden ("Three Sisters Garden Workshop" 2015) between the years of 2008 and 2015. In the fifth year, the cultural programming included workshops that specifically focused on sustainable Native garden designs, histories of the Three Sisters (i.e., corn, beans, and squash), and film discussions about *Save the Farm*, *The Harvest*, *Thirsty for Justice*, and *Dancing Salmon Home: A California Tribe Reunites with Salmon Relatives in New Zealand*. During the film showing of *Save the Farm*, we were able to invite activists Liz Chavez and Ernesto Tlatoa, who were involved in the South Central Los Angeles Farm mobilization. Also, during the film showings of *Dancing Salmon Home*, we were able to invite Chief Caleen Sisk, who has been involved in restoring salmon, protecting sacred sites, and raising awareness about the implications of the "twin tunnels" in Northern California. These film showings and events about food in culture and ecology history were announced in the local newspaper and were excellently attended. Participants engaged in discussing their desires for community gardens, cooking programs, and healthy food to low-income community members. These and other series of events over the years created the social, cultural, and human capital needed for organizing *Semillas y Culturas* conferences at the college in Fall 2014 and Fall 2015.

To support the Ethnic Studies program's goals and objectives, students and community members were invited and encouraged to engage. The purpose of this conference was to create a space to share knowledge and skills about ways to engage in sustainability practices that support cultural food—especially among low-income Native and Chicano families. This grassroots effort was sponsored by the USDA and a local center for families. Information about the *Semillas y Culturas* Conference for this chapter came from five primary sources: participant observation, photographs, newspaper, debriefs with interns, and surveys of conference participants. During one year of organizing preliminary foodways events and two years of conference organizing, I took on various roles in and outside the classroom, facilitating discussions and doing outreach. These conferences were the first of their kind, and they were attended by community college, high school, and university students as well as teachers and community members. The first year, 125 students and community members attended the conference, and the second year, 225 students and community members attended. Surveys were administered and summarized by conference interns. The surveys were given to all participants; 63 were returned the first year, and 104 were returned the second year. For both conferences, the majority of participants rated the conference as "excellent." The first year, 67 percent rated it excellent, 29 percent good, 3 percent average, and 1 percent unknown. The second year, 58 percent rated it excellent, 32 percent good, 7 percent average, and 3 percent unknown. Nobody rated the conference as "poor" or "very poor."

The *Semillas y Culturas* Conference organically brought together experts from many disciplines who were willing to volunteer their time and share their cultural and ecological knowledge. The first year, volunteer keynote speakers were Dr. Jennie Luna, from the CSU Channel Islands Chicana/o Studies department, and faculty David Serena, from the CSU Monterey Bay Humanities and Communications department. Both keynotes received standing ovations, after highlighting the importance of Native cultural foods and the challenges of engaging in the consumption of safe foods, especially for the younger generations. The second year, conference keynote speakers were Jasmin Vargas, from Communities for a Better Environment, and Michael Preston, a leader of the Winnemen Wintu tribe. Both shared their perspectives on the connection between the food justice and environmental justice movements. They emphasized the connection between culture, ecology, and politics. The participants were impressed by both of these young adult speakers, who inspired them to learn more about both food and environmental justice issues.

To provide foodways literacy, in addition to keynote speakers, the conference included volunteer panel presentations and discussions. In the first conference, the panel featured soil expert George Sellu from the Agriculture and Resource Department at Santa Rosa Junior College, Malin Alegria, who works with the Traditional Native American Farmers Association and who is a creative writer featured on NPR, and also Rafael

Aguilera of the Environmental Defense in the California State Assembly and founder of Liberation Permaculture. In the second conference, the panel featured Dr. Luz Calvo, Professor of Ethnic Studies at CSU East Bay, and Dr. Catriona Rueda Esquibel, Professor of Ethnic Studies at San Francisco State University. They are both coauthors of *Decolonize Your Diet: Plant-Based Mexican-American Recipes for Health and Healing*, which was printed third times during its first year when it was published in 2015. This panel also included Pomo/Coast Miwok fisherwomen and gardener Jacqueline Ross and food justice advocate and educator Jianna Robinson. The discussions with audience allowed for discourses of awareness regarding safe foods and concern about protected heritage seeds. The panels were followed by active workshops on the topic of soil improvement, heritage food harvesting, Native horticulture, cooking with Native foods, solar cooking, heritage seeds, and sustainable home and garden design. These workshops were led by Native educator Poncho Redhouse; Indigenous permaculture leader Guillermo Vasquez; organizer of the Festival de Maiz of Stockton, Luis Magana; Chicana/o Studies faculty Susy Zapeda; seed saver advocate Adriana Murgia; Chief Javier Pinzon; solar cooker Ray Daystar; La Defensa de Nuestro Maiz leaders Sergio Nesaulakoyotl Martinez and Angelica Tletlyolotl Delgado; the director of Sol Collective, Estella Sanchez; artist Luis Ramon; artist Francisco "Xico" Gonzalez; Osage Nation tribal member and Pacific tech assistant with IAC Cassandra Lepe; and others.

The support for foodways literacy took many forms. On the day of the conference, organizers on the ground included the community college students, high school students, and local community members. In addition to a series of workshops, there was music about culture shared by Dee Jay Novela, a schoolteacher who also received a major community award from the local university for her service. The conference cultural workers and performers included the local Folkórico group led by teacher Teresa Ramirez, as well as award-winning poet Francisco X. Alarcón. There were others who expressed interest in offering conference educational support but were unable to attend. Among them were Chief Caleen Sisk of the Winnemem Wintu tribe; Native educator Diana Almendariz; former South Central LA Farm activist Liz Chavez; author of *Tending the Wild*, Kat Anderson; and others. The human capital exceeded the financial capital offered for this conference.

At both conferences, *semillas* (seeds) were highlighted as a topic, along with indigenous *culturas* (cultures). The first conference ended with the opening of a cultural exhibition called *Danza Mexica*, co-organized with Dr. Jennie Luna. The exhibition was the first of its kind focusing on contemporary Meso American indigenous dancers who honor harvests. It included ten oil paintings by Artist Ruby Chacon, photographs of *danzantes* of the Sacramento Valley by Francisco "Xico" Gonzalez, prints of Mesoamerican foods by artist Veronica Perez, poems about indigeneity by poet Alarcón, and cultural items belonging to Dr. Luna and local *danza* teachers. The exhibition's opening speech was offered by Mexica-Aztec elder Mama Cobb, who has been described by Dr. Luna and Dr. Rose Borunda as one of the leading founders of contemporary *Mexica Danza* culture in the state of California (Borunda and Moreno 2014; Luna 2011). The second conference ended with the showing and discussion of the award-winning Native film *Beyond Recognition*, featuring Corrina Gould, Chochenyo Ohlone tribe leader and co-director of Indian People Organizing for Change with Johnella LaRose. Gould facilitated a discussion that empowered and inspired those who attended to learn more about Native sacred sites and land trusts.

Surveys from the conference indicated excellent ratings and a great demand for this kind of conference to exist and continue. For the 2014 conference, 90 percent of the surveys answered "yes" when asked, "Do you plan to attend another conference?" and for the 2015 conference, 87 percent of the surveys answered yes to this same question. To answer the question "What did you like most about this conference?" some participants stated the following:

- Themes of social justice, sustainability, healing through reconnecting to Mother Earth
- Meeting new people with common interests and values, and passionate speakers
- Everything—this was an amazing conference that needs to keep happening
- Community connection and connection to self-sustainability and community
- The atmosphere of learning, activism, poetry, and wonderful healthy food
- Educational points
- The panel gave the opportunity for the audience to participate in the sharing of experiences and keynotes
- The workshops were fun and interesting
- There were lots of interesting things to choose from
- The community!
- A safe space and feeling community; food!
- Community-centered feel
- Dancers!
- Question-and-answer discussion
- *Familia* oriented
- Student groups
- Many speakers from around [the region]
- I got a new experience
- The food was amazing, and I loved the discussion
- Seeing all the work that's happening around food … the food, connecting with people, free…
- Community feeling
- The sense of community and all the options for wonderful workshops
- "The Soil Is Alive" workshop

These responses suggest that the sense of belonging and community resonated with most participants. Most participants further cultivated their social and cultural capital. Most presenters of the conference expressed that they were amazed at being able to share knowledge in a space of mostly members of communities of color concerned about foodways and food justice. Most of the presenters had attended or presented at past conferences or workshops with this focus but with predominantly White environmental justice leaders and participants.

CONCLUSION

Creating spaces for foodways literacy at colleges and universities needs to take place—first, with an acknowledgment of the Native land and peoples and with various degrees of collaborations. The *Semillas y Culturas* Conference provided students in Native and Chicana/o Studies and community members with a lifelong learning opportunity to engage in education. Organizers and educators involved with the *Semillas y Culturas* Conference assumed that the topic, concepts, and practices of foodways could be engaged by students and community members. It also assumed they had cultural capital concerning cultural food, agricultural labor, and more. To engage, they used the cultural capital concerning their culture and cultural food, as well their family labor histories—including agricultural labor. Although I had previously lectured in many classes and organized many events to develop critical thinking and global awareness about culture and history, none had resonated with so many as the *Semillas y Culturas* Conference did. Despite the semi-rural setting, there was an excellent number of Native and non-Native students, community members, and experts who chose to participate and engage in discussions about food justice, cultures, and sustainable ecology. The attendance increased from 125 to 225 from one year to another, perhaps because of the equal involvement of Native and Chicana/o Studies students organizing the event, the engagement of students and community members alike, and the collaboration with community organizations. The participants expressed their engagement during conference discussions. They also indicated that new connections and educational interests emerged.

This space, created by the school's Ethnic Studies program, normalized the importance of Native cultural food sources for the first time in this community. In general, in our society the normalization of the foodways topic can be seen with the increased number of academic and nonacademic publications and even in social media, as well as summits on this topic. It can also be seen in the number of urban garden projects and pantries in schools, colleges, and the larger society addressing various realities of food deserts, food insecurity, and health issues (Chabrán 2015; Counihan 2013; Peña, Calvo, McFarland and Valle 2017). However, this topic is not addressed as much in semi-rural communities. Although Peña writes that there is an effort for "ecological democracy" to rise in urban core communities across the US (2010, 3), for some it is not clear that "ecological democracy" has risen in rural or semi-rural areas where massive agricultural food production is central to the context. During the conference participants did articulate the need to care for the local ecology and to dismantle racism in the food system, which is apparent in the quantity and quality of healthy food access, and food distribution gap throughout the various ethnic groups in this and other regions in the nation.

Also, educational institutions and their leadership, especially at Hispanic Serving Institutions, need to continue learning about the interests of students and community members. We need to better position our districts, colleges, and faculty to meet the needs of students at our semi-rural areas. Although foodways literacy is usually nowhere to be found explicitly in the educational master plan of colleges, it is certainly a concept that can be addressed through course topics at all levels and systems of education. For example, at CSU East Bay the Ganas Program has made it a point to require all their incoming transfer college students to take the Ethnic Studies course called "Decolonize Your Diet: Food Justice in Communities of Color" during their first year; this course is intended for academic and self-care preparation to succeed through the educational pipeline. At the community college where the *Semillas y Culturas* Conference was held foodways is addressed in the Mexican American history course in a teaching unit on the Mesoamerican agricultural revolution. Also in the Introduction to Chicana/o Studies course when addressing the indigeneity movement there is a focus on the care for the environment and the role of danza. In the History of Race and Ethnicity course, when discussing the Los Angeles race riots' aftermath, it is explained how racial ethnic alliances and coalitions were created to build the South Central Los Angeles Farm to address serious issues of food deserts and food insecurity. In the Introduction to Native Studies course, when addressing contemporary issues, there is a focus on Native seed protection. It is not about one discipline—for example, agriculture—being the only one assumed to discuss the topic of food. It is about all disciplines with their own approaches (i.e., anthropology, communication, ecology, English, ethnic studies, family consumer studies, political science, sociology, etc.) playing a part in preparing students to think critically about their futures with education and food in environments that value diversity and civic responsibility. We need to intervene in "silo thinking," a framework that overlooks the fact that it is not about a discipline, but about all disciplines creating a "whole" student.

As Peña has indicated, Chicana/o Studies has much work to do to normalize the topics of foodways and food justice in our field. It is not enough to develop lectures or units on food justice; rather, we need to continue creating entire classes. We especially need lower-division classes so that community college instructors can teach out of the shadows without being perceived as encroaching on the field of agriculture or others.

These kinds of courses would indeed encourage student engagement and an appreciation of the cultural capital that our Native, Chicana/o, and Latina/o students bring to our college campuses, resulting in student success and institutional change. Teaching about the concepts of foodways or food justice cannot be understood simply as an "honorable act"; rather, it should be understood as a practice of significant literacy that can engage all students and their communities. We need to continue supporting faculty leadership, full-time faculty hires, and curriculum development in Ethnic Studies so that we can continue serving students and their families in addressing their needs and everyday social realities. Also, we need to seek opportunities to teach and learn more about foodways in order to increase student retention and graduation rates across all educational systems and levels; by doing so, we will enrich the lives of our students and further the cause of affirming our colleges as safe and welcoming communities.

DISCUSSION QUESTIONS

1. What is your ancestral, cultural, or traditional food? In what ways is it sustained and protected?

2. What does land mean to you and what is your relationship to agriculture or to the food system?

3. What does it mean to have access to affordable, healthy, and traditional food?

4. What is your understanding of the food system and its relationship to the institution of family?

5. How is the increase of fast food chains and processed foods impacting health and family relationships?

6. What does it mean to decolonize your diet?

WEBSITE LINKS

www.nativeseeds.org

www.rareseeds.com/get-to-know-baker-creek/petaluma-seed-bank

www.facebook.com/DecolonizeYourDiet

http://ejfood.blogspot.com

AUDIOVISUAL MATERIALS

Ron Finley: A Guerilla Gardener in South Central LA: www.youtube.com/watch?v=EzZzZ_qpZ4w

Seeds of Our Ancestors—Native Youth Awakening to Foodways: www.youtube.com/watch?v=nEAg7KQiSbw

South Central Farm: www.youtube.com/watch?v=Qs-3f678vys

TEDxTC, Winona LaDuke: Seeds of Our Ancestors, Seeds of Life: www.youtube.com/watch?v=pHNlel72eQc

REFERENCES

Algert, S. J., A. Agrawal, and D. S. Lewis. 2006. "Disparities in Access to Fresh Produce in Low-Income Neighborhoods in Los Angeles." *American Journal of Preventive Medicine* 30(3) 65–70.

Alkon, A. H., and K. M. Norgaard. 2009. "Breaking the Food Chains: An Investigation of Food Justice Activism." *Sociological Inquiry* 79(3): 289–305.

Anderson, K. 2013. *Tending the Wild: Native American Knowledge and the Management of California's Natural Resources.* Berkeley: University of California Press.

Bauer, W. J. 2016. *California through Native Eyes: Reclaiming History.* Seattle: University of Washington Press.

Borunda, R., and M. Moreno. 2014. *Speaking from the Heart: Chicana, Latina, and Amerindian Women.* Dubuque, IA: Kendall Hunt Publishing Company.

Brecher, J., J. B. Childs, and J. Cutler. 1993. *Global Visions: Beyond the New World Order.* Boston, MA: South End Press.

Burawoy, M., A. Burton, A. A. Ferguson, K. J. Fox, J. Gamson, N. Gartell, L. Hurst, C. Kurzman, L. Salzinger, J. Schiffman, and S. Ui. 1991. *Ethnography Unbound: Power and Resistance in the Modern Metropolis.* Berkeley: University of California Press.

Calvo, L., and C. Rueda Esquibel. 2015. *Decolonize Your Diet: Plant-Based Mexican-American Recipes for Health and Healing.* Vancouver, Canada: Arsenal Pulp Press.

Chabram-Dernersesian, A., and A. de la Torre. 2008. *Speaking from the Body: Latinas on Health and Culture.* Tucson: University of Arizona Press.

Chabrán, R., ed. 2015. "Mestizaje y Gastronomia / Mestisaje and Gastronomy: What Latinos Eat" [special issue]. *Dialogo: An Interdisciplinary Studies Journal* 18(1).

Childs, J. B. 1993. "The Value of Diversity for Global Cooperation." In *Global Visions: Beyond the New World Order,* edited by J. Brecher, J. B. Childs, and J. Cutler, 17–25. Boston, MA: South End Press.

Childs, J. B. 1998. "Transcommunality: From the Politics of Conversion to the Ethics of Respect in the Context of Cultural Diversity: Learning from Native American Philosophics with a Focus on the Haudenosaunee." *Social Justice* 25: 143–169.

Childs, J. B. 2002. *Transcommunality: From the Politics of Conversion to the Ethics of Respect.* Philadelphia: Temple University Press.

Collins, P. 1990. *Black Feminist Thought: Knowledge, Consciousness, and the Politics of Empowerment.* New York: Routledge.

Counihan, C. 2013. *Food and Culture: A Reader*. New York: Routledge.

Dadigan, M. 2015. "CA Indian Leaders Discuss Lasting Effects of the Gold, Greed and Genocide Era." *Indian Country Today*, January 28. http://indiancountrytodaymedianetwork.com/2015/01/28/ca-indian-leaders-discuss-lasting-effects-gold-greed-and-genocide-era-158891.

Deeb-Sossa, N., and M. Moreno. 2015. "No Cierren Nuestra Escuela: Farm Worker Mothers as Cultural Citizens in an Educational Community Mobilization Effort." *Journal of Latinos and Education* 15(1): 39–57.

Forbes, J. D. 1973. *Aztecas del Norte: The Chicanos of Aztlan*. Greenwich, CT: A Fawcett Premier Book.

Fox, J., and G. Rivera-Salgado. 2004. *Indigenous Mexican Migrants in the United States*. La Jolla, CA: Center for U.S.-Mexican Studies.

Gonzalez, J. 2000. *Harvest of Empire: A History of Latinos in America*. New York: Viking.

Gramsci, A. 1971. *Selections from the Prison Notebooks*. New York: International Press.

Guerin-Gonzales, C. 1994. *Mexican Workers and American Dreams: Immigration, Repatriation, and California Farm Labor, 1900–1939*. New Brunswick, NJ: Rutgers University Press.

Hayes-Bautisa, D. E. 2004. *La Nueva California: Latinos in the Golden State*. Berkeley: University of California Press.

Irazabal, C., and A. Punja. 2009. "Cultivating Just Planning and Legal Institutions: A Critical Assessment of the South Central Farm Struggle in Los Angeles." *Journal of Urban Affairs* 31(1): 1–23.

Jacob, M. 2013. *Yakama Rising: Indigenous Cultural Revitalization, Activism, and Healing*. Tucson: University of Arizona Press.

Jiménez, K. P. 2006. "Start with the Land: Groundwork for Chicana Pedagogy." In *Chicana/Latina Education in Everyday Life: Feminista Perspectives on Pedagogy and Epistemology*, edited by D. D. Bernal, C. A. Elenes, F. E. Godinez, and S. Villenas. New York: State University of New York Press.

La Duke, W. 1999. *All Our Relations: Native Struggles for Land and Life*. Cambridge, MA: South End Press.

Loo, C. 2014. "Towards a More Participative Definition of Food Justice." *Agriculture Environmental Ethnics* 27(5): 787–809.

Luna, J. 2011. *Danza Mexica: Indigenous Identity, Spirituality, Activism, and Performance*. Davis: University of California, Davis.

Middleton, B. R. 2011. *Trust in the Land: New Directions in Tribal Conservation*. Tucson: University of Arizona Press.

Moreno, M. 1997. *Thesis: Chicana/Mexicana Community Mobilization in the San Joaquin Valley, 1979–1983*. Feminist Studies Thesis, University of California, Santa Cruz Department.

Murphy, K. 2016. "Cal State Professor Teaches Students to 'Decolonize Your Diet.'" *Mercury News*, January 6. www.mercurynews.com/health/ci_29347835/cal-state-professor-teaches-students-decolonize-your-diet.

Noriega, C. A., E. R. Avila, M. K. Davalos, C. Sandoval and R. Perez-Torres. 2001. *The Chicano Studies Reader: An Anthology of Aztlan*. Seattle: University of Washington Press.

Peña, D. 1998. *Chicano Culture, Ecology, Politics*. Tucson: University of Arizona Press.

Peña, D. 2005. *Mexican Americans and the Environment: Tierra y Vida*. Tucson: University of Arizona Press.

Peña, D. 2010. Proceedings from 2010 National Association for Chicana and Chicano Studies Annual Meeting on Chicana/o Environmental Justice Struggles for a Post-Neoliberal Age, Seattle, Washington.

Peña, D., L. Calvo, P. McFarland and G. R. Valle. 2017. *Mexican-Origin Foods, Foodways, and Social Movements: Decolonial Perspectives.* Fayetteville: University of Arkansas Press.

Pérez, E. 1999. *The Decolonial Imaginary: Writing Chicanas into History.* Bloomington: Indiana University Press.

Pulido, L. 1996. *Environmentalism and Economic Justice: Two Chicano Struggles in the Southwest.* Tucson: University of Arizona Press.

Rodriguez, R. C. 2014. *Our Sacred Maiz Is Our Mother: Indigeneity and Belonging in the Americas.* Tucson: University of Arizona Press.

"Seeds and Cultures Conference at College." 2015. *Daily Democrat,* October 8. www.dailydemocrat.com/article/NI/20151008/FEATURES/151009889.

Solis, P. S. 2017. "Del Alivio y Coraje la Tuna Nacera: A Re/membering of Land and Place." In *Mexican-Origin Foods, Foodways, and Social Movements: Decolonial Perspectives,* edited by D. Peña, L. Calvo, P. McFarland, and G. R. Valle. Fayetteville: University of Arkansas.

Szasz, A. 1994. *Ecopopulism: Toxic Waste and the Movement for Environmental Justice.* Minneapolis: University of Minnesota Press.

Takaki, R. 1993. *A Different Mirror: A History of Multicultural America.* New York: Little Brown and Company.

"Three Sisters Garden Workshop Offered at Woodland Community College." 2015. *Daily Democrat,* February 20. www.dailydemocrat.com/article/NI/20150220/FEATURES/150229990.

Trueba, H. T., C. Rodriguez, Y. Zou, and J. Cintron. 1993. *Healing Multicultural America: Mexican Immigrant Raise to Power in Rural California.* London: Falmer Press.

Turner, C. S. 2015. "Lessons from the Field: Cultivating Nurturing Environments in Higher Education." *Review of Higher Education* 38(3): 333–358.

Wildcat, D. 2009. Red Alert: Saving the Planet with Indigenous Knowledge. Golden, Colorado: Fulcrum Publishing.

Witte, D. 2014. "Merced College Los Banos Campus, Breaks Ground on Food Forest." *Merced Sun Star,* November 17. www.mercedsunstar.com/news/local/article3989069.html.

Zavella, P. 2016. "Contesting Structural Vulnerability through Reproductive Justice Activism with Latina Immigrants in California." *North American Dialogue* 19(1): 36–45.

From Mexico to the United States: Discovering and Advocating for Social Justice

By Cristobal Salinas Jr.

In this chapter, I write about my ongoing journey in discovering and advocating for social justice. My experiences of privilege, oppression, and marginalization and my social identities (i.e., race/ethnicity, linguistics, immigration, and sexual orientation) have helped me develop a framework for my research, pedagogy in education, social justice, and leadership. Migrating from Mexico to the United States during middle school and adapting to a new culture, all while learning a new language, provided me with an awareness and understanding of the challenges that exist within education. I will frame this chapter based on my life and professional experiences. The ultimate goals of this chapter is to inspire others to lead and to advocate for social justice.

I start this chapter with the picture of my role model. My real role model is my father. My father has provided me with the foundation of my early education, transformative life lessons, and remarkable values that I will carry with me and practice for the rest of my life. I acknowledge that I am privileged to have a father, a role model, who has guided me and given me advice multiple times. I say I am privileged because many of my peers grew up without a father. One of the main values that I learned from my father is the importance of family. This picture was taken during a Thanksgiving family reunion in 2012 in Madison, Nebraska.

I am personally challenged to share the picture of my father, as I hardly ever publish any pictures of my family members on any social media platforms. Also, I am personally challenged to start writing this chapter as I share my family's story—a story that has completely changed my life. I grew up in Atolinga, Zacatecas, Mexico, in a small town—beautiful, colorful, rich in culture, and with a long history. In early 1998, my father was kidnapped on his way back home to Atolinga. He was kidnapped by—we believe—police officers from a neighboring town. When I share my story with

Figure 4.7 My role model

other individuals, the first question that I get asked is, "Was your dad kidnapped by a drug cartel? Did he do drugs?" My response: "No he did not do drugs, and he was not kidnapped by a drug cartel. But he is fine—thank you for asking." It is important to mention that he was kidnapped by police officers, and that he was not kidnapped by a drug cartel, because drug cartels are a major issue that communities in Mexico are currently facing. In this chapter, I do not expand on how or why my dad was kidnapped; rather, I focus on the kidnapping's effects and how that event changed my life completely.

After my dad was released from the abduction, my parents decided to relocate to the United States. In December 1999, I arrived in Madison, Nebraska. Madison is a small town with a population of approximately 2,367, of which 75 percent were White at the time (United States Census Bureau 2000). When I arrived in Nebraska, my reality seemed unreal. The *pozole* and *menudo* transformed into chicken noodles, the *tamales* into pizza, the *pastel de tres leches* into brownies, and the beans into french fries. Everything was different. I was forced to learn English fast, as there were not too many Latinos/as around with whom I could have communicated in Spanish. I learned to adapt to a new culture, to speak a new language, to try new foods, to celebrate new holidays, and even to tell the difference in types of corn, as well as how to detassel corn, because that was the way society did things around there. Through these experiences, I learned how to navigate a new world; yet, there were multiple times I felt lost and invisible from society and school. As I learned to navigate a new world, I learned to survive in an ideology of Whiteness.

During my eighth-grade academic year, I was not invited to my class field trip because I was an English as a Second Language (ESL) student. I remember vividly how my ESL teacher advocated for me because the teacher who coordinated the field trip did not invite me or other ESL students. I also remember how my classmates, and even some teachers, would make fun of me because of my appearance, my inability to speak English, and my lack of knowledge about American culture and the educational system. These are some of my early experiences that I encountered where I felt that I did not fit in at the school and that some of my teachers were not inclusive of other students that sounded or looked like me. I questioned myself: How could I learn from teachers who were not inclusive of ESL students? This experience was critical in my development as an educator, because I choose to major in Spanish Education and ESL. I wanted to teach other students my native language and culture, and to help, inspire, and advocate for ESL students to continue with their education, regardless of how often they were experiencing rejection by the educational system.

Once I completed eighth grade and one semester of my freshman year, my parents decided to relocate to Schuyler, Nebraska. Moving to Schuyler was a new opportunity for my parents to seek new jobs. The move to Schuyler was positive; I had already moved from Mexico to the United States, so moving from one town to another town was an easy transition, as I had already learned some English, and I had some experience with the educational system in the United States. In my previous school, I learned from observation that the only way to fit in was by being involved. Once I arrived at Schuyler Central High School, I got involved in student government, show choir, one-act plays, speech, and Spanish club. This was an opportunity for me to get involved, feel like I fit in, and make new friends in my new school. Being involved in student groups was not the only way for me to be successful in high school; my teachers also played a significant role in my development as a student, and in my academic success. All my Schuyler Central High School teachers were supportive, caring, and inclusive, and they challenged me academically to become the best high school student I could have been.

After high school, I attended the University of Nebraska at Kearney (UNK). UNK provided me with a lot of opportunities that I will never forget. During my undergraduate career, I was actively involved in a variety of activities/organizations, such as student government, the Sigma Lambda Beta International Fraternity, the Hispanic student association, and the Nebraska Cultural Unity Conference. These activities/organizations helped me become more organized, more responsible, and a better leader. I refer to my UNK experience as a "buffet of activities." I had so many positive experiences at UNK that is hard to remember all of them.

One memory that I will never forget is from my junior year, when my friend Pat Ackerman and I decided to run for student body president and student vice president. This was a new and exciting leadership opportunity. I was the first Latino and student of color to run for student body president at UNK. During the campaign for student body president, I received an anonymous letter that stated, "Chris, take your name off the ballot before you get hurt. We do not want a Mexican or fag as student body president."

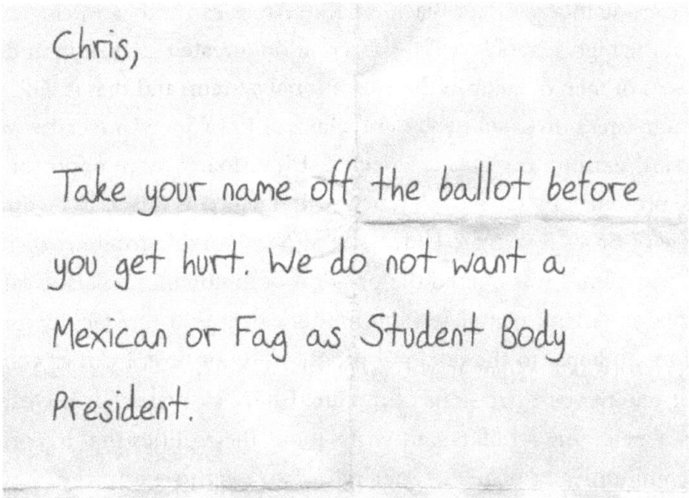

> Chris,
>
> Take your name off the ballot before you get hurt. We do not want a Mexican or Fag as Student Body President.

Figure 4.8

This note changed my life. First, I questioned my safety—I did not know what this actually meant for my security. I called my parents, but I could not explain to them what had happened. It was challenging, as I had a lot of emotions, and they do not speak English, and did not understand the American higher education system. I asked myself and friends, "Who would write such a hateful note? Why would someone attack me for my social identities?" Then I questioned whether I was a victim of institutionalized racism. The university did not do anything in regard to this hate crime, and I had negative experiences with the university policy when the report was being conducted. After I received the hateful note, Pat and I decided to keep our names on the ballot, but to no longer campaign. Pat and I were not elected. It was a difficult situation, but also a motivation to keep doing my best and to not give up. As I reflect on this painful experience, I like to think that Pat and I did not lose. We won! I won and gained many new experiences, new friendships, and new leadership opportunities that came my way.

After my undergraduate college career, I worked for Senator Michael Bennet from Colorado, thanks to the Congressional Hispanic Caucus Institute (www.chci.org). While I was working in the US Senate, I met so many senators, among other national political figures. It felt as if I were living in a reality TV show of politicians. During my stay in the US Senate, I got the opportunity to see Justice Sonia Sotomayor during her hearings after being appointed to the US Supreme Court by President Barack Obama. Seeing Judge Sotomayor in action is one of my favorite memories. It was the first time I saw a woman of color, a wise Latina, to be appointed to one of the most important jobs in the country.

After my experience in DC, I had the opportunity to relocate to Houston, Texas, where I taught Spanish at Elsik High School. Teaching at Elsik was another important moment in my career as an educator and researcher. At the time, I noticed that retention and graduation rates for Black/African American and Latino males presented a challenge at the high school level. My observations created interest in understanding the experiences of men of color in the educational system, and that is when I decided to apply for a master's program in student affairs at Iowa State University. While I was working toward earning my master's degree, I had many more opportunities to do research and present at national conferences with faculty, as well as to do an internship at the College of Brockport, State University of New York. During my second year of the master's program, I was offered the position of multicultural liaison officer for an academic college. After I completed my master's degree, a few faculty and mentors encouraged me to apply to the doctoral program. As of now, I can say, that earning my PhD was one the best decisions of my life. I have earned academic capital, and I get to educate emerging scholars and write about the realities that historically marginalized communities of people are facing. Also, I get to work with other scholars across the country through my work with the National Conference on Race and Ethnicity (NCORE) and the *Journal Committed to Social Change on Race and Ethnicity* (JCSCORE), in addition to many other organizations and journals.

Throughout my career, I have received multiple awards, I have visited more than thirty states across the United States, and I have traveled to five different countries to speak at conferences, high schools, and universities. Over the past five years, I have given more than eighty conferences, lectures, and talks across the country. While there are not a lot of career trajectory differences between me and other academics, there is a significant difference in some of the negative interactions I have with other people. For example, while I was at a university giving a speech on diversity, someone in the audience said to me, "You are stupid." I asked him, "Why?" and his response was, "Because you have an accent." Interactions like this have taught me to be strong and stay positive. Also, I learned that *if you do not know who you are, anyone can name you. And if anyone can name you, you will answer to anything.* It is human behavior to make assumptions about others, but what it is challenging to process is when other people judge and criticize me for my social identities. Comments on my research and scholarship are different from attacks on my social identities.

As I reflect on the past sixteen years, I have been successful, privileged, and honored. I have had the opportunity to learn the unexpected. I have learned about my own historical context, the historical context of Mexican Americans and other races, ethnicities, and cultures, and historically underrepresented communities of people in the United States. I have learned to discover and filter the meaning of powerful and hurtful words. I have learned to educate myself, by learning about the experiences and development of marginalized and targeted populations, and engaging in work that attempts to improve the climate for those populations in society. I have learned that with hard work, passion, and dedication, I can achieve the "American Dream," which, to me, is the Brown Dream.

My experiences of privilege, oppression, and marginalization and my social identities have helped me develop a framework for my pedagogy in education, social justice, and leadership. When I am out in public or private spaces, I cannot always hide my racial and ethnic identities, because these aspects are detectable visually and audibly to other people. Individuals often stereotype me because of my physical appearance: my skin color, height, and hair texture and color, among other characteristics. Despite the experiences of marginalization I have faced, I recognize that I am privileged to study and understand the complexities of my racial and social identities, advantages, and oppressions, while this is not the case for my peers back home. My journey in discovering social justice started through the understanding of my experiences of oppression and marginalization because of my social identities (i.e., race/ ethnicity, linguistics, immigration, and sexual orientation).

Despite the experiences of oppression and marginalization that I have faced, I have learned to always believe in myself; to take risks and have the courage to start new initiatives and leadership positions; to always be proud of who I am and where I come from; to find mentors who can provide me with support and guidance; to always reflect on and think about my lived experiences; and, most important, to always has a positive attitude. These characteristics have helped me with my development as a scholar and leader.

Also, I understand the power of words and numbers. For example, we can make each letter of the alphabet correspond with a number—A is the first letter of the alphabet, so it matches up with the number 1, B matches up with 2, and Z is the last letter, so it matches up with 26 (Cabrera 2002). It is fascinating to see how attitude complements everything we do in life. For example, when analyzing and completing the equation for the terms *knowledge*, *hard work*, and *attitude*, the results are as follows (Cabrera 2002):

Knowledge
K(11) + N(14) + O(15) + W(23) + L(12) + E(5) + D(4) + G(7) + E(5) = 96%
Hard work
H(8) + A(1) + R(18) + D(4) + W(23) + O(15) + R(18) + K(11) = 98%
Attitude
A(1) + T(20) + T(20) + I(9) + T(20) + U(21) + D(4) + E(5) = 100%

Figure 4.9: J. Cabrera, *What's on your Backpack? Packing for success in life*, p. 48. Source: Fig. 4.9: J. Cabrera, What's on your Backpack? Packing for success in life, p. 48. Copyright © 2002 by Liberty Publishing Group.

Knowledge equals 96 percent. Hard work equals 98 percent. And attitude equals 100 percent. When I work with people, in everything that I have done, and in new projects, I always give 100 percent positive attitude. A positive attitude has taken me far in life;

especially when I experience oppression and marginalization. Using the terms *knowledge*, *hard work*, and *attitude* has inspire me to overcome the challenges I encounter every day and to advocate for social justice.

My formative experiences, shaped by my educators and my parents, have framed my teaching and research interests. I believe that education is a conscious and purposeful activity aimed at developing the human potential for life. I know that humans learn through different means, methods, and modes. I believe it is my responsibility as an educator and researcher to provide learning experiences that will both challenge and allow others to think and grow. I know that we humans are the engines of education and society. And that we all can and should be inventors of our own theories, critics of other people's ideas, analyzers of evidence, and makers of our own personal marks on this most complex world. I believe in the power of social justice education to change lives, institutions, and society. Through higher education, educators and students can bring social justice issues to the forefront in order to continue promoting access and equity in higher education. I believe that the opportunity to study, learn, and teach is the greatest privilege; therefore, we all should be prepared to question power and privilege.

REFERENCES

Cabrera, J. 2002. *What's in Your Backpack? Packing for Success in Life*. New York: Liberty Publishing Group.

United State Census Bureau. 2000. *Census 2000 Data for the State of Nebraska*. www.census.gov/census2000/states/ne.html.

Indigenous Immigrants from the Mexican State of Oaxaca Residing in Monterey County, California: The Search for Meaning and Agency

By Renata Funke

Figure 4.10: Renata Funke, indigenous fiesta held by Triqui residents of Monterey County, April 2013

Adults from Oaxaca who settled in the Salinas Valley of Monterey County, California, in expressing a desire to develop English language skills, provided the impetus for research with a culturally and linguistically isolated indigenous population. Largely from the Triqui language group, its members started to arrive in California in the 1980s, and in greater numbers after the North American Free Trade Agreement (NAFTA) went into effect in 1994. In its aftermath, "more people moved from Mexico to the United States than in almost any other period in our history" (Bacon 2008, 51). Many of them had been subsistence-level peasants from rural areas neglected by the Mexican government. After Mexico's financial insolvency in 1982, the country favored foreign investors and large-scale landowners able to export goods, leading to the migration of Oaxacan farmworker families. Their arrival in Greenfield, California, raised issues around unauthorized immigration while at the same time boosting the local economy; it also presented all community members with considerable challenges to coexistence. The initial engagement phase through my work at a local college later led to regular interaction with the Triqui population in my role as volunteer tutor. It grew to include that of accompanier, cultural broker, and research participant. In the process, the inquiry emerged as a search for meaning making and new arenas of agency.

RESEARCH OBJECTIVES THAT EVOLVED OVER TIME

The contact with members of the local Triqui-speaking community of six thousand in a town of seventeen thousand was initiated by a leader of the *Unión Indígena* ("Indigenous Union"). To help me determine specific needs for their English instruction, he invited me to staff a resource table at a *fiesta* held at a local park, featuring traditional Oaxacan dance, clothing, music, and food. I identified fifty adults through my interaction with the participants, communicating in Spanish and noting their phone numbers and names if they had difficulties with writing. Once teachers and classroom space were arranged, a first challenge was to locate methods used for teaching literacy to adults from an oral culture, "bridging oral tradition and the written form of language, which are structurally and psychically different" (Bernstein 2005, 134). This was to occur in ways involving the students as active participants in their learning, allowing for self-determination, one of the four core values of community psychology (Nelson and Prilleltensky 2010, 35). The others are holism, health, and caring, compassion, and support for community structures.

Valuing self-determination and learner engagement quickly pointed to a series of questions on delivery modes. Given centuries of marginalization by fellow Mexicans and recent incidents of interracial strife between mestizo and indigenous Mexican students (Fox, Rivera-Salgado, and Santiago 2013), ways to decolonize the instruction had to be identified. Was Spanish translation appropriate, or was a Triqui interpreter needed in the classroom? Would the adults with literacy issues require additional tutoring, or should they be placed in separate groups altogether? Last, what mechanisms could encourage ongoing input from participants? While the teachers worked with the students on these questions, they also invited suggestions on areas of interest, alleviating the imbalance between newcomer/host and student/teacher through joint exploration, often after class.

As procedural issues were addressed, more fundamental questions emerged. What generative themes would allow for literacy to become a way of reading the world, in the sense suggested by Freire (1987)? The teachers and I ended up dialoguing about what we and the students needed to understand about their life-world beyond the classroom, including work constraints, displacement from their homeland, family issues, and acculturation stress. The critical praxis of community psychology focuses on empowering marginalized community members and promoting social change (Prilleltensky and Nelson 2009, 138). When attending a symposium in Oxnard, California, I was struck by the number of programs a local indigenous advocacy group had created there, from parenting workshops to youth support and literacy classes—all geared "to encourage the empowerment of the indigenous immigrant community in Ventura County" (Mixteco/Indigena Community Organizing Project 2016). In a keynote address, one of the Oaxacans' leading advocates, Gaspar Rivera-Salgado, called on the symposium participants to attend to the need for cultural brokering between indigenous and host populations. The purpose of my research eventually pointed me to an exploration of ways in which cultural brokering and accompaniment could help immigrant newcomers develop a sense of belonging.

METHODS OF DATA COLLECTION, ANALYSIS, AND INTERPRETATION

Philosophical assumptions central to my work with the neighbors from Oaxaca reflected a view of reality as subjective and value-laden, expressive of a variety of perspectives, allowing for a growing, collaborative relationship between researcher and participants as well as personal interpretation of knowledge by either. The method for the inquiry into the target population relied on a process that responded to experiences as they presented (Creswell 2007, 17). Research participants were two teachers, one from Oaxaca who had studied English at a Mexican university, and a local Californian of Native American descent, joined by two indigenous gatekeepers who provided services to the Triqui-speaking community.

The overall research design reflected constructionist and participatory worldviews. This allowed for meaning to be co-created and "an action agenda for change" (Creswell 2007, 22) to be advanced. In order to increase understanding about two issues—learner engagement and the effects of displacement—distinct approaches were selected for two research phases. The earlier study was guided by a grounded theory approach to identify a process that included steps and mechanisms needed for a culturally attuned service delivery model; the study also allowed for elements of phenomenology, describing and comparing invariant living conditions and the well-being of farmworkers. The later study called for a narrative approach, with its emergent focus on the effects of oppressive labor conditions and other stressors experienced by displaced noncitizen farmworkers; it was complemented by elements of critical ethnography and postcolonial theory, describing members of the Triqui culture as experiencing "dislocation, economic and material stratification, strategies of local resistance, as well as issues of representation, identity, belonging, and expressive traditions" (Mertens 2009, 180).

Qualitative research data described by Creswell (2007, 38) were collected and summarized in tabled form. They included desk research on cultural and language acquisition theories from various countries; journal entries and personal reflections on dream work; observations gathered in the field; pictures taken at various sites; protocols of informal interactions with indigenous service providers, interpreters, and students; surveys on learner interests; structured interviews on well-being and healthcare practices, and semiformal group interviews that had elements of storytelling (Creswell 2007).

In a chapter on "Education, Research, and Action," Brydon-Miller and Tolman argued that what set participatory action research (PAR) apart was the use of strategies including "group discussions, community seminars … and storytelling," besides traditional methods such as surveys (2001, 81). In a reference to Freire, Brydon-Miller and Tolman affirmed that "critically informed inquiry generates a form of knowledge that results in and grows out of the liberation of those generating the knowledge" (2001, 79), as illustrated through a graph (2001, 82). The latter also sums up the outcome of our interview process, "generating a theory illustrated in a figure" (Creswell 2007, 79), typical for the grounded approach. The graph in Figure 1 demonstrates how the indigenous Triqui community collaborated with our research team in order to identify, in a setting of popular education at a library, issues that allowed for community-based research with an eye to social action. The results were computed, discussed with the team, translated, captured in a table, and later shared with local healthcare providers.

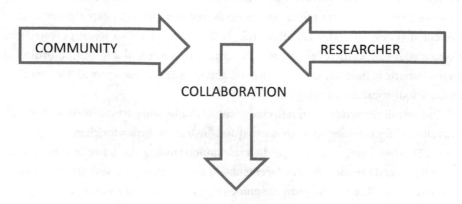

Figure 4.11: Making Meaning

As a type of community self-survey, introduced by Wormser and Selltiz in 1951 (Torre et al. 2012, 173), it also served as a strategy intended "to interrogate the gap between dominant ideologies and human lives, using deeply participatory methods accountable to the goals of social justice (Torre et al. 2012, 171). Indeed, the California Rural Legal Association (CRLA) registered complaints by Triqui-speaking community members not receiving legally mandated access to culturally sensitive care at a local hospital (Gatlin 2014), prompting the formation of a language access advisory group to which I and indigenous representatives were subsequently invited. One of the items on the interview protocol on well-being addressed language issues with local health providers. The analysis showed that 87 percent of the farmworkers who had used healthcare services in the past year encountered difficulties with being provided interpreters in their language of choice.

Some of the other data obtained in the interviews corroborated findings from Ventura County, conducted by an advocacy group gaining momentum through national sponsors and community support (Vargas 2014, 5). Gender composition was 70.6 percent male for Ventura County farmworkers (Central Coast Alliance United for a Sustainable Economy [CAUSE] 2015); our sampling similarly showed 70 percent male representation. Whereas 32 percent of the farm laborers in Ventura County had injured their hands, legs, or backs at work, the Monterey County results showed 55 percent of the workers reporting work-related backaches.

Since the local Triqui-speaking research team wanted to probe for indicators of pesticide exposure, the interviews also checked for headaches and allergies. Sixty-five percent of the workers indicated headaches, and 45 percent complained of allergies; 65 percent attributed their headaches and allergies to work. In checking chronic backaches at 55 percent and insomnia at 15 percent, they also listed markers that could be stress-related. CAUSE reported on major stressors in terms of "the extreme overwork needed in order to earn enough to survive" (2015, 9); the local group's survey highlighted trauma suffered during border crossings from Mexico into the United States. Eighty-five percent of the indigenous farmworkers indicated this *("batallarse mucho cruzando la frontera")*.

Importantly, data collected during earlier field work ended up informing questions asked further on. I incorporated some of them into a *semi-structured life world interview* designed "to understand the everyday world from the subjects' own perspectives" (Kvale and Brinkmann 2009, 27). The group interview was conducted with three indigenous men ages forty-five to fifty-five who, it turned out, had been living apart from their immediate family members in Oaxaca for five to ten years in order to support them with slightly higher incomes earned in California. The interview content was transcribed and analyzed using an *inductive content analysis* that could "identify underlying *themes* across informants" (Foster-Fishman et al. 2005, 280). However, my transcription was never confirmed by all three participants, due to some unexplained absences at subsequent meetings, possibly because of harvest schedules requiring late evening hours. I used a salient excerpt from the transcription to write a narrative from my perspective, condensing it into a table with columns for text units and central themes, as suggested by Kvale and Brinkmann (2009, 206). It turned out to raise many questions, including some about my positionality.

In interpreting themes identified with the three men, it struck me that they would much rather do seasonal work in California and freely return to Oaxaca to be with their families in the off-season—something the earlier trans-migrant status had allowed before the border became increasingly militarized, and illegal crossings with coyotes became both unaffordable and life-threatening. The three interviewees seemed resigned to the work they were able to obtain in California, yet showed indication of resentment to the oppressive working and living conditions in California. In a book entitled *Fresh Fruit, Broken Bodies* (Holmes 2013), the author pointed to permanent stress experienced by Mexican undocumented farmworkers, reflected in shocking statistics on morbidity and numerous instances of structural violence. Similarly, a UC Berkeley professor (Bloemraad 2016) reported on research findings during a California Community College webinar indicating that recent Mexican immigrants, upon arrival in California, had better health, fewer criminal records, and more intact family connections than they did years into their stay in the United States. Some reasons may include the harsh working conditions encountered. For instance, CAUSE reported "a lack of state enforcement, widespread labor violations … [resulting in] a culture of fear in farm work, where this highly vulnerable population is largely afraid to file claims and report labor abuses" (2015, 8). In addition, the hourly pay rate for pickers in the fields has not kept up with the increasing cost of living in California, making overtime pay, available to farmworkers only after sixty weekly work hours, more essential (Bacon 2016).

The interview with the local Oaxacan farmworkers revealed similar issues. It is worth noting that it occurred at their suggestion, prompted by a discussion after a tutoring session. I had taught them the phrase "I would like to . . ." in order to generate some responses on their hopes and wishes, and they had revealed being homesick, wanting to see their families in Oaxaca. An instructional activity had facilitated the men's spontaneous disclosure, as a result of "critical literacy development" (Benmayor 1991, 161). In Benmayor's practice, this Freirean approach around socially relevant themes led to *conscientization* by presenting learners with "an intense cognizance of shared conditions of poverty and class exploitation" (1991, 166). Benmayor concluded:

> Situations like these remind us of the heavy responsibility of working with life history and of the importance of not working alone. Action research has the potential to reposition the researcher/subject power relationship in many ways. … By

creating a space for testimony, literacy and empowerment are advanced. (1991, 172)

When the three men of few words came to me asking what they could do about their situation and whether I would help them, it marked a major shift toward what Benmayor considered an "organic connection to community" (1991, 172). The men had opened themselves up to their feelings, admitting their pain over the separation from their families. Moreover, the scenario of displacement and separation they struggled with emotionally may also have contained the seeds for a thinking-based response, generating a call to action. It suddenly mattered to find a way in which their story could be told, to start thinking about what type of change they wanted to bring about. And it mattered to me to offer something I could realistically do to help. It was a memorable, mutually transformative moment.

CONCLUSION

Dimensions of change and transformation in a PAR project involving undocumented migrants were explored elsewhere (Lykes, Hershberg, and Brabeck, 2011, chapter 2). Some members of Lykes's research team situated these dimensions as "consciousness-raising processes through which participants and collectivities develop agency that sometimes leads to wider efforts towards social change and transformation" (2011, 31); others identified more with providing services, "thereby temporarily changing some conditions for individuals in under-resourced organizations" (2011). My work with the group from Oaxaca seems to reflect both transformative and ameliorative interventions. As my knowledge of the complex context of displacement and emplacement deepened, the relevance of a more organic inquiry into my neighbors' challenges and my own positionality as a child of Central European refugees emerged. In a discussion of organic research methods (Clements 2011), inquiry was described as "a living and therefore mutable process" (2011, 131), one that invited transformation for heart and mind by using both feeling and thinking styles. It seemed as if my ongoing inquiry placed me in a space that, in the context of indigeneity and the Maya, was likened to a labyrinth:

> If one begins with universal criteria, such as experiencing colonialism, the maintenance of a separate identity since the colonial invasion, distinctive traditions, and a different phenotype, one soon enters a labyrinth of social and historical details that are unique to a nation, region, town, and even home. (Metz 2012, 1)

The image of the labyrinth presented itself in several ways. I heard about a labyrinth in Palenque; the Triqui men spoke of endless meanderings through the desert between Mexico and Arizona; I started training in the *Capacitar* modality (Cane 2003) to learn about a somatic, grassroots self-care system for traumatized populations—and discovered instructions for building therapeutic labyrinths in the training manual (2003, 204–210). After completing an experiential exercise on inspiration in organic inquiry proposed by Clements (2011, 141–147), mythic Ariadne, ancient Greek mistress of the labyrinth, came to mind. Having visited the palace of Knossos on the island of Crete years before, the embodied outcome of the exercise offered welcome guidance. Ariadne as muse could accompany this evolving, confounding project. Her ball of wool that helped a mythic hero find his way out of confusion offered a symbol for the courageous resolve to take one step at a time in the labyrinth, encountering a central issue and finding the way back to community praxis and social change.

The encounters with my neighbors from Oaxaca, combined with the growing awareness of mass migrations occasioned by globalization and the power structures of *coloniality* as "framework within which operate the other social relations of classes or estates" (Quijano 2010, 22), have pointed my steps increasingly in the direction of the psychosocial praxis of accompaniment (Watkins 2013), revealing to the practitioner how "his own complicity with the status quo harms others ... and when he acts to remediate this failure, his values are sharpened and his integrity deepened" (2013, p. 12). In my attempts to accompany my new neighbors, I am hoping to work on what Frantz Fanon called "collaboration with others on tasks that strengthen man's totality" (ibid.).

It seems that no individual's efforts, only synergistic collaboration with others, can create an infrastructure of inclusion in south Monterey County to help the newcomers from Oaxaca develop a sense of belonging, and to give the host community an increased awareness of man's totality. My inquiry into ways of facilitating this endeavor has brought not only troubling knowledge but also many connections with other possible collaborators in the process of—though more with gatekeepers than with the community members themselves. The inquiry has also pointed to advocacy groups elsewhere that may well become models for those in the community who wish to generate sustainable change. The literature on systems change in community psychology "has been slow to develop" (Prilleltensky and Nelson 2009, 129), providing few examples at the collective level of analysis. More research is needed to study collective impact.

DISCUSSION QUESTIONS

1 . When looking at the programs offered by the Mixteco/Indígena Community Organizing Project (MICOP 2016), what issues affecting indigenous immigrants and the established resident population of Oxnard do you think are being addressed by the project?

2 . Does the Central Coast Alliance United for a Sustainable Economy (CAUSE) stand a chance to gain momentum in other regions with large farmworker populations?

3 . Based on your reading of the online article by David Bacon on farmworker overtime (2016), how do you think current regulations for farmworkers affect the lives of their families, notably their children?

WEBSITE LINKS

California Rural Legal Association: www.crla.org

Center for Collaborative Research for an Equitable California: https://ccrec.ucsc.edu/projects

Mary Watkins, archive of articles on migration: http://mary-watkins.net/research-interests/forced-migration

AUDIOVISUAL MATERIALS

Rape in the Fields, PBS Frontline (educational film documentary)
La Cosecha/The Harvest, Shine Global (educational film documentary)

SUGGESTIONS FOR FURTHER READING

Bloemraad, I., E. de Graauw, and R. Hamiln. 2016. "Immigrants in the Media: Civic Visibility in the USA and Canada." http://sociology.berkeley.edu/sites/default/files/faculty/bloemraad/Bloemraad_deGraauw_Hamlin_Civic_Visibility_JEMS_2015.pdf.

REFERENCES

Bacon, D. 2008. *Illegal People: How Globalization Creates Migration and Criminalizes Immigrants*. Boston, MA: Beacon Press.

Bacon, D. 2016. "The Fight Isn't Over for Farmworker Overtime." http://davidba-conrealitycheck.blogspot.com/2016/06/the-fight-isnt-over-for-farm-worker_16.html.

Benmayor, R. 1991. "Testimony, Action Research, and Empowerment: Puerto Rican Women and Popular Education." In *Women's Words: The Feminist Practice of Oral History*, edited by S. Berger Gluck and D. Patai, 160–167. New York: Routledge.

Bernstein, J. 2005. *Living in the Borderland: The Evolution of Consciousness and the Challenge of Healing Trauma*. London and New York: Routledge, Taylor & Francis Group.

Bloemraad, I., E. de Graauw, and R. Hamlin. 2016."Immigrants in the Media: Civic Visibility in the USA and Canada." http://sociology.berkeley.edu/sites/default/files/faculty/bloemraad/Bloemraad_deGraauw_Hamlin_Civic_Visibility_JEMS_2015.pdf

Brydon-Miller, M., and D. Tolman. 2001. *From Subjects to Subjectivities: A Handbook of Participatory and Interpretive Methods*. New York: New York University Press.

Cane, P. 2003. *Trauma Healing and Transformation*. Santa Cruz, CA: Capacitar International.

Central Coast Alliance United for a Sustainable Economy (CAUSE). 2015. "Raising Up Farmworkers: Ventura County Report." htttp://causenow.org/sites/default/files/files/CAUSE%20Raising%20Up%20Farm%20Workers%20Ventura%20County%20September%202015.pdf.

Clements, J. 2011. "Organic Inquiry: Research in Partnership with Spirit." In *Transforming Self and Others through Research: Transpersonal Research Methods and Skills for the Human Sciences and Humanities*, edited by R. Anderson and W. Braud, 131–159. New York: State University of New York Press.

Creswell, J. W. 2007. *Qualitative Inquiry & Research Design: Choosing among Five Approaches*. 2nd ed. Thousand Oaks, CA: SAGE Publications.

Foster-Fishman, P. G., S. L. Berkowitz, D. W. Lounsbury, S. Jacobson, and N. A. Allen. (2001). Building collaborative capacity in community coalitions: A review and integrative framework. *American Journal of Community Psychology, 29(2)*, 241–261.

Fox, J., G. Rivera-Salgado, and J. Santiago. 2013. "Voices of Indigenous Oaxacan Youth in the Central Valley: Creating Our Sense of Belonging in California." https://ccrec.ucsc.edu/sites/default/files/eco%20english%20web%2C%20 final%20%288-23%29.pdf.

Freire, P. 1987. *Literacy: Reading the Word and the World*. Westport, CT: Bergin & Garvey.

Gatlin, A. 2014. "Triqui Speakers Win Claim against Mee Memorial." *The Salinas Californian*. www.thecalifornian.com/story/news/local/2014/08/18/triqui-speakers-win-claim-mee-memorial/14261991.

Holmes, S. 2013. *Fresh Fruit, Broken Bodies*. Berkeley: University of California Press.

Kvale, S., and S. Brinkmann. 2009. *Interviews: Learning the Craft of Qualitative Research Interviewing*. 2nd ed. Thousand Oaks, CA: SAGE Publications.

Lykes, M. B., R. Hershberg, and K. M. Brabeck. 2011. "Methodological Challenges in Participatory Action Research with Undocumented Central American Migrants." *Journal for Social Action in Counseling and Psychology* 3(2): 22–35.

Mertens, D. M. 2009. *Transformative Research and Evaluation*. New York: Guilford Press.

Metz, B. 2012. "The Labyrinth of Indigeneity: How Does One Determine Who Is an Indigenous Ch'orti Maya in Guatelmala, Honduras and El Salvador?" Lawrence: Center for Latin American & Caribbean Studies Scholarly Works, University of Kansas. https://kuscholarworks.ku.edu/handle/1808/12452.

Mixteco/Indigena Community Organizing Project (MICOP). 2016. "Programs." Retrieved from www.mixteco.org/programs.

Nelson, G., and I. Prilleltensky, eds.. 2010. *Community Psychology: In Pursuit of Liberation and Well-Being*. 2nd ed. New York: Palgrave Macmillan.

Prilleltensky, I., and G. Nelson. 2009. "Community Psychology: Advancing Social Justice." In *Critical Psychology: An Introduction*, 2nd ed., edited by D. Fox, I. Prilleltensky, and S. Austin, 126–143. Thousand Oaks, CA: SAGE Publications.

Quijano, A. 2010. "Coloniality and Modernity/Rationality." In *Globalization and the Decolonial Option*, edited by W. D. Mignolo and A. Escobar, 21–32. New York: Routledge.

Torre, M. E., M. Fine, B. G. Stoudt, and M. Fox. 2012. "Critical Participatory Action Research as Public Science." In *APA Handbook of Research Methods in Psychology*, edited by H. Cooper, 171–184. http://dx.doi.org/10.1037/13620-011.

Vargas, M. 2014. *Strategic Plan 2014–2018*. Ventura, CA: Central Coast Alliance United for a Sustainable Economy.

Watkins, M. 2013. "Accompaniment: Psychosocial, Environmental, Trans-species, Earth." http://mary-watkins.net/library/Accompaniment-Psychosocial-Environmental-Trans-Species-Earth.pdf.

Reincarnation

· ·

By Gloria Anzaldúa

Written in 1974, this previously unpublished poem resonates strongly with sections of *Borderlands/La Frontera* and "The New Mestiza Nation," indicating that even in the early 1970s, Anzaldúa defined herself in terms of multiplicity and transformation.

REINCARNATION

for Julie
     I
           slithered shedding
   my self
      on the path
        then
          looked back and
      contemplated
    the husk
       and wondered
         which me
           I had discarded
              and was it the second
              or the two thousand and
 thirty-second

and how many me's
would I slough off
before voiding
the core
if ever

June 20, 1974
South Bend, IN

REFERENCES

"Cornel West quotes." Find the famous quotes you need, ThinkExist.com Quotations.

Fessenden, Lee, Pecanha, and Singhvi. 2017. *Immigrants From Banned Nations: Educated, Mostly Citizens and Found in Every State*. The New York Times. Retrieved March 3, 2016 from https://www.nytimes.com/interactive/2017/01/30/us/politics/trump-immigration-ban-demographics.html?mcubz=1.

Golash-Boza, Tania. 2015. *Race and Racism: A Critical Approach*. New York: Oxford University Press.

Lopez, Gustavo, and Pattien, Eileen. 2015. *The Impact of Slowing Immigration: Foreign-Born Share Falls among 14 Largest U.S Hispanic Origin Groups*. Pew Research Center. Retrieved March 3, 2016, from http://www.pewhispanic.org/2015/09/15/the-impact-of-slowing-immigration-foreign-born-share-falls-among-14-largest-us-hispanic-origin-groups/.

Massey, Douglas S., and Capoferro, Chiara. 2008. "The Geographic Diversification of American Immigration." Pp 25–50 in New Faces in New Places: The Changing Geography of American Immigration, edited by Douglas Massey. New York: Russell Sage Foundation.

Ortman, M J., and Colby, L. S. 2015. Projections of the U.S Size and Composition of the U.S Population: 2014 to 2060. Population Estimates and Projections. Current Population Reports. Retrieved March 1, 2016, https://www.census.gov/content/dam/Census/library/publications/2015/demo/p25-1143.pdf.

"Overview of Race and Hispanic Origin: 2010" (PDF). 2011. Retrieved February 29, 2016, from http://www.census.gov/content/dam/Census/library/publications/2011/dec/c2010br-02.pdf.

Portes, Alejandro, and Rumbaut, Ruben. 2015. Immigrant America: A Portrait. 4th edition. CA: University of California Press.

United Nations High Commissioner for Refugees (UNHCR). 2015. *Global Trends: Forced Displacement in 2014*. Geneva: UNHCR. Retreived on March 3, 2016, from http://unhcr.org/556725e69.html#_ga=1.209789139.794806637.1437577173

Zong, Jie, and Batalova, Jeanne. 2015a (October 28). *Refugees and Asylees in the United States*. Migration Policy Institute. Retrieved on March 3, 2016, from http://www.migrationpolicy.org/article/refugees-and-asylees-united-states.

Zong, Jie, and Batalova, Jeanne. 2015b. (December 1) *European Immigrants in the United States*. Migration Policy Institute. Retrieved on March 3, 2016, from http://www.migrationpolicy.org/article/european-immigrants-united-states.

Zong, Jie & Batalova, Jeanne. 2016. Asian Immigrants in the United States. Migration Policy Institute. Retrieved on March 3, 2016 from http://www.migrationpolicy.org/article/asian-immigrants-united-states

Zuñiga, V., & Hernandez-Leon, R. 2005. New Destinations: Mexican Immigration in the United States. New York: Russell Sage Foundation.

CPSIA information can be obtained
at www.ICGtesting.com
Printed in the USA
BVHW090603160122
626298BV00002B/27

9 781516 533138